Ruth Dudley Edwards

Aftermath

The Omagh bombing and
the families' pursuit of justice

D0726452

Harvill *Secker*

LONDON

Published by Harvill Secker 2009

2 4 6 8 10 9 7 5 3 1

First published in Great Britain in 2009 by
HARVILL SECKER
Random House, 20 Vauxhall Bridge Road,
London SW1V 2SA

www.rbooks.co.uk

Addresses for companies within The Random House Group Limited can be found at:
www.randomhouse.co.uk/offices.htm

The Random House Group Limited Reg. No. 954009

A CIP catalogue record for this book
is available from the British Library

The publishers are grateful for permission to reproduce the images within this book. Every effort has
been made to trace and contact copyright holders and any mistakes or omissions will be corrected in
future editions.

Press Association Images: 'Market Street after the bomb', Philomena Skelton, Prince Charles, Colm
Murphy, Michael McKevitt, Bernadette Sands-McKevitt, Francie Mackey, 'Ex-Secretaries of State',
'Families after meeting the Irish Justice Minister', 'families outside Downing Street'; Reuters: Fred White,
'United in grief', 'Hillary Clinton lays a wreath'; Alan Lewis: Lorraine Wilson and Samantha McFarland,
Breda Devine, Ann McCombe, Seamus Daly, 'Families outside court on the first day of the trial',
'After the victory'; Collins: Liam Campbell; Camera Press/Paul Massey/*The Times*: H2O legal team;
Irish News/Hugh Russell: 'Families addressing the media'

The author would also like to thank the *Daily Mail* and the Omagh Support and Self-help Group
and their supporters for photographs.

ISBN 9780436205996

The Random House Group Limited supports The Forest Stewardship
Council (FSC), the leading international forest certification organisation. All our titles that are printed
on Greenpeace approved FSC certified paper carry the FSC logo. Our paper procurement policy can
be found at www.rbooks.co.uk/environment

Mixed Sources

To Nina, who thought I was mad to take this on but kept me going throughout, to all those in the strange and wonderful team who saw the case through, and, of course, to Victor, Michael, and to the brave and tenacious families of Omagh who won a famous victory

CONTENTS

PART I

First they came for the Jews and I did not speak out — because I was not a Jew.

Then they came for the communists and I did not speak out — because I was not a communist.

Then they came for the trade unionists and I did not speak out — because I was not a trade unionist.

Then they came for me — and there was no one left to speak out for me.

Pastor Niemöller,
quote pinned to the notice board of the Omagh Support and
Self-help Group

For evil to flourish it is only necessary for good men to do nothing

Attributed to Edmund Burke, this quote has been an inspiration
to Michael Gallagher

PROLOGUE

At 2.29 p.m. on Saturday, 15 August 1998, Maggie Hall, a programme assistant in the Belfast newsroom of Ulster Television, received a phone call via the switchboard. 'A male voice with a northern country accent spoke to me,' she would tell the coroner at the inquest on the dead of Omagh. 'I am unable to recall his initial words as I found him so difficult to understand because of his accent.' She believed him to be a man in his early fifties and in retrospect guessed that he had muffled his voice.

'At first I thought he was some sort of nutcase. I started saying "what" to him several times, in an effort to make him speak more clearly. I then heard him say, "Bomb Courthouse Omagh, Main Street, 500 pounds explosion, 30 minutes."' As was routine with bomb warnings, she asked for a code word and he said what she thought was 'Malta Pope' or 'Martha Pope'* and added 'Óglaigh na hÉireann't in the 'very thick accent' she found so impenetrable. She dialled 999 and was put through to George Mullan, Constable Controller of the RUC attached to Belfast Regional Control, at Castlereagh RUC station in Belfast: the tape records her saying: 'I'm only after getting a call from a man with a country accent, saying there's a bomb in Omagh main street near the courthouse,

---

* To demonstrate that they are serious, some terrorist organisations use codewords notified to the media, who pass them on to security forces. Terrorists are not long on humour, but the adoption of 'Martha Pope' as a codeword was the Real IRA's idea of a joke. An aide to Senator George Mitchell, broker of the peace talks that led to the Belfast Agreement, Martha Pope was alleged in 1996 to be having an affair with the notorious Gerry Kelly, a convicted bomber and high-profile Sinn Féin spokesman. The allegations were without any foundation whatsoever: Martha Pope won libel damages.
† 'Óglaigh na hÉireann' ('Volunteers of Ireland') is the correct title of the defence forces of the Republic of Ireland; however, since all IRAs (Provisional, Continuity and Real) believe themselves to be the legitimate government of Ireland, each appropriates the term for itself, as later did yet another breakaway group, which is given the abbreviation of OnH. It is mystifying to people with no knowledge of Irish: at the inquest in September 2000, the Coroner had to ask for a translation.

a 500-pound bomb. It's going to go off in 30 minutes. I asked him for a codeword and he said it was "Malta Pope" and he did repeat it.'

Mullan immediately phoned the enquiries room at Omagh to alert them and explain that 'Malta Pope' was a Real IRA codeword that had been used two weeks previously in the warning for a 500-pound bomb that blew the heart out of Banbridge and injured thirty-five. Constable William Hall, the duty officer, relayed to the communications room his notes: 'UTV, Main Street, Court, 500, Martha Pope.' Mullan by then was entering 'a computer record detailing this call, date, time, location, et cetera and a description of the contents of the call' and committing it to the Atlas Command and Control system that would send a written copy automatically to Omagh communications room, where it would appear on their computer screen for action. Under the heading BMBS (bombs, bomb scare), the substance of his message was 'Male caller to UTV bomb to go off in 30 mins near the courthouse Main Street, 500 pounds. Codeword, Malta Pope. No organisation mentioned.'

At 2.31, Hilary,* a volunteer worker with the Samaritans in Coleraine, received a call from a man with a gentle voice she thought was sober, and neither old nor young. He asked if he were through to Omagh and she said, no, this was Coleraine (to which calls from the Omagh office were diverted on Saturdays). He then said, 'This is a bomb warning', and that the bomb would go off in the centre of Omagh in thirty minutes. When asked if there was a codeword, he said 'Martha Pope', but he was speaking so fast it took three repetitions and his spelling it out before Hilary understood it. 'I then asked him to clarify whereabouts in Omagh as I do not know the town.' The bomb, he said, was 'about 200 yards up from the courthouse – High Street, the main street'. He hung up, she dialled 999 and she told Constable Gary Murphy at Coleraine communications: 'I have received a bomb call for Omagh town centre approximately 200 yards from the courthouse and the codeword Martha Pope was given.' The codeword meant nothing to him, but he passed the message to Omagh communications and then logged the information on the computer system with the description: 'bomb warning received at Samaritans centre Coleraine with effect that a bomb was going to go off in Omagh town centre near the courthouse (200 yards). Codeword given "Marta Pope"'.

---

* Because of the Samaritans' strict policy of anonymity, Hilary was screened at the inquest from all in the court except for the Coroner and the court clerk and was referred to as 'Hilary Unknown'.

2

Meanwhile, at 2.31, Maggie Hall at Ulster Television had received another brief message: 'Martha Pope, 15 minutes, Omagh town'; this 999 call was taken in Belfast Regional Control by Constable Wesley Francis, who likewise relayed the information to Omagh communications. They told him that a car was already responding to the initial call.

That the bombers did not know Omagh accounted for some of the vagueness in the warnings, though had they or their accomplices been concerned about loss of life, they would not have chosen a Saturday afternoon, and could – as was sometimes done – have given information about their car or the name of a shop near where they had parked. Both warnings had referred to 'Main Street' or 'the main street', but there is no Main Street in Omagh: there is a High Street, which runs from the courthouse to Scarffe's Entry, which runs south of the beginning of Market Street. It is 240 yards from the front of the courthouse to the corner of High Street and Scarffe's Entry and 380 yards to where the car bomb was parked. The warning to the Samaritans had mentioned the town centre, but, fatally, people had different views on where that was: some thought it meant Market Street and some thought it meant further up town – the Bridge Street and High Street area running up towards the courthouse.

Although there had been seventeen Omagh bomb scares already that year – some with codewords and some without – the police took the threat very seriously. Immediately on being told of the first warning by Constable Martin Millar, the Omagh communications officer, the duty sergeant, Philip Marshall, told him to instruct mobile police units to go and clear the area. 'I got all three bomb warnings together,' said Millar at the inquest, 'and I thought to myself, two say the courthouse, one says the town centre . . . my assessment was that there was a bomb in the general area of the courthouse and that that was the main place to be evacuated.' He 'wanted them to basically make a sterile area around the courthouse and then start pushing everybody back down, away from the courthouse, towards Market Street'. It was a rational interpretation of ambiguous information that would set the police herding hundreds of people away from safety and towards the bomb.

By 2.49, four local police cars had been assigned along with one from nearby Newtownstewart. Sergeant Marshall and Constable Norman Haslett, who had been expecting to lead a parade of carnival floats that afternoon, were clearing crowds from John Street up towards the Kevlin Road junction: 'We had some difficulty in moving patrons, some of whom were intoxicated, from the three public houses.' Their colleagues were also finding it difficult to get people to move. Lulled into a sense of security by the IRA's ceasefire, bored with hoaxes and convinced that only Protestant towns were threatened by the Real IRA, no one really believed anyone would place a bomb in a packed market town with a Catholic majority. 'It never actually entered my head there was a bomb,' said Marguerrita Larsen, who was at the bottom of Market Street helping another traffic warden, Rosemary Ingram, to follow the instructions of Constable Alan Palmer to block cars from entering the street. 'Over the years there were quite a few that came to nothing. Nobody seemed to think there was a bomb, there was quite a light-hearted atmosphere. A lot of people wanted just to go to their cars and go home. They were moving towards the lower end of Market Street. Everyone seemed to be heading off in that direction.'

Constable Tara McBurney, having cleared shops and premises in the bottom half of High Street and pushed back the crowd towards Scarffe's Entry, was with Constable Palmer when they sealed the road with police tape. 'We ran back to the top of Market Street and, as we were having difficulty moving people down the street, I told Constable Palmer to take the white tape and cross the road to SuperValu. I had the other end of the tape and we started to walk down Market Street clearing premises as we went, moving people along with the tape. People in general were very reluctant to move and I had to constantly push and shove them physically in order to keep them moving away from the courthouse.'

Just after Omagh communications warned Sergeant Marshall via his personal radio that there were only three or four minutes of the warning period left, he stood in front of the courthouse and looked down the High Street, John Street, Georges Street and Market Street, as far as Scarffe's Entry, and saw they were all clear of pedestrians. Now only the police were in danger: they had managed to clear almost two hundred premises. 'My initial thought was that it was perfect, that we couldn't have done better. Omagh was like a ghost town, I thought: if something goes up now, it's buildings only.' He walked down High Street, relaying a message to the station that he and his men were about to check the cars on both sides of the street for incendiary devices, though they could see no suspicious signs and no car that seemed heavily laden. They had just begun to look when, twenty seconds after 3.04 p.m.,* the bomb went off.

* * *

* The media wrongly reported the time as 3.10 and that is the time which is annually commemorated.

4

At about 4.15, my close friend Henry Reid, a farmer in County Tyrone, Northern Ireland, rang me in London to tell me to turn on the television: a huge bomb had gone off in his local town. He said his wife and two children, who had been there shopping, were safe. Fearful when she heard there was a bomb warning, Lorraine had packed the children into the car; they were still only a few feet away when the bomb exploded. 'They've gone to hospital,' Henry said, 'but they're all right. Just shock, I think, and trouble with their eardrums. I'm off to get them and then I'll ring you.'

I watched the horrifying television coverage all afternoon and evening as the death toll climbed into the twenties and the injured into the hundreds. Henry reported that though Lorraine's car had shuddered violently and was extensively damaged, it had been insulated from the worst of the blast by a wall of people. Only five-year-old Erin's and four-year-old Thomas's seatbelts had saved them from being sucked out by the vacuum caused by the blast. 'I hope Daddy wasn't killed in the bomb,' Thomas had remarked thoughtfully as they drove to the hospital, where Lorraine, in deep shock as well as pain from the effect of the suction on her whole body, was kept in overnight. Before he took them home, Henry brought Erin and Thomas to the children's ward to play for a while – amid shocking scenes – with some of the injured, frightened and lost. They tried to distract the toddler wearing just a nappy, whose legs, said Henry, 'looked as though she'd been pulled through a briar patch. Her head was shaved and she was crying with hunger but couldn't be fed because she was to have an operation.'

My emotions were frozen for hours. The anger came later, as it had in the wake of other terrorist atrocities in Ireland. I attended a 'Service in Solidarity with Omagh' at Trafalgar Square's St Martin-in-the-Fields a week later, where the names of the dead were read out. I had been to such commemorative events before, but this time it was personal: I knew Omagh very well, and my friends had almost died. Although, compared to many of their neighbours, the Reids had been very, very lucky, for a long time Lorraine would suffer from blinding headaches and survivor guilt, Erin have nightmares and Thomas organise other children to play games of hospitals and dead bodies.

For the next eighteen months, like so many victims and onlookers, I was intensely frustrated that – though the Real IRA had admitted responsibility for the car bomb and the police believed they knew the perpetrators' identities – only one person, a building contractor named Colm

Murphy, had been charged in connection with the case. All I could do was to carry on writing and campaigning against the political violence that had devastated so many lives in Ireland. And then, in January 2000, I had a call from Simon Shaw, a London friend from my crime-fiction world. Could he introduce me to Victor Barker, whose twelve-year-old son James had been killed in Omagh? Contemporaries at Cambridge University in the 1980s, they had met at a recent reunion and Victor had asked him if he knew anyone who could help him in his quest for justice for James.

'But there's nothing I can do for him, Simon. He'll be wasting his time.'

'You were the only person I could think of who has anything to do with Ireland,' said Simon, a note of desperation in his voice. 'And I had to suggest something. Victor's very persistent. That's what I remember best about him from Cambridge. He was incredibly dogged. Having been disappointed with his performance in his first-year exams, he gave up most of his social life, threw himself into his work and got a good degree.'

Reluctantly, I arranged to have a drink with them and another of their Cambridge contemporaries early in February in a small literary club in Soho. Victor, a short, bespectacled solicitor in his early forties who practised in a small English town, told me the story of how James had come to die in Omagh. Victor's Northern Ireland-born wife, Donna-Maria, had been homesick, and to give Estella, James and Oliver, the three youngest children, a better quality of life, she had moved with them to Buncrana, County Donegal, in the north-west of the Republic of Ireland, where her parents had settled on retirement. Their new house was across the political border from her Northern Ireland hometown of Derry, was surrounded by trees and had a wonderful view over Lough Swilly. Victor spent every third weekend there, and during the week lived in Chertsey, in Surrey, working in the solicitors' firm in which he was a partner. He was also a local Conservative councillor. He is a doer.

James had died because he went across the border for a day out with a group of Irish and Spanish children. Without self-pity – for he accepts the capriciousness of fate – Victor described to us something of how his family had been devastated by James's death and of what he had done in pursuit of his son's murderers. He spoke of what he had learned about some of those widely believed to have planned and carried out the bombing. He described fruitless correspondence and encounters with British and Irish police and politicians that had culminated in equally fruitless meetings with innumerable powerful people, including Tony Blair, then Prime

Minister of the United Kingdom, Bertie Ahern, then the Republic of Ireland Taoiseach, and Martin McGuinness, widely believed to be the ex-Chief of Staff of the Provisional IRA and Chief Negotiator of Sinn Féin. He told me a little about the Omagh Support and Self Help Group and its chairman, Michael Gallagher, another bereaved father who had become his friend and ally. He recounted how – in an attempt to highlight how badly victims were being treated – he had brought a claim against the state for compensation for James's school fees and other such expenses that was, as he expected, unsuccessful. And he laughed caustically – for Victor has a sharp wit and a very self-deprecating English sense of humour – about the people who in consequence thought him grasping, as well as all those who found him a confounded nuisance. As indefatigable as Simon had promised, he made it clear that he intended to go on and on. The trouble was, he had little idea where next to go.

Then he said: 'I've wondered about bringing a civil case against the bombers, but no one takes the idea seriously.'

CHAPTER ONE

VICTIMS

'With an explosion of this type, chance does play its part and it can be a
lottery who lives and who dies' – John Leckey, Coroner, inquest on the
Omagh bomb

All the thirty-one deaths left broken-hearted relatives and friends, but this
book deals only with the families who became involved in the civil case
against some of those they blamed for the atrocity. As it became clear that
the criminal justice systems in both parts of Ireland lacked the means, the
competence or the will to punish the bombers, these were the people who
would refuse to admit defeat. Anguished and frustrated by knowing the
names of those they believed were responsible and who were walking
the streets, they would decide to take on both those people and the Real
IRA. These were good men and women who – despite being sorely tempted
– would not take the path of violence, but when they found a legal route
to pursue justice for their loved ones, they marched down it.

In a criminal case, guilt has to be proven beyond reasonable doubt: a
civil case is decided on the balance of probabilities, though when the
allegation is murder, the bar is set higher. More important is that hearsay
is, under certain circumstances, admissible, which potentially makes
available significant evidence excluded from criminal cases. Suing the
people they held responsible for this vile act offered only limited justice,
but to these families it was a lot better than doing nothing. Money was
not the primary issue: what mattered was to name and shame at least some
of those they believed were liable.

It would take more than eight years after my first meeting with Victor
for the case to come to court. Throughout, as a friend, supporter and –
later – chronicler, I would be part of a story that was as inspirational as
it was harrowing. Along the way, these ordinary people would have to
take on not just a terrorist organisation, but most of the Dublin, Belfast
and London police, justice and political establishments, who for varied
reasons thought their actions misguided, counterproductive or unhelpful

to the peace process. They had to draw on reserves of courage, endurance and nerve they did not know they had in order to survive the innumerable disappointments and setbacks. Yet they attracted to their cause an extraordinary collection of mavericks and unlikely bedfellows who, between them, found a way of devising an unprecedented case and finding the millions to make it happen.

Not all the families stayed the course to the end, but all those I write of here, who talked to me so freely over the years, played their part in making it happen. What they did was done for love of their massacred children, siblings and spouses, who had woken up on a sunny Saturday morning looking forward to an enjoyable day.*

James Victor Barker, aged twelve, had been having a blissful time. A gentle, happy, athletic boy who made friends easily, he had adapted to Irish life and loved outdoor activities, particularly clambering over the seaside rocks. 'He was just a really sunny little guy,' said his father. A terrific runner, at Foyle and Londonderry Junior School he was goalkeeper for the football team and a member of the cub scouts. But he did miss his father, for whom he tried to stand in as the man about the house by changing plugs and generally being practical. Although he did not shine academically, he was bright and shrewd and determined to be a lawyer, as he explained in a rather uncertainly spelled school essay, 'because my dad is one and he had to work very harde to be a lawyer'. He would live in his father's house in England when he qualified, he explained, 'and dad can move over to Ireland to have a rest and I will work the same amount of hours as my dad did. I will study for a coarse from third year till upper 6, then my dad will teach me till I'm ready to take over the Joint.' It was for James a great bonus that Victor had flown over a day early this particular weekend, arriving on Thursday night with three close friends to play in a Pro-Am golf tournament at Ballyliffin, on Malin Head, where he was a member.

James was very keen on fishing, so Victor booked a trip with a local fisherman and on Friday afternoon they all went to Lough Swilly. 'We travelled up the coast by Rathmullen and back again, and I remember him sitting on my lap and saying, "Dad, this is a great place. The only sad

---

* Apart from many conversations with the families over the years, I have also drawn on their evidence to the High Court, media interviews and Graham Spencer's *Omagh: Voices of Loss* (2005). Where there are the minor inconsistencies that occur as time goes by, I have assumed the earliest testimonies were likely to be the most correct.

thing is that you're not here every day.'" Victor's friend Barry Hancock recalled an afternoon punctuated by laughter at his mock-resentment that James kept catching fish while Barry caught nothing. He would shove him up the deck demanding his space on the grounds that it was full of fish. 'My last memory of that afternoon,' recalled Tony Rattue, another of Victor's guests, 'was of Victor standing with his arms around James and James's were around Victor. At that instant I realised how much I missed having children. It was a wonderful moment.'

The following morning, James was intending to caddy for his father, but there was a change of plan. Lucrezia Blasco Baselga, an exchange student from Madrid, was staying with the Barkers, and on Saturday morning her twelve-year-old brother Fernando, who was staying with a neighbour, arrived early to ask James to come with him and some other friends on a coach trip to the Ulster American Folk Park near Omagh, which he had never seen. James's sister, Estella, had intended to go, but was unwell, so there was a spare place. 'Dad, can I go?' 'As was natural for a child,' Victor told the inquest, 'he would much prefer to be with his friends than lugging a golf bag around for his father, particularly given the state of my golf game, and he went on the trip.'

Victor, James and Lucrezia had breakfast around 7.30 a.m. Donna-Maria packed her son a lunch of ham sandwiches, cheese and onion crisps, sweets and chocolates and took the three children to catch the coach into town. He wanted to wear the new Chelsea shirt he had been wearing almost non-stop for two weeks, but she took it away from him to wash and he went off instead in his Three Lions England football shirt. 'He was out the back of the car so fast I didn't even get the chance to say goodbye,' said Donna-Maria later. 'I just saw him walking off smiling at me. He was always smiling.'

James, Fernando and Lucrezia joined twenty-eight Spanish children, their three youth leaders and nine local children, including James's friends Sean McLaughlin, who was also twelve, and eight-year-old Oran Doherty. After seeing the Folk Park, the youth leaders decided to visit Omagh for a shopping trip. The driver had parked the coach by 2.40, when he directed all his passengers towards the main shopping area in Market Street. When the alarm was raised several of the children ran back to the bus, but James, Oran, Sean, Fernando, Lucrezia and Rocio Abad Ramon, the young woman looking after them, were among those who stayed at the shops. Lucrezia, seriously injured, would be the only one to survive.

Most of the staff members of Wattersons drapers shop had been evacuated through a rear door by three o'clock, but three of the shop assistants – Geraldine Breslin, Ann McCombe and Veda Short – were in Market Street enjoying the sunshine. Geraldine had gone out through the front because she was helping a customer with a pram. The three of them had worked together for years: 'They were utterly dedicated, dependable and trustworthy,' said Tom Watterson later. 'They were employees,' said his wife Maretta, 'but they were very special friends. We were really one big family.'

Geraldine was forty-three. When she had met Mark Breslin, five years earlier, she was a single mother living with her parents, grandfather and nine-year-old son, Gareth. Mark, a quantity surveyor, had worked in Belfast for some years, but left after a colleague was shot by loyalist terrorists. After a while in London, he came home to Omagh. Quiet, easy-going and rather shy, he met Geraldine at a concert, was greatly taken by her outgoing nature, and 'I plucked up the courage to ask her out.' An attractive woman, who loved make-up and fashion, she greatly enjoyed her job and had many friends, not least among the hundreds of customers to whom she would chat. 'Religion or politics never came up in her conversations,' recalled a friend. Geraldine brought Mark out into a more lively world and gave him social confidence, they fell very much in love and, in December 1995, they married, both for the first time: by then, Mark regarded Gareth as a son. Their social life was put mostly on hold as they focused on making their house a home for the three of them.

That Saturday, like every Saturday, Mark gave Geraldine a lift to Wattersons, picked her up at 1.15, took her for lunch to their home a mile outside Omagh, dropped her back at the shop around 2.15, and went back to do some gardening.

Like Mark, Geraldine was a non-practising Catholic: her best friend, forty-eight-year-old Ann McCombe, was a devout church-going Protestant. There are parts of Northern Ireland in which cross-community friendships would be remarked upon or disapproved of, but they were nothing special in Omagh. Some areas might have been classified as more Catholic/nationalist or Protestant/unionist than others, but no-go areas did not exist. 'Omagh is a town where you are judged on who you are, not what you are,' said Independent Councillor Paddy McGowan a few days after the bomb. 'A good person is a good person and an evil person is an evil person.'

The McCombes had celebrated their silver wedding anniversary in June. Temperamentally they were opposites. Stanley, who was retired from the electricity board, was a part-time bookie, a member of a pipe band and an immensely gregarious drinker and smoker who seemed to know everyone in town; when not at work or singing in a local choir, Ann was a homebody, dedicated to looking after Stanley and their sons, Clive, who was twenty-two, and eighteen-year-old Colin, who had learning difficulties. She was a quiet perfectionist, who, said Stanley, 'never came downstairs without being properly dressed and with her make-up on'. Her husband thought her 'the kindest-hearted person that I've ever known and she cared for everybody'. Ann's parents, who had both died within the previous twelve months, had been nursed by her for years; sometimes she would visit them twice in a night. 'She was,' said Michael and Patsy Gallagher, who in the 1980s had lived beside the McCombes for several years, 'the nicest woman in the world.'

Ann and Geraldine were last seen chatting, standing together in front of Carland Newsagents.

Breda Devine was doing what she did every day. The youngest of three girls and one boy, at twenty months she was learning to walk and talk. She had had a tough start to life; born three months prematurely and weighing only just over two pounds, she had not been expected to live.

Breda had been taken into Omagh by her mother, Tracey, her uncle Garry and his fiancée Donna Marie, who were to be married the following week: Breda was to be a bridesmaid and needed new shoes. All four were crossing Market Street shortly after three o'clock.

Adrian Michael Gallagher, twenty-one, known as Aiden, had arrived in Market Street earlier. An adored only son and brother, and a cheery, hardworking, clean-cut young man with a great sense of humour and plenty of friends, he was mad about sports cars. Having taken the Light Vehicle Body Repairs course at Portadown College, he had spent two years building his own car business with his father, Michael, who attended to the mechanics: together they would watch programmes about rally driving. Aiden was ambitious. His business had outgrown the family garage so he had hired a larger one two miles away: Michael now worked for his son.

Aiden saved enthusiastically for whatever he wanted, so would have worked on a Saturday, for he needed money to renovate the old family cottage – across the street from the Gallaghers' new, bigger house – which his parents intended to give him. That Saturday, after a late night, he was slow to get up. His younger sister, Cathy, to whom he was very close (the age gap was only fourteen months and they made common cause over being laughed at for their ginger hair), came into his bedroom to extract information about what he had been up to the night before and which girl he might have been out with, but gave up when all she could elicit was a grunt. When Aiden finally got up, Cathy had gone out and Patsy, their mother, was busy cleaning the kitchen. In that part of the world, women are very houseproud: cleanliness really is seen as being next to godliness.

Aiden had a mock altercation with Patsy about a missing brown bag containing sausages – his favourite food – that he had brought home from a takeaway late the night before and that she claimed to have put in the bin. When, laughing, she finally retrieved the sausages from the refrigerator, he rushed out with them and went off to pay a work bill. He came back still peckish, searched for something to eat and found some noodles in a packet. He refused to let Patsy, who was still cleaning, cook them for him. When he had finished eating and chatting, he rang Sharon, his older sister, spoke to her partner, and then called his great friend Michael Barrett to ask if he would come to Omagh with him as he needed new jeans and work boots. It was a first for Aiden: his mother always bought his clothes.

'I'm away now, Mammy, to buy the jeans. What size am I?' 'Try them on,' she said. 'That's the best way.' Although he was in a hurry, he stopped for a couple of minutes to chat to his father, who had just come back from their garage, and ask his advice on where to park. 'It is lovely to remember those last few minutes that he was standing there,' said Michael later. 'He was just the way you would want him to be.'

'I won't be long,' said Aiden, as he left about 2.00 p.m. to pick up his friend. They went to Wattersons, but left when staff and customers were told to get out because there was a bomb scare at the top of the town. 'We just followed the crowd,' said Michael Barrett. 'When we got to Market Street we went into SuperValu and bought a drink and came back outside and stood in front of the shop for a few minutes.' Then they did as the police asked, and walked down towards Dublin Road.

Esther Gibson, thirty-six, the second eldest child in a family of five girls and six boys, worked at Desmond's clothing factory in Omagh as a despatch clerk. She lived at the family farm outside Beragh, was intensely religious and a Sunday School teacher in Ian Paisley's Free Presbyterian Church, which provided the focus for her social life. A second mother to her siblings, she was a steadying influence – particularly on the girls.

Exceptionally level-headed and selfless, she was a source of stability in the family and the first port of call for advice.

Esther would take her siblings to church fellowship meetings in nearby towns and villages, but she and the girls also enjoyed shopping together. She also found time to help look after the two children of her married sister Wilma Kyle. Most of her modest wages went on helping members of her family. She paid, for instance, for her sister Elizabeth to attend a private preparatory school.

Esther had been praying for a husband and family; in her much-thumbed Bible she had written: 'God, if it pleases you, send me a man of God to be my partner in life.' She had begun to fear she would never find someone who would both love her and share her religious principles, but the previous March she had met Kenneth Hawkes. Birthdays and anniversaries are very important in rural Northern Ireland, so they became engaged on Kenneth's birthday in March 1998 and were to be married on Esther's birthday in July 1999: she was ecstatically happy. But for the moment the family focus was on her sister Caroline's wedding six weeks hence, at which Esther was to be chief bridesmaid. 'Esther was kind and loving – the most generous person I have ever known,' said Kenneth. 'She loved children. She couldn't wait to start a family. We wanted a boy and a girl.' Planning excitedly with Kenneth for the house they wanted to build beside his family's farm, it was the first time Esther was thinking about her own happiness.

That Saturday, Esther and her mother had their hair cut in Sixmilecross, then went back home. As lunch was being prepared, she asked her sister Audrey if she would like to go into town, where she was going to buy flowers for the church, but Audrey was meeting her boyfriend. Their father asked her to collect his suit from the dry-cleaners, and Esther left without waiting for lunch. She parked in the car park beside Market Street, went to the bank and set off to run her errands.

Seventeen-year-old Samantha McFarland, vital, energetic and ambitious, and her friend Lorraine Wilson were spending Saturday working as volunteers at the Oxfam charity shop. Samantha's father, Gerald, ran a racehorse business and was separated from his wife, Doreen, with whom Samantha, their only daughter, lived. Mad about riding and academically bright, Samantha had left Omagh High School, was studying for her A-levels at Strabane Grammar School and hoped to read business studies at university. She and Lorraine often talked about their dream of back-packing round the world.

Samantha was a confident, big-hearted and witty girl, who made friends across religious and class divides and had an idealistic belief in the intrinsic goodness of others; her charitable activities included helping Riding for the Disabled and The Royal National Institute for the Blind and she worked in the Barnardo's shop as well as Oxfam. She had a very enjoyable life; at this time she was learning to drive her father's 4x4. Her closest friend was Lorraine, whom she had met on a skiing holiday; she was friendly, too, with Lorraine's big brother Garry, with whom she had started to go out.

Lorraine was two years younger than Samantha, but was so mature that there was no sense of an age gap. Nor were they divided by the difference in their financial circumstances. Lorraine's father, Godfrey, was a spray drier and team leader at the Nestlé factory, where her mother, Ann, worked as a cleaner. Although she had an elder sister, Denise, then twenty-one, who felt protective about her, once Denise left home to live with her boyfriend, Stephen, Lorraine was the maternal figure, full of energy and helpful around the house. She would make tea for Garry, who, like Denise, worked at the Desmond textile factory, and have dinner ready for her parents, as well as making Sunday lunch. She also looked after her younger brother, nine-year-old Colin, who had learning difficulties; she would make him toys out of cereal packets and cardboard. She did well at Omagh High School, where she played in the hockey team and collected money for charity. When she had any spare time, she would curl up in an armchair reading love stories.

They were a close and happy family, who all enjoyed socialising. Godfrey would take the children riding or cycling and their friends of both religions were welcome in their home. Lorraine often went out with her older siblings: Denise would drive Garry and Lorraine to clubs and parties, and, as Ann put it, 'We always knew Lorraine would look after the older pair. If they went to a dance and couldn't get in, it would be Lorraine who would phone to let us know what they were doing or where they were going.' To pay for her clothes or get the money to go horse-riding or go-karting, Lorraine had begun working in the Omagh chip shop that Denise ran part-time with Stephen. Lorraine's plans for the future included being an air hostess for a few years, then settling down at home and becoming a chef.

Lorraine was to work in the chip shop that day, but the cellar was flooded and there was a problem with Health and Safety officials. Instead, she went to work in the Oxfam shop with Samantha. When the bomb warning came, they closed the shop and walked together down Market

Street. They refused an invitation from a friend to go to the Kozy Corner pub for a drink, as they had the keys to the shop and wanted to be ready to reopen it. Just before the bomb went off, an acquaintance of Samantha's saw her sitting on the window sill of S.D. Kells.

Alan Radford, sixteen, one of an Omagh family of five children, was shopping with his mother, Marion, as he did every Saturday. Marion, who was born and brought up in Scotland by an Irish mother and an angry father, had had a tough life. Married at twenty, she was a gentle and loving woman who was a bad picker of men. She had had three unsuccessful marriages, all of which ended in divorce. Before she met her third husband, Alan's father, after she moved to Omagh in the late 1970s, he had been injured by a bomb outside the town.

From the mid-1980s she raised her three daughters and two sons alone. She suffered bouts of depression, for the failure of relationships greatly upset her, but she had been given a great deal of emotional support by members of the Mormon church to which she had converted. Life had become stable and contented, and she had been off antidepressants for twelve months and was doing well at her job as a supervisor in a cleaning company.

Alan had now left Omagh High, where Lorraine Wilson was still studying, and was anxiously awaiting his GCSE results; he wanted to go to college in the autumn to study catering. A cheerful and companionable boy, who shared his mother's Mormon beliefs, he showed no interest in football or clubbing but liked reading and helping people; he was happy, for instance, to baby-sit for neighbours. Described by Marion as emotional and caring, he had been moved by reading about the Irish Famine; his favourite film was *Titanic*, which he had seen three times, the last time with Marion, to whom he was very close. 'He always went shopping with his mum on Saturdays and carried her bags for her. He was such a good lad,' said his brother Paul.

The evening before, unusually for him, Alan had said he did not want to go shopping, but on Saturday morning he changed his mind. Because he wanted to visit a woman that he baby-sat for, he and his mother went out later than usual. They thought briefly of going to shops out of town, but dismissed the idea and walked on into Omagh. A girl they knew told them there might be a bomb and Marion wanted to return home, but Alan thought they should carry on and pay their electricity bill. After leaving Shop Electric, they intended to withdraw money from the machine at the Northern Bank to open an account for Alan, but could not get through the cordon. 'I remember saying to Alan, "I want to leave this country, as I am sick of it. You cannot go into the town but there are bomb scares."' Marion said again that they should go home but he said it was probably only a hoax. She suggested moving to another part of town, but Alan wanted to look in at another shop, so she went into the Salad Bowl. She was about to pay for lettuce and tomatoes when the bomb went off.

Elizabeth (Libbi) Rush, who was fifty-seven, was working in her shop. A quiet and serene woman, she had married the artistic, intelligent but volatile Laurence when they were eighteen and had lived with him for some years in London. When they returned to Omagh, he became a sign-writer and calligrapher, then taught lettering in the Art Department at Omagh Technical College and gradually built up a business.

As well as bringing up Siobhan, Anthony and Andrew, Libbi was a gifted dressmaker who had run a dress shop and now had a furniture shop, the Pine Emporium. She had many friends locally, not least because she was discreet and a good listener. The Rush marriage had gone through a rough period because of Laurence's drinking, but he had sought help and given up alcohol fourteen months previously, which had made Libbi very happy.

That Saturday, Laurence had gone swimming as usual at 9.00 a.m. and had called into the coffee shop for a chat. He bought some vegetables at the Salad Bowl and returned to Libbi with a bag of nuts as a present. She made a joke about them making her fat and he laughed and went off to see someone about buying chickens to keep in their garden. She was last seen alive standing at her shop doorway looking up the street to see what was going on.

Philomena (Mena) Skelton, from the little village of Drumquin, about ten miles west of Omagh, who was thirty-nine, had met her husband Kevin when she was fifteen and married him four years later. She was even more of a homebird than Ann McCombe, for, in addition to looking after teenagers Paula, Ray, Tracey and Shauna, she worked from home as a professional knitter. Like Ann, she was an old-fashioned wife. 'I couldn't have boiled an egg,' said Kevin. 'I was spoilt. Maybe that's being selfish, I don't know, but Mena was happy like that.' Kevin drove a lorry taking tar from a quarry, and was out most evenings, refereeing Gaelic football matches at club and county level. Dinner was on the table when he came home from work and his clean sports kit was neatly laid out; work clothes were ready every morning along with a packed lunch.

Apart from the grocery shopping every Thursday that she did with Kevin, Philomena rarely went out. She visited Omagh town centre only twice a year – at Christmas, and in August to buy school uniforms. That Saturday, Kevin had a bad back, so he drew only one load of tar, and was available to go with her and the girls to Omagh, where they arrived just before 2.00; Ray was on a fishing trip. Kevin left the family for a while to go to the travel agent. This was the second year he and Philomena had taken a child from a Romanian orphanage for a holiday in Omagh: he had taken the child back the previous week and now wanted to price a flight for his next journey.

When he had finished, he found Paula had gone off with her boyfriend but the other three were in Tyler's, a shoe shop. When they left, Kevin was told by a traffic warden that there was a suspected bomb at the court-house and they would have to move. He fetched his car from the front of the Royal Arms Hotel round to the car park at the back and then he, Philomena, Tracey and Shauna walked down the road, stopping by a small confectionery shop to buy pencils and pens. The police came in and told them to move further on. Kevin suggested they go home, but they still needed a pair of brown shoes, so they headed for S.D. Kells. 'Three women in a shop,' thought Kevin. 'I'll go for a walk somewhere else.' So he went into Mr Gees next door to look at ornaments. Tracey went to the lower part of the shop and Philomena and Shauna looked at shoes near the door. Having found the pair they liked, Philomena asked a shop assistant to get the right size.

Frederick White, sixty, from Omagh, had gone into town with his son Bryan, twenty-seven, to shop. Fred came from a farming background, had worked as a clerk in the Accounts Department of the local education board but had retired in 1989 after a brain haemorrhage. He occupied his time with practical jobs around the house and garden, and with growing prize-winning daffodils. A churchgoer, he was an office holder with the Omagh Ulster Unionist Association, and a member of the Orange Order, a Protestant fraternity. One of his brethren, Tom Reid, Henry's father, described him as 'one of nature's gentlemen', the highest praise one man can give another in County Tyrone. The minister at his church would describe him as 'a man we thought something of in this church and community. Mixed in Fred were many Christian graces, such as goodness, kindness, thoughtfulness for others, and a great love of God and for the things of God.' Fred had been married for thirty-two years to Edith, who taught Business Studies at Omagh College until Fred became ill and she retired to look after him.

Easy-going, sociable Bryan, who had graduated from York University as a horticulturalist, was a member of all his father's organisations and also a keen photographer. A part-time student of business and horticulture, he lived at home, had a girlfriend and a job in Strabane and had just been promoted.

Fred, Edith and Bryan had come back early that morning from a holiday in Aberdeen, where the Whites' daughter Linda, who had left home, had been to university; they had driven around, stayed in bed-and-breakfasts and visited friends. Edith, who was frightened about the bombs that had been going off in Northern Ireland, suggested they should buy a house in Scotland, but Fred told her not to worry: they would be safe in Omagh.

The ferry was late and did not dock till midnight. They toyed with the idea of staying in Belfast, but Edith was afraid of bombs and eager to get home, so they drove straight to Omagh, had a cup of tea and got to bed about 3.30 a.m.

Fred was medically forbidden from driving, so after their late breakfast they agreed Bryan would take him into town to shop for food while Edith did some housework. Before he left, Bryan, as usual, put his arm around her and said, 'Cheerio, Mum. See you shortly.'

Their last call was to the Salad Bowl, where customers were coming and going, unconcerned about the bomb scare. Fred mentioned to the shopkeeper that there had been a coded warning about the bomb, so it was serious, and then, after having made their purchases, he and Bryan left at a few minutes past three, just before Marion Radford paid for her shopping.

The deaths of these thirteen people would break the hearts of the families I write of here, as the loss of Fernando Blasco Baselga (12), Deborah-Anne Cartwright (20), Gareth Conway (18), Oran Doherty (8), Olive Hawkes (60), Julia Hughes (21), Brenda Logue (17), Jolene Marlow (17), Sean McGrath (61), Sean McLaughlin (12), Brian McCrory (54), Rocio Abad Ramon (23), Veda Short (56) and Avril Monaghan (30), her unborn twins, her daughter Maura (1) and her mother Mary Grimes (66) would devastate theirs. Yet even those relatives made up just a small fraction of the thousands whose lives were ravaged from that day onwards by grief, pain and physical and mental trauma.

CHAPTER TWO

THE BOMB

'There was a real sense of watching history in the making. We were all overwhelmed with solidarity and a pure determination to make [Gerry] Adams and Martin McGuinness accountable for their abandonment of Irish sovereignty. We were so confident. We could see that things were going to go our way, that we were going to win the argument and that people were going to join us. We were on the crest of a wave, there was no doubt about that. We felt great'[1] – Member of the Army Council recollecting the night the Real IRA was formed in Oldcastle, County Meath

It would be a very domestic atrocity. Early that Saturday afternoon, the main streets of the little market town of Omagh were more than usually crammed with shoppers; it was the time of year when mothers and children headed to S.D. Kells or Wattersons to buy new school uniforms. Nearly everyone about was from the town or the surrounding villages and countryside of County Tyrone, though an exotic note was provided by the Spaniards among the coachload of children from Donegal who had stopped in Omagh after their visit to the Ulster American Folk Park.

Encouraging more people to come to town was the uncommonly sunny weather in what is a rainy part of the world and the great parade involving over two hundred children that was to be the climax of a week-long cross-community festival. In the Roman Catholic calendar, 15 August is the Feast of the Assumption of the Virgin Mary into heaven, a celebratory day on which Catholics are required to go to Mass and sometimes there are children's processions. But on this day children of all faiths and none were involved in the Omagh carnival, and there were stilt-walkers, clowns, Teletubbies and bands – and five children's floats which were scheduled to pass through Market Street around twenty past three. It was to have been 'a day of dancing, singing and barbecues', a community group representative later told a journalist, trembling as he recounted that it was only a few days previously that the organisers had changed the original plan, which would have had the starting point only 200 yards away from where the bomb went off: 'There would have been thousands lining the streets waiting for the floats.'

Omagh – the biggest town in very rural County Tyrone, with a population then of around 18,000 – is an ordinary place in a beautiful location. Seventy miles west of Belfast and thirty-four miles south of Derry city, it nestles in an agricultural hollow at the centre of the county, at the foothills of the Sperrin Mountains, on the fringe of that fisherman's paradise, the glorious Clogher Valley. It is a town of three rivers: the Camowen and Drumragh flow into Omagh from the south-east, merging less than fifty yards from what would be the bomb site, where they become the Strule. Yet this peaceful countryside has known terrible violence over the centuries, a microcosm of that which periodically afflicts the whole island.

For such a small and isolated country, Ireland has a very complicated and violent history. There is a widespread myth (often used to justify terrorism) that the island was a happy unified Gaelic country until it was invaded by the English in the twelfth century, after which, for more than eight hundred years, the native population strove night and day to overthrow their foreign oppressors.*

The reality is less romantic. Until the eighth century, the island's savage warfare was mainly to do with the continuous struggle for supremacy between provincial kings. Thereafter, the indigenous population had also to contend with Scandinavian invaders turned settlers who were known as 'Norsemen' (from the north) or Vikings.

These marauders were tamed in the eleventh century, but in 1169 Ireland was invaded by their descendants – the Normans from France who had conquered England in 1066 and spread to Wales and Scotland – who had been invited by an overthrown provincial king to help him regain his throne. King Henry II despatched Welsh Normans, who took most of the south-east, including Dublin; in 1171, Henry went to Ireland and secured the submission of the Normans and many Irish kings. The conquest of Ireland was not complete until the end of the reign of Queen Eliza-

---

* 'Throughout history,' begins the 'History of the Conflict' page of the Sinn Féin website, 'the island of Ireland has been regarded as a single national unit. Prior to the Norman invasion from England in 1169, the Irish had their own system of law, culture and language and their own political and social structures. Following the invasion, the island continued to be governed as a single political unit, as a colony of Britain, until 1921. At various times over the next 800 years Irish men and women resisted British rule and attempted to assert Irish independence.'

beth I; she even managed to pacify Ulster, most of which, because of its inaccessibility, had always been a place apart.

It was Elizabeth's successor, James I, who was also King of Scotland, who in the early seventeenth century changed the face of Ulster by seizing almost four million acres and offering them to Scots as well as English settlers. Religion was now an important part of the equation: Elizabeth's father Henry VIII had set up a Church of England independent of the Pope, while Scotland had seen the rapid development of a more radical and puritan form of Protestantism inspired by the teachings of John Calvin.

The tens of thousands of Scottish immigrants who arrived in Ulster along with the English were mainly Presbyterians driven by poverty and religious persecution, for, under James, Protestant dissenters as well as Roman Catholics incurred the wrath of the state. Unwittingly, James created the ideal conditions for tribal warfare. Not only did vast numbers of native Irish have to relocate to inferior land or work as landless labourers, but they found the religion of their new masters alien. Religion was now an enormous obstacle to the intermarriage and assimilation that had been the hallmark of earlier colonists.

Four hundred years on, in that part of Ulster that in 1921 became Northern Ireland, religion is still political: it is assumed that Protestants will be loyal to the union with Britain while Catholics wish for an all-Ireland nation. Both tribes have imbibed at school and at home terrible folk memories. Protestants, for instance, remember how 12,000 settlers – men, women and children – were massacred in a Catholic uprising in 1641; Catholics speak of the horrors inflicted in 1649 by Oliver Cromwell's Puritan forces. The polarisation became complete when the war between the Catholic King James II and his Protestant son-in-law William of Orange spilled over into Ireland. Among the places devastated was Omagh town, which was burned by Williamites. Protestants are as proud as Catholics are resentful that James failed to starve the city of Londonderry* into submission and that William triumphed at the Battle of the Boyne in 1690.

The Orange Order, a defensive association loyal to the Crown, was set up by Protestants in 1795 to combat sectarian assaults from the Catholic militant agrarian Defenders; it celebrated the Boyne victory annually on

---

* 'Derry' became 'Londonderry' in 1613. Catholics call it Derry, Protestants call it Londonderry, fence-sitters call it Derry/Londonderry and humorists call it Stroke City.

12 July by parading with banners displaying their heroes and bands playing partisan tunes – providing the occasion of vicious tribal violence. (Catholics would develop a mirror image with the Ancient Order of Hibernians, which expressed peaceful nationalist aspirations for self-government under the British Crown, and now in Ireland is almost defunct, though republicans are inveterate and aggressive paraders.)

Ireland had become part of the United Kingdom in 1801, and in the nineteenth century, particularly after the terrible potato famine of the 1840s, British statesmen sought with some success to find benign solutions to Irish problems. Irish members of parliament, however, symbolised the continuing religious divide. With a few notable exceptions, Protestants were unionists who wanted to keep the status quo and Catholics were nationalists who wanted Home Rule. Occasionally, small groups would attempt a revolution. In 1798, exhilarated by the successful American and French revolutions, the United Irishmen, led by a few middle-class Presbyterians and Catholics who wanted religious equality, radical reform and an Irish republic, mounted an idealistic rebellion with the help of French troops. 'To unite Protestant, Catholic and Dissenter under the common name of Irishmen in order to break the connection with England, the never failing source of all our political evils' was the avowed aim of Theobald Wolfe Tone, its most famous leader. Disastrously, it attracted the sectarian Defenders and vast numbers of sectarian Catholics; there were mass atrocities committed by both government and rebels and a death toll of 30,000. In his speech from the dock Tone would lament that the 'fair and open war' for which he had planned had 'degenerated into a system of assassination, massacre, and plunder'. The Irish Republican Brotherhood (IRB), founded in the 1850s, were a tiny group who considered themselves heirs to the United Irishmen and were dedicated to achieving a republic through revolution. Their sister movement, the Fenian Brotherhood,* was based in the United States, beginning an Irish-American tradition of encouraging and funding revolution in Ireland. Riven by dissent and splits, it staged a doomed invasion of Ireland in 1867.

As a result of decades of political pressure from Irish nationalist members of parliament, and despite bitter opposition from their unionist counterparts, a Home Rule bill was passed in 1914; it was suspended a few months later on the outbreak of the First World War. In April 1916, a tiny IRB

---

* Named after the Fianna, a band of mythological warriors. 'Fenian' is a term of abuse used against Northern Irish republicans, who proudly use it of themselves.

cabal instigated an attempted *coup d'état* that sparked off an insurrection that led to around 450 deaths – mainly civilians – and much destruction in Dublin; it would become popularly known as the Easter Rising. Although fewer than three thousand insurgents were involved, and they had little support, the execution of sixteen of the rebels swung public opinion towards them and gave armed republicanism a pantheon of heroes – most notably Patrick Pearse,* a brilliant propagandist whose legacy of stirring rhetoric would make him in every generation the patron saint of uncompromising republicanism. The gulf between unionists and nationalists became a chasm: now unionists in the northern part of Ireland were ready to resist Irish unification to the death.

The 1918 General Election saw the defeat of constitutional nationalism at the hands of Sinn Féin ('Ourselves'), a hitherto tiny party committed to cultural, economic and political self-sufficiency which had been hijacked by republicans: its success owed much to intimidation as well as to its opposition to the threat of conscription. In 1919, its MPs refused to recognise the British parliament, set up Dáil Éireann ('Assembly of Ireland') in Dublin and declared a republic. Simultaneously, a group of physical-force enthusiasts assassinated two policemen and kicked off a guerrilla war against the British security forces that lasted until July 1921, was distinguished by brutality on both sides and would lead to about 1,400 deaths: its members would become known as the Irish Republican Army (IRA).

In Northern Ireland, plagued by IRA attacks and coping with a flood of Protestant refugees from the south, unionist resistance to all-Ireland home rule intensified, as did inter-communal fighting, with loyalists taking vengeance on Catholics for IRA violence. A British offer of limited devolution of power to parliaments representing the six north-eastern counties and the other twenty-six was accepted by unionists and rejected by Sinn Féin.

Although an Anglo-Irish treaty setting up a twenty-six-county Irish Free State with dominion status was signed in December 1921, approved by the Dáil and endorsed by the electorate, Sinn Féin and the IRA split, and an obdurate minority took to the gun. Around two thousand died in the ensuing civil war between the forces of the Free State and those known as Republicans: the atrocities committed by both sides would leave a legacy of terrible bitterness. Northern Ireland unionists shrank further into isolationism.

* He is also known as Pádraig MacPiarais or Pádraig Pearse.

Republicans surrendered in 1923 and in 1926 the majority abandoned Sinn Féin and the IRA — both of which refused to recognise the state — to enter electoral politics as Fianna Fáil ('Soldiers of Destiny'), which soon became and still is the dominant party. Like the first Free State government, Fianna Fáil would deal with the IRA by hanging, imprisoning and interning those they could not seduce from violence.

The pattern was set. Henceforward, intransigent republicans would weary of pointless violence and the degeneracy 'of assassination, massacre, and plunder', and would either retire or become drawn into the political process, leaving an irreconcilable rump behind to plot another round of carnage. In 1939, for instance, calling itself the 'Government of the Irish Republic', the IRA Army Council formally declared war on the British government and embarked on a bombing campaign in Britain which lasted until the killing of five civilians in Coventry in August 1939 brought a wave of repression throughout the British Isles. Pro-Nazi during the Second World War, they had an ineffective campaign in Northern Ireland. Reduced to two hundred members in the mid-1940s, they regrouped and began to rearm, announcing they would no longer try to overthrow the government of the Republic but would concentrate on freeing Northern Ireland. What was known as the Border Campaign, in which southern guerrillas (known as flying columns) launched attacks in the north on security targets, lasted from 1956 to 1961, when internment north and south and a lack of popular support caused the Army Council to call it off.

As with the persecution of Protestants in the early years of the Irish Free State, the consequence of every wave of terrorist violence was to make the unionist majority in Northern Ireland ever more paranoid about the Catholic minority: gerrymandering (manipulating) electoral boundaries and petty discrimination was the hallmark of its governments.

What was left of the IRA hijacked the civil rights movement that began in 1968 and split in two in 1970: the anti-sectarian Marxist Official IRA recognised the legitimacy of the Irish government and were turning against violence; the Provisional IRA were in the Defender tradition, maintained an abstentionist position on the Dáil and were committed to fighting for a united Ireland. They would tack towards Marxism themselves during their long war, which would lead to more than three thousand deaths, of which 56 per cent were civilian. When in 1986 the Provisionals agreed to recognise the Irish government, there was another split which led to the formation of the Continuity IRA. The IRA's political wing, Sinn Féin, which had been in the doldrums for years, was by now revived but also split between Official Sinn Féin, Provisional Sinn Féin and Republican Sinn Féin. The next revolutionary groundhog day would come in 1997 when a splinter group rejected the Provisionals' abandonment of violence and founded the Real IRA: this would lead to the devastation of Omagh.

A garrison town for centuries, and about twenty-five miles from the border, Omagh is home to Lisanelly army barracks, which is now vacant but in 1998 was still used by the Royal Irish Regiment (RIR) and visiting units of the British Army, and was over the years a popular target for local republican terrorists. However, the car bomb that wrecked the town was left outside the drapers S. D. Kells, one of three family businesses (the others were in Enniskillen and Lisnaskea) owned by Roy Kells, who has bravely borne much trouble and tragedy in his life.

As a part-time member of the Ulster Defence Regiment, loathed by republicans for its implacable resistance to terrorism, Roy lived through the murders of eleven of his company. As a member of the security forces he was what the Provisionals called 'a legitimate target'; by 1998 he had survived three assassination attempts and his Lisnaskea shop had been burned three times, bombed a dozen or so times and completely destroyed once. But nothing compared with what would now happen in Omagh; nine people would die in Roy Kells's shop.

Apart from the rivers, there is nothing much to look at in Omagh but churches, graveyards, pubs and takeaways, a modern shopping centre, a variety of small provincial shops and the fine nineteenth-century neoclassical courthouse, with its Tuscan-columned portico, that looks down over the town. Yet this unpretentious little place has always been a constant target of the notoriously ruthless and active East Tyrone Brigade of the IRA. One of Omagh's most famous sons, the novelist Benedict Kiely (1919–2007), was a non-sectarian Irish nationalist who came to loathe the evil done in Ireland's name. His novella *Proxopera*, published in 1977, about the kidnapping of a retired schoolmaster forced to drive to town a creamery can loaded with explosives, is a savage indictment of the brutality of the local IRA. As the novelist Colum McCann put it, 'Kiely knew the poison of narrow lives, and where empathy could trump it.'

The people of Tyrone had suffered severely from the poison of narrow, violent nationalism for almost three decades, particularly in those parts on the border with the Republic of Ireland: it suited republican terrorists to be able to avoid the British Army and the police by skipping across to a more friendly jurisdiction. There are bitter sectarian hatreds in such areas that go back to the arrival of the seventeenth-century Scots Presbyterian settlers whose descendants love the land their forebears cultivated as passionately as do the descendants of those they dispossessed. At the same time, over the centuries, there have been many local people whose empathy for their neighbours transcended political or religious differences.

Almost four centuries on, there were members of the Provisional IRA (known by the army as the PIRA but popularly known simply as the IRA) near the border who found excuses vengefully to kill Protestant farmers and their sons in the hope of forcing land on to the market and buying it back into Catholic hands. My friend Henry Reid has gone to many a wake for murdered neighbours.

County Tyrone has had more than its share of major atrocities. No local will navigate the Ballygawley roundabout, on the A5 to Omagh, without remembering horrifying accounts of the carnage in 1988 when eight soldiers were killed and nineteen injured by an IRA landmine. At Teebane crossroads, on the Omagh–Cookstown road, they will remember just as clearly that, in 1992, eight Protestant workmen were blown up there by a landmine: the East Tyrone IRA brigade's justification was that the men worked for a construction company that had been carrying out repairs at Lisanelly barracks. Omagh town itself suffered on numerous occasions during the 1970s and 1980s when IRA bombs devastated its centre: in the most tragic incident, in 1973, five off-duty soldiers were murdered by a bomb in the car park of Knock Na Moe Castle Hotel where they had been attending a dance.

Yet by August 1998 most people in Omagh believed the Troubles were over. The IRA ceasefire of July 1997 had held, and the Good Friday Agreement* of Easter 1998 had been ratified in May by referenda north and south of the border, with support respectively from 71 and 94 per cent. A religiously mixed town with a small Catholic majority and little sectarianism, Omagh hungered for peace: it had voted overwhelmingly for a deal that included the release of both republican and loyalist prisoners in exchange for the abandonment of violence. The formal acceptance by Sinn Féin, the IRA's political wing, that a united Ireland could not be brought

---

* Terminology in Northern Ireland is often loaded. Nationalists tend to refer to the Good Friday Agreement and unionists to the Belfast Agreement. (Some evangelical Protestant churches do not recognise Good Friday as a day of atonement: others find the republican cult of Easter 1916, with its themes of sacrifice and resurrection, sacrilegious.) I am opting for the better-known option.

about without the consent of the majority in Northern Ireland, was the main price it paid for the right to join a government devolved from Westminster and operated by a power-sharing executive.

Elections to the new Northern Ireland Assembly in June 1998 had produced a solid majority of pro-Agreement candidates, and Sinn Féin had polled sufficiently strongly to demonstrate that republicans were largely behind its peace strategy. In July, power-sharing took symbolic form with the election by the Assembly of the Ulster Unionist Party leader, David Trimble, as First Minister (designate) and Seamus Mallon of the nationalist Social Democratic and Labour Party (SDLP) as Deputy First Minister (designate): preparations for devolving power from London were well underway, though the refusal of the Provisionals to disarm was causing a delay. British and Irish attempts to construct a settlement acceptable to nationalists and unionists had been going on for several years but had come to fruition after a year of intense effort and high-wire negotiation by Northern Irish political parties and the British, Irish and US governments: Prime Minister Tony Blair, Taoiseach Bertie Ahern and President Bill Clinton were being lauded around the world as the brokers of a deal that had brought permanent peace to Northern Ireland.

Not even ugly sectarian violence in July, connected with disputed Orange parades, could dampen the general belief that Northern Ireland had a peaceful future in prospect. There was little appetite among politicians or the populace at large to worry about the activities of dissident republicans, despite threats and occasional violence from the homicidal Irish National Liberation Army (INLA), Continuity IRA and, most significant of all, Real IRA. The Provisionals had realised that their campaign to bomb Britain out of Northern Ireland and the unionist population into a United Ireland was a lost cause and they had better settle for power-sharing: the few hundred spread around INLA, the Continuity IRA and the Real IRA intended to carry on the violence. Widely dismissed as the last ineffectual gasp of violent republicanism, these groups helped each other informally, but were becoming increasingly isolated. Events had moved on, and it was generally felt that history had passed them by.

The Real IRA* was formed in November 1997 following a bitter confrontation over the peace strategy of Gerry Adams and Martin McGuinness.

* The group's wish to be known as Óglaigh na hÉireann was never realistic. Early in 1998, when some of their followers set up a roadblock in South Armagh, they told motorists: 'We're from the IRA. The Real IRA,' and the name stuck.

Outmanoeuvred in mid-October at a Provisional Extraordinary General Army Convention at Falcarragh in County Donegal, the Quartermaster General, Michael McKevitt, recognised that he and his eight or so supporters had lost the internal debate and on 26 October they resigned en bloc. The Continuity IRA, who were cock-a-hoop at having wrecked the Protestant village of Markethill the previous September with a van bomb, hoped for a flood of recruits, but McKevitt despised their leadership and wanted to run his own show.

McKevitt, who was forty-eight, was a builder from a republican family in Dundalk; he had joined the IRA in his teens. In his twenties he had been shot in the knees by members of the Official IRA; this punishment, known as knee-capping, is a favourite of Northern Ireland paramilitaries and was carried out in revenge for McKevitt's involvement in knee-capping an Official in Newry. During his career McKevitt took part in shootings and bombings and for many years had efficiently managed arms procurement and distribution; he knew the location of the arms bunkers that held the IRA's enormous cache of weapons he had helped to import from Libya in the 1980s.

Totally trusted, reliable, security-conscious, efficient and discreet, McKevitt was number two in the Provisionals to Thomas 'Slab' Murphy, the millionaire smuggler and brutal Chief of Staff, who disappointed him by choosing to side with the Adams/McGuinness leadership. McKevitt was a warped idealist who saw compromise as treachery; Murphy was a pragmatist who knew that to leave the Provisionals would be to put his criminal empire at risk from two governments who were turning a blind eye only because he supported the peace process. Without either the mental agility that enabled the Sinn Féin leadership to pretend that being ministers of the British Crown was a republican victory or the empathy to understand the Irish people's desire for peace, McKevitt clung to the militarism of past generations and their belief that – in the words of Mary MacSwiney, a fanatical opponent of the 1921 Treaty – 'the people have no right to be wrong'. In principle, McKevitt was prepared to see the last republican volunteer fall fighting the last British soldier; anyone else who died in the process was regarded as expendable.

Eamon Collins, an IRA informer later murdered by ex-colleagues, described McKevitt as 'a violent, secretive man', whose weakness was his 'impetuosity'.[2] His intransigence was matched by that of his partner of many years, Bernadette Sands, who styled herself Bernadette Sands-McKevitt*: her elder brother Bobby was the first and most famous of the IRA hunger strikers (who died trying to force the British government into granting terrorist prisoners political status†); he was elected to the House of Commons in a sensational parliamentary by-election for the constituency of Fermanagh and South Tyrone three weeks before he died of starvation‡. In a message from prison he had recommended to the Provisional leadership his young sister. 'She's in Dundalk, south of the border – on the run,' he wrote. 'Firebombs went off in her pocket. She can't come up here, but if groomed would do down there.' This encomium helped her gain a high profile in republican circles, unusual for a woman in such a male-dominated world.

Irish republicans wallow in necrophilia, their dead are hero-martyrs, the merest foot soldier blown up by his own bomb will be annually commemorated and may even have a Sinn Féin branch named after him. Bobby Sands had rapidly become the most famous of their heroic martyred dead since 1916: 100,000 mourners followed his coffin in Belfast, while there were riots in Dublin and angry protests in many European cities. Sinn Féin exploited the twenty-seven-year-old's death in May 1981 to brilliant effect in the international media, while Prime Minister Margaret

---

* They met in the early 1980s in a factory making electronic components and formed a relationship. He secured an annulment from the Roman Catholic Church but divorce was not legal in Ireland until 1997. She took his name but they did not marry until 9 September 1999.

† It was important for the republican psyche to be classed as political prisoners rather than criminals, but such status also offered privileges like free association with other prisoners that would make it easier to control and influence jailed IRA members. The hunger strikes also won the Provisionals tremendous support at home and abroad.

‡ The first child of a family of four, Bobby Sands was born in 1954. In 1972, by far the worst year of the Troubles, loyalists intimidated him out of his job as an apprentice coachbuilder and his family out of their home. He joined the IRA in Twinbrook, West Belfast, was arrested, and married his pregnant girlfriend while on remand on the charge of possession of weapons. Sentenced in 1973 to five years' imprisonment, he was released in April 1976 and arrested in October as part of an IRA team which fire-bombed a local furnishing company and fought a subsequent gun battle with the police. He was sentenced to fourteen years for possession of a gun, and his wife, who had lost their second baby when he was arrested, divorced him. During both periods in jail, Sands became an enthusiast for the Irish language, Irish nationalist writing and international revolutionaries like Che Guevara; he wrote propagandist articles and sentimental poetry and when he initiated the 1981 hunger strike, he kept a hidden diary on toilet paper.

Thatcher's crisp comment in the House of Commons that 'Mr Sands was a convicted criminal. He chose to take his own life. It was a choice that his organisation did not allow to many of its victims,' was thought unfeeling. Nine more hunger strikers died over the next three months, the last on 20 August, the same day that Sands's election agent won the by-election. (It would be claimed decades later, though denied by the Provisional leadership, that they had been secretly offered enough concessions in time to save the lives of six of the hunger strikers, but chose instead, for propaganda reasons, to let them die.[3])

Sands was rapidly adopted as an iconic pin-up for Marxists, revolutionaries, the down-trodden and the gullible all over the world, becoming almost a competitor to his hero Che Guevara: the countries in which there are memorials to him and streets named after him include Cuba, France, Iran and the United States. He inspired much mawkish prose, poetry and song. An enormous portrait of him painted on the gable wall of the Sinn Féin office in Belfast's Falls Road reproduced his dictum: 'Everyone, Republican or otherwise, has their own particular part to play. No part is too great or too small; no one is too old or too young to do something.'

The Sands cult helped fill the IRA's coffers – particularly in the United States – and give their spokesmen a new legitimacy abroad. Selective quotes from him were also used by the republican leadership over the years to justify whatever strategy they were selling at the time to their grass roots: in due course he would be cited as an inspiration for the peace process. He certainly assisted the Provisionals' electoral success as they moved to what became known as the strategy of 'the armalite and ballot box'*: the IRA would go on murdering but Sinn Féin would look for votes.

For the McKevitts, however, the true Bobby Sands was expressed in such quotes as 'We must see our present fight right through to the very end.' As far as they were concerned, the Provisionals had sold out and betrayed their martyrs. Their objective was to bring the IRA back to uncompromising basics. McKevitt saw himself, he would confide in a

---

* 'The People's MP' was a song that ended 'Forever we'll remember him that man who died in pain/That his country North and South might be united once again/To mourn him is to organise and build a movement strong/With ballot box and armalite, with music and with song.'

friend, as part of the relay race that was Irish republicanism: he now had the baton which, if necessary, he would pass on to another.[4]

The Real IRA's structure was modelled slavishly on that of the Provisional IRA, as its political wing, the 32 County Sovereignty Committee, later Movement (Ireland has thirty-two counties: intransigent republicans call Northern Ireland 'the Six Counties' and the Republic 'the Twenty-Six Counties'), was based on Sinn Féin. The only difference, according to David Rupert (who gave evidence against McKevitt at his trial), was that McKevitt felt that the same people should run the 32CSM and the Army Council*,[5] although, as with IRA/Sinn Féin, real power was in the hands of a tiny clique. It suited McKevitt to give the nominal title of Chief of Staff of the Real IRA to someone else, and continue to call himself by his Provisional title of Quartermaster, but there was no doubt who was in charge. McKevitt was very strong about the importance of discipline: anyone challenging his authority was left in no doubt that the penalty for disobedience was death.

In a decision that would spell disaster for the people of Omagh, thirty-five-year-old Liam Campbell became Director of Operations for Northern Ireland. He was a cabinetmaker, farmer and smuggler of tobacco, alcohol and fireworks; conveniently, he lived at Faughart, right on the border in County Louth, not far from McKevitt's home in Blackrock, a seaside village three miles from Dundalk.† Campbell too came from an IRA background: one of his brothers had been blown up by his own landmine, another served fourteen years for terrorist offences. But Liam was more hardline than either of them; in 1983 his terrorist activities on the border had resulted in the British government taking the exceptional step of banning him from setting foot in Northern Ireland, over the road from where he lived. Campbell ignored those of his colleagues who worried that car bombs could prove counterproductive if civilians perished: the Provisionals, after all, had killed hundreds of civilians over the years and had usually got away with it.

The haemorrhage of recruits from the Provisionals had been staunched

---

* Membership of the Real IRA has been specifically denied by a number of 32CSM members, including Francie Mackey.

† Dundalk took in trainloads of Catholic refugees from Belfast during an intense period of sectarian violence in 1969; a significant section of them were intransigent republicans, or became so in their flight and exile. Later, the IRA began to use Dundalk as a base for moving weaponry and housing for members on the run and the town became a centre for republican smuggling and racketeering. It was popularly known as 'El Paso' because of its lawlessness.

when – after a few weeks in denial – the Army Council had sent in heavy-hitters around the country to persuade and threaten waverers to stay loyal, yet the Real IRA had retained a substantial number of disillusioned Provisional recruits. Having squirrelled away Provisionals' explosives, they were quickly the strongest and best armed of the dissident groups. McKevitt had recruited several experienced engineers – bomb- and weapon-makers – but had few people who knew how to transport bombs efficiently and the organisation was short of money. The Real IRA had still not made its presence known to the public when, on 8 December 1997, Bernadette Sands-McKevitt told the world about the 32 County Sovereignty Movement, set up the previous day in County Dublin at the seaside village of Rush.

Although she had three young children, and ran The Print Junction T-shirt, picture-framing and souvenir shop in Dundalk (sample T-shirt logo: 'When Irish eyes are smiling, you know they're up to something'), thirty-nine-year-old Bernadette was as dedicated to the republican cause as McKevitt. She was described by American journalist Kevin Cullen as 'gracious, modest, almost shy' and dressed 'in understated, handsome suits that make her look like one of the yuppies who have done well in Ireland's booming economy'. 'A spin doctor's dream', said the *Irish Times*: 'bright, well-groomed and friendly . . . her obvious skills, her easy command in a leadership role, are noticeable.' It was her hard work, eloquence and charismatic pedigree that brought the 32CSM quickly into existence and for a while won it extensive media coverage as the new political entity on the block.

Her brother's generation 'didn't fight for peace', she explained. 'We don't want to see peace, we want independence.' Like McKevitt, she was the key figure who gave the top title to someone else: Francie Mackey – a Sinn Féin councillor in Omagh until he was suspended over his opposition to the peace process (which he said should be resisted 'by whatever means') and now an independent – became Chairman. Yet it was Vice-Chair Sands-McKevitt who launched the group in Ireland and the US, where she soon developed a support base with the help of New Yorker Martin Galvin.* Their Movement, she explained, was 'a one-issue, broad-based'

---

* Martin Galvin, a Bronx lawyer and armchair general, was a committed activist for Sinn Féin for many years, helping as a propagandist and fundraiser. He had resigned from its US fundraising arm, the Irish Northern Aid Committee (NORAID), in protest at the first IRA ceasefire in 1994.

group committed to defending Irish sovereignty. The acceptance by Sinn Féin of the principle that there could be no end to partition without the consent of the people of Northern Ireland was 'a unionist veto dressed up in another way' and was therefore unacceptable.

While she claimed to be in favour of the IRA ceasefire, Sands-McKevitt's explanation that her concern was 'for future generations because [partition] has been proved time and again to create conditions to cause insurrections' made her true position obvious. She wanted donations, begging Americans not to be misled by Sinn Féin's change of heart, and she made it abundantly clear that Sinn Féin would have a tough time holding on to the Bobby Sands brand name. Having told Radio Free Éireann, a New York republican station, in January, that the 32CSM were 'watchdogs over Irish sovereignty', she concluded by saying that, as she had been waiting for the station to call her, she had 'happened to lift Bobby's book' which opened at his diary entry on the very first day of his hunger strike. 'I just think it's very poignant that I happened to open at this particular page.' She read a long passage beginning:

> I'm standing on the threshold of another trembling world. May God have mercy on my soul. My heart is very sore because I know that I have broken my poor mother's heart and my home is struck with unbearable anxiety. But I have considered all the arguments and tried every means to avoid what has become the unavoidable. It has been forced upon me and my comrades for 4½ years of stark inhumanity. I am a political prisoner. I am a political prisoner because I am a casualty of a perennial war that is being fought between the oppressed Irish people and an alien unwanted repressive regime that refuses to withdraw from our land. I believe in the God-given right of the Irish nation to sovereign independence and the right of any Irish man or woman to assert this right in armed revolution. This is why I am incarcerated, naked and tortured.

Unlike Bobby Sands, though, the Real IRA were not in the business of dying for Ireland. Like him in his pre-prison career, they wanted to kill. By January 1998, they were ready to begin a bombing campaign led by Liam Campbell. The purpose was to devastate populated areas, kill police and soldiers, demonstrate to the world that, despite the Good Friday Agreement, it was business as usual for republican terrorism, and thereby demoralise unionists and kill off political negotiations.

In the ensuing months, the Real IRA was responsible for sending letter bombs, planting incendiary devices and the occasional minor mortar attack on RUC stations in Counties Armagh and Down; in January 1998, a 500-pound car bomb was defused in Banbridge, County Down; a similar bomb exploded at an RUC station in Moira, County Down, in February, causing extensive damage to commercial and private property and slightly injuring eleven people, mostly RUC officers; severe damage to business premises was caused by a 300-pound car bomb in Portadown, County Armagh, three days later.

By March 1998, as the multi-party talks were edging towards what became the Good Friday Agreement, the 32CSM were worrying Sinn Féin: 'It is emerging as a pressure group of substance,' wrote John Mullin in the *Guardian* in March 1998, in an interview with Bernadette Sands-McKevitt, who spoke of what she saw as the selling-out of republicanism; she was all for negotiation, but only after 'England' had agreed to leave Ireland. Dundalk had become 'a flagship': she and people like her had 'decided we would try and do something, instead of sitting in the background, grumbling': 32CSM committees were, she claimed, springing up all round the country.

Still the peace.process rolled remorselessly onward, culminating in the Good Friday Agreement of 10 April, which the 32CSM leadership had decided to contest at the United Nations. Bearing a lengthy submission challenging the legality of British involvement in Ireland and consequently that of the Agreement, Sands-McKevitt and Rory Dougan from Dundalk set off to America. To his deep chagrin, Francie Mackey, who was to join them, was refused a visa – for what he rightly described as 'political reasons' – because of his conviction in the early 1990s for assaulting a member of the RUC.

Through the intercession of Congressman Peter King, Sands-McKevitt addressed members of the Ad Hoc Committee on Ireland on Capitol Hill. She and Dougan were politely and seriously received at the UN, which troubled UN representatives of the Republic of Ireland, and the ill-informed New York City Council presented them with a proclamation addressed to the Movement's leaders for their role as an advocate 'for peaceful and progressive change in Ireland'. In O'Lunney's bar on West 43rd Street, sitting under a ceramic portrait of her brother, she denounced the forthcoming referendum on the Agreement as illegal and was heartily applauded for calling for independence rather than peace.

In a highly significant snub, the Sands family refused to attend the Sinn Féin commemoration of Bobby's death on 5 May 1998. In their view, as

Bernadette put it, the Sinn Féin/IRA leadership were hypocrites: 'A united Ireland is what our people have bombed and shot for all these years . . . Bobby did not die for cross-border bodies with executive powers. He did not die for nationalists to be equal British citizens within the Northern Ireland state. The cause of conflict in our country is the presence of a foreign government, the British government, that has imposed its will against the will of the Irish people.' The pro-Agreement referenda were a 'dupe' and a 'con'.

The McKevitts were in Dublin on 8 May for the funeral of the first Real IRA hero/martyr, twenty-seven-year-old father of three Ronan McLaughlin. After a tip-off from informers, McLaughlin, whose republican mother had long been wanted by the RUC, had been shot dead by a female garda while attempting, as part of a six-man armed gang,* to fundraise by robbing a Securicor van.

Sands-McKevitt wore black and McKevitt, bizarrely, wore a baseball cap with 'AMERIKA' in red-stitch lettering. Like his old boss Slab Murphy, McKevitt liked to stay out of the public eye with the help of a scarf and a cap, but this time he was caught walking past gravestones by a television camera: the resulting clip would be shown all over the world after the Omagh bomb. The writer Kevin Toolis compared McKevitt's small band of supporters to 'the last dregs of an old army as they gathered outside the run down Dublin council house, peeling with paint. Their faces, men and women, were exhausted, wracked by fags and poverty.'

Francie Mackey gave the graveside oration: 'Ronán MacLochlainn [the Gaelicised version of his name] remained loyal and true to the IRA constitution when others have used and usurped it,' he said. Councillor Mackey said many republicans would 'make the right decision' and 'develop the struggle against British rule in Ireland'. No amount of 'spin-doctoring or fudging' could legitimise the British presence. Republicans had a duty to do 'whatever is necessary' to prevent the dilution of Irish national sovereignty, he said. A long interview with Sands-McKevitt published in the *Irish Times* the next day finished with her smiling statement: 'We've broken the mould so far, we've done a lot of things that are very unpredictable. We're trying not to make the mistakes of the past.' The following day, in a phone call to the UTV newsroom, a man claimed responsibility for a

---

* Their arms included an AK-47, a pump-action shotgun and a Magnum .357, all weapons frequently used by the IRA, as well as a simulated hand-held rocket launcher of a deadly type manufactured by IRA engineers.

mortar attack on an RUC station in County Fermanagh, on behalf of the 'true IRA', the 'real IRA'. Alarm was growing in official circles that the 32CSM was clearly gaining strength politically and the Real IRA militarily.

It was at this time that the Irish government decided to try direct diplomacy and sent a secret message to the 32CSM through Father Alec Reid, a priest in the Redemptorist monastery in the Falls Road, who had been the conduit between Sinn Féin/IRA and successive Dublin governments from the 1980s. Once again, Dublin's emissary was a diplomat, who from 1981 had become a devoted member of Fianna Fáil and a close adviser to its leaders. Dr Martin Mansergh, although a Protestant born in England, brought up in Cambridge and educated at King's School, Canterbury, and Christ Church, Oxford, was of Irish stock and from childhood a romantic Irish nationalist. He was trusted by republicans: although he deplored contemporary violence, he was a proud apologist for the physical-force tradition in Irish history until the end of the Irish Civil War in 1923 and himself had shown great sympathy for republican aspirations for a united Ireland. 'He articulates the diehard Republican agenda in a posh English accent,' said Ulster Unionist MP Ken Maginnis of him in 1992.

Mansergh is in the tradition of the poet and playwright Alice Milligan (1865–1953), an Omagh Protestant who became a romantic nationalist in the 1890s. My IRA-supporting grandmother gave me her *Collected Poems* when I was ten, perhaps hopeful that I would emulate the child in 'When I was a little girl', who tells how her siblings quivered with fear at their nurse's warning that the Fenians were coming:

> But one little rebel there,
> Watching all with laughter,
> Thought 'When the Fenians come
> I'll rise and go after.'

> Wished she had been a boy
> And a good deal older –
> Able to walk for miles
> With a gun on her shoulder;

> Able to lift aloft
> That Green Flag o'er them
> (Red Coats and black police
> Flying before them).

Milligan lived to wring her hands over brother killing brother in the civil war and to see a Fianna Fáil government under the republican Éamon de Valera, a 1916 leader who had been on the losing side in the civil war, dealing brutally with former IRA colleagues, but she was dead before the lethal feuds of the 1970s between the Official and Provisional IRA and the Irish National Liberation Army that continued the long, grim tradition of murderous splits between pragmatists and diehards.* A new round was about to begin.

Around this time Martin Mansergh wrote: 'Ideological rigidity is nearly always associated with the politics of failure, as the real and the ideal move further and further apart. The unwitting repetition of history decades later is often frustrating.'[6] As an historian, Mansergh recognised that today's diehard was tomorrow's pragmatist; after years of nudging Provisionals towards compromise, he was faced with a splinter group that thought that accepting reality was selling out. Yet he was prepared to try. Mansergh not only understands much of the hearts and minds of intransigent republicans; he is also a man of extraordinary patience, when he deems it necessary, ready to listen courteously and for as long as it takes even to the mad, the bad and the boring.

The Real IRA were pleased with the overture. To be meeting Mansergh was a sign they were being taken seriously by Dublin. In a Dundalk monastery – a venue arranged by Father Reid – Mansergh and a colleague met four leaders of the 32CSM: Sands-McKevitt, Francie Mackey, Rory Dougan and Joe Dillon, a Dubliner who had put together the claim to the UN that the British government was in breach of the International Covenant on Civil and Political Rights, the International Covenant on Economic Social and Cultural Rights, the United Nations Declaration on the Granting of Independence to Colonial Countries and Peoples and the Declaration on Principles of International Law Concerning Friendly Relations and Co-operation Among States in Accordance with the Charter of the United Nations.

In a long meeting, Mansergh, said one of those present, 'used the language of understanding our position and repeatedly nodded his head, but that was probably him being clever. There were some frank moments when we

---

* My pacifist brother was scheduled to speak about this at the 1998 Alice Milligan Summer School. Scheduled to run in Omagh for a week from Monday 17 August, it was cancelled after the bomb.

put our side and he countered it – but there were no rows. It was quite civilised.' Just as Gerry Adams, Martin McGuinness and Pat Doherty would insist they were representing only Sinn Féin, so Mackey insisted to Mansergh that they were representing only the 32CSM. 'Bombs along the border don't help,' said Mansergh. 'If there is somebody here who can pass the message on, then fine.'[7]

It was clear to the quartet that Mansergh wanted to communicate directly with the Real IRA rather than listen to elaborate arguments about international law. A republican source told a journalist that this made some of the Real IRA people conclude that 'because the government was concentrating on ending the war, that was all that counted. It made some [Real IRA] army people believe that war was the only thing the Irish government would listen to.'

Mansergh left further fruitless meetings to Father Reid, to whom he sent a letter rejecting the 32CSM's case: 'No breach of international law existing at the present time can be established that would . . . now justify further or continued armed insurgency.' Still Bernadette Sands-McKevitt trudged grimly on, though her message was not reaching many. On 10 August, in Dundalk, she launched the Movement's newspaper, *The Sovereign Nation*, in the presence of one journalist and one photographer.

The prime reason why Mansergh was not prepared to talk further to the 32CSM was that the Real IRA were continuing on a ruthless campaign of devastation, in conjunction with the Continuity IRA and the INLA: essentially, the INLA stole cars and the Real IRA turned them into bombs which were usually delivered by the Continuity IRA. In June, despite a fifty-minute warning, a 200-pound car bomb close to the local RUC station injured six in Newtownhamilton, County Armagh, wrecked the town centre and caused over £3 million-worth of damage to property; and on Saturday 1 August, a 500-pound car bomb in the centre of Banbridge seriously injured thirty-three civilians and two policemen and caused millions of pounds' worth of damage.

The higher number of casualties in Banbridge was the result of a crucial change in strategy. Frustrated by their failure to kill members of the security forces, Liam Campbell had altered the orders: henceforth, they would be less concerned about warnings. Although they did not necessarily mean to kill civilians, they were very eager to kill police and were becoming more relaxed about what they called 'collateral damage'.

To an extraordinary degree, few politicians or journalists showed much concern. After all the crises and cliff-hangers and near disasters and, finally, the apparent political triumphs, of the previous few months, fatigue had set in. A dissident bomb in Banbridge in which no one died was not going to excite Number 10 Downing Street or stop Tony Blair or Mo Mowlam, the Secretary of State for Northern Ireland, from going on holiday. The RUC and the Irish gardaí were worried about the Real IRA, but believed it so well infiltrated by informers as to be under reasonable control. The location of the car bombs apparently indicated that it was confining itself to operations in Protestant towns near its safe haven on the Louth/Armagh border.

Police chiefs were also well aware that their political masters were plugging the message of 'normalisation': army and police were encouraged to keep a low profile. In the euphoric post-Agreement climate, wishful thinking was rife. People revelled in a world where their local town centre was no longer cordoned off, where there were no helicopters overhead and no security zones or concrete 'dragon's teeth' preventing them from parking near the shops. The predominantly Catholic Omagh was a most unlikely target, but even had the police station been fully staffed, there would not have been enough police to check the hundreds of cars coming into town. And that day, because of an officer's wedding, instead of one inspector, four sergeants and up to twenty constables, there were only two sergeants and eight or so constables.

The Vauxhall Cavalier that would devastate Omagh had been stolen early the previous Thursday from Carrickmacross, County Monaghan, and fitted with a false Northern Ireland number plate; the boot was loaded with 150–200 kilograms of improvised explosives – probably a mixture of fertiliser, sugar and some Semtex. A booster charge and a timer power unit housed in a plastic Addis lunchbox probably sat in the front passenger glove compartment.

On Saturday, the Cavalier – preceded by a scout car – was driven from Dundalk to Omagh. The pair of two-man teams communicated via mobile phones that had been provided by a Continuity IRA member: telephone traffic would later provide crucial evidence.

The bombers had not yet reached Omagh when my friend Lorraine Reid arrived there not long after two o'clock. She saw a parking place outside S.D. Kells, on Market Street close to the junction with Dublin Road, but decided to park closer to the shopping centre between Moira's Fashion Shop and Richardson's Jewellers: later she would feel irrational guilt that she had left the space clear for the bomb car. At about 2.20, no one took any notice as the bombers parked the red Vauxhall Cavalier, registration number MDZ 5211, set the timer by adjusting a black plastic knob and two metal switches, and walked away through the crowds to the getaway car; they seemed relaxed, and one of them smiled at a female passer-by as he left. As Detective Chief Superintendent Eric Anderson would put it: 'The people who left the bomb had three deliberate voluntary acts to perform before they left the car in order, first of all, to ensure their own safety, which was paramount to them; secondly, to arm the bomb; and, thirdly, to be away from the scene a fair distance when it exploded. The bomb would not have gone off without all three tasks being performed and, as they did it, they would have seen hundreds of people stretching up towards the courthouse at the other end of the street. They had a choice.'

They had another choice when they phoned accomplices, including Real IRA Director of Operations Liam Campbell, who were to make the warning calls. Had they been concerned about loss of life they could have identified the Cavalier or given the name of a shop near where it was parked. Instead – unwilling to give any hostages to forensic scientists – they gave vague warnings about the location. Unconcerned for the grief they might cause, they had set out to kill and destroy, not to initiate a public relations disaster for the Real IRA. But that was what their stupidity and callousness were to achieve.

CHAPTER THREE

AFTER THE BOMB

'I am very proud of what my officers did that day. I would also like to mention that the fire service and the ambulance service were tremendous. Even more so, in the initial 10 or 15 minutes of mayhem, the local people of Omagh were tremendous . . . I just kept shouting at everybody, and my reason for that was, I did not want anybody to start to think about what they were actually doing, keep them active, keep their mind active, keep them physically active and that is how we got through it. It was a combined effort from the whole community, including the police service' – Sergeant Philip Marshall, RUC[1]

From the high ground ten miles west of Omagh, Constable Peter Thompson had a clear view. It was pleasurable sitting in the sun with eight soldiers, waiting to be flown back to the army base after an enjoyable and uneventful foot patrol.* But when he heard by radio at around 3.00 p.m. that part of the town was being evacuated, uneasiness descended, not least because he thought his wife and child would be there around this time. A few minutes later, as he gazed in the direction of Omagh, watching anxiously for the helicopter, he saw a large, dense, mushroom-shaped cloud of smoke rise into the sky, and, after what seemed a long time, heard a boom. 'It's gone up,' came the cry from the radio transmission, followed by a plea for medical help for the casualties strewn everywhere. Thompson recalls being consumed by a sense of helplessness and a desperate desire to get to the scene and assist as best he could, but also by great fear of what lay ahead. Would he and his colleagues be able to cope?[2]

Constable Tara McBurney was a lot closer, just outside Spick and Span,

---

* From the early 1980s, in areas like South Fermanagh, West Tyrone and South Armagh, rural patrols were carried out on foot because of the threat posed by large roadside bombs that were usually placed in culverts (underground water conduits). A solitary police constable accompanied by military personnel would be taken in and out of the patrol area by helicopter; he would carry out routine police enquiries and check vehicles, always moving from one point to another over land, never by road.

the dry-cleaners where Thompson's wife helped the owner, her brother, on Saturdays; she was a few yards behind Constable Colin Doherty when she heard the explosion. 'I felt a strong wind and my breath was taken away for about five seconds. I felt debris flying past my body from behind, clipping me as it went. I opened my eyes and realised that a bomb had exploded and that we had walked right into it. I then realised that my ears had been affected by the blast and held them. I looked down Market Street for Constable Doherty and saw him standing uninjured but surrounded by dead bodies and body parts. Everybody was screaming and hysterical and covered in blood.'[3] A bomb blast, as the pathologist Dr Derek Carson explained to the inquest, can damage people in three ways. 'One can be affected directly by a blast wave hitting the chest and with air going down, under force, the windpipe. Or one can be thrown against solid objects by the blast. Or solid objects can be thrown against you by the blast.'

Sergeant Peter Salter and his patrol, who, at around 2.50 p.m., had been diverted from driving to Kilkeel to police a potentially contentious band parade, had arrived in John Street as Phil Marshall left it, and Salter and his colleagues began following him on foot. When they heard the blast they got back in the Land Rover and drove to Market Street, where they all plunged into the acrid, black smoke. 'There were approximately two hundred people in Market Street at this point,' said Salter, 'with the majority of them injured, some lying on the ground, some walking towards me and others walking past. The injuries to these people ranged from what appeared to be severe shock and lacerations to severe head, chest, stomach and limb injuries ... there were also numerous people lying about the road and pavements, some injured and some obviously dead.'

The blast had torn down buildings, cut telephone and electricity power lines, created a three-metre-wide crater in the road and fractured a water main; bloody water was flowing down the street carrying pieces of people; naked, blackened corpses lay face down in it. 'Lying in the roadway were large amounts of belongings including handbags, shoes, clothing and prams, as well as parts of human bodies including arms, legs, hands and parts of face and head.' And everywhere were desperate people scrabbling in the rubble in search of relatives and friends.

Constable Louise Stewart, one of Salter's crew, remarked on 'the dreadful smell of burning flesh and blood – a stench that would hang over Omagh for a long time – children lying dead on the street ... I saw people who had parts of their bodies missing. I ran from one side of the street to the

other and saw more dead and injured. I just felt completely helpless . . .
Sergeant Philip Marshall then took charge.'

'You have to understand,' Marshall would explain at the inquest, 'that
in the first ten or fifteen minutes there was a lot of confusion. It had got
to the stage that if you were begging for help, you were not ignored, but
you had to move on, because if they were able to talk, they were not as
bad as the person lying a couple of feet away.' He tried 'to switch off as
a human being, because even though I was traumatised I needed to remain
as level headed and coherent as possible to relay information and give
directions to those at the scene'. But the sight of a baby's body in the
window of the Salad Bowl that he at first believed was that of his own
daughter would haunt him forever.

Reinforcements were arriving, and within a few minutes there were
twenty-seven police officers in Omagh. Radioing for ambulances, doctors
and nurses, Marshall was also trying to locate and deal with living casualties before it was too late, and to establish priorities. 'I moved up and
down the street grabbing uninjured members of the public and police and
tried to allocate two people to remain with each of the seriously injured
casualties, such as persons with missing limbs or whose breathing had
stopped.' His rationale was that one would administer first aid or whatever medical assistance they could while the other talked and talked to the
casualty. 'I can assure [the families]', he told the inquest, 'that there was
somebody with their loved ones on the day, there was somebody talking
to them and at no time did they die alone.'

His colleagues had reacted instinctively, and were saving those they
could. Tara McBurney, for instance, had been galvanised into action by a
screaming girl pointing to another one with 'a piece of mangled and twisted
metal about five inches long protruding from her chest. I grabbed her arm
and walked her to my police car parked at Scarffe's Entry junction with
Market Street and put her inside.' She located other shocked and bleeding
casualties and began ferrying them the half mile or so to Tyrone County
Hospital, commonly known as Omagh hospital.

Constable Alan Palmer, who was searching under rubble for survivors
and giving first aid to the injured, was completely unaware that his back
had been lacerated by flying glass and that he was bleeding copiously until
one of his colleagues ripped his shirt open and told him he needed medical
attention. Having helped take injured people to hospital, he would end up
having twenty-seven stitches.

The blast had caused Constable Colin Doherty to curl into a ball on the ground just beside Lorraine Reid's car: when the debris stopped falling around him he ran down Market Street through the choking dust, where he saw the flailing arms of a woman trapped underneath the burning axle and two wheels of a car. 'I tried to push it off her but couldn't. Other people then started pushing it while someone put the fire out . . . I grabbed the girl's arm and kept a constant pull on it, the axle rocked over and I was able to pull her out. Her legs were on fire and I tried to put it out, but a man took off his coat and wrapped her legs in it, which put out the fire.' Then an ex-soldier with a first aid kit took over and Doherty moved on to help carry the injured to the makeshift transport.

While the police had their training to fall back on, most members of the public had little idea how to help and there were desperate pleas to Councillor Paddy McGowan, whom everyone knew, and who was on the scene within three minutes of the bomb going off. A long-serving volunteer fireman, McGowan had seen terrible sights in his time, including the carnage at Ballygawley and at the Knock Na Moe Castle Hotel, but nothing as bad as this. 'Everyone was shouting, "What can we do, Paddy? What can we do?"' He organised people to take shelving and doors from shops for stretchers, and duvets to cover the dead. 'I recall myself and this little chap who worked in the hardware shop in the town and we wanted duvet covers to cover a body, charred, badly burnt. This duvet cover was rolled up, so I said "We've got this one here", and we opened it and somebody had rolled a child up in it, obviously dead.' Even the experienced McGowan was traumatised. He recognised not a single corpse, and yet found later that he knew almost everyone who had been killed except the Spaniards and the children from Donegal: he had simply blanked out the faces.

It took several minutes after the bomb before ambulances or fire engines began to arrive. McGowan would later speak of 'the forgotten people of that day, the ordinary Joe Bloggs of this world, the women and men who done Trojan work before anybody. I'm sure some of them saved lives that day in their own way.'[4] McGowan, who was the Omagh manager for Ulster Bus, flagged down two buses to take victims to hospital. So terrible were the injuries, he said later, 'that the blood was flowing down the steps out of the buses on to the road. When it was over we had to take those buses out and all the seats had to be taken out and destroyed.' One of the bus drivers, Michael McNally, recalled the screams of pain when he went over the speed bumps at the hospital.

At the inquest, there would be evidence of many moments of heroism and humanity in the midst of horror. An especially striking image from the inquest is from the testimony of one such Joe Bloggs, Robert Bonar, who fetched first aid kits from Boots, where he worked, and tended to casualties up and down the street as well as disconnecting blaring burglar alarms: 'I saw one young girl, about fourteen or fifteen years old, sitting on the ground amongst all the dirt and grime, holding the hand of one of the dead girls. I asked her what she was doing and she said, "I am just holding her hand." I asked her did she know who it was and she said "No. I don't want her to be alone."' There were innumerable other unsung heroes, including the injured who refused treatment and went on trying to help those in a worse state than themselves.

When the living casualties had been cleared, Sergeant Marshall decided to take charge of the scene, still noisy with pealing burglar alarms and screaming and sobbing. 'The only way I could attract everyone's attention was to stand in the middle of the road and yell at the top of my voice.' He ordered everyone to the bottom of the street, telling someone to put police tape across the junction at Market Street between Nicholl & Shiels and the Kozy Corner public house. 'I then instructed all police to form a line in front of the white tape and instructed them to carry out a systematic search of all the buildings in the immediate vicinity to try and locate any further living casualties.' Grimly, they sifted through the charnel house Market Street had turned into, their uniforms caked with grime and blood and some of them crying.

One of Marshall's colleagues turned up. A brave man who had dealt with innumerable terrorist atrocities, he was visibly dazed by what he saw: it was all too much. 'Phil,' he said, 'you're on your own,' and he departed the scene to less harrowing duties. Over the next five hours senior officers would come and go, but Sergeant Marshall was always left in charge, perhaps because his seniors realised they could not do a better job.

The doctors and nurses and ambulances Marshall had been calling for had still not turned up: he did not realise that all the medics in the vicinity were looking after the crowds of bleeding, broken people who had reached the hospital or were staggering towards it. Desperate to have the dead pronounced dead, so they could be taken out of the public view, and now being told there were several more bodies in and around Kells's shop, he suddenly saw a man in a fluorescent jacket reading 'doctor' materialise beside him.

As soon as they heard the blast, Royal Irish Regiment soldiers based at the nearby Lisanelly Barracks had rushed down to the town and the regiment's doctor, Captain Samuel Potter, had gone to the barracks' medical centre and organised his staff. After about fifteen minutes they were ordered to the scene and he was with Sergeant Marshall before 3.30 p.m. Marshall asked him to check for signs of life in all the corpses. 'The reason why we tried to get the bodies identified so quickly – pronounce life extinct so quickly – was, to be honest, I was conscious of the media. I knew it would not be long until they arrived and I wanted to get everybody off the street and out of sight. I think we achieved that and in doing so everybody was treated with the utmost respect and dignity and the compassion shown by everyone concerned was unbelievable.'

Between 3.30 and 4.10, with Marshall beside him, Captain Potter pronounced life extinct on twenty bodies, numbered 1–20, and a body part, an arm. The inevitably matter-of-fact nature of Potter's interrogation at the inquest is imbued with a horror of its own. Asked by the Coroner – who was aware that some of the bereaved feared live people might have been erroneously declared dead – what criteria he looked for in reaching a decision, he explained:

> Obviously the first thing we need to look for is: are the injuries surviv-able? If somebody does not have a head, obviously they are not survivable. The next thing I would try to assess is the airway and the breathing. So I would make an assessment to feel breath, using my stethoscope I would listen to the lung fields and assess whether there is air entry into one or both lungs. I would then assess the pulse, the carotic pulse up at the neck, and then using my stethoscope again listen for heart sounds. Using my torch assess for brain death, assessing the pupils themselves, and if I had enough time, I would also move the tip of my finger across the front of the eyeball to assess if there is a reflex there or not.

This Potter did for all bodies, ensuring categorically that there was no chance anyone was alive. Because some of them had been moved (from the flowing water, for instance), at the inquest there would be some confusion as witnesses sometimes disagreed about exactly when an individual had died. A barrister asked if 'the condition of the bodies [was] such that you would have been able to make an easy determination as to whether they were male or female, elderly or younger, that sort of thing?'

'That was relatively easy,' explained Captain Potter, 'except for the people who were decapitated.'

As each person was pronounced dead, they were covered with curtains, blankets, towels and sheets and any other coverings taken from the shops, and were carried to where even cameras with telephoto lenses could not pry. They included, said Sergeant Peter Salter at the inquest, 'adults, youths, children and infants of both sexes and many of the bodies were horribly mutilated and in poor condition to the extent that when I attempted to lift some, the body parts would come apart in my hands.' The first four-teen bodies were moved to a small alleyway called Market Street Entry that led to the SuperValu car park, and the other six and the arm were placed in Moira's clothes shop.

Meanwhile, an army bomb disposal officer arrived to guard against the high possibility that there might be – as there often was – another bomb planted to target rescuers and the fire brigade as they arrived and joined in the frantic search for bodies. 'One crew', recalled Marshall, 'went mad digging this person out and then found that it was a bloody shop mannequin.' Mindful at all time of the need to treat the dead in a way that might bring some shred of comfort to their loved ones, Marshall had detailed individual police to remain with specific bodies and accompany them in the ambulance when they were removed to the temporary mortuary at the Lisanelly Barracks.

Acting Duty-Inspector Billy Williams was already in a troubled state before the bomb as he was awaiting an operation for a hereditary cancer that had killed his father and uncle. He had spent the earlier part of the afternoon ferrying casualties and was then part of a team searching build-ings in Market Street, all the while terrified that his daughter had been killed or injured, having met his son-in-law searching for her. At one stage he saw a pair of multicoloured glasses in the street that he thought were hers, but, asking colleagues to look out for her, he went on with his job; to his immeasurable relief she appeared at the cordon not much later, and he began helping move bodies out of public view, his feet squelching in shoes sodden with red water.[5]

When all the bodies were recovered, Williams told Phil Marshall that he knew from local emergency disaster plans that there was a suitable place in Lisanelly Barracks for a mortuary. He then went to the camp with a team to set it up: it turned out to be a covered area for playing football or basketball known as the Bubble Gym. 'We set blankets on the ground with a further blanket and a folder with paper and writing implements, so when a body would come in we would number it as it had been numbered at the bomb site. So the first body was No. 1 and had No. 1 against it and remained there so we could account for where people had come from.' Working for him that day were some young probationers who were already in a state of shock and now had to cope with sights such as the body that had intestines trailing on the ground behind the stretcher, the baby dressed only in a partial nappy and the headless elderly woman with a tuft of blue-rinse hair attached to the back of her neck. When there was a lull in the admissions, they put on latex gloves and began looking for anything that could help identify a corpse: watch, hair colour, gold teeth, dentures, jewellery. 'You had the gloves on but very often you had to search in round the body and there was pools of blood in the clothing or had seeped through the clothing and you could feel the wetness even through the gloves.' Pulling back eyelids to record eye colour was particularly terrible for some.

Phil Marshall continued directing the teams until, after two systematic searches of buildings and rubble had been made, almost five hours after the bomb had gone off, he left Omagh with the last batch of bodies. 'At this point I knew continuity was important,' he told the inquest, 'and I had to reluctantly order my "body team" to accompany me into the mortuary and help unravel, strip and examine each deceased person. In the cold atmosphere of the temporary mortuary and my knowing some of the dead I found this particularly distressing. I then systematically examined each of these bodies for descriptions and other clues to assist with identification.'

It was terrible at the mortuary, he said later – the horror alleviated only slightly by the clergy who stayed with the bodies saying prayers. 'They weren't fully formed people, fully clothed; some had no head, some no legs, and maybe just a pair of black underpants.' The police had begun working individually, 'but then a couple said "I don't want to do this" and I said "Right, we'll all do this together. We'll move from one to the next as a group and we'll mentally as well as physically support each other through and if you feel like shit just walk away from this one and some-body else can step forward." And that was really, really tough.'

'These kids performed heroics,' Marshall said later of the RUC's young. 'Nobody cracked, nobody ran away. No human should have to do the things I asked them to do. A lot of them are local, and knew the people involved.'

For Constable Peter Thompson, Marshall is a hero: 'Phil is an amazing man. How he did what he managed to do seems unbelievable.' Thompson was one of those who spent hours trying to control the cordon points after civilians had all been cleared out of the area. First, they had had to repel desperate relatives who wanted to search for their missing loved ones. Then there were the journalists and the cameras.

It was the job of journalists to get to Omagh as fast as possible and send graphic photographs, film and reports back to base, which put them in conflict with police who were trying to ensure the dignity of the dead and the integrity of the crime scene. 'If I took my eye off him for a minute,' said Thompson of one well-known journalist, 'he was trying to slip past.'

Later would arrive the shopkeepers who wanted to clear up their premises or retrieve their money. And, of course, there were the gawkers.

'Looking back on it,' Thompson said later, 'I regard myself as being extremely lucky because I didn't have to face or deal with some of the things that my colleagues had to. I then worked for a few days with colleagues who really did suffer and maybe at the time they didn't realise it but then after a while they had to take time off to try and sort themselves out.' Seamus Mallon, the Deputy First Minister of Northern Ireland, visited Omagh police station that evening and found officers in tears.

The time-honoured RUC method for getting through terrible experiences was to get drunk on whiskey with colleagues: psychological counselling was for sissies. But whiskey offered little protection from the Omagh experience. Years later, I met one policeman who had been in the control room from 3.00 p.m. onwards who could not speak of what he had heard without dissolving into tears. Some of those who helped that day were never able to return to a normal life and none ever fully recovered. A policeman who had wandered up and down the street carrying a head had to be invalided out of the RUC, as eventually was Eddie Gibson, a member of the full-time reserve* who had worked with the injured and bereaved until midnight, knowing all the while that his sister Esther was missing. Billy Williams held together and also recovered from his cancer, but his daughter's marriage – one month old at the time of the bomb – was a casualty. He had not known when he saw her at the cordon that she had disappeared briefly because, in a state of shock, she had gone home to

---

* Local reserve officers were engaged full- or part-time to support the regular force in security-related policing work.

wash shrapnel and debris out of her hair. Like her husband, whose trousers had been covered with blood from a body part that landed at his feet, she suffered from terrible nightmares and other traumatic symptoms. Their marriage eventually fell apart.

Phil Marshall held together too with the help of two years of therapy, but it was three and a half years after the bomb before he could walk into Market Street Entry without being physically sick.

CHAPTER FOUR

LATER

'My strong view was that it would have been quite wrong for me to have engaged in an exercise whose purpose was to sanitise or dilute the horror perpetrated on behalf of the Real IRA. I believe that would not have served the interests of justice and it would have been unfair to the memories of those who died so tragically. Also it would have marginalised the important role played by those involved in rescuing the injured and the recovery and identification of the bodies . . .

The age of Robocop has not yet dawned; it is still a film. The police officers who confronted the horror were real men and women, not robots without feelings and emotions. I am sure all who assisted in any way as a consequence of what happened – police officers, traffic wardens, civilians and members of the emergency services, are grateful for the way the bereaved families acknowledged their efforts' – John Leckey, Coroner

Constable Mark Benson saw James Barker lying about eight feet from a burning car, apparently unconscious, but gasping for breath. Benson noticed the deep wound in the boy's chin and the cuts to his leg; he could feel the broken bone sticking out of it. 'A man came over and put the boy's head in his hands to comfort him,' he told the inquest. 'Another civilian, Nicky Craig, put a cushion under the boy's head.' Benson applied some field dressings, and when an ambulance arrived with a paramedic, and they lifted him on to a stretcher, James moaned, though Benson was sure he was still unconscious. He was put into a Land Rover and driven immediately to Omagh hospital, and Benson went back to searching for the injured and the dead.

In hospital, James was sometimes semi-conscious, though probably not aware of what was happening to him. He had massive abdominal bleeding and staff tried to raise his blood pressure by giving him first intravenous fluids and then blood transfusions, and to help him breathe by putting a tube in his windpipe. At 5.20 p.m. Dominic Pinto, the consultant surgeon, operated to try to stem the blood loss, but James had a cardiac arrest and all attempts at resuscitation failed. The post-mortem would show that he had multiple injuries, particularly of the internal organs, and that he might have survived had Pinto and a medical team been able to operate earlier. But, as it was, Pinto was operating in battlefield conditions.

At 6.30 p.m. Pinto pronounced James dead. At around 7.30 his body was delivered to the temporary mortuary at the barracks, where Constable Benson recognised him as the boy he had helped earlier.

After the bomb went off, Sean O'Hagan, who had been evacuated from SuperValu, saw a woman lying in the middle of the road opposite McElroy's shoe shop. She told him she was Geraldine Breslin and she started calling for her husband. 'I told her he was OK. I could see she had head injuries and knee injuries and was bleeding. I stayed with her until other people came to help me. We placed her on a shop sign and put her in a green estate car.'

Geraldine was still conscious when she arrived at Omagh hospital. She was operated on unsuccessfully in casualty to stem the bleeding and then transferred to the Royal Victoria Hospital in Belfast where, despite further surgery, she died at 11.30. She had multiple injuries from innumerable fragments of shrapnel, including the fracture of eight ribs, the base of her skull and her left leg. But what killed her was the laceration of her liver which caused uncontrollable bleeding. On Monday 17th, her body was taken back to the Omagh hospital mortuary.

Geraldine's friend Ann McCombe was luckier, for she died instantly. She had broken legs and four ribs and her chest was badly injured, but what rendered her immediately unconscious and killed her shortly afterwards was the piece of jagged shrapnel that tore through her face, jaw and neck and caused major damage to her pharynx, oesophagus, thyroid gland and voice box. Captain Sam Potter was one of those who found her in S.D. Kells, into which she had been blown. 'As we went into it,' he said, 'three of the main beams and joists within the shop had fallen over, so the bodies were covered with rubble and lumber. As well as that there was a small fire in the back of the shop and there was smoke around.' She was lying more or less on top of the almost headless corpse of Brian McCrory, a crane driver who a week previously had been putting the roof on Henry Reid's new silo and then wandered around the farm admiring the calves. When their bodies were moved, hers was put into the care of Constable Colin Doherty, along with those of Rocio Abad Ramon and Frederick White.

Breda Devine's uncle Garry was thrown through the air and regained consciousness to find he was on fire. Having torn off his burning shirt he began looking for baby Breda and found her under rubble and a shop sign, in the buggy which his unconscious fiancée was still holding. He first carried Breda to her injured mother but then realised she needed medical help and ran to a policeman who took her. Breda was put into the arms of traffic warden Rosemary Ingram, Ann McCombe's sister-in-law, who had been crying for help for her multiple injuries when a police car stopped beside her. 'There were injured people in the car. I got into the front seat and somebody handed me a wee baby. The baby was black with debris. I could see an open wound on its left cheek. The baby was not moving, it was like stiff, but I could find a strong heart beat. We were driven to the Tyrone County Hospital. I got up and my legs just left me. I fell on to my back, still holding the wee baby. I shouted for someone to please take the wee baby, which somebody did.'

Breda was one of the first victims to arrive at the hospital, but she was burned and had many injuries; the one that defied the efforts of the medical staff was the major skull fracture with associated swelling of the brain. She was pronounced dead at 3.50 and taken to the hospital's temporary mortuary.

Young Aiden Gallagher and his friend Michael Barrett had been moved by the police down Market Street and were still walking together towards the Dublin Road when the bomb went off. Michael put up his hand to save his face and was blown down the street. Although his left foot was injured, he got through the devastation to Slevin's 'and then I realised that Aiden was not with me. I then headed back up the street to look for him, but I was too weak and fell on the footpath outside the Kozy Corner public house.'

Constable Gary McClatchey, who had raced down from Foundry Lane when he heard the bomb, saw the body of a young, ginger-haired man who would turn out to be Aiden lying face up in the middle of the road. Believing him dead, he left him to help pull the young girl from under the burning axle and then tried to save the life of a young woman who would turn out to be the daughter of his colleague, Constable Cartwright, and who died later in hospital.

A neighbour of the Gallaghers who had been playing bowls in the Leisure Centre had also run to the bomb scene with two other men. 'I saw Aiden Gallagher lying on his back in the street,' James Quinn would tell the inquest. 'I went over to him and there were two men leaving him, who said he was dead. I said I did not think he was because there was a wee bit of movement. He turned his head away from me and let out two big sighs and then he was gone.' Aiden had been struck in the face by a piece of shrapnel which destroyed most of his mouth and passed backwards, fracturing his spinal cord. His body was moved to the alleyway and in due course taken to Lisanelly Barracks along with those of James Barker's friend Oran Doherty, Esther Gibson and an arm.

Esther had been killed instantly from behind by shrapnel that broke her skull into several pieces. At the barracks she was recognised by an officer from Omagh, who turned to Billy Williams and said, 'That's Eddie Gibson's sister.' Williams knew Eddie, who was attached to Omagh station, and he also knew his sister Caroline, who worked in the canteen. He recognised the family resemblance.

Samantha McFarland was seen by former neighbours lying on the road outside Nicholl & Shiels a couple of minutes after the explosion. They thought she was dead, but she still had a pulse so she was put on a makeshift stretcher and taken to an ambulance where she went into cardiac arrest. She responded to the paramedic's first attempts at cardiopulmonary resuscitation, but not to the second, and was dead when she arrived at the hospital shortly after 3.30. She had died not from the fractures of her collarbone, right leg and sixteen ribs, but from her damaged chest and a blow to her head that had fractured her skull. She was taken later to Lisanelly, still attached to her yellow holdall.

Lorraine Wilson — who also had multiple injuries — probably died a few minutes before her best friend. In her case the fatal injury was the perforation of the carotid artery that supplies the head and neck with oxygenated blood. Lying in the water cascading down Market Street, she bled to death and her life was pronounced extinct by Captain Potter.

A red and yellow velcro wallet with the name of Alan Radford was picked up later outside the Salad Bowl. Alan, who had been struck by many fragments of shrapnel and debris, was lying face down in water outside Nicholl & Shiels with some of his clothes blown off. The pathologist thought that the most serious of his multiple injuries, and those that, in combination, caused him to die quickly, were the perforation of his right eyeball, the fractures of the upper jaw, a rib, the right shoulder, the left leg, the laceration of the aorta, the left lung, the bowel and a major artery in the pelvis. His body was taken on a trolley by Constable Haslett to Market Street Entry and thence to Lisanelly.

Sergeant Peter Salter found Libbi Rush lying where she had been blown backwards into the Pine Emporium, detected no sign of life, and, after searching for any other casualties, went back outside to help the living. She had been facing the bomb and had multiple shrapnel injuries, and would have died quickly from the laceration of her right lung, liver, diaphragm and ribcage. She, too, was moved to the alleyway and was one of the bodies accompanied to Lisanelly by Sergeant Phil Marshall.

Kevin Skelton had turned round when he saw the front of Mr Gee's ornament shop 'coming to meet me. As the glass shattered I just burst through the door and saw the explosion travelling down the street, bouncing off each building. One would blow in and the next one out.' As they fell in like a pack of cards, they reminded him of a Hollywood film: 'I saw the Kozy Corner just disintegrate into rubble.' When he rushed into Kells's, 'my wife was lying like a rag doll, face down, the clothes blown off her back. I knew she was dead but I felt for her pulse anyway.' A Gaelic football-playing fireman he had often refereed came in, lifted her arm and, realising she was dead, dropped it. 'My next thought was the three children. I just went wild, scrabbling through the rubble. The police dragged me out of the shop, but I fought them off and went back, again and again.' Local priest Father Kevin Mullan remembered 'falling into the arms of a man from here, Kevin Skelton, all bloody, and him saying his wife was dead, and his daughter was missing, and just crying. And then I said some prayers where people were lying covered.'

Kevin's dead wife Philomena was naked, blackened, burned and mutilated. Her injuries included the breaching of her abdomen, which left coils of bowel protruding, but what the pathologist concluded would have killed her within a minute or two were terrible neck injuries and bleeding over the brain surface. She was subsequently moved to the alleyway and thence accompanied by Sergeant Haslett to Lisanelly along with James Barker's friend Fernando Blasco Baselga, who had been almost uninjured save for the shrapnel that penetrated his neck and fatally damaged his spinal cord.

There was no doubt about Fred and Bryan White being dead, for they had walked out of the Salad Bowl straight into the explosion and were the closest to the Vauxhall Cavalier. Fred was killed by his multiple injuries and Bryan by gross laceration of the brain.

After reading this chapter, my brother told me of an old woman from Kerry who had once said to a friend of his: 'If ever you see cruelty, boy, write it in the sky, and then people won't stand for it.' The sickened journalists who were on their way to Omagh would play their part by writing the cruelty in the sky.

CHAPTER FIVE

THE FAMILIES

'I heard the bomb blast, contacted the hospital and made my way, but the roads to the hospital were choc-a-bloc, bumper to bumper, and I had to drive on the wrong side of the road with my lights on to try and get me to the hospital . . .

What greeted me when I got into the main corridor was sheer pandemonium. This was not a major incident, but a major disaster of battlefield proportions. There were people lying in the corridor adjacent to the Accident and Emergency Department, overflowing to the Radiology Department, with the A&E Department full to capacity and more injured arriving and seeking help. There were some 240 injured people arrived within the first forty-five minutes. The Department was staffed for a normal Saturday afternoon – Dominic Pinto, consultant surgeon, Tyrone County Hospital, Omagh'[1]

Donna-Maria Barker was out with thirteen-year-old Estella when she heard on the car radio that there had been a bomb at Omagh. 'I turned to my daughter and said: "Some people are going to get some very sad news today."' Victor heard about it as he had lunch at the golf club before going back to the course. Neither of them worried about James, whom they knew was miles away from Omagh. They did not see the image on television of his bloodied face, photographed being stretchered into hospital.

That evening, Victor and his friends and Donna-Maria met for dinner at a Buncrana restaurant: her mother was to collect James, Fernando and Lucrezia from the coach. It was just about the time when James's body arrived at the mortuary that Donna-Maria looked up from her soup to see her mother walking in. 'She told us there had been a terrible accident and that James hadn't come home.' After a fruitless visit to the meeting place for the coach, they went immediately to the garda station, where they were told that all the phone lines to Omagh were down, so they began ringing all the major hospitals in Northern Ireland. By then it was known that victims were being taken to six other hospitals, ferried by ambulances, jeeps and army helicopters.

It was around 10.00 p.m. that they discovered that Lucrezia was in a Belfast hospital. Victor was in a state of indecision: he felt responsible for Lucrezia, who had been in the Barkers' care, but was still desperate for news of James. He decided to wait for another hour and then investigate the Ulster American Folk Park, but then the local priest, Father Bradley, phoned and said they should go to Omagh, a place Victor knew nothing about, so the three of them set out. On being told he was looking for his son and two Spanish students, police directed Victor to the Omagh Leisure Centre, now transformed into a makeshift headquarters for victims and support agencies.

Among hundreds fearing their loved ones were dead and waiting to identify them were relatives of the badly injured and many bomb victims still covered with dust and debris. There was blood on the floor and crying and screaming. First-aiders stayed all night dealing with people in shock. The atmosphere, said one of the Gibson sisters, was that of 'terror and fear'. And for residents of Omagh and its locality, there was the added horror of seeing distressed friends and acquaintances and hearing news of others who were dead or injured. One drunken father was shouting anti-English abuse, blaming 'the fucking Brit occupation of Ireland' for the bomb.

For hours, the Barkers were part of what was called 'the long wait'; the families of James's friends Oran Doherty and Sean McLaughlin were there, too. Victor was asked if he was the father of an English boy and questioned about hair colour and distinguishing marks, but no one could say if James was alive or dead or where he was.

It was not until 6.00 on Sunday morning that, with the Dohertys and McLaughlins, they were taken by bus to the temporary mortuary in the army barracks, whose walls were draped in black. Then they realised James must be dead. There were about seven other families waiting to identify children and it was an hour or so before they saw James's body. 'To see him lying there with half of his head gone and those beautiful green eyes looking out at me, as if he was waiting for me, was devastating,' said Donna-Maria. 'I never realised how green his eyes were. That image will stay with me for the rest of my life. They have taken away my baby, they have robbed him of his future and for what? I will never forgive the evil men who carried out this deed.'

When they were driven back to the Leisure Centre, they learned that Fernando too had died.

Geraldine Breslin's husband Mark was gardening when he heard a loud explosion from the direction of the town centre that he immediately recognised as a bomb. He also heard a helicopter starting its engine and saw it hurriedly taking off vertically and concluded that there was a serious emergency. He rang Wattersons and was told by a distressed member of staff that everyone had been evacuated, that not everyone had returned, that the bomb had gone off outside Nicholl & Shiels and there was at least one fatality.

Mark was now worried also about his sister, Elizabeth, who usually had coffee in the café above Nicholl & Shiels at this time on a Saturday. He rang his father and heard that his mother and sister had both gone into town, but, to his relief, a few minutes later a call came to say they were safe. Switching from channel to channel on the television, Mark began to see news of a major bombing incident as well as appeals for all medical staff to go to local hospitals: from all over Northern Ireland, off-duty doctors, nurses, surgeons, laboratory staff, radiographers, paramedics, pharmacy workers, porters, security workers, chaplains, social workers, first-aiders and volunteers were rushing to their local hospitals.

When Mark rang Wattersons again, the line was dead. Shortly after 4.00 p.m., he wrote notes to Geraldine telling her he was safe, stuck them on the front and back doors, set off in his car but had to abandon it because of terrible traffic, and, through a chaotic scene of distraught people, finally entered Wattersons via the back door to find staff worrying about their missing colleagues. He found his car, drove home, told Gareth to wait in case Geraldine returned and set off on a frantic search for her. He drew a blank at her parents' house, then went to his parents: his father drove him to the nearest dropping-off point to Omagh hospital, which was in a state of complete pandemonium.* He first searched the casualty department, where corridors were crammed with bloodied victims, desperate

---

* As Dominic Pinto pointed out at the inquest, there were numerous unique features of this disaster: the huge number of casualties; the high number of elderly, women and children; the hospital so near the explosion that it became the centre of the event; the high number of casualties suffering from blast and shrapnel injuries and the relatively low number of head injuries; the number of staff who had relatives killed or injured and who were known to the victims; and the serious damage to the telecommunications system which led to major disruption of the hospital's telephone link with other services.

relatives and a priest administering the last rites, gave Geraldine's name to the hospital staff and searched all the rooms in the nursing centre. His brother Peter, who had arrived to give blood, helped him calm down, and then Mark continued searching wards for Geraldine until he finally discovered that she was in intensive care and might have to have a leg amputated. She had been able to give a nurse her name, address and phone number, which encouraged Mark to believe she was going to live.

As the phones were still not working, Peter had to go and tell the family about Geraldine and leave Mark waiting alone outside the intensive care unit. For a while he was joined by some Wattersons staff looking for Ann McCombe. After almost three hours, during which he had seen innumerable bloodied and bandaged victims as well as a corpse, he was told by a surgeon that Geraldine's leg had been amputated, that another operation was needed and that there was damage to her liver. He was allowed a brief visit to a semi-conscious Geraldine, whose head and an eye were bandaged, whose face had burn marks, but who managed to say 'I'm sorry.' At 8.30 p.m., he was told she had to be flown to Belfast Hospital and he accompanied the trolley bearing his unconscious wife to a helicopter. Shocked and confused, he went home and Peter drove him to Belfast, where they arrived at 11.30 p.m. and met their other brother and their sister. They were then told that Geraldine had died. He sat with her body for about half an hour, holding her hand, before going home to break the news to her son.

Stanley and Clive McCombe were spending a few days in Scotland with several others from Omagh for the World Pipe Band Championships in Glasgow. In mid-afternoon, Stanley was told there had been a huge bomb in Omagh. He was relieved to be told it was near the courthouse, well away from Wattersons, and he knew Ann would have been evacuated through the back of the shop. Then someone else told the McCombes a lot of people had been killed at the bottom of the town.

It was impossible to get through by phone and although Stanley believed his wife would be safe, he was worried about his son Colin, who he knew would have been playing snooker at an arcade only 100 yards from the bomb. But then he was told that Veda Short, Ann's colleague, who would almost certainly have been with her, had been killed. Now very frightened, he reached the coach that was to take them back to the hotel in Ayr, to be informed that his sister Rosemary Ingram, the traffic warden, was dead. Stanley recognised that the man who told him was protecting him from hearing it on the radio news. 'I just went to pieces.'

The coach journey was a nightmare, with everyone fruitlessly trying their mobiles and Stanley flicking through radio channels hearing the death toll rising and rising. As he knew almost everyone in town, Stanley realised that he would know most of the dead, whoever they were. He tried to ring his brothers when he got back to the hotel, but it was still impossible. Eventually, someone made contact with an Omagh resident and was able to tell Stanley that his sister, though badly injured, was in fact alive and in hospital. It was after 8.00 p.m., when the coach driver managed to reach Stanley's brother David, who sent a message saying 'Colin is safe. He is with me. Ann is missing.' Stanley crumpled, virtually certain she was dead: it was inconceivable that she could be missing for five hours and have survived.

Frantic attempts to find transport home culminated in the ferry company giving the Omagh group an early crossing. For the McCombes, the journey was torture. They got back to Omagh at about 10.00 on Sunday morning. 'You could feel death in the air,' Stanley remembered. In the familiar places, there was no one about. Even the dogs weren't barking.

With his six other siblings he went to the Leisure Centre through the banks of television crews and reporters, where they found themselves among hundreds of distraught relatives – many of whom he recognised – in various stages of shock: he was told to return on Monday. After another sleepless night, he was told that Ann's body had been identified by the minister at their church. He was determined to see her himself and was finally shown her on Tuesday. Her injuries were so terrible he was allowed only to see her face; as well as being badly burned, her left jaw was gone, her right jaw was burned black and she had a metal bolt sticking out of her head. 'That image,' he said years later, 'stays in my head and will be in my head until the day I die.'

Labourer Paul Devine identified his daughter Breda at 7.20 on Saturday evening at the Omagh hospital and then left to cope with a family of three small children who had lost their baby sister, whose mother was unconscious in intensive care and whose uncle and his fiancée were also seriously injured in hospital.

Michael Gallagher was working in Aiden's garage when he heard a loud explosion, the noise of which was amplified by the corrugated iron roof. He looked up and saw a pall of smoke rising from the centre of the town: Michael had lived through many years of the Troubles, so he knew this was serious and went home immediately. Patsy and Cathy were agitated and then the elder girl, Sharon, arrived and put on the Teletext, which told them that ten people were dead. Against the background of helicopters and ambulance sirens, Michael set off to search for Aiden.

Realising that the town centre would be cordoned off, he went straight to the Omagh hospital casualty department, about half a mile from the bomb site; he had to leave his car because abandoned vehicles were blocking the approach roads. The injured were all around him – walking up to the hospital or being ferried in ambulances and cars. People were calling for a stretcher for a young woman who had been transported on a shop sign in a van with blood all over its floor. Helicopters were taking off with patients bound for other hospitals.

Inside the hospital, 'there was blood everywhere – on the floor, on people's faces and bodies – you felt you were walking through blood'; a woman's corpse lay on a stretcher. In a state of blind panic, he tried and failed to get into any of the eight reception areas and then began searching the wards; he even walked into an operating theatre to see if the patient's clothes were familiar.

Some victims were so bloodstained that their faces and clothes could not be identified, so he looked for people of Aiden's size and then at their shoes. Eventually, dazed by the terrible scenes, but relieved that Aiden wasn't there, he went home, for there seemed nothing to do but wait. He would always remember that Cathy had placed a candle in the window.

At home he found the father of Aiden's friend Michael – who was also missing – and with him went back to the hospital, where they located Michael, who told them about the moments before the bomb. He went home again, where Patsy and Cathy were sitting in a state of suspended animation, watching Sky news, hearing the number of fatalities grow and also facing the realisation that, since Omagh was so small, they would know people killed or injured.

Cathy found herself bargaining with God and all the saints that if her brother was alive she would clean his room forever and make him cheese sandwiches on demand. When the phone came back on, her sister Sharon started contacting hospitals; Michael then left to check the car park he had recommended to Aiden, where he found the familiar white Toyota MR2 parked beside just one other vehicle: 'That moment was the nearest I came to collapsing. I was struggling to stop myself from losing it. It was just the realisation that the car was still there and he hadn't rung.' He understood then that his son would not be coming home. On the advice of a soldier, after another visit to the hospital, he went to the Leisure Centre where – like the Barkers, whom he didn't know – he waited for hour after hour.

It was not until 5.30 a.m. on Sunday that he was told Aiden was dead and his body was in the temporary mortuary at the army barracks. He went with his brother James to the room being used for identification, but could not bring himself to look at Aiden. 'If I had looked at Aiden and seen an image that was horrible it would have stuck with me for the rest of my life. There was no way I could do that – not ever.' So James looked under the sheet, and though the bottom of Aiden's face was injured, he recognised and identified him.

Robert Gibson, who helped his father on the family farm ten miles outside Omagh, was checking some cows on land they owned near Omagh when he heard an explosion. He went straight home, heard that his sister Esther had gone to town and watched a newsflash on television. The family began phoning hospitals but could find out nothing and at various times of the afternoon and evening searched for her: her fiancé Kenneth found her parked car with shopping bags in the back, as, later, did Eddie and then Robert and their father. Caroline Gibson checked Erne hospital and, separately, Liz and her fiancé and Robert and his father all tried to find Esther in the nightmare that was Omagh hospital.

Ultimately, they were directed to the Leisure Centre, where they gave a detailed description of Esther: after 2.00 a.m. on Sunday, Eddie – now off duty – Liz and Esther's fiancé were taken to Lisanelly to the identification room. Liz would never forget that what looked like beads of polystyrene (but may have been fertiliser particles or building insulation) were embedded in the dried blood on her sister's face. 'I cannot even bear to think about the people who did this,' said Kenneth later. 'The only person on my mind is my Esther, my lovely Esther, the best thing that ever happened to me and now this. This is the worst.'

That Saturday afternoon, Gerald McFarland as usual was watching the racing on television at his home about sixteen miles from Omagh; he intended to meet his daughter Samantha when she finished at Oxfam and go for a drive. The broadcast was interrupted by a bulletin about a serious explosion in Omagh. Unable to make contact with his wife Doreen, or his grown-up sons Richard and Jonathan, he finally spoke to a friend who lived near Omagh who said that the injured were being taken to the hospital. He drove to Omagh hospital where he met Doreen and Richard and finally determined that Samantha was not there. Advised to go to the Leisure Centre, and now joined by Jonathan, they waited interminably among many familiar faces until, in the middle of the night, they were told that Samantha was dead. Numb with shock, just after 6.00 a.m. on Sunday, Gerald and Jonathan identified her in Lisanelly.

Denise Wilson, visiting the family that day, had promised to meet Lorraine in town to give her some wages she owed her so she could buy new school shoes. Just before 3.00 p.m., Godfrey, Ann, Denise and Colin went into town, but though they reached the back of the Oxfam shop, it had been evacuated and there was no sign of Lorraine and nothing to do but go home. A few minutes after getting inside, the family heard a very loud explosion and saw rising smoke and debris, which terrified them. For reasons she could not understand, Ann, who was on the phone to her mother, immediately said, 'Lorraine's dead.'

Denise and Garry left the house and ran into town, but though they got as far as Slevin's, they did not realise that a body lying across the road was Lorraine's. When Godfrey and Ann were unable to get into town by car, Godfrey went in on his bicycle and Ann, by now in a hysterical panic, sent Colin to his grandmother. Denise went home to ring hospitals and the rest of the family went to Omagh hospital, where they met Doreen McFarland at the front entrance, asking if they knew anything about Samantha and Lorraine. Like thousands of others, they were experiencing hours of appalling confusions, delays, frantic searches, random encounters, misleading rumours and downright panic.

The Wilsons, too, had the experience of walking through pools of blood among hysterical, injured people as they searched the wards. The terrible scenes were made even worse because this was the hospital where their son Gavin had died many years before of pneumonia at the age of two months. Colin turned up, and was again sent to his grandmother's, but they later found him sitting watching stretchers being loaded into helicopters. Eventually they were told Lorraine was not in the hospital.

They tried the Tyrone and Fermanagh Clinic, but ended up at about 5.00 p.m. at the Leisure Centre, where they spent the whole night. At about 8.30 a.m. on Sunday they were told by a policeman that it was pretty certain that Lorraine was in the morgue. And it was there, at 11.30 a.m., that Godfrey, Garry, Denise and Ann's father identified her. Like Esther Gibson, her body also appeared to be covered with polystyrene beads. Lorraine was cold and still damp, but her face was dry. Godfrey found himself checking her teeth and her hair, of which Lorraine had always been proud: her teeth were intact but her straight, fair hair was dirty and dishevelled. Then Godfrey saw what he thought was a teardrop under one eye, which he gently removed, put in a matchbox and took home.

After being blown backwards by the blast, Marion Radford found a big piece of glass embedded in her head and pulled it out, along with a large shard from the back of her neck. Hearing all the screaming outside, she left the shop to look for Alan. She did not notice his body, only yards away from her in the middle of the hell around the bomb site. A man asked her for her overcoat to cover up a body she had nearly stood on and that she would later learn was Lorraine Wilson. A girl came from behind, took off Marion's cardigan, wrapped it round her bleeding head, told her she must go to the hospital and sat her with others to await an ambulance. Still pleading to be allowed to look for Alan, Marion was coerced into the ambulance and promised that her son would be found.

From Omagh hospital Marion rang home. Her son Paul arrived with David, a friend, and helped to ferry hideously injured people from the vehicles that kept arriving. Having been told by an uninjured young woman that Alan had been standing beside her, Paul assured his mother that he would be fine; but it turned out to be another Alan.

Marion went home, still bleeding and covered in particles of glass and too shocked to go out again. Paul and his friend continued the search, ending up, like so many others, spending hours and hours in the Leisure Centre. It was not until 1.30 p.m. on Sunday that he, his sister Elaine and two friends identified the body.

Laurence Rush had got home at about 5.00 p.m. and was chopping sticks when his young grandson came in, ashen white and in a cold sweat. Laurence drove down to the town like a madman and, when stopped, abandoned his car and ran up the hill to what he described as resembling the 'fucking killing fields'. Like so many other desperate relatives, he checked every face in every ward, and also checked out the operating theatre.

Having run to the Leisure Centre, he stayed until the following morning, willing his wife to live, until he was ushered into a room where a priest and a minister were saying prayers for the bereaved. Having denounced them for daring to pray when Libbi hadn't been declared dead, he was taken away by his sister and brother-in-law. Libbi was eventually identified at 3.15 on Sunday afternoon by her friend Hugh Slevin.

After a frantic half hour searching the area for his daughters, Kevin Skelton had gone back to his wife's body and found Tracey kneeling beside her trying to find some sign of life. He found Paula, later, but there was still no sign of Shauna. Then a man shouted from across the street to ask if Kevin had a ginger-haired daughter and when he said yes, told him she had been taken to hospital. He found her there just as she was about to be taken by helicopter to another hospital. One side of her face was badly damaged, but she was alive: her mother had taken the full force of the blast and had saved her. 'I will never forget those two hours running about, not knowing whether people were dead or alive, and smelling burning flesh.'

With his children, Kevin spent all night at the Leisure Centre among people he mostly knew; his brothers and their wives went to stay with Shauna. 'There were lists going up for Omagh hospital, Enniskillen hospital, Dungannon and Belfast. Every time a list went up people ran to look for the names of their loved ones.' He did not see Philomena's body until 10.00 on Sunday morning when he went to the barracks and identified her and then left to go to the hospital to tell Shauna her mother was dead.

Edith White heard a bang and first thought her washing machine had exploded. Then she went outside and a neighbour came over to tell her a bomb had gone off. After a while, getting anxious, she walked as far as a cordoned-off area. She was told there were only a few minor injuries, so she went home and waited. The amnesia from which she has since suffered means she cannot remember how she got to Omagh hospital or, later, the Leisure Centre, or what happened in either place: one of the Gibson sisters saw her and her daughter in the Centre, uncontrollably hysterical. Nor does Edith remember why they did not remain to identify Fred and Bryan – a job done by two policemen – but she does have a clear memory of being at home when her GP arrived at midday on Sunday and said: 'Edith, there is only a short way to talk about this. They are both dead.'

CHAPTER SIX

THE BURIAL OF
THE DEAD

'I live now in a town of ghosts. Each of us here in Omagh has been revisiting in our minds the still-cordoned-off section of Market Street at the lower end of town. The people in the dress shop, best dressed or about to be so – half-naked, limbless, lifeless. Those in the paper shop, now to be read of themselves in the newspapers of the world. The once-happy Saturday afternoon shoppers, betrayed by a lie as to the location of death, and herded towards and not away from destruction.

Ghosts that are going to wander always around this corner of the street as surely as Molly Malone's ghost wheels her barrow through Dublin. The daughter, mother and granddaughter – the foreign children who stepped singing off their bus – the son and father returned that morning from holiday – the twenty-eight[*], at least, who will neither see nor be seen here any more' – Father Kevin Mullan[1]

Within hours, the dead and injured of Omagh were public property at home and abroad. Television ran a film taken by Pat McElhatton, a local man who had brought his video camera into town to film a cycle race and found himself recording the chaos after the bomb. Gazing at the pictures of the ravaged little town, people all around the world could relate to the sheer ordinariness of those who had been targeted so brutally. The statistics spoke for themselves: of the twenty-eight so far dead, eleven were children and twelve were women, one of whom was thirty-four weeks pregnant with twin girls. Then there was the international dimension. Although most of the victims lived in or near Omagh, two were from the Irish Republic, two from Spain and James Barker was English: they included Protestants, Catholics and a Mormon.

Well briefed by British and Irish diplomats, world leaders queued up to

---

[*] Sean McGrath, a retired baker, did not die until 5 September.

condemn the atrocity and to urge that it not be allowed to derail the peace process. The bombing was 'a barbaric act intended to wreck Ireland's aspirations for peace and reconciliation,' said President Clinton. 'Once again,' said Pope John Paul II, 'blind violence is attempting to impede the difficult path of peace and productive harmony which most discerning people are convinced is possible.' President Nelson Mandela urged political leaders to continue to strive for peace and 'not allow this repulsive act to deter them'.

Dignitaries began to arrive. On Sunday, the day after the bomb, the President of Ireland, Mary McAleese, was at the Leisure Centre meeting relatives, describing the bombers as being 'off the Richter scale of decency', urging ordinary people to help the police north and south and thanking Sinn Féin for bringing the Provisional IRA to ceasefire. The UK Deputy Prime Minister John Prescott arrived in Omagh, but Prime Minister Tony Blair flew in from holiday in Toulouse to Belfast on an RAF flight and, after meeting selected staff, victims and relatives, went straight back to France.* Victims who resented him not coming to Omagh were unappeased by an article in his name on the Tuesday describing how he had been moved to tears in the Royal Victoria by the terrible injuries of some young victims. 'I think, as any parent would, of my own sons, or daughter. I know I would go mad with grief should it happen to them.' His message was that the Provisionals were innocent of any connection with the bomb and that his job was to continue with the peace process.

The Prince of Wales walked through the rubble of Omagh and visited the hospital on Tuesday, along with First Minister David Trimble and the Secretary of State for Northern Ireland, Mo Mowlam. His message was subtly different from President McAleese's. Asked if this reminded him of Enniskillen, he said it did: 'And I remember only too well feeling deeply angry when my great uncle Mountbatten and other relations were blown to small pieces.'†

---

* In his memoir, *Great Hatred, Little Room: Making Peace in Northern Ireland* (2008) Blair's chief of staff Jonathan Powell erroneously said: 'The day after the bomb, Tony came back from holiday in France to visit Omagh. He was appalled by what he saw and particularly upset by a little girl who had lost her sight in the explosion.' In fact, Blair did not go to Omagh until 25 August.

† On 27 August 1979, a Provisional IRA bomb murdered Prince Charles's seventy-nine-year-old uncle, Louis, Lord Mounbatten of Burma, on his boat off Mullaghmore, County Sligo, along with his fourteen-year-old grandson, Nicholas, his daughter's eighty-three-year-old mother-in-law and the fifteen-year-old boat boy.

Most of the bodies were released to their families on Monday after the post-mortems. Relatives, friends, priests and the police liaison officers assigned to each family, along with other people of goodwill, embarked on organising funerals in such a way as to maximise community involvement. Father Kevin Mullan, who on Saturday had led prayers in Market Street, spoke later of those few days. 'The Tuesday and Wednesday night before the funerals, the whole of Omagh and the surrounding district was just one long pilgrimage. I was in tears watching it, going from one house to the next. Then, late on in the night, some of the bereaved families themselves started to visit other bereaved homes. The solidarity and comfort they gave one another was absolutely amazing.'

Celts are generally much better than Anglo-Saxons at acknowledging and marking death ceremonially, and most of the inhabitants of Northern Ireland are of Irish or Scots stock. Pamela Dix, secretary of the pressure group 'Families Flight 103' which sought justice for those killed at Lockerbie*, told me once of her family's experience after the death of her brother Peter: the Scots farmers on whose land these bodies had fallen from the sky ran out and covered them all and generally dealt with bereaved relatives without embarrassment. When Peter's body was taken back to his native Dublin, hundreds turned up to his parents' house to offer their condolences face to face. Afterwards, in London, where he had lived, his widow received many kind letters from people offering to help but neither visiting nor phoning lest in any way they intrude on her grief.

Victor Barker is English, but his wife was Irish and the family home was in Ireland. He was trying desperately to do the right thing in impossible circumstances. On Sunday morning, after the identification of James's body, Victor took his hysterical wife home, and then had a heart-rending telephone conversation with the mother of dead Fernando and badly injured Lucrezia, for whom this was a nightmare relived: her husband had been seriously injured in 1992 by shrapnel from an ETA car bomb.

After a brief rest, Victor went to the hotel to tell his golfing friends what had happened. In the foyer he saw on the front page of the *Mail*

---

* On 12 December 1988, a Boeing 747 on its way from London to New York was blown up by a bomb and its wreckage landed on the small Scottish town of Lockerbie; all 279 on board died, along with eleven townspeople from Sherwood Crescent, who included a family of four. A group of families and friends of the dead carried on a relentless campaign for justice.

on Sunday a photograph of James that he did not then know had already been beamed around the world; James was lying on a stretcher with his face bloodied. The caption was 'Victim of the Omagh Bomb'. As Victor's friends came down to ask if James was all right, Victor said, 'Look what they've done to my boy,' and broke down. But then he pulled himself together and with his friends drove to Belfast Airport to collect the mother of Fernando and Lucrezia and to take her to the hospital; he was consumed with a feeling that he had somehow failed her daughter.

Typically, Victor went the following day to Omagh and insisted on being taken to the bomb site, which was where he believed James had died. He then rang the *Mail* to ask how they could print a photograph of his dead son, forced them to have the photographer call him and they met on a bridge in Derry. It was only then that he learned that James had been alive at the time he was carried out of the town.

Victor felt railroaded into burying James in Ireland: Buncrana was a town stricken by grief as well as by guilt. On Monday, a Mass had been held there for the Spanish students by Father Shane Bradley, who told them: 'I hope you can forgive us, remembering the real Ireland instead of the "Real" IRA. The one of the thousand welcomes rather than the one of the thousand bombs. What an evil sacrilege in my home town. I can say nothing else to you, only "Sorry."' The Barkers went to Omagh to collect the body and waited in a car park for more than three hours. James's body and those of Oran Doherty and Sean McLaughlin were escorted from Omagh by the RUC: at the border, the gardaí took over and both sets of police officers saluted. In Buncrana, where the families arrived after midnight, hundreds lined the main street, many of them holding lighted candles. 'Men and women wept openly,' reported an *Irish Times* journalist, 'and the sound of uncontrolled sobbing and wailing filled the air at the first sight of the small coffins. The families of the boys, visibly distraught, followed in cars.'

The custom in rural Ireland is to have a body in the house until the funeral, an open coffin and an open house: neighbours and friends show their concern in practical ways, bringing sandwiches and cake and milk for the endless cups of tea.

'It's our religion in this country,' said Liz Gibson later. 'A Protestant wake would be from nine a.m. until twelve o'clock at night, whereas a Catholic wake may go on all through the night. The wake provides a kind of closure, but it also allows for respect to be given. To see the thousands of people coming showed that there was a widespread disgust for what had happened and that people needed to show they wanted no part in it.' But Victor hated having the coffin open and found it impossible to handle the crowds (which included President McAleese, Bertie Ahern and the Nobel Laureate leader of the SDLP, John Hume) tramping through his house to look at James and sprinkle holy water over him; he particularly resented visits from politicians delivering platitudes. When Martin McGuinness sent a messenger to enquire if he could visit, he was told he would not be welcome.

Nevertheless, on Wednesday morning, along with the families of Oran and Sean, the Barkers walked through Buncrana behind the hearses of the three boys at the head of a procession of thousands on its way to a Requiem Mass at 11.00.

What made Victor ever afterwards regret having James buried in Ireland was the sight of politicians in the church, particularly Gerry Adams and Martin McGuinness. Desperate to distance themselves from the Real IRA, the Sinn Féin leaders – whose stock in trade for thirty years on being asked to condemn IRA violence had been to say they did not believe in the politics of condemnation – had for the first time actually committed themselves: 'I am totally horrified by this action,' said Adams. 'I condemn it without any equivocation whatsoever.' Yet Victor was one of many who believed that the Omagh atrocity was in essence no different from those like Bloody Friday, Claudy, Enniskillen* and La Mon† perpetrated by the Provisional IRA. He would point this out to them frequently in the future. Paul Durcan expressed the sentiment well in a poem purporting to have been sent by 'the Omagh Quartermaster' to Gerry Adams: 'What I would also like to know is' said one verse:

---

* On Friday 21 July 1972, when Adams was adjutant of the IRA's Belfast Brigade, ten people were killed and 130 injured when twenty bombs went off in central Belfast; on 31 July 1972, nine people were murdered in the tiny Londonderry village of Claudy by three car bombs planted by the South Derry IRA; on 8 November 1987, eleven people, including three couples, were killed by an IRA bomb as they waited for the beginning of a Remembrance Sunday ceremony at the Enniskillen war memorial.
† On 17 February 1978, twelve people, including three married couples, were burned to death by an IRA incendiary bomb while attending the annual dinner-dance of the Irish Collie Club at La Mon House. The strain of savagery that permeates violent republicanism was exhibited by a former IRA commander who remarked at the time to a colleague, Sean O'Callaghan (an informer), that he didn't know what 'all the squealing was about. They were only Orangies anyway.'

'Are you seriously positing that Omagh
Is a different kettle of fish to Canary Wharf?*
By the way, remember the name of the Paki
We topped at Canary? For the life of me, I cannot.

There were sixteen funerals of Omagh victims that day, all attended by thousands. 'On Wednesday I attended one of the funerals near Omagh,' wrote the journalist Lindy McDowell. 'And as I drove along wee country roads I passed car upon car of black-tied mourners travelling to this funeral or that one. There were people walking. At times it seemed as if every man and woman and child in the country was on foot following behind the coffins of their neighbours and friends.' Breda Devine's Mass was at the same time as James's, but her mother was not at her funeral: she would not know Breda was dead until she woke from her coma two months later. Nor were Breda's uncle Garry or his fiancée there: both were in hospital fighting for their lives, with third-degree burns to 35 and 65 per cent of their bodies respectively. Her father carried her little white coffin into church in the crook of his arm and listened to Dr Edward Daly, the former Bishop of Derry, promise that good would triumph over evil. 'Breda's short life is over,' added the parish priest, 'through the cruel action of a stranger. May God forgive him for his terrible sins.'

The funerals of Aiden Gallagher and Alan Radford were at noon.

When Michael Gallagher had returned home to his wife and daughters early on Sunday morning, 'I really did not have to say anything. They knew, they knew it was over.' For Michael, however, it was not just grief that was beginning. It was a crusade.

In 1984, Michael's twenty-six-year-old taxi-driver brother Hugh had been lured to an address outside Omagh where he was murdered by the IRA. His crime was to have once been a member of the Ulster Defence Regiment; he left a wife and two children. For weeks, Michael had been unable to move: he lay on the sofa watching news programmes and Patsy had to run his taxi business, sometimes, in the evenings, with young Aiden keeping her company on the road. 'It took me a good five years even to start getting over Hughie's death,' Michael said later.

Like most murderers in Northern Ireland, Hugh's were never brought to justice. This time, intending to do everything in his power to let the

* Two newsagents, Inan Ul-haq Bashir and John Jeffries, were killed on 9 February 1996 by an IRA bomb in Canary Wharf, London.

world know about both the victims and perpetrators of the Omagh catastrophe, Michael decided to make the media his allies. That Sunday, less than twenty-four hours after the bomb, a team from the *Mirror* rang the doorbell and Michael welcomed them. 'Nobody must be turned away,' he said to Patsy and the girls afterwards. From then onwards, this natural communicator made himself available to any and every journalist and photographer, day or night.

But first, he and his family had to get through the next few days. The Gallaghers lived in Omagh and were well known and there were thousands, Catholic and Protestant, passing through his house. Because of his injuries, Aiden's coffin was closed. The church and its car park were crammed with people, including the MP for West Tyrone, Pat Doherty of Sinn Féin, probably Adams's and McGuinness's closest colleague. Father Kevin Mullan spoke of 'our happy, handsome Adrian', whose future had been blasted from him. 'From the ruins of our town and the ruins of our hearts, let the world of the murderous past be gone. Build our memories of Adrian and his poor pitiable companions into a future for us here until we join them, and slowly wipe away our tears.' Michael fought back tears as he gave an address after Mass, but when he reached the line 'We are very frightened by what has happened and we are broken-hearted that you are no longer to exist upon this earth,' he broke down and could not continue.

Marion Radford had screamed and screamed when she heard that Alan was dead until a doctor came and calmed her with valium. By Monday, though, lifted by the strength of her Mormon faith, she touched Alan's face in his coffin and accepted that he really was dead. She was distressed when she stepped back and saw stains where blood had seeped through the coffin, but she understood that the undertakers had been extraordinarily stretched in these terrible circumstances.

While Aiden's Mass was going on, there was a private family service at the Radford home at which a member of the Mormon church and Bill Harper, the headmaster of Omagh High School, spoke: Alan, he said, had practised the Christian* principles in which he strongly believed. Harper was struggling to come to terms with the deaths of two current (Alan and Lorraine Wilson) and three former pupils (Deborah-Anne Cartwright,

* The Mormons are the Church of Jesus Christ of the Latter-day Saints, and hence Christian, but with additional scriptures and revelations.

Esther Gibson and Samantha McFarland) and the hospitalisation of eight more. Afterwards, the throng waiting outside followed the cortège to the cemetery, where, through her sobs, Marion quoted Gandhi: 'There is enough love in the world to neutralise the hatred of millions.'

Lorraine's funeral was next. Because of pressure on the mortuaries, her body had not been returned until Tuesday, but her funeral took place at 2.00 p.m. on Wednesday. As the crowds came to pay their respects, Godfrey's tears gave way to merciful shock and he was able to greet the many hundreds of visitors with a handshake and a smile. Lorraine was wearing her mother's wedding dress, which she had tried on a fortnight before she was killed; when Godfrey told her she looked lovely in it, she had answered in another eerily prescient moment, 'If I die before you two, just bury me in this.' The high lace collar hid many of her injuries.

Lorraine's coffin was carried into church by Godfrey and her brothers Garry and Colin, flanked by a guard of honour of classmates from Omagh High. A friend sang 'Candle in the Wind' as the coffin was carried out of the church. The Church of Ireland Bishop of Derry and Raphoe reiterated the message being given by most clergy: 'The bombing has only served to strengthen everyone's determination to work for peace. The dark cloud of evil is being penetrated by numerous acts of love and goodness which are happening all around us.'

Fred and Bryan White were next, their service being held at Ballynahatty Presbyterian Church: David Trimble had time to get from the Buncrana joint funeral Mass – where the congregation had applauded him* – to that of the Whites, whom he knew through their involvement in his party. '[Fred's] death and the death of his son is a tremendous tragedy for me personally,' said Trimble. 'His family are in a terrible state.' Among the mourners was Fred's sister Betty Wright, a volunteer at the Oxfam shop where Lorraine and Samantha had worked.

Dazed and drugged, Edith White could barely tell what was going on that week. She has no memories of the church service, where the minister said that what had happened in Omagh 'was an act of medieval savagery' and spoke of having witnessed 'the anguish, bitter grief and hot, hot tears

---

* Like almost all unionist politicians, David Trimble is a member of the Orange Order, which bans attendance at any Roman Catholic service, including funerals. After Omagh, as Catholics and Protestants showed unprecedentedly deep, strong unity in grief, he deliberately chose to attend the most high-profile Catholic funeral.

of this family . . . waiting, waiting, and waiting, through the long watches of the night. Hoping, hoping and hoping against hope that with the coming of the dawn word would come that Fred and Bryan were safe. It was not to be. The powers of evil and wickedness had done their worst.' The Presbyterian Moderator denounced 'the evil, wicked men who planned and perpetrated this vile obscenity' whose 'desperate depravity' was known to God. Fred and Bryan were buried a mile up the road in a country churchyard.

Philomena Skelton's funeral was the last of the day. As he was a well-known Gaelic football referee, Kevin Skelton's tragedy had attracted even more mourners than most of the others. From the time Philomena's coffin arrived home on Tuesday, thousands came to the house from all over Ireland, though they would not be viewing her, as she was too mutilated for her coffin to be open. Kevin went outside to the driveway at 4.00 in the afternoon and did not get back inside until midnight because people were continually arriving to shake his hand. With her jaw wired and heavily bandaged, thirteen-year-old Shauna was released from hospital for a few hours to attend the packed funeral, where the coffin had a guard of honour of referees. The priest made a Christian demand beyond what Kevin could agree or cope with when he said the congregation had a duty to pray for the bombers so they might repent.

There were eight more funerals on Thursday, a day of biting wind and driving rain. The first was that of Geraldine Breslin, whose coffin had not come home until Tuesday; it was not open. Numbed by his experiences, her husband Mark found it difficult to deal with the queues at his house and the crowds at the funeral. There were, he said, 'too many photographers, too many people'. Her son Gareth's classmates formed a guard of honour and the Mass was said by the priest who had married the Breslins three years earlier. He spoke of a daughter who loved her parents, a sister who adored her siblings, a mother who doted over her son, a wife who dearly loved her husband, and a person who was 'a real friend to all. Those she worked with, she cherished. Her friends became part of her family.'

Mark was slightly disconcerted by the arrival of the Bishop of Derry, Dr Seamus Hegarty, whom he had not expected, but like British and Irish politicians and other dignitaries, bishops and moderators and other senior clergy were racing from funeral to funeral to display their solidarity with the bereaved. Bishop Hegarty said he hoped the crossing of the sectarian barriers in Omagh would be held up as an example for the rest of Northern Ireland and won a round of applause when he said: 'We are in it together. We will come out of it together.'

Laurence Rush had asked the funeral director to make Libbi look better, but was eventually warned not to open the coffin: 'I couldn't fix her,' said the undertaker, 'I just couldn't fix her.' Confused and desperate and maddened with rage, Laurence tried to get rid of the innumerable visitors, but, mercifully, he never got the opportunity. 'I'm not coping. I'm a mess,' he told reporters. 'There is nobody in this world that knows me like my Libbi did. I have lost my soulmate.' He walked behind her coffin, 'nestling up to it', in the words of one observer. Libbi's funeral Mass was attended by both David Trimble and Seamus Mallon and a Dublin government minister. The priest observed that the bombing had brought Omagh 'the kind of fame we neither sought nor deserved'. And an angry bishop cried to the bombers: 'Shame on you for killing and maiming, shame on you for bringing so much pain and loneliness into so many homes.'

Like Lorraine Wilson, Samantha McFarland had a guard of honour of classmates at her Church of Ireland funeral, so crowded that all her father Gerald could remember of it was a sea of faces. A clergyman wrote later: 'Mrs McFarland took me to see Samantha in her coffin. I am accustomed to funerals but when I laid a hand on Samantha's head she was so cold for one so young and so pretty.' The officiating minister spoke of an aspect of her death that would particularly torment those who loved her and Lorraine: she had died because she was an Oxfam volunteer: 'How cruel and ironic it is that it was because of her very desire to help those afflicted by poverty, injustice and oppression that she herself and her best friend should lose their lives.' As her coffin left the church, 'Spiegel im Spiegel', a serene piece of music for piano and violin, was played, to the accompaniment of sobbing and wails of grief.

Ann McCombe's service was held the same day, in Mountjoy Presbyterian Church in Omagh where she had sung in the choir. Lamenting 'a genuinely bright, positive, happy character with a smile that encouraged others to smile with her', the minister tried desperately to muster a message of hope: 'Undoubtedly designed to drive a wedge through this community, I believe time alone will show this was the decisive act in unleashing a fierce determination from the people of Omagh to stand together as a community.' The invitation to Father Kevin Mullan to address the congregation was a symbol of anti-sectarian solidarity, but easy-going

Stanley McCombe sat through proceedings discovering for the first time in his life what it was to hate.

Ann McCombe was another victim whose facial injuries had been so terrible that her coffin was closed. Though her face was badly marked, that of Esther Gibson, who was buried on Friday, was open, much to the distress of some of her siblings. As the eldest brother, it was Eddie's job to stand next to the coffin, and he stood there for the two days of the wake making sure that nobody of the thousands paying their respects touched her, for she had no back to her head or chest. Not even when the body began to decompose could the police liaison officer persuade Esther's mother to close the coffin.

As the family set out to follow the hearse, Esther's mother, a natural stoic, instructed them that that no one was to cry in public. The service was held in the church where Esther had taught Sunday School and the mourners were addressed by the Reverend Ian Paisley, who in 2007 would become First Minister of Northern Ireland, with Martin McGuinness as his Deputy. Saying that the British government had forfeited its right to government, Paisley accused successive governments of having 'surrendered the sword to evil-doers and praised evil-doings, whilst gaining the wrath of those seeking to do right . . . Omagh and its people have been cruelly hurt in the last few days. Today we feel for them all. No matter what their religion, no matter what their beliefs, no matter what their political principles may be, we feel for them all.'

At the end of the week, when all the funerals had taken place and all that remained was to grieve, Lindy McDowell expressed the raw emotion of the average Ulster person in an open letter to Tony Blair: 'I heard Mo Mowlam on the radio the other day talking about how people here are "determined". But I live here, Mr Blair, and I see no signs of this "determination". All I see and feel around me is complete and abject despair. I do not think, Mr Blair, you can understand the depth of the raw, real hurt that every one of us has felt this week. You cannot imagine how many tears we have shed between us or the sense of hopelessness that now hangs over our entire land.'

The Real IRA leaders, meanwhile, were contemplating what they had done in killing two babies (and two about to be born), three schoolgirls, four schoolboys, six students, four housewives, three shop assistants, a despatch clerk, a shopkeeper, a crane driver, a mechanic, a horticulturalist and a retired accounts clerk. They had realised soon after the bomb went off that they were in trouble. A member of their Army Council later recalled to the journalist John Mooney:[2] 'I was at home when the first reports came on at around 3.20 p.m. or 3.30 p.m. My first thought was, "That's interesting, that's the first time they have brought the war over to Tyrone." Then the news said there had been casualties and I knew straight away it was bad. Then it came through that there were three dead, then five, then seven, then ten. Then thirteen. The death toll kept rising. I knew we were fucked. I knew there and then the entire army was fucked.'

The afternoon of the bombing, Seamus Daly went with his friend Seamus McKenna to their favourite haunt, Colm Murphy's Emerald Bar in Dundalk. Murphy was there. Some hours later, a drunken Daly sniggered to Terence Morgan, who had innocently lent his phone to Murphy[*]: 'You're the boy that driv[†] the yoke[‡] to Omagh today.'

The Real IRA were stunned at the extent to which they had brought the anger of the world down on top of themselves. With Omagh teeming with journalists, photographers and camera crews, Francie Mackey of the 32CSM was particularly vulnerable as a local councillor; he and the 32 County Sovereignty Movement were desperately trying to head off the backlash. On Sunday, the Chief Constable, Ronnie Flanagan, had put it bluntly: 'It's fair to say our focus at this point in time would be on those who call themselves the 32 County Sovereignty Movement and those close to them. They are out to murder people for the sake of murdering people. That's what they have done.'

That night, the 32CSM had responded by issuing a statement claiming their shock and devastation at the 'terrible tragedy . . . We share the grief and sorrow of everyone on the island of Ireland and we offer our sincerest sympathy to the injured and the bereaved and their family and friends at this moment in time. The killing of innocent people cannot be justified in any circumstances. We are a political movement and not a military group. We reject categorically any suggestion that our movement was responsible in any way.'

The next day, Mackey had to face an emergency meeting of Omagh council. The DUP's Councillor Oliver Gibson, a cousin of Esther's, was present. 'It made my stomach churn to be in the same room as him,' said

[*] See pp. 96–7.
[†] Drove.
[‡] An all-purpose Irish slang term for 'thing' which in this case can be assumed to mean 'bomb'.

Gibson afterwards. 'I could not take my eyes off him – I make it my business to know my enemy. I just sat there thinking of Esther and looking at him.'

Mackey said he would have to leave the meeting early, as his son Shane had been arrested, and he 'went on to state that neither the 32 County Sovereignty Committee, of which he was a member, nor himself or any member of his family had any involvement in the bombing of Omagh and he was critical of those who had intimated that the 32 County Sovereignty Committee had been involved'. He also asked that the council 'support his family, as constituents of the district, in order to alleviate the trauma which had been inflicted on them since the bombing of Omagh'. Afterwards, Mackey was mobbed by the media.

While under pressure at the meeting he had agreed to a statement 'collectively' condemning the bomb, but in public he preferred the weasel words he had learned in his many years in Sinn Féin. Persons unknown had come to Omagh and planted a bomb, he said, which was a terrible tragedy, but while there was no justification for it, he would not engage in the 'media's word games' of condemnation. Mackey also accused the government and the RUC of 'looking for a public face, like myself. At all times I have been open and honest in expressing the Republican analysis. They are demonising me for that honest and open expression of political opinion. This also happened to me when I was in Sinn Féin.'

The following evening, a spokesman for the rattled Real IRA dictated a statement over the telephone to a journalist on the *Irish News*, admitting responsibility, but blaming the police: 'This is about the explosion, this is Óglaigh na hÉireann. There were three warnings put in, there were forty minutes' warning on each of them – two to UTV and one to the Samaritans in Coleraine. Each time the call was made it was very clear and the people talked back. The location was 300 to 400 yards from the courthouse on the Main Street. At no time was it said it was near the courthouse. It was a commercial target. Despite media reports it was not our intention at any time to kill any civilians. It was a commercial target, part of an ongoing war against the Brits. We offer apologies to the civilians.'

Such utterances did nothing to alleviate the condition of the beseiged McKevitts, pariahs terrified they might be lynched and followed wherever they went by gardaí and media. Michael McKevitt was also aghast that the Continuity IRA had broken an agreement to take partial responsibility for the bomb. After Father Desmond Campbell, a Dundalk priest, had said during Mass on Sunday that it was disturbing that the chief suspect for the Omagh attack lived in his parish, he had a hysterical phone call from Bernadette Sands-McKevitt: 'She was crying so much she could hardly speak . . . She said she was frightened because there was a march planned and she was afraid that somebody would hurt her children.' Michael McKevitt came on the phone after she broke down, and, according to Father Campbell, 'was tougher . . . What he did say, and I find it hard to disbelieve him − I won't say I believe him − he said he had neither hand, act or part in this thing.' He added that 'They are going to march on the house apparently and my partner is very upset about it, but I want you to know that I had nothing whatsoever to do with it.'

On Monday, photographers and journalists clustered around the McKevitts' Print Junction shop, outside which appeared bunches of flowers with cards and black ribbons (symbols of grief); there were calls to talk shows saying the McKevitts should be burned out and ostracised, and their shop assistant walked out. The shop was closed on Tuesday and reopened the following day, but hundreds of people held a silent candle-lit vigil in Blackrock, the McKevitts' village, though they refrained from marching to their house, from which the children had been sent away. A spokesman said the message to the 32CSM and the Real IRA was 'that there will be no hiding place in Dundalk or Co. Louth for their activities' and promised a mass peace rally for the following Saturday. On Friday, Sands-McKevitt found the locks on the shop had been changed and she was told she could no longer do business there. The shop was never reopened, nor did anyone take it over. Rumours abounded that the Provisional IRA might assassinate McKevitt and some of his associates.

With the McKevitts panicking, the British and Irish governments threatening a savage crackdown and Sands-McKevitt being refused a visa by the US government, the Real IRA was trying to limit the damage. 'It was very glum,' said one member of the Army Council apropos their emergency secret meeting. 'There was a debate about what we should do next, after this disaster. We knew we were in a deep hole and some people said we could and should bomb our way out of it. But in reality there was only one thing we could do − call a ceasefire.'[3]

Real IRA 'sources' continued to brief journalists that they had not set out to kill civilians, which would have been 'illogical' and counterproductive, and that they had immense 'regret' for what had happened. On Irish radio, Sands-McKevitt attempted to distance herself from the bomb, but, asked to follow her quasi-condemnation by calling on groupings such as the Real IRA to disband, she answered: 'I don't think that's for me to do because I don't think people are listening in that sense. It's up to them to do.'

In New York Martin Galvin also refused to condemn the Real IRA: 'People have to not simply react to the immediate but to look at the bigger picture,' he said. He flew in on Saturday – a week after the bomb – to visit the McKevitts at home on a day when television news programmes were dominated by scenes of services and prayer vigils in towns and cities all over Ireland, as well as in London, Madrid and New York. In Omagh, more than 50,000 attended, including the Irish President and Taoiseach, the British Deputy Prime Minister, David Trimble, Gerry Adams and the Duke and Duchess of Abercorn: in Dundalk there were around 12,000, who came, said the Chairman of its District Council, 'in affirmation of our determination as a community – and within the rule of law and order – never to tolerate in our midst those who would support or practise violence in furtherance of any political end'. And for Sands-McKevitt, there was a savage little poem by Dermot Bolger in the *Sunday Independent*:

> Hovering like Christ above the mourners
> The ghost of Bobby Sands
> Smiled his boyish Bay City Roller smile
> And held out withered hands.

> As they lowered each the coffin
> Of someone's daughter or son
> He called like the piper of Hamelin:
> 'Come little children, come.'

On 22 August the INLA had declared that it was abandoning violence for good. Michael McKevitt, meanwhile, was trying to organise negotiations with the Irish government through Father Reid, only to be told that a ceasefire was a necessary pre-condition of any talks. Terrified by threats of draconian security measures that might include internment, the Real IRA, cynically to buy time, announced first the 'cessation'* of its activities,

---

* Another instance of slavish copying of the Provisionals. On 31 August 1994 the Provisional IRA announced 'a complete cessation of military operations', which wishful thinkers took to mean a total ceasefire, but which they thought entitled them to go on killing and torturing in their own community in the name of housekeeping. On 9 February 1996 they returned to bombing and the murder of members of the security forces. The 'cessation' was finally restored on 20 July 1997.

and then, on 7 September, after a meeting of its convention, a ceasefire it privately regarded as temporary. With the Provisional IRA leadership threatening to kill any member of the Real IRA who stepped out of line and the Irish government promising to lock up the perpetrators of Omagh, the Real IRA leadership hunkered down to wait out the crisis.

CHAPTER SEVEN

INVESTIGATING IT

'I do not like to say "I told you so" but for sixteen years I have opposed the IRA in all its forms, in my native town of Dundalk in County Louth in general and in this Chamber . . .

The tragedy of Omagh in which so many women and children were killed was such that violent republicanism will be dead in Ireland for several years to come. The rats who have murdered people for the past thirty years have retreated into their bolt holes. Some of them will hopefully be bolted up for good but some will escape. I do not believe violent republicanism is dead. Like Dracula, it would be necessary to drive a stake through its breast to achieve that . . .

These measures we have been forced to take are an indication of how much out of control this country has been for the past thirty years when death stalked the land – death promoted by Adams and McGuinness, the IRA's chief of staff, who are guilty by association of the deaths of hundreds of Irish people. Now they are being hailed as international statesmen. They are the bastards who have brought Ireland to its knees'
– Brendan McGahon,* Dáil Éireann, 2 September 1998

The blind, the limbless, the mutilated, the bereaved and the traumatised drew what comfort they could from the torrents of sympathy expressed in the weeks after the bomb. Around eight hundred books of condolence with around two million signatures were delivered to Omagh, along with many thousands of messages by post and through email from all over the world. They became a potent symbol of comfort to locals trying to come to terms with the impact of the bomb.

Omagh District Council showed commendable imagination when it decided to employ Carole Kane, a Northern Irish artist, to find a way of preserving these tributes for posterity. She taught local people, including

* A Fine Gael parliamentarian, McGahon loathed the IRA, responded to their threats to him and his town with utter contempt and was the only deputy to support the death penalty for terrorism.

dozens of children, how to make textile art from dried flower heads and paper in a project called 'Petals of Hope' – intended to symbolise 'the thoughts, prayers, love and friendship which emerged worldwide as a result of the atrocity'. Each bereaved family was given a framed piece of art and three larger pictures were given to the towns of Omagh and Buncrana and the city of Madrid as a tribute to those who had died. It is only in listening to victims that one appreciates how much consolation can be derived from such imaginative thoughtfulness, and how crucial it is to give suffering people hope.

However angry and desolate were the bereaved, they had in common the wish that their tragedy would help bring a permanent peace to Northern Ireland: to hope that a loved one's death has not been in vain is a common human response to loss. On the evening after Aiden's funeral, Michael Gallagher said on television: 'The peace process is the only way forward,' and his daughter Sharon added, 'It is all we have left. I don't want Aiden to have died for nothing.'

On a long-planned visit to Ireland with his wife Hillary, taking place at the height of the Monica Lewinsky scandal, Bill Clinton made a detour to Omagh, almost three weeks after the bomb. His US Air Force heli-copter landed at Lisanelly army camp at 4.00 p.m. on Thursday 3 September, followed by a dozen more carrying the aides and the cars for the presidential cavalcade that drove straight to the Leisure Centre, where Tony and Cherie Blair and around six hundred of the bereaved, injured and their relatives were gathered. The great communicator received a standing ovation from the victims, many of whom were revisiting a place of terrible memories, and he thanked them for 'standing up in the face of such a soul-searing loss, and restating your determination to walk the road of peace'. The cameras left as soon as the public part of the event finished: Hillary had an appointment elsewhere, but Bill Clinton and the Blairs stayed and went round and spoke to everyone.

'To me, it helped,' said Kevin Skelton afterwards. 'Every little bit helps. And the most important thing was that it was completely private. There were no television cameras being pushed in your face.' Clinton spent around five minutes with every family, gave autographs and posed freely for photo-graphs; he conveyed so much warmth and empathy as to soften the hearts of even his greatest critics. (When I went a few days later to see Henry Reid and his family, he rather shamefacedly showed me a photograph of Clinton, whom he had never liked, with his arms around Erin and Thomas.)

After perhaps two hours, the cavalcade took off past cheering crowds to Market Street, where Clinton and Blair unveiled a memorial plaque* outside S. D. Kells, and then proceeded to meet 1,500 invited guests in the High Street, including members of the emergency services and Sergeant Phil Marshall.

The visit was a tremendous morale boost for the town, but there was never any doubt that Clinton was bearing a political message as well as sympathy: 'What happened here on August the 15th was so incredibly unreasonable, so shocking to the conscience of every decent person in this land,' he had said in the Leisure Centre, his voice cracking with emotion, 'that it has perversely had exactly the reverse impact that the people who perpetrated this act intended. By killing Catholics and Protestants, young and old, men, women and children, even those about to be born, people from Northern Ireland, the Irish Republic and abroad – by doing all that in the aftermath of what the people have voted for in Northern Ireland, it galvanized, strengthened and humanized the impulse to peace.'

For most of the survivors, though, while they wanted peace – though not necessarily the Good Friday Agreement – what was most important was the hope that the bombers would be brought to justice. And they had plenty of encouragement from Bertie Ahern and Tony Blair to believe they would be. The day after the bombing, having met Blair, Ahern had promised to take any necessary steps to 'crush' the Real IRA and the 32CSM, which he insisted were one and the same organisation.

The two governments, he said, shared 'an unrelenting determination ... to pursue the perpetrators. I'm determined to do whatever is necessary.' Blair hailed the 'unprecedented cooperation between our two governments as we take our plans forward.' He and Ahern were 'absolutely clear' that the bombers 'will be dealt with and taken off the streets'.

The two governments introduced emergency legislation simultaneously at the beginning of September. Ahern's new legislation was tough, certainly: it included longer detention periods, curtailment of the right to silence, provision for the confiscation of property used in subversive activity and five new offences including 'direction of terrorism'. Blair's made it easier to secure convictions for membership of proscribed organisations

* 'In remembrance of the men, women and children who died in the terrorist bombing of August 15th, 1998/May their memory serve to foster peace and reconciliation/Presented on the occasion of the visit by the President of the United States William Jefferson Clinton and First Lady Hillary Rodham Clinton/September 3rd 1998'

and gave police the power to seize the assets of persons convicted of such membership if they were being used for terrorist purposes. But in general its provisions were far milder than their Irish equivalents. Sinn Féin denounced the security package as 'repressive' and claimed the laws could jeopardise the peace process.

In both parliaments, as the legislation was rushed through, some thoughtful voices protested about the pitfalls of hastily written law. The Fine Gael justice spokesman, Jim Higgins, spoke tellingly about the Irish government's failure to confront the Real IRA threat in time: 'The reality,' he said, 'is that this time last year the Real IRA was a small group, ill-equipped and isolated. If their identity was so well known why was there no round the clock surveillance on these people to monitor their location, movements and activities? They should have been subjected to exactly the same scrutiny, surveillance, vigilance and frustrations as was meted out to the drug barons.'* If the problem was inadequate legislation, 'why was this legislation not introduced as a matter of urgency as soon as possible after the British–Irish Agreement in order to head off the seepage of members, guns and explosives to the new movement?' One glaring consequence of having delayed legislation was that although membership of the Real IRA was now a crime, members could be prosecuted only for their post-Omagh involvement.

The Provisional IRA had their own steps in the choreography, producing a lofty article in the Sinn Féin newspaper *An Phoblacht: Republican News*, on 3 September, intended to put the Real IRA in its place. Without a shred of irony, this pronunciamento, from an organisation that had killed more than two thousand people, described the Omagh bomb as a tragedy 'in human terms', which had caused damage 'to the struggle for Irish independence and unity' and was aimed at destabilising Sinn Féin's peace strategy. The perpetrators, it was explained, having failed in an IRA leadership bid, had resigned. 'Their lack of credibility among volunteers or our support base has caused them therefore to seek to gain legitimacy by trying to hijack the name of Óglaigh na hÉireann, and, by extension, trying to put themselves and their views in the proud tradition of eighty years of struggle.

---

* When in 1996 the journalist Veronica Guerin was murdered on the orders of a drug baron, the Irish parliament rushed through legislation to enable the seizure of ill-gotten assets, and the gardaí also gave much higher priority than previously to chasing criminals in the world of illegal drugs.

'While they have failed on both counts, many republicans feel none-theless aggrieved that they have tarnished the name of Óglaigh na hÉireann and many are justifiably angry at their use of the term "RIRA". The grouping have done only disservice to the republican cause. They have no coherent political strategy, they are not a credible alternative to the Irish Republican Army. In the immediate aftermath of the Omagh bomb they announced a temporary halt to their actions. This is insufficient. They should disband and they should do so sooner rather than later.' It was as though Hitler had been accused of brand infringement.

'Republicanism is a family affair,' wrote the commentator Fergus Finlay after the Omagh bomb, 'and there's no feud more bitter, more deep-seated, more bloody, than a family feud. The row between the purists and the rest is not about history, or politics, or aims or methods – it's about owner-ship of the grail.'

On both sides of the border, representatives of the Provisional IRA were despatched to put the frighteners on dissidents, and there were some ferocious beatings, but though the ceasefire was announced on the 7th, it was not because McKevitt was alarmed by IRA threats or prepared to abandon the quest for the grail. Though McKevitt was no political animal, he could see that with Adams and McGuinness sitting in the Assembly, aspiring for Sinn Féin to be part of a power-sharing executive and under great pressure to secure decommission of all the IRA's weapons, assassinating dissidents was not an option for the Provisionals. So McKevitt bided his time.

Not even the Irish legislation provided the stake in the heart that Brendan McGahon sought, not least because what his colleague Jim Higgins referred to as the 'enormous capacity for ambivalence' of the Irish was to be seen in the words of the Taoiseach. Referring to Omagh, he said those who organised and carried out the act had a stark choice: 'They can heed the will of the Irish people now and tell us – and convince us – that their violence is at an end for good. Or they can defy us to put them out of business. If they do, they should not be in any doubt about this Government's determination to crush and dismantle any organisations that still engage in violence. We are determined that the victims of Omagh will have justice.'

Implicitly promising a deal if the Real IRA offered to repent was not what the surviving victims considered justice. There was disappointment that cross-border internment,* which really could have taken the Real IRA, the Continuity IRA and indeed loyalist paramilitaries off the streets, was ruled out, mainly because Mo Mowlam objected to it on principle and had taken it off the statute book the previous year. While she had promised that the government would 'leave no stone unturned to make sure that the people who did this are caught', she also said she was against 'using a sledge-hammer to crack a nut'. In any case, both governments were nervous of upsetting republicans, whom they were now hoping would bow to public opinion and disarm.

There was certainly no appetite whatsoever in the higher echelons of government for the solution that would have appealed to many of the Omagh survivors. It was articulated the morning after the bomb to a jour- nalist in the Leisure Centre by David Graham, who had spent the best part of seventeen hours with his friend Paul Radford looking for his brother Alan and now knew he was dead. 'What peace process?' asked Graham. 'Sorry, have I missed something here? The only solution is to take an Israeli attitude. Shoot to kill and annihilate the terrorists. Give the RUC, the British Army and the Royal Irish Regiment a free hand for forty-eight hours. Let's see how brave the bombers are then.' Many of the relatives wanted vengeance: as the months dragged by and the law failed them, the miracle was that no one took up a gun.

Councillor Francie Mackey, a very visible figure in Omagh and a psychiatric nurse at the hospital which the Real IRA had turned into a charnel house, was well known to be Chairman of the 32CSM. His nineteen- year-old son Shane was one of those temporarily arrested in connection with the bombing but released without charge after three days. Everyone knew about the McKevitts, and newspapers were full of speculation about other people linked with both organisations. The police had said that the investigation 'would be brought to a speedy conclusion' if the public came forward with information, but gradually it became clear that poten- tial witnesses were too terrified to speak.

Ronnie Flanagan, the RUC Chief Constable, had assured the world that

* Internment without trial of suspected terrorists, which had been used north and south of the border at times of crisis, was introduced again in 1971 in Northern Ireland and so thoroughly botched that it became utterly discredited and helped IRA recruitment: few politicians were prepared to listen to those who pointed out now that if it were intro- duced by both governments simultaneously it could destroy the Real IRA and other intransigent paramilitary groups.

he had no doubt that the bombers would be caught: 'We are determined,' he said, 'to bring to justice the people who carried out this.' Flanagan, an ex-head of Special Branch, was thought by some colleagues to be too cerebral to be head of an organisation which had been through such fire and trauma as had the RUC. But at the time of his appointment, when the killing had almost stopped, what was needed was the politician and skilled communicator that he was rather than a policeman's policeman.

Even though the IRA had gone back to terror in February 1996, the month Flanagan was appointed Deputy Chief Constable, it was clear that this was a hiccup in the peace process and that in negotiations between governments and local politicians, the future of the RUC would be a bargaining counter. Republicans loathed the police,* while unionists wanted to keep the RUC intact. By November, when he was appointed Chief Constable, Flanagan had completed the RUC's 'Fundamental Review of Policing', designed to demonstrate that the force accepted that it needed to be reformed and to make concrete suggestions for how this could be done without damaging policing.

In line with the promise in the Good Friday Agreement of 'a new beginning to policing in Northern Ireland with a police service capable of attracting and sustaining support from the community as a whole', the British government set up an Independent Commission on Policing for Northern Ireland in June 1998, ten weeks before the Omagh bomb. Led by Chris Patten,† this commission sat in towns around Northern Ireland listening to the views of locals about the RUC. Fearful that they were being sacrificed to appease terrorists, most police viewed the Patten Commission with suspicion and deeply resented the vicious anti-RUC propaganda orchestrated by Sinn Féin at many rancorous meetings and in the international press.

The publication of the Patten report in September 1999 would be followed by a consultation period and fierce political warfare for another year. So during the first two years of the Omagh investigation, the RUC's Chief Constable was also contending with trying to salvage a decent future

* Three hundred and three Northern Ireland policemen and policewomen were killed by paramilitaries between 1969 and 2004, 273 of them by republicans; the RUC were responsible for 50 deaths in total, of whom only 15 were republican paramilitaries.

† A Roman Catholic Conservative politician who served as a junior minister in Northern Ireland from 1983 to 1985, a Cabinet minister from 1989 to 1992 and Governor of Hong Kong from 1992 to 1997.

for his demoralised force. From his perspective, the practical handling of the Omagh investigation was the responsibility of those he had appointed the day after the bomb went off: Task Force Commander was Detective Chief Superintendent Eric Anderson, whose experience included the investigation of around three hundred murders; Detective Superintendent Hamilton Houston was Senior Investigating Officer. Initially staffed by 150 CID and uniformed RUC officers, they were supplemented for a time by a team from the Bomb Squad of the London Metropolitan Police, who brought with them specialised equipment.

In theory, Anderson, who was the head of the Criminal Investigation Department (CID), was the obvious person for the job, not least because until the previous year he had been in charge of the North Region, which includes west Tyrone. One of his successes had been in finding the loyalist gunmen who murdered six Catholics and two Protestants in 1993 in what they saw as a Catholic bar in Greysteel, County Londonderry. Yet many felt he was out of his depth in an investigation of the unprecedented size and complexity of Omagh. As his critics observed, Anderson knew how to talk the talk better than walk the walk. Hamilton Houston, on the other hand, was viewed as solid and hardworking but a poor commmunicator.

In April 2000, nearly two years after the bomb, as the clamour grew about the failure of the RUC to charge anyone with murder, an uneasy Flanagan commissioned an internal report. The review team, staffed by officers who had not been involved in the investigation, and with some advice and assistance from senior English officers and HM Inspectorate of Constabulary, were charged to examine the work, the line and conduct of the early inquiry for thoroughness and accountability and to ensure that nothing had been missed. In his report of November 2000, Detective Chief Superintendent Brian McVicar acknowledged 'the extreme pressures and stress the Senior Command faced in this investigation. It was the worst single atrocity of the troubles, and never before had Senior Detectives in the RUC been faced with such a massive murder investigation.' The crime scene was 'unprecedented' and 'complex, difficult and compromised from the outset by the presence of so many injured persons'.

The first problem was that it had been impossible to preserve the forensic integrity of the scene. No one ever questioned that he had got his priorities right, even if, from the forensic point of view, Phil Marshall technically had not been complying with procedures when he had bodies moved out of Market Street to maintain their dignity in death and spare their families needless agony. That Saturday evening, traumatised police had made a quick search for obvious evidence, clothing and personal effects, and, after a cursory examination, a forensic scientist had a path brushed up the right-hand side of Market Street to allow access. The police were focused mainly on the identification of bodies and the safeguarding of obviously vital exhibits: the need to take scrupulous protective measures to avoid the contamination of evidence – particularly in respect of DNA opportunities – was not top of the list. Nor did anyone yet know anything of low copy number (LCN) DNA that would be such an important feature of the only prosecution mounted in Northern Ireland and which demanded stringent anti-contamination procedures.

There were five days of fingertip searches, but political pressure meant that from Saturday evening onwards, despite an order to close the scene overnight, Market Street was being tramped on by VIPs, staff from the Northern Ireland office, local politicians, senior police, army officers, shopkeepers, and – later – journalists, as well as the repairmen needed to allow the town to open again for business.

Police and politicians were faced with two mutually exclusive priorities: to nail the bombers it would have been wise to make the town completely off-limits for a week and maintain it in close to laboratory conditions; but the overwhelming emotional demand from the public was to face down the bombers by restoring some semblance of normality as quickly as possible.

The Forensic Science Agency (FSNI) was doing its best, although it was enormously hampered in its work by having had its large explosives section greatly reduced in size during the peace process, but, under the supervision of Senior Scientific Officer Denis McAuley, bomb components were collected. The damaged blue Addis lunchbox lid, the black battery connector with three batteries and a slightly damaged toggle switch were enough to indicate that the bombers of Omagh were linked to several earlier attacks.* Additionally, thirteen skips of debris were filled and removed by the following Saturday, when the 50,000 sympathisers and senior politicians took over the town. Among the strange objects that ended up with the forensic scientists were the two phone boxes used to

---

* Similar Timer Power Units (TPUs) had been used between January and July 1998 in two hoax devices, two explosive devices, five mortar attacks and six car bombs.

give the warnings, which were cut out of the ground in Forkhill and Newtownhamilton, two small villages in County Armagh.

The desperate efforts of a grief-stricken community to get on with life were visible on Monday 24th, when the shops that reopened included some that had lost members of staff. Tears were shed as people passed the hundreds of bouquets left outside damaged and ruined shops. The town's Chamber of Commerce president, Michael Gaine, urged the town to face up to practicalities: 'Many of those able to return to business feel uneasy,' he said. 'There are shops that cannot physically open as they are wrecked. There are shops that are fine physically but can't open because they have lost staff, and there are shops that are fine but feel ashamed to open. It is going to be terrible for some people but we really have to start over again.' The manager of Oxfam told a journalist that all the volunteers had come in that day to be together. 'We lost Lorraine and Samantha and Betty Wright lost her brother and nephew but all our volunteers believe that reopening the shop is what Lorraine and Samantha would have wanted.'

As the victims struggled to function, the investigation swung into gear. Its scale was huge, involving the two police forces, who in the first year conducted more than six thousand interviews, carried out more than three thousand house-to-house enquiries and took more than 2,500 statements while sifting through the dialling records of some five hundred million calls on the day of the bombing. The Irish police are much less accountable than those of Northern Ireland, so investigative deficiencies on that side of the border can only be guessed at. But it was clear from McVicar's meticulous 286-page report that, despite the dedicated work of at times hundreds of officers, the RUC investigation had often been sloppy, understaffed and badly coordinated: the innumerable inadequacies and missed opportunities in the police investigation that he pointed out included inadequate resources, lack of suitable accommodation, untrained staff, a lack of understanding of the capabilities of the Home Office Large Major Enquiry System (HOLMES) data base, a confused command structure and poor coordination of intelligence analysis. There were many instances of interviews being badly indexed and simply not followed up, meetings were rarely minuted and there was little communication between the Forensic Service and the investigating officers.

There were serious specific oversights. After forensic examination, the shell of the car and other car parts were left in the car park at the back of the FSNI under a tarpaulin cover, where, month by month, rust eroded any potential for future enquiry teams equipped with new technology or forensic techniques. Incredibly, there was no collation of tape recordings of Real IRA warnings or tapings of the voices of suspects, with a view to having them examined by a voice analyst.

Such revelations would cause enormous public rows when they became known in 2001. By then another of McVicar's findings had also become independently obvious to many observers: though Eric Anderson would tell the inquest that there was daily contact between the two police services ('with full and frank interchange of information, intelligence and joint co-operation'), for public relations reasons he was putting a rosy veneer on the reality that there was no properly structured relationship between the RUC and their counterparts in the Irish Republic, An Garda Síochána,* the police of the Irish Republic. Although there were good individual relationships, there was a long history of institutional mistrust between the two forces. The RUC perspective was that over three decades many people in Northern Ireland had been the victims of murderers from the south whom gardaí and twenty-six-county politicians had done little to put out of business. It was summed up trenchantly by an RUC Special Branch officer in the late-1990s: 'After nearly 30 years of protests from the guards that we were asking too much of them on the border, when the BSE† crisis came there were suddenly vehicle checkpoints every night of the week and more security than ever before. A very good source who was also a smuggler told us that in the 20 years he had been operating until BSE broke out he had no problem and then suddenly he couldn't move for guards.'[1]

The basic problem was that the murders had been carried out in Northern Ireland, so the RUC 'naturally assumed primacy' in the investigation, as McVicar put it, yet the car, the explosives, the phones and most of the suspects came from the Republic. Senior RUC officers, said McVicar, 'should have had the capacity to influence the course and direction of the An Garda Síochána investigation, to access relevant intelligence, suspects' details, timing of arrests and consultation during and after arrest'. There should have been 'an open and joint enquiry'.

---

* Irish for 'Peace Guard of Ireland'; garda is singular; gardaí plural.
† Bovine spongiform encephalopathy (BSE), otherwise known as 'mad-cow disease', which was threatening Ireland in 1996–7 and had infected Britain and Northern Ireland.

Instead, the gardaí carried out their investigations independently: of all documentation on the Omagh database only 2.8 per cent related to garda enquiries, even though the gardaí had made seventy arrests. So despite public expressions by Blair and Ahern of their joint determination to track down the murderers, and occasional publicised meetings between Chief Constable Ronnie Flanagan and Garda Commissioner Pat Byrne, the RUC and the gardaí for the most part went their separate ways. There was no formal structure in place to manage the exchange of documents and information, and while Task Force Commander Anderson had a genial relationship with the gardaí he met from time to time, Senior Investigating Officer Houston and his deputy were frequently frustrated at the failure of gardaí to deliver on their requests. It was demoralising usually to have no more notice of garda arrests than did members of the general public. And details of interviews with suspects were frequently not passed from the gardaí to the RUC.

There was nothing sinister about the lack of cooperation: police forces in separate jurisdictions like to do things their own way. The gardaí loathed the perpetrators of Omagh and gave known sympathisers a hard time, secure in the knowledge that – unlike in Northern Ireland – complaints of harassment and human rights abuses from republicans would both be muted and get short shrift from the political establishment. One member of the Real IRA Army Council recalled that the Irish Special Branch 'would be waiting for you outside the house and would follow you everywhere, a few feet behind the car. They used to run people off the road all the time. They were covert and very overt. They sat outside one volunteer's house in Cork for two months after Omagh.'[2]

The gardaí made the first serious breakthrough in March 1999 when they charged forty-six-year-old Colm Murphy. After being imprisoned for the first time as a nineteen-year-old for firearms offences, he had escaped from the Curragh Military Prison but was recaptured after seven months. Murphy was jailed again for firearms offences and membership of the IRA. He was jailed in 1983 in New York after an FBI sting for attempting to purchase twenty M-16 rifles.

Returning to Dundalk in 1985, Murphy stayed out of jail and built up an impressive business portfolio of land, bars and construction firms in Dundalk and Drogheda. His Emerald Bar in Church Street, Dundalk, with prominent photographs of the hunger strikers, made non-republicans feel unwelcome.

He was on friendly terms with his customers and the allegation is that Murphy handed over his phone and that of his unwitting foreman, Terence Morgan, at the request of Daly. This was a time when few would have had any inkling that phone masts could pinpoint the location of a phone when a call was made. The finding in the civil case was to be that the inference that Murphy provided these phones to the bombers was 'irresistible', but it should be noted that Murphy has yet to be re-tried on a criminal charge that he did so.

Towards the end of February 1999 the analysis of the mobile phone networks was pointing inexorably towards Morgan and Murphy, and the RUC and the gardaí cooperated and made simultaneous arrests: Morgan was interrogated by the RUC and Murphy by the gardaí.

Morgan, who was then thirty-one and lived on his grandfather's farm in Mullaghbawn in South Armagh with his wife and two children, was virtually illiterate and had no interest in politics. A bricklayer, he had begun working for Murphy, who was his mother's first cousin, around 1996 and from December 1997–8 had been his foreman on the Dublin City University site, in charge of fifty or sixty men. Six mornings a week he would drive the twelve miles to Dundalk where, with several others, he would be picked up at 6.20 by one of Murphy's vans and transported to the Dublin site, which they would leave at 5.00 p.m. His wages were supplemented by UK unemployment benefit.

Morgan was terrified of saying anything that might get him into trouble. 'I just mind me own business, do me day's work,' he kept telling the police. Confronted with telephone records showing his phone had been to Omagh on 15 August, he had no option but to admit he had given his boss his phone the day before when Murphy said his own was 'on the blink'. Police were satisfied Morgan was innocent of any involvement in the bombing and no charges were ever brought against him.

Charges were brought against Colm Murphy, however. On 24 February, after being charged with conspiracy to cause an explosion likely to endanger life or cause injury, he was taken to the Special Criminal Court in Dublin. He was denied bail and despatched to Portlaoise Prison, where he exercised his right to join the segregated republican wing until he was released on IR£100,000 bail.

The gardaí were jubilant. But for the families, one arrest on a peripheral charge meant little. Especially since many of them believed that the Real IRA were going back to war.

PART II

And yet who knows what's yet to come?
For Patrick Pearse has said
That in every generation
Shall Ireland's blood be shed

W.B. Yeats

CHAPTER EIGHT

SURVIVING IT

'We feel the politicians have not done their job and would just want to forget about us, but we will not go away or be forgotten about. We have too many friends who are willing to help us keep the peace process within the media spotlight' – Michael Gallagher, August 1999

It was eighteen months after the bomb that a group of relatives decided to take the law into their own hands. By then they had begun to transform themselves from passive victims into activists for justice.

Shock can mask pain temporarily. But when the funerals were over and the families had to try to re-engage with normal life, the agony truly began. It is human nature after an unnatural death to talk of the deceased as a perfect human being: children are all angels, mothers are devoted and fathers lived for their families. Yet it would be hard to find anything but good to say of the dead of this group. Breda Devine was a toddler; James Barker a cheerful, kind boy; good-natured, hard-working Aiden Gallagher was widely popular; Esther Gibson was a selfless mainstay of her large family and her community; Samantha McFarland and Lorraine Wilson brimmed over with the desire to make the lives of family, friends and strangers better; best friends Geraldine Breslin and Ann McCombe were regarded as treasures by their employers and customers; Alan Radford stood out among his peers for his helpfulness and consideration; Libbi Rush was a confidante to troubled neighbours and friends; Philomena Skelton's instinct to nurture extended to a Romanian orphanage; Fred White was decent, easy-going and uxorious; and sociable Bryan White worked hard at a profession he loved. Every one was an unmitigated and crushing loss to a wide circle of people.

To determine their right to claim damages for injury, a psychiatrist would later individually assess the plaintiffs who were suing the Omagh bombers. Two years on, most still exhibited symptoms of post-traumatic stress disorder and several were clinically depressed. Dr Cooling listed innumerable symptoms displayed by those he examined, which included anxiety, physical aches and pains, anger, irritability, loss of appetite, weight loss, weight gain from comfort eating, impaired concentration, acute stress, insomnia, claustrophobia, tearfulness, flashbacks, tension, nightmares, poor memory, low energy, jumpiness, suicidal urges, obsessional behaviour, mood swings, panic attacks, sweating, palpitations, hallucinations and breathing difficulties. Misery is not an acknowledged medical term, but all the plaintiffs were plunged into it and many were broken by it. Their suffering was intensified by what the psychiatrist described as their conviction 'of the intentional nature of the acts' that killed their relative. 'If it had been an illness, or even a car accident,' said Esther Gibson's sister Liz, 'you could maybe have accepted it in time, but to make a bomb and plant it where you knew there would be so many children!'

Many relatives also suffered from senseless but powerful guilt. Michael Gallagher blamed himself for recommending that Aiden use a particular car park; Victor Barker felt he had let James down by not being with him when he most needed his father; Donna-Maria blamed herself for the family move to Donegal; Edith White tortured herself because she had let Fred and Bryan do the shopping; and so on and on and on with many of the others. Some siblings endured the common affliction among young people of survivor guilt: 'My brother/sister is dead. Why am I alive?'

Those that have never seen tragedy at close quarters find it hard to imagine the sheer irrationality of grief and the way in which it drives the bereaved apart. Terrible patterns emerge, most of which were to be seen among the bereaved of Omagh. I grew up with some sense of how victims react. My reticent father was marked for life by the unexpected death of his eighteen-year-old brother and only surviving sibling. He wrote a brief diary every day, and in his seventies would still note the anniversaries of Ralph's birth and death and sometimes speak of his brother as if he had died yesterday. His mother was so traumatised that at first no one mattered to her except her dead son, and she had little sympathy to spare for her husband or surviving child. My father never forgave or recovered from the experience of his mother coming home from church a few days after Ralph's death and reporting that the priest had said the best one had died. I saw something similar when one of my aunt's two boys was killed – also at eighteen. She was not cruel to her husband and surviving son, but her anguish detached her from them.

Some couples, like Godfrey and Ann Wilson, who were mourning Lorraine, are brought closer by joint sorrow, though, as happened in their case, that can alienate the surviving children. As well as displaying many of the classic symptoms, Godfrey cried for much of every day for months and months. Their daughter Denise and son Garry, like Ann, began to drink heavily; Colin, who had learning difficulties, had temper tantrums and insisted on sleeping in his parents' bedroom. All of them had problems with work, changing jobs, staying away for long periods or, in Godfrey's case, eventually stopping work completely because neither his mind nor his body could cope.

'People don't realise what goes on behind closed doors in a situation like this,' said Godfrey later. 'There have been attempts in the family to take life, which we have had to deal with. Trying to take your own life because of an act that other people have imposed, it's demented. But for one family member finding out in time we would have been attending another funeral . . . To find a loved one trying to kill themselves, people don't realise what you have to deal with. You're trying to be as strong as you can for your family and then there's Ann and me sat up at night wondering if someone is taking tablets to end it all.'

More often, as in the case of Victor and Donna-Maria Barker who would end up divorced, couples become divided because they grieve in radically different ways: traumatic bereavements are often followed by divorce.* Often, the mother wants only to grieve and thinks her husband heartless, while the father wants to take action against those responsible for the disaster and feels his wife self-indulgent. The Barkers were a classic instance of this. Donna-Maria enveloped herself in grief and was barely conscious of those around her; Victor, on the other hand, was trying to look after his family, earn a living and do whatever he thought necessary to get justice for James. By September 1998 he was already in battle with officialdom about compensation.

Most of the families had little or no money and would not even have been able to afford the funerals of their dead, but they were told they could apply for criminal injuries compensation. Within a few days of the bomb, notices ran in the local press telling anyone who had sustained a physical or mental injury 'that they need to *forthwith* report their injury' to the police and to consult their solicitors. A notice of intention to apply for compensation had to be lodged within twenty-eight days: as Victor

---

* Two such couples were the parents of Stephen Lawrence, stabbed to death by racist thugs in 1993, and Sarah Payne, murdered by a paedophile in 2000.

realised in talking to his Buncrana neighbours, the families of Oran Doherty and Sean McLaughlin, traumatised people with little knowledge of the law or officialdom did not really know where to start. So Victor filled in the forms and made a claim on behalf of the three families. And for a time, he became the champion of the four little boys – James, Oran, Sean and Fernando – who had gone merrily from Buncrana to their deaths.

Bureaucracies, however, have rules, and to vulnerable people these rules can seem heartless and arbitrary. For instance, unless claimants could prove dependency and future loss of earnings, there was a statutory bereavement award with a top limit of £7,500 payable to the spouse of a victim or the parents of a victim under eighteen.* So the Gallaghers and the Gibsons were not entitled to compensation for the murders of Aiden and Esther, while Edith White was eligible for the loss of her husband but not her son. Everyone was entitled to up to £1,000 towards funeral expenses and £750 for a headstone.

Nor are the traumatised and bereaved very logical. So the Wilsons, for instance, perceived that the state thought the loss of Lorraine was worth only £7,500 and the Gallaghers that the loss of Aiden was worth nothing. To the state, of course, as a minister explained in a letter to Michael Gallagher, such sums do not place 'a monetary value on a human life', which would be impossible, but are merely 'a gesture of recognition by society to the relatives of the victims of violent crime'.

Victor, who had already begun channelling his anger into challenging authority, was enraged that the Irish government had offered the Buncrana families no financial help whatsoever, and were passing the buck to the Omagh Memorial Fund, set up within a few days of the bomb, into which was pouring hundreds of thousands of pounds. Furious at rumours of compensation payments to jailed paramilitaries for damage to personal property, as opposed to 'the derisory compensation' paid to the families of deceased children, he pointed out to his MP that he had spent about £30,000 on James's school fees alone. 'It seems to me a cruel world where the lives of innocent hardworking people are ruined by acts of cruel inhumanity and the victims of crime seem to be treated far worse than the perpetrators which society now seeks to "re-house".'

---

* Compared to how victims of terrorism were treated in the earlier days of the Troubles, these sums were relatively generous. The amount awarded for children murdered in the bomb in Claudy in 1972 was £63.

Victor would regard himself as fortunate in having no choice but to go back to work nine days after James's death. Not only had he a family to support, but the house in Donegal had cost a fortune to buy and renovate and he was a partner in a two-man law firm; the work had to be done. Being based far from Omagh and living in a tranquil English community was another apparent blessing, though he learned some harsh lessons about how people respond to tragedy. While most of his clients and his many friends were immensely supportive, some – embarrassed by grief and terrified by any association with terrorism – shunned him, or broke off business links.

The commuting to Donegal was now even more gruelling because the weekends were spent in a house which Donna-Maria had turned into a shrine dominated by an enormous photograph of their dead son. Like her mother, Estella was possessed by an intense grief but also by a deep, irrational guilt because James had taken her seat on the coach trip; four-year-old Oliver missed his big brother and did his best in a volatile environment. Donna-Maria's parents, neighbours and Father Shane Bradley were kind and supportive, but Victor worried for his whole family.

Compared to the terrible condition of many of the bereaved, Victor, although desolate and angry, was managing to cope. Yes, it took him half a bottle of wine to get to sleep, which for this sparing drinker was serious excess, and he was uncharacteristically short-tempered, but mostly he got on with his job, his duties as a local councillor and his family responsibilities. But as a way of channelling his terrible rage, every day, when he had finished a morning's work, there would be what he called James Time, when he would think of practical things to do for his dead son. That involved trying to find out what exactly had happened, to help bring the perpetrators to justice, to support other victims, to stop the Real IRA from killing again and to raise money for Omagh-related good causes: letters were despatched to politicians, police and officials. In his spare time, Victor organised a Golf Day in Surrey in James's memory in June 1999, which raised around £75,000 for the Omagh Fund.

For the families in and around Omagh, life was in many ways more difficult. In Surrey and Buncrana, no one was faced with the relentless reminders of tragedy that the Omagh relatives had every day. In a world of close family links, the ripple effect caused great suffering to grandparents and aunts and uncles and cousins as well as immediate parents, children and siblings: Aiden Gallagher's maternal grandfather died ten days after the bomb having uttered hardly a word from the moment he learned of Aiden's death.

The town and the surrounding villages and everyone who lived and worked there were to a greater or lesser extent traumatised. Many of the police were consumed with guilt because they had unwittingly directed people towards the bomb. 'We are trying to help each other through it,' said Sergeant Phil Marshall. 'We are on the phone every day. We will overcome it by doing little things like walking back up the town. The scenes will haunt us for the rest of our lives.'

More than six hundred people consulted the Omagh Community Trauma and Recovery Team, which included doctors, nurses, social workers and a range of therapists, though many of the bereaved and injured could not even bear to go near the town for years and some have never been back. Many places of work were contaminated, too. When, after a year off, Denise Wilson went back to the Desmond factory, where Esther Gibson had worked too, she was very upset to learn there was graffito in the men's room reading 'RIRA 29-0' and left to find work elsewhere. Real IRA supporters are a depraved bunch: in the years after the bomb Omagh was plagued by hoax bomb scares. One disruptive call came on Christmas Eve 1998.

Geraldine Breslin's widower, Mark, who was looking after his fifteen-year-old stepson, went back to work as a surveyor after about six weeks, but found it harder and harder to cope and finally quit after eighteen months. Michael Gallagher could never bring himself to go into the garage where he had worked with Aiden, and though his daughter Cathy went back to college, she took a job well below her capabilities when she graduated. Esther Gibson's mother developed leukaemia, her sister Audrey gave up her job in the police canteen because she could not endure seeing officers she associated with the bomb, Caroline was unable to work at all, Liz resigned as a filing clerk because it involved dealing with the registrar of deaths and took up part-time bar work, Eddie found his job as a policeman virtually impossible and eventually retired in February 2001, Robert lost his job in May 1999 and Wilma took periods of sick leave before changing to a less stressful job. Samantha McFarland's father Gerry gave up his equestrian business, Alan Radford's mother Marion could not go back to work, his brother Paul's bitterness caused him to leave Northern Ireland, and Ann McCombe's widower Stanley lost his job because he could not concentrate. Philomena Skelton's widower, Kevin, was also unable to work, but though physically ill and domestically inept, battled to acquire the skills to look after his four children.

Edith White had no work to go to. In a confused state of denial and grief, she filled her time driving long distances in the hope of finding Fred and Bryan, yet also in visiting their graves twice a day. What saved her sanity was the Omagh Support and Self Help Group (OSSHG).

In the weeks after the bomb, Michael Gallagher had forged a close friendship with Stanley McCombe. They had known each other in the 1980s when the Gallaghers had been forced to leave their house because it had been damaged by a bomb and had ended up being rehoused beside the McCombes. They had seen little of each other in the intervening years, but after the bomb Patsy Gallagher recalls Stanley sitting night after night at the kitchen table with Michael as they sobbed their hearts out. Libbi Rush's widower, Laurence, who was in a desperate state, also called in from time to time, as did the Wilsons, and gradually the idea of having a proper support group developed. As Michael put it later, 'After the funerals, there was a sort of emptiness, a gap where no one seemed to know where to turn. Then some of us got together to talk about what happened. We were able to relate to each other's feelings.'

They also decided they wanted some control over their fate. In late October, Laurence booked a room in an Omagh hotel to which around fifty people came: more than half of the bereaved families were represented along with many of those injured and maimed. Laurence had expected to be chairman, but so all-enveloping was his rage that he was thought by some too much of a loose cannon: Stanley and Godfrey proposed Michael, Stanley became Vice-Chair, Laurence Treasurer, and Mandy Walker, whose mother Olive Hawkes had been decapitated, was Secretary. Most Northern Ireland victims' groups are tribal: the OSSHG, however, included hardline and moderate unionists as well as nationalists, although republican supporters mostly avoided it; religiously, there were Catholics, Anglicans, Presbyterians, Free Presbyterians and the Mormon Marion Radford.

From the beginning Michael made it clear that politics and religion would play no part in the group. 'Its aim,' he said, 'is to support and help the bereaved and injured in any way we can.' And to that end he cultivated every journalist he could. One reason why Omagh has never been forgotten by the media was that Michael Gallagher always took phone calls and answered questions fully and courteously.

Money was the first priority. The Omagh Fund had collected over a million pounds by now, but nothing had yet filtered through to victims: well-heeled, middle-class people have little understanding of how important comparatively small sums can be at a time of disaster. As Michael Gallagher would point out, there would have been merit in having 'ordinary people' on the board as well as 'people of station'. As late as December, Stanley, for instance, was living on £55.70 per week sick pay. In the ensuing months, the OSSHG formed a good relationship with the Trustees of the Omagh Fund and money began to reach those who needed it.

The Omagh Fund existed because of the urge to give money as a response to tragedy. More than £6 million would be donated by individuals and through innumerable events like concerts and football matches: around £4 million went directly to the injured and the families of the dead. But, as with all such funds, there were resentments about who got what, and the well-meaning great and good from Northern Ireland and the Republic who were the Trustees would be shaken by the virulence of some of the criticism. Unhappy, grief-stricken people can be difficult and angry and fall out with outsiders and each other easily: there were tensions in the OSSHG itself between relatives of the dead who thought the injured were lucky and people in pain who thought the bereaved had no idea how it was to suffer physically day after day.

One of the key virtues of the group, however, was that it offered the chance to talk about agonies with others who understood. 'There are tears,' said Stanley, 'and there is anger. And the main thing is none of us is afraid, or embarrassed, to show the way we feel.' And it gave its members confidence. A donation of £20,000 from an event at Shelbourne Park Greyhound Racing in Dublin provided enough to find premises of their own – a Portakabin on the outskirts of Omagh town – where they could sit over cups of tea and talk about what outsiders could not comprehend.

Few in the OSSHG would ever have met anyone famous or powerful before the bomb, but, only days after its formation, representatives were meeting senior civil servants and politicians. Within a few weeks they were impressed by no one and felt let down by many. The unimaginativeness and unintentional cruelties of the compensation system were a daily affront that became a focus for anger. Complaining about the rigidity of the Compensation Agency and its slowness in assessing pecuniary loss, Michael told the press in February that 'in the aftermath of the bomb, when the Prime Minister, the US President and the Taoiseach visited, they said they would do anything they could. When they left, the promises left with them.'

There was no doubt that while society in general and governments in particular wished the victims of Omagh well, what was hoped was that they would quieten down and support the peace process. A telling passage in the 2002 autobiography of ex-Secretary of State for Northern Ireland, Mo Mowlam, addressed Omagh very briefly. What was important, she explained, was that victims deal with their grief by helping others and by backing the peace process. She singled out for admiration a handful of people who had become peace activists after being bereaved during the Troubles, including Colin and Wendy Parry, whose son had been murdered in Warrington in 1993, and Rita Restorick, whose soldier son was murdered by an IRA sniper in 1997. 'Of course,' admitted Mowlam, 'many of those who lost loved ones had to find other ways of handling their grief differently from Rita and Colin. The pain of losing a loved one may be too great to do anything but try to cope with your emotions in whatever way you can.' There was no indication from anything Mowlam wrote that she understood those who felt anger, or who craved justice.

While it is obviously unwise to encourage victims to hate, society's impatience for them to forgive and shut up can be hard to bear. One public figure with empathy was Bob Geldof, who made a memorable contribution to Irish television's star-studded *Late Late Show* tribute to the victims of Omagh, three months after the bomb.

Entertainers and celebrities had rallied swiftly and generously to help the survivors. The racing driver Eddie Irvine and the champion boxer Barry McGuigan had been sitting beside injured children within days and over the ensuing months visitors to Omagh would include Heather Mills, who inspired amputees, and Boyzone, who put on a tribute concert. Among the stars of this *Late Late Show* were U2 and The Corrs, who, with performers Enya, Sinead O'Connor, Daniel O'Donnell and Van Morrison, had contributed to *Across the Bridge of Hope*,* an album compiled to raise money for the Omagh Fund. The Northern Irish actor Liam Neeson read poetry on the album, and also donated a considerable sum to the Omagh Fund.

---

* The title was that of a poem which twelve-year-old Sean McLaughlin of Buncrana and five classmates had written and performed for President Mary McAleese three months before he was murdered. 'Orange and green it doesn't matter/United now don't shatter our dream/Scatter the seeds of peace over our land/So we can travel hand in hand across the bridge of hope.'

But while victims were grateful for the concern, the relentless propaganda for the peace process was an affront to those who thought it morally repugnant to negotiate and share power with former terrorists. And the equally relentless urgings from the well-meaning to the relatives to rise above their sufferings seemed at times impertinent to those still in a state of raw grief.

The extract Neeson read from Seamus Heaney's 1990 play, *The Cure at Troy* begins appropriately enough with 'Human beings suffer,/they torture one another,/they get hurt and get hard', but then proceeds: 'History says, Don't hope/on this side of the grave./But then, once in a lifetime/the longed for tidal wave/of justice can rise up,/and hope and history rhyme.' The last four words had long since been hijacked by politicians and transformed into a cliché of the peace process.*

The *Late Late* producers had managed to find, with one exception, a collection of brave and stoical victims who all said positive things about hope and peace and forgiveness and good coming out of evil: Michael Grimes, whose wife, daughter and unborn grandchildren had died, had no harsh words; fifteen-year-old Claire Gallagher (no relation to Michael), who had been blinded, was back at school and immensely positive, as were the burned and the amputees. The exception was Donna-Maria Barker, who spoke passionately about her intense anger at James's murder.

Among the guests were Bertie Ahern, who lauded the peace process, and Father Brian D'Arcy, an Irish celebrity priest who spoke eloquently about the importance of rising above negative emotions. He did not impress Bob Geldof, who had always been implacably anti-IRA, and was in no mood to consider the peace process or to mince his words: 'You were asking where everybody was [when they heard of the bomb],' he said to Gay Byrne, the host. 'I was in London. My reaction was very typically extreme. I got sick. I mean I literally got sick with rage. I thought it was finally done, that the boil had all been lanced or whatever cancer that exists in the soul of this country was done with now. And then these pigs crawled out again from under whatever rock and did this to these people. You sit in the face of these people and the whole country is humbled and humiliated. I still feel an intense anger. I'm not at the point like Brian

* Bill Clinton published *Between Hope and History: Meeting America's Challenges for the 21st Century* in 1996; Jack Holland *Hope against History: The Ulster Conflict* in 1999; Gerry Adams *Hope and History: Making Peace in Northern Ireland* in 2003.

D'Arcy was saying. I sympathise with the woman who is angry. I think we must remain angry.'

To Donna-Maria's delight, his voice shaking, Geldof raged on: 'I cannot forgive and because I can't forgive I will never ever forget it. And what we have to learn is Omagh was our – I always quote Yeats, you know, that great poem where things fall apart and the centre cannot hold. At some point he talks about the rough beasts slouching towards Jerusalem to be born.* And I think Omagh was the Jerusalem. That was our rough beast; and out of it was born – and in this horror was encapsulated – the entire horror of the last thirty years which none of us that I've ever met ever wanted. So in whose name were these three and a half thousand people maimed, murdered, beaten up, killed? In whose name? How dare they! How dare they! And the intellectual path that these people have crawled through for thirty years to arrive at this point that we were all at previously? It's just a waste, an entire waste of a country. And maybe because you live abroad it strikes you worse, but the shame of the thirty years, the horror of it, everything summed up in that blast.'

At which stage, Gay Byrne also challenged the consensus. 'Am I out of step,' he asked, 'by wishing these people rot in hell forever? Am I out of step?' A Protestant clergyman was worried. 'It's exactly what I would feel initially but I mean I don't want anyone to be in hell. Look at what hell is doing to people in here. Who wants more people to be in hell? What I want is conversion and reconciliation.'

'I'm not disagreeing at all in any sense,' said Father D'Arcy, 'and I don't want tonight to be a night in which there is disagreement at all, but I think the people of Omagh that I know and these people who are suffering a lot – they have to come through suffering in a more positive way. If we let suffering demean us then we have let those people take our soul too and I will not let them hijack my hope.'

But there was no assuaging Geldof with such flights of sentimental rhetoric. While it was right for Bertie Ahern 'to keep the peace process going, and it's our duty to make sure he does', it was also right 'personally to

---

* W. B. Yeats's 'The Second Coming', an apocalyptic poem of 1921 about a disintegrating old world being replaced by a new, is often drawn on to illustrate aspects of violent Irish history: the lines most commonly used are: 'Things fall apart; the centre cannot hold;/Mere anarchy is loosed upon the world'; 'The best lack all conviction, while the worst/Are full of passionate intensity'; and the climax – 'And what rough beast, its hour come round at last,/Slouches towards Bethlehem to be born?'

remember to loathe it, to remember the anger, to wave Omagh in any one's face and say "That's what this nonsense leads to." Anyone who ever contributes to "the boys . . . collecting [for republican terrorists] in the pub". Shame on them! Shame on them! Exactly. May they rot in hell!'

Befitting his accustomed role in their partnership as global activists, Bono played soft cop to Geldof's hard cop. 'The only grain of hope that you can possibly glean from this terror,' he said, 'is that this has to be the end of it. That was the moment that marked the end of the Troubles. We have to believe that – the politicians, the police and the paramilitaries and priests and whoever, that they will go that extra mile now to understand their adversaries and then go one mile further. That's the only thing that we can hope for.'

Irish politicians had been so anxious to go that extra mile to understand their adversaries that Martin Mansergh was despatched by Bertie Ahern in December 1998 to talk to Michael McKevitt in person and persuade him to disband the Real IRA. Wishful thinking was operating at a high level in Dublin, where despite garda intelligence about the regrouping of the Real IRA after Omagh, senior ministers appeared to believe that nothing more would happen to disturb the precarious peace.

It was a brief meeting. Unimpressed by McKevitt's argument that disbandment was impossible because it would leave the Real IRA member-ship defenceless against Provisional assassins, Mansergh left. It had been another foolish move by the Irish government: every such meeting with any dissidents gave an illusion of legitimacy and further convinced people like the McKevitts that, whatever they did and whomever they killed, it would always be possible in the end to negotiate a deal that kept or let them out of jail.

This final breakdown of government–terrorist dialogue left the gardaí free to pursue the Real IRA without political interference. As McKevitt tried to get the organisation up and running again, he was tracked, moni-tored and his group infiltrated further by informers. That was one of the reasons why the McKevitts decided to have a new Army Council, although Liam Campbell stayed on. Henceforward, McKevitt gave priority to trying to unite dissidents of all varieties under the umbrella title of Óglaigh na hÉireann and he gained recruits from the Continuity IRA and disen-chanted Provisionals. He had made the decision to stop taking public responsibility for Real IRA attacks, and even sometimes attributed them to the Continuity IRA.

Bernadette Sands-McKevitt had embarked on a three-year computer course to make herself a more useful member of the 32CSM. Progress was being made on recruitment and in the case of the Real IRA also rearming. In May 1999 came a perverse boost with the trial and jailing of three young Irish university students for conspiring to cause explosions in London the previous summer. That the Real IRA could attract lily-whites – people with no terrorist background – proved that it was not just an organisation for middle-aged and old men too stupid to see that violence was counterproductive. And in that same month, McKevitt sent three men to Croatia to buy weapons: the resulting arms shipment provided ample supplies of guns, detonators, rocket launchers and other instruments of death.

This appalling information was not then available to the victims of Omagh, but they were feeling gloomy enough. In January, Detective Chief Superintendent Eric Anderson had told a newspaper: 'We have a fair idea who did it. We probably know about half a dozen who were involved. We are trying to work out their actual roles.' However, he added, the evidence was not available to 'put them away. It's a long, protracted process involving many avenues of investigation,' he said, 'and we're not there yet.'

This had caused an uproar in the Omagh District Council. How could it be, asked Paddy McGowan, who had helped load bloodied people on to Ulster buses, that if the police knew who committed the crime, they could not bring them to justice? A motion was passed asking the Secretary of State to intervene and give the police special powers to arrest those responsible. Francie Mackey abstained, protesting that the council would be going down a very dangerous road: 'We don't want to be part of the injustices that legislation in the past has thrown up.' Nothing came of the motion.

A major concern for the self-help group had been to assist each other to face the first anniversary of the bomb. Stanley had been unable to go to Mountjoy Presbyterian Church since Ann's funeral, because the choir would be singing without her, but on the day of the anniversary Michael went with him. Afterwards they drew comfort from the huge crowds at the memorial ceremony in Omagh and the plans for a permanent garden of remembrance. Yet, as Stanley told a journalist, 'For the families of the victims, normality will be a long long time in coming, if ever. It is as painful today as it was twelve months ago. People say to you that things will get better and life will move on. But that does not really happen.'

The group were by now proud of how they had bonded and developed collectively and how that had strengthened them individually. Nothing could dull the pain, but it helped that they felt they were having an effect on public opinion, particularly in putting pressure on politicians, governments and statutory bodies to recognise the needs of the victims, 'which, sadly,' said Michael correctly, 'up to this point have to a large extent been neglected'. For this was the most remarkable aspect of the OSSHG. During thirty years of violence, there was no precedent for a group of victims challenging the system who were neither attached to nor under the wing of a political party. Yet in all their inexperience, they had learned to use some of their suffering in a practical way. 'What we have found,' said Stanley, 'is that because we are a group representing people who have been bereaved in the worst atrocity in Northern Ireland, people do listen to what we have to say and at least as a group we have an opportunity to meet these people.'

Besides helping victims practically and psychologically, many of them also, in Michael's words, 'felt they had to do something so the bomb would have some effect on those intent on ruining the lives of others'. They wanted the Real IRA to know what it had done and to be put out of action.

At the funeral of Fred and Bryan White, Dr John Dixon, the Presbyterian Moderator, had made a powerful plea:

> Coming into the house of God can give us a new perspective. It did for David the Psalmist. He lived in a violent, sin-ruined society, too. We can resonate with his feelings as he writes in Psalm 73, 'I had almost stopped believing, I had almost lost my faith . . . I saw wicked people doing well. They are not suffering . . . they wear pride like a necklace and put on violence as their clothing. They say, "How can God know? What does the most high God know?"'
>
> The psalmist continues, 'I tried to understand all this, but it was too hard for me to see until I went to the temple of the Lord. Then I understood what will happen to them . . . You, Lord, cause them to be destroyed. They are swept away by terrors. Lord, when you rise up, they will disappear.'
>
> May those words stabilise the people of God today, particularly those who mourn, are maimed and suffering and all who, like the psalmist, are unsettled by the activities of evil men.

Such sentiments, allied to a strong faith, had over the decades helped thousands of grieving people to cope when it became clear a loved one's murderer would never be brought to justice. It did not work for Edith White, who had lost her religion along with her husband and son. What was especially terrible was the realisation that the bombers did not seem to care about what they had done. 'When you hear of arrests and then people being released,' said Esther Gibson's sister Liz, 'your heart bounces and hits the floor. There must be wives, sisters, who know their menfolk were in some way connected and yet they say nothing. How could anybody do that?' Laurence Rush was devastated when a garda detective 'said to me, and I will never forget it, "Don't think for a second that these people have a conscience. Don't think that they know what they did here." He says he sees the men police believed were the bombers walking about, spending their giros on pints and fags, and trips to the bookies, and that's their life, and they don't give a damn about what they've done.'

Indignant journalists stoked that fire. 'SMILING BOMBER MAKES A MOCKERY OF POLICE SHADOWS' read a headline in the *Sunday People* on the first anniversary of the bomb. It concerned an unnamed bomber, born in South Armagh, who had left his 'signature' on the timer of the Omagh bomb. The man visited friends in South Armagh and Dundalk, but 'mocks the RUC and gardaí whenever he spots them', as he knows they don't have enough evidence to bring him to book. 'The IRA, ourselves and everybody else', said 'a source close to the investigation', 'seems to know who he is – but nobody is prepared to help us arrest and charge him. It's a shame. He may just get away with all these murders and that's something we just have to face up to.' He smiled and waved at police on his trail, it was alleged. 'Like most hardened, committed terrorists, he probably just feels that the twenty-nine dead are par for the course.'

Anger, Laurence would say, kept him functioning. His raw emotion was in evidence in October 1999, when he went to Dublin to see Colm Murphy appear in the Special Criminal Court to be given a date for his trial. 'I finally had seen the guy. I was angry that this [the court appearances] was going to continue and continue. I went to leave and he was just standing there laughing with his counsel in the foyer. My anger boiled over. He was standing there free as a bird. I went over and cried: "You're a bastard for killing my wife." He was pleading with me that he didn't do it.' Sympathetic gardaí led Laurence from the court and Michael came to his defence, describing him as 'an unbelievably kind and warm person' who 'from time to time gets very upset. But that's understandable. He was married for forty years and now he's in his home on his own.'

The OSSHG moved steadily but slowly and found help where they could. Michael and Victor were in touch and they consulted and supported each other, but, for most purposes, Victor Barker was a one-man tornado. As he tried to teach himself about Irish history* and politics, letters were fired off demanding information from police and politicians on both sides of the border about everything from the progress of the case to the state of the peace process. As a Conservative councillor, he had easy access to the opposition, but, where government was concerned, he made no progress with Mo Mowlam; he found her security minister, Adam Ingram, much more approachable and helpful. Ingram wrote sympathetic letters, genuinely tried to answer the flood of questions and attended Victor's fundraising golf event.

Victor's persistence and thoroughness were dismaying to authority. In October 1999, after the OSSGH had persuaded the RUC to brief them on the investigation, Victor gave Michael a three-page list of questions for tabling at a meeting with senior policemen, including Detective Chief Superintendent Eric Anderson and Superintendent James Baxter, the most senior officer in Omagh, who had been on leave almost two hours' drive away from the town when he heard about the bomb. Victor's questions were *inter alia* about security pre-15 August, the timing and relaying of the warnings, the level and methods of policing on the day of the bomb, the absence of army back-up, the nature of the investigations, the identity of suspects and the names of their solicitors, the number of eyewitnesses and what was holding up the inquest.

Half the bereaved families were represented at a two-and-a-half-hour meeting that reassured Michael. 'We were left in no doubt,' he reported, 'that it remained a very active, ongoing, joint and cross-border inquiry. And we were also convinced of the determination and ability of the police teams involved to see it through to a fruitful end ... We were

---

* Victor never really got to grips with Irish history. In May 2000, he sent a letter to the Shadow Secretary of State for Northern Ireland, Andrew MacKay, enclosing a letter from the 32CSM to an Irish emigrant newspaper, in which they quoted Patrick Pearse: 'War is a terrible thing but it is not an evil thing. It is the evil things that make war necessary.' Victor concluded that Pearse was the PRO of the 32CSM. 'It is my personal belief that people like Padraig Pearse', he wrote crossly, 'should not be allowed to publish this sort of war nonsense.' It is a shame he did not send this to Bertie Ahern: Pearse did indeed produce much inflammatory rhetoric before his execution in 1916, but his reputation is sacrosanct in nationalist Ireland and his photograph was on the Taoiseach's office wall.

pleased with the meeting, but we will never really be pleased until the perpetrators are brought to justice and put behind bars', not because of vindictiveness, 'but rather as an assurance that no other person would lose a son, a daughter, a loved one in similar horrific circumstances as we have'.

Victor was less satisfied. In all his dealings with officialdom, he was restless and insatiable, could not be fobbed off with evasion or kind words and was learning fast how to cut through the layers of bureaucracy. In a typical exchange, a long and helpful if vague letter from Tony Blair in March 1999 was met with a request on 1 June from Victor for a private meeting to discuss the state of the investigation and issues concerning victims.

Blair's office was sent a reminder on 26 June and another on 13 July which ended: 'I wonder how the Prime Minister would feel if he had to spend some sleepless nights in the depths of despair as do I and my family wondering what suffering and torment my twelve-year-old son endured. And he protested at the negotiations with Sinn Féin 'with whom the Prime Minister seems only too keen to "do a deal" at what to some now appears to be any cost.'

On 2 August, on what would have been James's thirteenth birthday, Victor wrote again expressing disappointment and anger at having had no response. 'It is now with some regret that my only alternative is to seek a more public forum to discuss the matters that I have sought to raise with you in private.' He was, he explained, convinced that for political reasons the government had failed to pursue the murderers. 'Indeed I take the view that your government has failed in its constitutional duty to ensure that the rule of law prevails and is enforced in ALL PARTS of the United Kingdom, particularly in South Armagh and Carrickmacross, and other areas close to the border with Eire, where these evil men live, and where, as admitted by one of your ministers, the rules of normal civilised society do not prevail.' He was now, said Victor, intending to take advice on what options were open under UK and EU law to sue the government for its 'misguided faith in the political wing of the IRA'. As a law-abiding citizen, he asked, 'am I not entitled to have the protection of the law and our constitution, for my wife and children, which for example the Lawrence family are entitled to, or do I have to resort to other methods to seek justice for the soul of my twelve-year-old son murdered by Mr McKevitt and his private army?'

Victor had pressed the right button by mentioning the Lawrence family.

In 1993, Stephen Lawrence, an eighteen-year-old black student, was murdered in London. The Metropolitan Police botched the investigation, a private prosecution taken by his highly articulate and charismatic parents failed, and sensationally, in 1997, the *Daily Mail* branded the five suspects murderers and challenged them to sue for libel. After a ferocious public outcry, the Home Secretary ordered a public inquiry. Published in February 1999, the MacPherson report labelled the police 'institutionally racist', raised a media storm and led to major reforms in the Met. The last thing the government wanted was another articulate, bereaved parent on the war path.

Victor was amused to receive a letter from Blair's Private Secretary, dated 5 August but ostensibly replying just to his July letters: 'The delay has been caused not by inaction but because we have been paying particular attention to this correspondence.' 'I refer to my letter to you of the 2 August which for some mysterious reason appears to have crossed with your letter of the 5 August,' responded Victor. 'I note what you have said. Perhaps you should telephone me to discuss why you have been "paying particular attention to this correspondence".' Unconvincingly, Downing Street wrote again claiming they had never seen the letter of the 2nd and asking for a copy. On 17 September, Victor reminded them it still had not been answered, 'which may of course be an indication of how low on the government's agenda the interests of the victims are as opposed to the interests of the perpetrators of violence'.

A swift reply assured him there were no grounds for his fears: 'The Prime Minister, the Government, the RUC and the Garda Síochána are totally committed to bringing those responsible for the Omagh atrocity to justice.' In November, Victor finally got his private meeting at Number 10 Downing Street.

Blair's genius for connecting with people has been compared* to a radio receiver constantly trying to lock on to his interlocutor's signal: people are so charmed they forget to make the arguments they arrived primed with and leave believing he has agreed to everything they asked for. But he did not succeed in getting Victor to take his eye off the ball or to stem the unremitting flow of questions and requests, to which Blair eventually responded at the end of January. By this time Victor's bombardment of the Irish government and the gardaí had resulted in a meeting with the Irish

---

* By Sir Christopher Meyer, former British Ambassador to the US.

Taoiseach, Bertie Ahern, at which Victor had had a warm reception to the idea that, on the second anniversary of the bomb, the two prime ministers should make a joint appeal to the public to help convict the killers.

The following Blair–Barker exchange is not only a good illustration of Victor's relentlessness, but of how ministers and the ordinary man find it almost impossible to communicate; the minister thinks the ordinary guy fails to see the big picture; the ordinary guy thinks he is being taken for a mug:

31 January 2000
Dear Victor,

It was good to see you at our meeting in November, and my thoughts remain with you, Donna-Maria and your family. I am also very grateful for the commemorative china plate* which you gave me.

I appreciate and share your determination to see James's killers brought to justice. As you know, the police investigation into the Omagh bombing continues. One person has been charged in the Republic, and his trial commences on 29th February. The Police and Garda co-operation on this investigation has been unprecedentedly close. You will not be surprised to hear that catching those responsible for Omagh and combating the threat from dissident republicanism is the main priority of all the agencies involved in counter-terrorist work in Northern Ireland.

The most encouraging news in Northern Ireland in recent weeks has, of course, been the successful formation of the devolved administration. Things remain uncertain on the decommissioning front, in particular, but I am convinced that political progress will continue to erode any remaining support for violent political action. I believe we are already seeing signs of this.

At the meeting you expressed concerns about the adequacy of counter-terrorist powers. The Counter Terrorism Bill currently before Parliament provides what we see as the necessary tools for the Police in Great Britain and Northern Ireland to continue their work in countering terrorism. The Government continues to believe that the powers you referred to in chapter 14 of the White Paper would mark a significant departure from the established criminal law, and they do not feature in the Bill. Our position

* This was a plate prepared for the James Barker Memorial Golf Day in aid of the Omagh Fund; it had a decoration of Ireland with two doves, one flying from north to south, the other from south to north.

remains, however, that we do not rule out introducing further powers if they were effective and proportionate to the level of threat.

I continue to consider with the Secretary of State for Northern Ireland the best time for an appeal for added co-operation with investigations into terrorist crime. The new political landscape offers unparalleled opportunities to create a political structure that has broad allegiance from both communities and a policing structure to match. This is why we have made the very difficult decisions on the implementation of the Patten Report. I hope the results of this will be a much greater readiness to act to support the security forces in their investigations.

Once again, thank you for sharing your views with me in November, and for all the work you have done on behalf of the victims and bereaved of Omagh.

Yours ever,

Tony Blair

This letter arrived just as Peter Mandelson, who had replaced Mo Mowlam as Secretary of State the previous October, was preparing to suspend the devolved administration at Stormont because of the refusal of the IRA to honour the understanding in the Agreement that they would get rid of their arsenal – or, in euphemistic parlance, to decommission. In fairness to politicians and officials, their dealings with the Omagh relatives would be happening against the permanent backdrop of crises in the peace process. For Bertie Ahern, Martin Mansergh, Tony Blair and his Chief of Staff, Jonathan Powell, who were involved at every stage of the negotiations, what some saw as their anxiety to pander to republican sensibilities made them regard protesting victims as a potential threat to peace.

9 February 2000

Dear Prime Minister,

Thank you for your letter dated the 31st January, which somewhat surprisingly did not arrive here until the morning of the 9th February.

Whilst I am grateful to you for taking time to reply, I am very concerned indeed about the fact that a number of issues have not really been dealt with, in any substantive fashion.

In particular, the question of an Appeal, which I was asking you to consider specifically in relation to the Omagh bombing. It is quite clear to me, after some one and a half years since the 15th August 1998, that the police investigation is not making any serious progress, and stands no

This photograph showing the bomb car was taken just before the bomb went off; the camera was found in the rubble. The subjects survived

Market Street after the bomb, Saturday 15th August 1998

James Barker

Aiden Gallagher

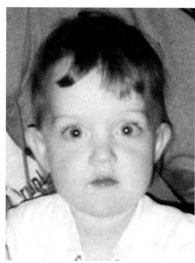

Breda Devine

Lorraine Wilson
and
Samantha
McFarland

Bryan White

Fred White

Alan Radford

Philomena Skelton (her husband Kevin holding
their wedding photograph)

Ann McCombe

Geraldine Breslin

Esther Gibson

Elizabeth Rush

United in grief in Omagh:
the 50,000 at the Act of Prayerful Reflection,
a week after the bomb

Hillary Clinton lays a wreath at the
bomb site, 3rd September 1998

Prince Charles visits the scene,
18th August 1998

Colm Murphy

Liam Campbell

Michael McKevitt

Seamus Daly

Bernadette Sands-McKevitt

Francie Mackey and Donna-Maria Barker, London, November 2000

Ex-Secretaries of State for Northern Ireland pledge support for the civil case:
Peter Brooke, Tom King, Peter Mandelson and Lord Merlyn-Rees, March 2001

Peter Mandelson with Victor Barker, Stanley McCombe, Elizabeth Gibson and Ann Wilson,
campaigning in Westminster, February 2001

David Greenhalgh, Victor and Donna-Maria Barker, Henry Robinson and Sean O'Callaghan after Victor's first marathon in 2002

The trustees: Paul Le Druillenec, Máirín Carter and John Lippitt

chance of doing so. The only hope for progress on the investigation is for people to come forward and give evidence. After all, how many times can a man turn his head, and pretend that he just does not see?

I would ask you, Prime Minister, again to consider an urgent public appeal. At my recent meeting with the Taoiseach, he promised to do all he can, and as quickly as possible.

My concerns about the adequacy of counter-terrorist powers have also not been addressed. I am particularly concerned about the lack of security before the Omagh bombing, the fact that the army were effectively confined to barracks, and the failure of your government to implement the powers referred to in Chapter 14 of the White Paper. I note your comment that they mark a significant departure from the established criminal law, but here we are dealing with unscrupulous people, who have no conscience or morals, and are prepared to murder innocent children in cold blood.

Finally, Prime Minister, whilst I appreciate that your letter was written on the 31st January, I was saddened to hear of the potential suspension of the devolved administration. It is clear to me, beyond doubt, that Sinn Fein and the IRA are inextricably linked. Whilst it has been alleged that the Real IRA, and Continuity IRA are break away groups, they are all intimately known to each other. I think that it is notable that neither Mr Adams or Mr McGuinness have volunteered any help, after our approaches to them, in respect of the Omagh investigation.

I remain, Sir, with disappointment,

Yours sincerely,

Victor E. Barker

Unsurprisingly, the response to this was a note saying that his correspondence had been transferred to the Northern Ireland Office. An 'insulted and saddened' Victor sent a thunderous letter to Blair about what he saw as his 'sickening' appeasement of the IRA.

In a recent economic forum on Northern Ireland, a close friend of mine who is a director of a prominent bank, asked Gerry Adams on no less than four separate occasions why he would not come forward and identify the Omagh bombers to the RUC, the Garda or any other source.

On four occasions he refused to answer the question.

How long will you go on giving in to people who at the same time have a gun pointed firmly at your head?

I do not intend to let this matter rest, believe you me, I will go to my grave still pursuing these people even if you are not prepared to help me.

I know that you won't admit it because you are a politician, but your overriding concern is not to ensure that justice is delivered to people such as myself who have suffered as a result of your policies, there is simply an overriding desire to eliminate Republican attacks in London.

I wonder what your reaction would be, if one of your colleagues was seriously injured or hurt in another Brighton bomb?

Yours sincerely,

Victor E. Barker

'I am aware that everybody probably regards my correspondence as a complete pain in the arse,' Victor would disarmingly confess later to Bertie Ahern. But the sense of injustice that drove him allowed for no slacking. In early 2000 he was about to take his quest on to a new plane. And I was the unwitting agent.

CHAPTER NINE

THE LONDON
CONNECTION

'I would love to move on. But James is still part of me. It's not a question of closure, but I can't just leave that little guy as an image on the front of the Sunday papers and say, "Well, that's what happened; we can't change it"' – Victor Barker

It was clear when I first met him that February night in Soho in 2000 that Victor was not going to leave it. Indeed, his determination to understand what had happened and to do something about it was all-encompassing. There was plenty to be worried about for the future as well as in the past.

The previous October, gardaí had found a Real IRA training camp in Stramullen in County Meath, where the weaponry included an RPG-18 rocket launcher; this demonstrated that the Balkans arms shipment garda intelligence had heard about had indeed landed in Ireland. Ten people, including Seamus McGrane, McKevitt's close friend and Real IRA Director of Training, were arrested and would be convicted: the gardaí would later learn that they had been just too early to arrest McKevitt too. The Garda Commissioner and the Minister for Justice, John O'Donoghue, were bullish: all necessary resources would be made available to ensure the group did not undermine the Belfast Agreement. Yet the Real IRA were defiant: their New Year message promised that they would fight on. The 32CSM too were regrouping and recruiting. Councillor Francie Mackey spoke of the 'demonisation' he and others had suffered, but insisted that the movement was unaffected. 'British interference in Ireland is the root cause of the problem here. That must be addressed before we can move forward.'

Victor struggled to understand. Much though I already liked him, I became irritated by how, showing traditional English liberal anxiety to see the other chap's point of view, he could lean over backwards so far as to overbalance: 'My wife is from Derry,' he said. 'She sang in the choir at a service for the men killed on Bloody Sunday,* so I know something about the treatment of Northern Ireland Catholics. After all, Martin McGuinness was turned down for a job as an apprentice mechanic because he was a Catholic.' I recall pointing out acidly that in my twenties I had been turned down for several jobs because I was a woman, but did not feel that justified me in joining a band of feminist paramilitaries.

That aside, I was very moved by Victor's passion, integrity and sheer decency and his determination to see his mission through. 'I'm only a provincial solicitor,' he said, 'but I refuse to believe some way can't be found of making the law work.' He reminded me of Alastair Logan, a 'provincial' solicitor in Guildford who by chance in 1974 came to represent eleven people who became known as the Guildford Four and the Maguire Seven – innocent people wrongly convicted respectively of mass murder and bomb-manufacturing. Although it exacted a terrible personal toll on him, Logan stuck with his clients in the teeth of public opinion, until their convictions were quashed many years later. He was described in a letter to *The Times*[1] by Lords Devlin and Scarman as 'one of those pilgrims of the law who, when Justice beckons, pick up the staff and the scrip and walk. Legal aid has long since dried up. He is walking still.'†

True, Victor's desire for justice was personal, but the similarities still struck me as profound. Both men would have been content to lead quiet lives in quiet branches of the law: Logan specialised in family law, Victor in conveyancing. Yet both believed in meeting unexpected challenges head-on and both believed that British justice, however flawed, would triumph in the end. Victor and Michael had been talking vaguely about legal remedies for some time. In a letter to a senior garda in April 1999, Victor had demanded Colm Murphy's full name and address, 'as I shall require these in due course in relation to a civil suit which will be instigated . . . both

---

* On 30 January 1972, on what became known as 'Bloody Sunday', British paratroopers killed thirteen apparently unarmed civilians on a prohibited civil rights march in Derry, massively boosting IRA recruitment. At the time of writing the Savile Inquiry into the events of that day, set up in 1998 as a sop to Sinn Féin during the peace process, has cost over £180 million and has not yet reported.

† Logan was ignored in the film *In the Name of the Father*, about the Guildford Four; Emma Thompson won an Oscar for her portrayal of the lawyer, Gareth Peirce, who became involved in 1989.

by myself, and I believe a number of other families who have lost loved ones as a result of the bombing atrocity'.

Victor's first legal foray came soon afterwards, and was a protest against what he saw as the inhumane treatment of victims by the Compensation Agency. Of course officials had the duty of ensuring that taxpayers' money was not wasted, but, in balancing between accountability and insensitivity, the latter won far too often. Stanley's sister, Rosemary Ingram, would later publicly describe what she felt to be degrading treatment. Her husband had sent the Agency photographs of her raw sores and scars, taken after she was discharged from hospital; her claim was backed by reports from doctors and surgeons, who also described the pieces of shrapnel that still moved about her body and sometimes painfully broke through the skin on her legs, back and cheek. Yet she was called to a room at the High Court in Belfast and asked to strip down to her underwear and show her scars to six lawyers – three of them male – one of whom pulled her bra strap aside to look at a scar on her shoulder; her husband wrapped his jacket around her to lessen her humiliation. 'Apparently they need to see the scars after they have healed,' she said, 'so they can cut the level of compensation . . . What they don't see are the emotional scars and the terrible nightmares.' Discharged on medical grounds from her job as a traffic warden, it took more than four years for her to receive her compensation.

Such stories were rife among the Omagh victims, most of whom experienced the incredible pettiness of officialdom: school results were examined to calculate the potential lost earnings of teenagers; receipts were demanded for clothes blown off people during the explosion. The way compensation claims were handled had been addressed in a report[2] published four months before the bomb by Sir Kenneth Bloomfield, then Northern Ireland Victims' Commissioner. He had concluded that the method of awarding compensation was completely inadequate and simply added to the trauma of serious injury or bereavement. Any action on his recommendation that the system be made less painful and more equitable would, however, come too late for the victims of Omagh.

Rosemary would later discover that she would have been within her rights to refuse to take off her clothes, but, like most of the injured and bereaved of Omagh, her upbringing had accustomed her to obeying rather than challenging authority. By contrast, Rugby School, Cambridge and local politics had left Victor unimpressed by those in power at any level:

to draw attention to the inadequacies of the Compensation Agency, he took it to Omagh County Court in October 1999 in a civil action unprecedented in common law or criminal injury legislation. Though Victor had mooted the idea, he was not keen to see it through, but Donna-Maria persuaded him and the OSSHG gave full support. It was agonising for the Barkers to go back to Omagh and sit in the courthouse, but they were united about it being right to make a stand to get media coverage, and it helped that there was a good turnout of members of the OSSHG.

By this time the Barkers had received compensation of £13,010.70 (bereavement award of £7,500; funeral expenses of £1,160; associated funeral expenses of £2,780.70; £1,000 towards the cost of James's headstone; and £570 for the cost of school uniforms bought for the Belfast preparatory school he was to board at in September 1998). Victor submitted that there should also have been compensation for the £28,770.55 that had been spent on James's education: by paying private school fees, he argued, the state had been relieved of a financial burden. The fees had been paid for James's benefit, but became 'wasted expenses at the moment of his death and resulted directly from his death'. If the court found in his favour, he argued, it would be making some acknowledgement of the plight of the victims of crimes that had blackened the history of Northern Ireland for decades.

Victor had explained outside the court that he was seeking 'to draw attention to the way compensation is dished out to victims of crime. It is just an appalling system, and it gives no assistance to the ongoing problems that many people suffer. We are among 3,500 people to suffer in Northern Ireland since 1968 and I think it is high time the Government . . . started treating the victims a little better than the perpetrators.' Victor can be naïve. High-minded himself, he can be surprised when others see low motives. Years later he still smarted from the interviewer who asked him on television after he left the court: 'It's all about money, Mr Barker, isn't it?'

The defence had unsurprisingly pointed out that, if Victor won the case, it would 'open the flood gates' in respect of the costs of bringing up a person until the date of their death, but the judge's dismissal of the application was based on the words of the relevant article in the legislation. Complimenting Victor on the 'dignity of his submissions', the judge concluded: 'I have come to the view that Mr Barker's interpretation of Article 3 was ingenious, but flawed. The words are clear and school fees already paid are not recoverable under the present legislation.' Victor was in Surrey when the judgement was made: it was Donna-Maria and Michael Gallagher who were in Omagh to speak to the media. The fight to highlight the vast disparity in the treatment of victims of terrorist crime and the perpetrators would go on, Donna-Maria promised. 'In what direction we move I don't know,' said Michael, 'but we are looking at it. It is active and ongoing and this is certainly only the beginning.' Donna-Maria and Michael added that, if necessary, they would take the issue to the European Court of Human Rights.

I had expected my meeting with Victor to be short and final. Instead, he enlisted me for his as yet ill-defined campaign. Twelve days after our encounter, on 21 February 2000, I had an article in the *Daily Telegraph* headed 'We know who the Omagh bombers are – so why are they still free?'

> 'I would go mad with grief if it were my kids,' wrote the Prime Minister in August 1998, after two babies, five children and a pair of unborn twins were murdered along with 22 adults in Omagh.
>
> Other people's kids are another matter. Eighteen months on, Tony Blair shows little interest in helping bring the bombers to justice. Although, as they put it in Ulster, 'the dogs in the street' know the names of those in the Real IRA who planned and executed the bombing, no one has been charged in the United Kingdom and only one in the Republic of Ireland. Many of the bereaved believe there is no political appetite for prosecuting republicans and justice has once again been sacrificed to the 'peace process'.

Blair had assured us that Gerry Adams and Martin McGuinness were 'committed to treading the path of peace', but 'what they are definitely not committed to is treading the path of justice' since they refuse to ask their supporters to help the Omagh inquiry.

> Victor Barker says Mr McGuinness admitted to him privately – sweating with embarrassment – that the names of some of those involved in killing his 12-year-old son James had been published accurately in Ireland.* But

---

* Although Victor had refused to allow McGuinness to attend James's wake, he got in touch with him a few weeks later and they met in a Buncrana hotel. Asked if he or his organisation had anything to do with James's death, and, if not, who was responsible, McGuinness handed him a copy of an article and said Victor had only to read that. The article on the RIRA included some familiar names. McGuinness added, however, that he could not help bring the bombers to justice as it was against his 'code'.

he offered no help. On the anniversary of the atrocity, he was asked on television by Sarah Montague, an unusually brave and persistent BBC interviewer, if he thought the bombers would be charged. The top priority for the bereaved families, he responded, was the implementation of the Belfast Agreement. But 'would you urge anybody who knows anything [to give] that information to the RUC?' asked Miss Montague. Of course, owing to the unacceptability of the RUC since partition, explained Mr McGuinness, he couldn't. 'Fine,' she said, 'but they could give the information to the Garda.' At which moment Mr McGuinness plunged into shifty gibberish about Garda involvement with British military intelligence at the time of the Dublin and Monaghan bombings, which was his way of saying 'no'.* Richard McAuley, Mr Adams's chief sidekick, recently explained to Mr Barker that Mr Adams could not ask republicans to help send the bombers to trial in a British court.

As a lawyer, Mr Barker is doubly outraged that his son's killers and their apologists can be seen walking freely on British and Irish streets. A week ago, Francie Mackey, an Omagh councillor and spokesman for the Real IRA's political front, the 32 County Sovereignty Committee, held a meeting in London at which he hinted at the possibility of further violence. The security forces know the Real IRA is in cahoots with Continuity IRA, who recently bombed a hotel in Fermanagh, as well as with members of the Provisional IRA whose commanders let them moonlight.

The allegedly 'draconian' measures rushed into law by Blair and Ahern had yielded no results, not least because witnesses were unwilling to come forward. Victor was trying to persuade Blair and Ahern to launch a public plea for witnesses, but Blair was stalling, and seemed keener to let terrorists out of jail than punish the Omagh killers. 'Victor Barker's last hope', I ended, 'lies with those people in the United Kingdom whose sense of right and wrong has not been blurred into moral equivocation by the exigencies of the "peace process". If those who believe that justice should be done to the murderers of James Barker and those who died with him were to write to the Prime Minister and to their MPs, Mr Barker's request

---

* In another interview, Martin McGuinness was asked why the Omagh killers had not been caught and said angrily, 'But they didn't get away with it. We've told the people responsible that this [killing] has to stop.' When asked why he would not tell the police who the bombers were, he replied, 'I am not an informer.'

might be granted. One million Spaniards recently protested against ETA. How many letters will it take to persuade Tony Blair and his colleagues to be as tough as the Spanish government?'

I have no idea how many letters were launched by that article, or by another on the same theme but from a different perspective that I wrote in March in the Irish *Sunday Independent*, but to my surprise, one arrived for me from Secretary of State Peter Mandelson. He had thought my *Telegraph* article timely, he said, 'and felt it raised a number of issues which I should like to comment on further'.

> I agree with you entirely that everything possible should be done to try and bring those responsible for the Omagh bomb to justice. The RUC are doing everything they can; the investigation has not been closed and I can assure you the security forces continue to do everything possible to ensure further violence from the 'real' IRA is prevented, so that there is no repetition of the events of 15 August 1998 in Omagh.
>
> I wish I could include in this letter news that the security forces, either North or South, had new leads in the Omagh bombing case which could bring it to a rapid conclusion. Sadly that is not the case. As I am sure you are aware, establishing credible prosecution cases against members of terrorist groups such as the 'real' IRA, which provide their members with specific training and equipment designed to frustrate evidence-gathering by the police, is a time-consuming business, often relying on an element of luck on the part of the police, or error by the terrorists, to produce a result. This is true regardless of the skill and dedication of the investigating officers, in which I have every confidence.
>
> Finally I should say that I think that articles in the media such as yours, which highlight the human damage terrorism does, play an important part in changing the environment in which the terrorists operate. The more this can be brought home to those who commit these acts, and those who give them protection, either actively or simply through their silence, the safer a society we shall all live in.

Victor, who within a few weeks of Mandelson taking up the job had been complaining to the press about his failure to tackle Omagh, was not as impressed with this as I was. I had once been a Whitehall civil servant and knew plenty of politicians through my involvement in matters British–Irish, so I was aware how unusual it was for a minister to send an unsolicited letter that he had obviously written himself. It was also amazing that, at a time when the British government were wooing Sinn Féin, the Secretary of State was encouraging the media to highlight the human cost of terrorism.* At the very least, Mandelson was distancing himself from Mo Mowlam, who had always seemed more comfortable with ex-terrorists, Catholic or Protestant, than with their victims, and whose perceived indifference to the Omagh relatives had been scandalous. I had been no fan of Mandelson in his role as the New Labour spinmeister, but I began to think there was more to him than I had realised.

Writing a couple of helpful articles was, however, the least of what I had got myself into as a result of my meeting with Victor. When he mentioned the idea of a civil case, I had replied: 'Well, I do have a friend who has been thinking along the lines of a civil case for a long time. You need to know, however, that he's an ex-terrorist.'

Henry Robinson joined the Marxist Official IRA (OIRA) in 1977 as a sixteen-year-old. The seventh of eighteen children of a manual worker, he lived in Downpatrick, and had a passion to change the world for the better. The flood of Catholic refugees coming into the town after sectarian violence in Belfast persuaded Henry to join what he saw as a resistance movement against Protestant oppressors. His terrorist career came to an abrupt end when he was instructed to carry out an operation against OIRA's main enemy, the Provisional IRA, by shooting one of its members in the leg.

Henry is very intelligent, but on this occasion he was foolish enough to take off his balaclava too soon and ended up in jail. In his early days in the Maze prison, he was regularly beaten up by Provos or had his head stuffed down the lavatory. Already wondering where all this violence was getting anyone, his conversion came as he lay in the infirmary recovering from a particularly vicious attack. The Wimbledon championship, as foreign to him as elephant polo in India, was showing on a television which he was unable to switch off. Despite himself, he grew fascinated by the sheer gentility of the proceedings which, improbably, would develop in him a longing for a different way of life. But his crusading urge would never leave him.

Henry left jail at Christmas 1983 after serving two and a half years,

---

* Alastair Campbell would record in his diary in May 2000 that Mandelson felt Tony Blair 'was too prone to buying the line from Adams'. Mowlam had disliked the security services, but Mandelson appreciated the trauma caused by the Patten report, tried to make it more police-friendly and arranged that the George Cross be awarded to the RUC collectively in recognition of their heroism and suffering.

took a diploma in social work, worked with Irish travellers and then found his niche as a co-founder of Families Against Intimidation and Terror (FAIT) in Belfast, which helped ordinary people stand up to all varieties of paramilitaries. When Margaret McKinney came to him to ask his help in finding the body of her twenty-two-year-old backward son Brian, murdered by the Provisionals in 1978 for stealing £70 from an IRA-run social club, he helped her set up the Families of the Disappeared. This group represented seventeen families: they would seriously embarrass Sinn Féin as they attracted international attention in their largely successful campaign to force the IRA to give them the information to locate the missing remains of their loved ones.

With editing, Henry can produce arrestingly provocative journalism; for a time he had a column in the *Sunday World* challenging thugs and murderers. One ran with a title along the lines of 'YOU DON'T FRIGHTEN ME, KING RAT!', addressed to Billy Wright,* the most sinister loyalist sectarian murderer of the time. After five years of saving children from being knee-capped and publicly challenging terrorist organisations that threatened to kill him, Henry was eventually worn down by poverty, fourteen-hour days and the squabbling that seems inevitable in voluntary organisations. He abandoned Belfast and went to England, where he discovered his inner entrepreneur and made enough money in the private childcare world to buy a large house in Hertfordshire, dabble in property and race greyhounds.

We had been allies and close friends for five years when the Omagh bomb went off, and spoke often of the authorities' failure to bring the perpetrators to justice. Henry kept talking about the possibility of a civil case; he had been greatly interested in how the steely determination of Lockerbie families had kept the hunt for the killers alive, and inspired by the successful civil action taken against O. J. Simpson.† Knowing the burden of proof is

---

* A highly intelligent, mesmerising fanatic who left me shaken when we had a conversation at a contested Orange parade in Drumcree in 1996, Wright was responsible for the murder of around twenty Catholics, of whom only a few were members of the IRA; he was murdered in jail by dissident republicans in 1997.

† To much incredulity and outrage, in 1995 O. J. Simpson was found not guilty of the murder the previous year of his ex-wife Nicole and her friend Ronald Goldman, but in 1997, in a civil case, a jury unanimously found him liable for their deaths and the Goldman family was awarded $33.5 million. Though little money would ever be extracted from Simpson, the victims felt that some justice had been done.

lower in a civil than in a criminal case, Henry had been floating the possibility of victims suing terrorist organisations: no one took the idea seriously.

Victor was happy to meet Henry, they got on and the three of us went next to the London house of another friend and ally, Robert, Lord Cranborne (now the Marquess of Salisbury), whom I had got to know in the mid-1990s when he was Leader of the House of Lords in John Major's government. In December 1998 Robert was sacked as Shadow Leader of the House of Lords by the then Tory leader William Hague over a deal with Tony Blair to save ninety-one hereditary peers from the axe of the Lords reformers, so he had more time on his hands than hitherto.

Robert is kind, and is one of the very few British politicians with a keen interest in, and deep understanding of, Northern Ireland, as well as an intense concern for those devastated by terrorist violence. He and I tried fruitlessly to save the Orange Order from its own stupidity when Sinn Féin/IRA were using their parades as an excuse to stir up communal violence. And we were now – along with Henry – much involved in the *Daily Telegraph* 'Defend the RUC Campaign' – intended to minimise the damage to the effectiveness of the police caused by the Patten report's more dangerous proposals, to show brave people that Middle England appreciated their sacrifices and to help them lobby in London and Dublin.

I had warned Victor that the three of us were questionable allies as we carried a lot of political baggage. Unlike Henry, Robert and I had at least stayed out of jail, but Robert was regarded with deep suspicion by Irish nationalists: according to Jean Kennedy Smith, who was made US Ambassador to Ireland in 1993 by Bill Clinton, Gerry Adams believed Robert to be the most dangerous man in Britain.* I come from a Catholic Dublin background and my friendship with Ulster Protestants like David Trimble and my sympathetic book the previous year about the Orange Order[3] had not endeared me to my own tribe any more than did my anti-republican journalism (even though I was even-handed in my hostility to all paramilitaries). In Ireland, if you build a bridge to the tribal enemy, you can usually rely on your own side to blow it up after you, so I was accused of being a turncoat, a neo-unionist, a lickspittle to the British Establishment and, in some quarters, a spook.

In Northern Ireland, smearing people as British spies was often used as an excuse to murder them, so in the mid-1990s Henry was forced to

* 'I wish,' was Robert's response.

discourage potential assassins by taking and winning a libel action against a magazine that said he was an agent of MI5. And, although Henry, Robert and I had all campaigned for the 'yes' side in the referendum on the Good Friday Agreement, our objections to the appeasement of Sinn Féin and the sacrifice of the political middle ground were widely regarded as being as 'unhelpful' as our championing of the RUC.

Victor was not to be dissuaded: he needed any friends he could get. Indeed, within two days of meeting Henry, he had sent a letter to the Taoiseach's office displaying a magnificent ignorance of Irish sensitivities by announcing the glad news that he had made contact with the journalists Ruth Dudley Edwards and Henry Robinson.

At our meeting in early March, Robert was immediately sympathetic to Victor's idea of taking a civil case; he offered a generous amount of seed-corn money and Henry was delegated to find a suitable lawyer. As he began his search, Henry was simultaneously inspiring Victor to take anti-Real IRA action in new directions. His letters now contained demands that the Irish government seize the assets of Colm Murphy,* who was still on bail† and had given £240,000 to his children; and that the British government close down terrorist sympathisers' bank accounts. Urging Peter Mandelson to act, Victor told him that 'it is only if they are forced to carry their ill gotten gains in plastic bags in their cars, and keep out of the public gaze that ordinary decent people will be able to live their lives without having their children murdered'. He extended his range by appealing to BBC journalists to take up the issue of Omagh: one who took an interest was John Ware of the BBC *Panorama* programme, to whom Victor sent a dossier of all his correspondence.

My popularity with the Irish government was not enhanced in May 2000 when I accompanied Robert and a delegation of RUC widows and the Police Federation to Dublin to meet Bertie Ahern and Martin Mansergh. I was in friendlier territory at the end of June, at an anniversary dinner organised by Henry Reid's parents, where Henry introduced me to Michael Gallagher.

I had often seen Michael on television and had been impressed by the articulate and reasonable way in which he made a tough case: he knew of

---

* 'He is so fucking depressed he is hard to talk to,' reported an American visitor in late February.

† The ease with which suspect terrorists get bail in the Republic has been a constant affront to Northern Ireland victims, but there is a constitutional provision that bail is refused only when the accused is considered likely to commit a serious offence.

me through Victor and from what I had been writing about the case. In person, Michael's manner is very easy, but when presented with anyone who might help the cause of justice for his son, he is as intense as Victor. From Michael I learned a great deal about what life was like for the families of Omagh, about how disillusion had set in after the initial belief that justice would be done, how desperately frustrating it was for them when people were arrested and then released and how nothing mattered any more except that the murderers would be brought to court.

Influenced by the uniqueness of the Omagh bomb in killing citizens of three states, the self-help group had been investigating the possibility of prosecuting the Real IRA in an international court on the grounds that targeting civilians was a war crime under the Geneva Convention.* 'People are being prosecuted for war crimes in Bosnia and Kosovo in front of an international court in The Hague, so why shouldn't we do the same to get justice?' asked Michael. We discussed the notion of the civil case, which he was sure several of the families would be supportive towards.

'I knew Michael Gallagher for years just as an amiable taxi-driver,' said Henry Reid afterwards. 'I never realised he was so deep.' Michael himself would admit that Aiden's murder had brought out qualities he had never realised he had. I found him thoughtful and intelligent, and a perfect complement to Victor, whose boundless energy, indefatigable research and gift for putting the families' case was an enormous asset to the OSSHG. Writing was not Michael's forte, but he was a very good talker, who had taught himself how to produce the right sound bites and cultivate the innumerable journalists who threw all cynicism aside when it came to the Omagh victims. Additionally, Michael had lived through decades of terrorism, understood the politics of Northern Ireland and had some feel for the south, while Victor would never fully get over his Anglo-Saxon bewilderment at the Celts' oddities. And, where Victor was impetuous, Michael was wary. Yet he never avoided raising difficult issues.

At this period, for instance, the group were being highly critical of Omagh District Council: they were moving slowly over a permanent memorial to the victims, there were administrative problems with the Omagh Fund and councillors had considered it inappropriate to take a vote of no confidence against Francie Mackey. Laurence Rush's approach

---

* This was probably a non-starter, since though the Provisionals called their campaign a war, the government called it terrorism.

was to barrack Mackey from the public gallery of the council chamber; Michael's was to tell the media he found it unacceptable that the council 'would have a person like that associated with a group of people who tried to completely wreck this town and cause the worst atrocity of thirty years'. He accepted, he said, that the OSSHG was reaching a stage when they were labelled as troublemakers for raising what they felt were legitimate concerns, but that was not going to stop them.

Michael spoke eloquently to me of the OSSHG, particularly of his pride in how so many of its members had crossed barriers of religion and politics. As I would see in practice, he had the vision and the patience to weld this disparate group into a considerable fighting force. It was important for their recovery, he explained, that they reassert control of their lives and of the search for justice. He empathised with each individual in the group, respected their qualities and accepted their deficiencies. Unable to work, he was utterly obsessed with the plight of victims, for whom he had all the time in the world. Michael was also concerned that the group should widen its horizons by helping other victims: in July they would send a contingent to Claudy to take part in the unveiling of a memorial to its dead.

Michael was as anxious as Victor that a way be found to take a civil case. In February 2000 the Real IRA had restarted their campaign: a bomb at an army barracks in Londonderry had caused structural damage and there was an abortive attack on a base in Tyrone. The group had been cast into despair when in March the Garda Commissioner, Pat Byrne, asked if those behind the Omagh bomb were likely to escape conviction, had replied: 'Sadly, possibly and maybe probably.' Without evidence, he said, intelligence was worthless, and the people on whom he had been trying to gather evidence were trying to ensure it was not available. 'If I could prosecute people for all the intelligence information I had on them, I can tell you a lot more would be in jail. There is a price to be paid for democracy – that a person is innocent until proven guilty.'

Many bombs had been stopped getting to Northern Ireland, said Byrne: the Omagh bomb was one that had got through and he believed it was a mistake. 'Look at the bombs that happened before that we didn't intercept,' he said. 'Look what happened there. They were commercial targets. I am the last person to make an excuse for any terrorist, but I have to be very accurate in how we fundamentally analyse the situation. And I do believe in relation to Omagh that it was a tragic cock-up.' As for the future: 'I have always said that we cannot provide 100 per cent security. I can't assure anyone that we can prevent it happening again, other than that we are going to do our level best to ensure that it doesn't happen again.'

The families were outraged. This, said Michael, 'was relegating murder to manslaughter'. 'To hear that the Garda chief knows who planted the bomb which killed my wife and her two work colleagues from Wattersons shop,' said Stanley, 'but has no evidence against them, is nothing short of a disgrace.' He called on the Irish government to bring in the necessary changes to the law.

Also in February, Victor finally received a letter from Gerry Adams in response to his requests for him to use his influence to encourage anyone with information on the bombers to give it to the police or the gardaí.

14 March 2000

Mr Barker a chara*

My apologies for the delay in responding to your letter and phone calls.

The issues raised by your letter required serious and considered discussion.

The protracted efforts to end the crisis in the peace process, establish the new political institutions, and then try to save them from collapse, all intervened in delaying my response.

As you know Sinn Féin took a very strong stand against those who carried out the Omagh atrocity. My public condemnation of the attack, and Sinn Féin's vigorous opposition to those unrepresentative groups opposed to the peace process, played a decisive part in isolating these groups and thwarting further attacks.

While there were and are political as well as personal risks involved in this, the issue of peace in Ireland is more important than anything else and we will continue our efforts to achieve this.

---

* Irish for 'friend' and the Irish equivalent of 'Dear Mr Barker'. Even members of Sinn Féin who do not speak the Irish language make a political point of using it for the record, hence the entry in James's memorial book that reads: 'A chara James, The work of justice and Peace will continue until we succeed. When we do, that will be a most fitting memorial. Siochán [peace] Martin McGuinness.'

Victor sometimes tried to be culturally sensitive by using Irish phrases in correspondence and usually made a grammatical hash of it, as in 'Dear An Taoiseach', which means 'Dear the Leader'. He had to consult me on several occasions when he was wrestling with 'Óglaigh na hÉireann'.

The peace process is the best hope the people of Ireland have of achieving a permanent end to conflict.

It is our best hope of ensuring that more lives are not lost, that no other families suffer the loss that you have. The loss of a loved one, especially a young person like your son James, is more than anyone should have to bear.

You ask that I call upon citizens to give information, if they have it, about the Omagh atrocity.

There are historical, as well as contemporary reasons for not doing this. Not least of which is our continuing concern at the Criminal Justice system in the north, and the existence and role of the RUC, which must inevitably be involved in any prosecutions even if information is given to the Gardaí.

I appreciate this is not the answer you would have hoped for. But be assured that it is my earnest desire to do everything I can to ensure that no one else dies because of conflict in my country.

We can best do this by ensuring that there is no popular support for those who carry out actions like Omagh, while at the same time changing the situation here so that conflict is ended forever.

Is mise le meas*

Gerry

Gerry Adams MP

Enclosing a copy of Adams's 'evasive answer', Victor wrote to Adam Ingram at the Northern Ireland Office: 'It is incredible that a man who purports to stand for peace in Northern Ireland will not assist in bringing these terrorists to justice. I find it even more staggering in that, as a further means of showing your government's intentions to appease Republicans some 10.5 million pounds has been spent to date in relation to the "Bloody Sunday" enquiry and, it is estimated that between a further 100 million and 200 million will be spent on that enquiry into events when fourteen people were killed by English paratroopers who were acting under great provocation. The bombers in Omagh killed 29 people but none have been arrested: "where is our public enquiry?"'

Like all useful correspondence, Adams's letter was passed on to Michael and the OSSHG, encouraging Laurence Rush to ambush Adams at the Sinn Féin annual conference at the beginning of April. Adams

* Literally, 'It's myself with respect'.

pacified him by agreeing to go to Omagh for a meeting that the OSSHG declined to attend in a 'formal capacity'. Nothing came of it, but it increased the group's self-confidence: they were now scheduled for meetings with the Taoiseach and the Garda Commissioner, as well as the Secretary of State.

The Barkers were in a condition of high emotion at this time. They had been deeply upset in the spring of 1999, when, as Victor wrote to the Irish Minister for Justice in June, 'at the graveyard in Buncrana where my son is buried, some weeks ago a sign appeared not more than 20 yards away from my son's grave with the words "In memory of all those who died in the cause of Irish freedom". Although the sign has now been taken down, at my request, I do not think I could have imagined anything that was more insensitive, particularly to my wife who is a resident of Buncrana and who visits the grave on a daily basis.'

Knowing now what went on in Buncrana graveyard every Easter to mark the rising of 1916, the Barkers could not stand keeping James there any longer. 'In the light of the refusal from Gerry Adams,' Victor told the press, 'we found it unbearable to think that republicans would be honouring their dead close to James's grave.' The family left Buncrana for good before Easter and took James's body with them: his exhumation, as Victor wrote to Ahern, caused ill-feeling with some of the neighbours* and, he believed, led to his ill-treatment by the local council. James's coffin was taken home for a few hours, his mother put white lilies on it and lit candles, and then it went by road and air to Surrey, where it was reburied in the grounds of his Surrey prep school. Donna-Maria draped the coffin in the flag of St George. 'We find it difficult to be in Ireland,' she said. 'We thought by now they would have got someone, but that's politics. I am very angry. I have been angry from the start. But Victor and I will keep on the fight in England.'

A lengthy response from Victor to Adams's letter complained about republican double standards in using the legal system when it suited them. 'The conclusion therefore, that you reach in your response, concerning the involvement of the criminal justice system in the North of Ireland, I find very difficult to understand. It is hypocrisy in the extreme to refuse

---

* They would end up selling the house at a considerable loss. People were reluctant to live in a place associated with tragedy and the local council refused to give the Barkers planning permission for their surrounding land.

to ask those with information to co-operate with the authorities, not only for yourself, but for the whole of the Republican movement. Those who demand justice for themselves and their supporters have no excuse in seeking to deny it to others.

> I am further astonished by your stance, bearing in mind that I am particularly referring to the death of my son, and three other *innocent children*. These children were denied the right to a future, at a time in their lives when they had no political affiliation, nor had an opportunity of making a choice about the way they chose to conduct their future lives. It is not a question therefore of a Republican or a Unionist being killed because of their affiliation, but innocent lives being destroyed by a bomb, which was at best planted in an act of wanton recklessness.

Surely, he said, politics were irrelevant: in any democratic society the murder of innocent children would be regarded as a crime which ought to be punished. 'As the leader of the Republican movement, and as a man now committed to peace and democracy, I once again call upon you to honour your duties and responsibilities in bringing those responsible for this horrific murder to answer for their crime.'

> Everyone in the island of Ireland, irrespective of their political beliefs or religious affiliation, bears a responsibility to ensure that such individuals as those who committed the Omagh atrocity are no longer able to ply their bloody trade. Such a responsibility is owed to each and every one of those who died or who were injured on the 15th, but particularly to Sean McLaughlin, Oran Doherty, Fernando Blasco and James Barker.
>
> I await your response with eagerness.
>
> Yours sincerely,
>
> Victor Barker

June 19th 2000

A chara Victor

> Thank you for your letter.
>
> As you know several colleagues and I met with a number of relatives of the Omagh atrocity several months ago.
>
> We had a long discussion in which I outlined Sinn Féin's abhorrence of the attack and our desire to help the relatives in whatever way we can.
>
> You will also be aware that we continue, despite all the difficulties, to advance the peace process.

I note the positions that you outline in your letter. While I understand the argument the objective reality is that there are huge deficiencies in the judicial and policing system here.

All of us concerned to bring about a democratic settlement of the conflict have to deal with all the issues involved within our own lights.

My position on these matters is in no way at odds with my opposition to those who killed your son.

You accuse me of hypocrisy, but be assured that your assertion that 'everyone on the island of Ireland, irrespective of their political beliefs or religious affiliation bears a responsibility to ensure that such individuals or those who committed the Omagh atrocity are no longer able to ply their bloody trade', is one which I am totally committed to.

Is mise le meas

Gerry

Gerry Adams MP, MLA

Victor suggested to Adams they meet, and that he would be happy for Martin McGuinness to be present, too. The latest stone-walling letter was distributed widely, as the acerbity of Victor's letters increased. He ended one to Peter Mandelson, whom he thought an insufficiently assiduous correspondent, with: 'In case you do not have the necessary facilities to reply to my correspondence, I enclose a stamped addressed envelope, a sheet of writing paper and a pen, for your kind reply.' Tony Blair, who had been shamed back into correspondence, was told by Victor that Gerry Adams was quite right to criticise the Northern Ireland criminal justice system, not least because 'there is not one at all. Almost all the killers, butchers, bombers, torturers, knifemen and knee-cappers have been released unconditionally, and will not return to jail, regardless of whether or not the paramilitaries they have the signal honour of belonging to, return to war, but I suspect that this is not what Gerry Adams meant in his letter. What he meant, is that there is no atrocity so vile, so monstrous, or so disgusting, or so inhuman as to warrant assisting the RUC.'

These outbursts achieved more than enabling Victor to let off steam. He was still pushing for a Blair/Ahern joint appeal for witnesses to come forward and was making progress by comparing Blair's concern for victims unfavourably with that of Ahern. Once again, he pressed a key button. 'I was recently asked in a radio interview whether I felt it was better to remain silent about the Omagh bombers if at the end of the day peace was achieved in Northern Ireland. I wonder how Stephen Lawrence's parents would have felt if the same proposal were made to them in the interests of peaceful race relations?' Michael Gallagher expressed some of the anger of the OSSHG in the protest letter he presented to the Prince of Wales at the June Hillsborough garden party, an occasion Victor refused to attend and Stanley dismissed as a 'highfalutin day out' that he did not need. The group were concerned, said the letter, at 'the lack of progress of the criminal investigation in both jurisdictions. The civic representatives and our international statesmen are not publicly supporting the criminal investigation and some are totally opposed to any investigation.' Prince Charles was understanding, sympathetic and 'genuine', said Michael to the media, adding mollifying words about how the party had lifted some people's spirits.

But frustration was turning some decent people sour and unreasonable. 'Could you please stop treating me like a child?' wrote Victor to Mandelson, who had been more sympathetic than most. 'It would assist me enormously if you tried to respond to my letters in some meaningful way rather than to regurgitate the "spin" which I have received from your office on many occasions in the past.' 'Et tu, Brute,' he wrote to the ever considerate Adam Ingram, accusing him of adopting 'Peter Mandelson's method of selective reply . . . When I met you at James's golf day, I found you to be a sincere and honest person who was keen to help in any way possible. I don't, I am afraid, share that opinion of the Secretary of State.' He followed this with a demand to know how much had been spent on the Jill Dando* investigation compared to that into Omagh.

Such relentless importuning paid off when, on the second anniversary of the bomb, Ahern and Blair issued a joint statement appealing for those with information to come forward. They had been galvanised, perhaps, by an acceleration in the Real IRA bombing campaign.† Both governments,

---

* There was a year-long investigation of the murder in 1999 of this popular BBC presenter.
† There were three attacks on London in 2000: a small explosion at Hammersmith Bridge on 1 June; an aborted attack on a railway line between Ealing and Acton on 19 July; and a successful grenade attack on the HQ of MI6 on 20 September. Attacks in Northern Ireland included, in April, placing a small bomb inside the fence of Ebrington army barracks in Derry, putting another in the grounds of Hillsborough on 19 June, blowing up the Belfast–Dublin railway line on 30 June, bombing an RUC station in Stewartstown, County Tyrone, and a mortar attack on an RUC station in Armagh in September. There were no casualties.

they said, were resolute in their commitment to prevent those still bent on violence from 'pursuing their evil plans . . . That is what society, especially those who have suffered so grievously in Omagh and elsewhere, has a fundamental right to expect.' This was echoed by Adam Ingram, who on behalf of Mandelson, who was away, said publicly that Adams and other republicans should help the police. 'I hope anyone who wants to see a different Northern Ireland and a better Northern Ireland should just reflect on the grief of those families and the demands and requests of the families. They should reflect on whether they want to see another Omagh. If they want to satisfy the demand that there should not be another Omagh, then they should do what the two prime ministers ask – if they have any information they should bring it forward.' 'Now that Sinn Féin have their stepping stone onto politics,' echoed Lorraine Wilson's father, Godfrey, 'they should do the honourable thing and come forward and make sure that these people are treated for what they have done through the justice system.'

When forced to comment, Sinn Féin spokesmen stuck to the existing party line.

More practically, on behalf of the OSSGH, Geraldine Breslin's widower, Mark, had been monitoring dissident websites, and the group were drawing to media attention an Allied Irish Bank Dundalk account in the name of the Irish Republican Prisoners' Welfare Association (IRPW),* a group associated with the 32 Counties Sovereignty Movement, who were requesting donations for twenty-four 'anti-Stormont' prisoners. The AIB, like the Bank of Ireland, said they had no authority to close down accounts held by legal entities and the governments were prevaricating about tightening up the law. The 32CSM were prosperous enough to send Francie Mackey and a few others on the political side in August to a so-called human rights conference in Geneva, where McKevitt, who was anxious to form links with other so-called freedom movements, hoped a relationship could be struck up with Palestinians. To McKevitt's chagrin, Mackey failed to make any connection. However, McKevitt drew what little consolation he could from Mackey's report that they had become very friendly with Native Americans, who had offered to use their lawyers to help the 32CSM get US visas. Back home, the OSSHG had become

---

* Republicans have traditionally got around bans on collecting for the IRA by fund raising for prisoners. Each IRA has its own prisoners' organisation.

involved in their first public protest, organised with the help of Henry Robinson.

Henry is a seasoned demonstrator. His exploits have included picketing the White House to protest at Gerry Adams being a guest there when the Provisional IRA were torturing and mutilating people in their own community – a practice euphemistically known as punishment beating or shooting. He understands how to make a protest eye-catching and media-friendly. I had watched him in October 1999 in London before a demonstration outside Downing Street explaining eloquently to two broken-hearted mothers of murdered young RUC officers how political protests involve forgetting your inhibitions and rising above embarrassment; what matters is to stand up and be counted.

Most of the Omagh group were not the kind who went on marches or waved placards, but they were learning to do many things they had never dreamed of doing. The occasion that turned them into protestors was a fundraising event for the IRPW, held by the 32CSM, news of which had caused great distress to many of them. 'There were tears in my house when we heard of it,' Michael told a journalist. Victor initiated the protest, and Henry organised posters that would become a familiar sight on television, and taught the participants some of the tricks of his old trade.

One evening, seventeen of the relatives travelled up from Omagh to join Henry and some journalists for their first public protest, held outside Brennan's Bar in Hannahstown, West Belfast. It was Friday 18 August 2000, two years and three days after the bomb, so it was an emotional time. What was more, the long-delayed inquest which the families needed but dreaded was due to begin in Omagh at the beginning of September: an appeal to cancel the Brennan's Bar event had been ignored.

The organisers of the event had described it as a night of 'Craic agus Ceol' (fun and music) with a speech from the McKevitts' close friend and US ally, Martin Galvin. 'There has been little singing in the home of the relatives of the 29 victims (and the many maimed and injured) since the Real IRA exploded a massive car bomb following misleading warnings, in Omagh Town Centre' read the OSSHG press release. 'Here tonight we have Catholics and Protestants on this protest, united against all those who preach against peace and preach the views of a very small minority who criticise the peace process as a "sell out", when it is supported by the vast majority of all the people in the island of Ireland.'

As they stood in one of the bar's car parks, holding placards showing photos of their dead, a pretty, middle-aged woman came out and told them they were on private property and should leave. When they moved to another car park, she emerged again and asked them to go to the public road. They later found out she was the Old Bailey bomber, Marian Price, whose story typifies the tangled nationalist/republican web, the smallness and incestuousness of Northern Ireland and the fanaticism passed from generation to generation.

Price and her sister Dolours, daughters of a lifelong IRA man, were part of the Provisional IRA group including Gerry Kelly who wounded many and killed one in a bomb at the Old Bailey. They had planted four car bombs in London and warnings had been given an hour before detonation; two had been defused. A detective who questioned Price – then a trainee nurse in Belfast – after she was picked up at Heathrow Airport, on 8 March 1973, recalled that just before 3.00 p.m., when the bombs were due to go off, she calmly looked at her watch and smiled. In jail, the Price sisters went on hunger strike for two hundred days and were force-fed. Suffering badly from malnutrition, they were released from jail on humanitarian grounds after seven years.

Unlike Gerry Kelly, who trod the pragmatic route and ended up a minister in the Northern Ireland Executive at Stormont, Dolours, now divorced from the actor Stephen Rea,* is a highly emotional critic of what she sees as the treachery of the peace process and the betrayal of republicanism by the Adams leadership: Marian became a stalwart of the 32CSM and later its secretary. Both still defend 'armed struggle'.

For two hours the Omagh relatives handed out leaflets. They were well received by locals and ignored or angrily rejected by some of the 250 or so attending the fundraiser. One person got out of his car, turned to Laurence Rush and told him he was nothing but a sad old zombie. Some women, by contrast, covered their faces. But most of those going into the bar were very young. 'They are running their army on teenagers,' said Michael's wife, Patsy. 'A few young lads walked past us and they were shaking.' She was pleased with the protest. 'I said before we left Omagh that I would be happy if the protest stopped even one person from taking part. We did that. To me it was a success. It gave them something to think about and it also let them see that everybody is not scared of them.'

* From 1988 to 1994 eleven loyalist and republican organisations were banned from direct access to broadcasting in the United Kingdom, so actors had to speak their spokespersons' words; Rea was the best-known voice of Gerry Adams.

Stanley, meanwhile, told the media that the Irish government should sequester the group's money, and Victor denounced Adams for demanding justice for himself but not for victims of terrorist violence. 'I am not saying I want him to inform on all his former colleagues, but he should make it clear he does not believe violence and murder are acceptable.'

Martin Galvin – who the press release said 'is contributing nothing to the people of Ireland only misery' – did not show his face. But inside the bar he was complaining of the deliberate misrepresentation of the event: 'The *Irish News* actually published a story that the event was cancelled, and an editorial applauding the cancellation. There has been an orchestrated campaign to vilify and intimidate people. If that campaign had succeeded, if this event were cancelled, the real victims would be the wives and children of Irish political prisoners, and the Republican prisoners themselves, whether in Maghaberry, England or Portlaoise. That is something which will never be.'

The real victims, however, were outside, talking tough. Michael Gallagher told the press that relatives intended to lobby the US government to curb funding to dissidents' groups. And he echoed the press release's angry rebuke to the two governments for permitting the 32CSM – with its associations – to hold bank accounts, run offices and conduct public activities. 'All people committed to democracy and peace in Ireland should be prepared to stand against them.' The Real IRA had no right to put Omagh behind them, said the press release. 'We, therefore, turn to the Irish, British and American governments in our call for setting up a joint approach to use all legitimate, democratic means at their disposal, within a human rights context, to campaign against the further growth of this "hate and murder movement".'

The 32CSM issued their own press release later, expressing sympathy with the suffering of Michael Gallagher, who had been bereaved 'as a result of the conflict in Ireland'. However, it continued, 'the people of this country have endured much tragedy and suffering and we must all work towards the solution bringing an end to it all'. They referred obliquely to Victor as 'a sinister British element': he had now achieved Henry's and my distinction of being an alleged agent of MI5. Indeed, they seem genuinely to have believed that: McKevitt told a confidant a few days later that the protest had been orchestrated by the state.[4]*

Not all those objecting to the event were as peaceful as the Omagh

---

* It is a republican trait to assume their opponents must be government puppets.

families. Brennan's Bar was gutted ten days later and one of its walls daubed with loyalist paramilitary graffiti, though there were Real IRA supporters who believed the Provisional IRA were the arsonists. As McKevitt told a friend, that event had been more to do with turf than fundraising: by holding it in the lion's den of the Provisional stronghold of West Belfast, they were making a show of strength. Their republican opponents agreed. On 13 October, Joe O'Connor, a ruthless killer who had left the Provisionals for the Real IRA and was one of the event's organisers, was shot dead by erstwhile colleagues, though their involvement was denied by the leadership. Marian Price gave the graveside oration, in which she asserted that Martin McGuinness was now a member of the British Establishment.

'How do you think the relatives of the Omagh victims feel when they are told to move away by Marian Price, a person responsible for so much fear and horror in London?' asked Victor of Adam Ingram. 'There seems to me to be no alternative to direct action and if you are not prepared to roll your sleeves up, I certainly am.

'I intend to take this campaign to Dundalk and to Dublin. You wouldn't allow the Ku Klux Klan to run a bank account in England, so *why* the so-called "Republican Prisoners' Welfare Association"?'

'How long are these people to be allowed to operate in the manner which they do without being challenged?' he asked in another letter. 'You know as well as I do that they are inextricably linked with the Real IRA.' Responding to Ingram's assurance that the government was still determined to see those responsible brought to justice, Victor said at the end of September: 'I have had these platitudes on many previous occasions. Nothing ever seems to happen! Last week the MI6 building – what next?'

What was next for the families was to go on enduring the concentrated agony of hearing exactly how those they loved had died.

CHAPTER TEN

THE INQUEST

'Having lived for two years with the memories of that day, the families of those who lost their lives share a strange bond – a bond reinforced by the horrors of the inquests and the painful reality of the incredible carnage that occurred' – Victor Barker, 12 October 2000

The inquest into the deaths of the twenty-nine victims began on Wednesday 6 September 2000 in the Omagh Leisure Centre, where so many people had spent terrible hours after the bomb: there simply was no other suitable building in the area and the Coroner was determined the hearing should be in Omagh rather than Belfast. Victor had to keep working and could not attend the main proceedings, so had arranged with the Coroner that James's inquest would be the last. He would represent himself by choice and necessity, for legal aid provisions did not apply to coroners' courts in Northern Ireland. Although Lord Irvine, the Lord Chancellor, had agreed to provide the necessary funds because of the 'exceptional' circumstances, the families would be means-tested: about a quarter did not qualify. Legal fees for the twelve families represented would total over £200,000, but, as Michael pointed out, it was anomalous that, had the victims died in a car accident, their insurance companies would have paid for legal representation.

For the most part, the Omagh group approached this ordeal in a spirit both apprehensive and combative. Some of them had accepted an invitation from the Northern Ireland Human Rights Commission and attended a training session on what inquests involved. They knew they would have to endure harrowing evidence, and that the Coroner's finding would have no practical impact on the police investigation, but they did hope that what emerged would put further pressure on the bombers.

John Leckey – the most senior and best-regarded Coroner in Northern Ireland – had presided over many harrowing inquests, though, as he admitted, he would find this one 'an emotional experience the like of which I have never encountered previously'. He showed enormous sensitivity to the families from the beginning, making every possible concession to protect and accommodate them. At a preliminary hearing in the court-house on 31 August, because of the large number of witnesses and 'the international dimension' of the tragedy, he took a landmark decision to give lawyers and families prior access to the depositions of the 154 witnesses, and to maps and other related documents.

Michael Gallagher, Mark Breslin, Stanley McCombe and Gerald McFar-land also had no lawyers. At the pre-inquest hearing, Michael spoke of how encouraged the families were by the decision about the documents and how they hoped 'these proceedings will carry on taking into account the new Human Rights legislation which would allow this inquest to have wider latitude than probably previous inquests had'. This would not prove possible.

Michael asked, too, that Colm Murphy (who was still awaiting trial) be added to the list of witnesses as he was then the only person charged in connection with the bomb. He also wanted Francie Mackey: as he was chairman of the 32CSM, 'it would be useful if he could be called and some clarification given as to the nature and status of the organisation he represents'. Bernadette Sands-McKevitt was furious: 'The disgraceful use of a tragedy, such as Omagh, as a whipping stick to serve a particular political agenda,' she said, 'only adds to the suffering of all the victims of Omagh, including the many families whose loved ones have been wrongfully accused.'

Leckey had arranged for information about the inquest to be passed to Murphy and Mackey so that they could give evidence to the inquest if they wished, but he heard nothing from either of them. Before he had even made a decision on Michael's request that they be required to attend, he was annoyed that the 32CSM issued a statement designed to obfuscate: 'Francie Mackey has been formally notified [untrue] that he will not be subpoenaed as a witness in the Omagh inquest. He clearly has no involve-ment or relevant information about this tragedy, and the publicised attempts to raise his name seem to be a diversion away from the truth in the service of an apparent personal political agenda.' As it happened, Leckey rejected Michael's request: Murphy lived in another jurisdiction and he could not subpoena Mackey on 'speculation without an evidential basis'.

Considerable thought had gone into turning the Leisure Centre into a suitable venue: construction costs and a state-of-the-art technology system came to over £1.4 million. A fully carpeted false floor (for cabling) and

wood panelling around the walls had been installed in its Minor Hall –
usually the venue for indoor football – with seating for families of the
victims, members of the public and the media. There were video screens,
and, in the overflow annex built behind the Leisure Centre, separate accommodation where families could find some privacy as well as a separate
entrance that enabled them to avoid the media. John Leckey and his two
barristers, Gemma Loughran and Richard Bullick – whose job was to
present the evidence on the coroner's behalf – commuted daily from
Belfast, which is about ninety minutes from Omagh. Before court proceedings began every morning, in the Youth Centre, local clergy conducted a
five-minute inter-denominational service of prayer and meditation called
'With Grace and Truth'. On the makeshift altar, along with flowers and
a candle, was *Lost Lives*, a book telling the story of every death resulting
from the Troubles.

Leckey spelled out the inquest's limitations on the first day: this was
not a public inquiry,* a criminal trial or a civil action: 'it is a form of
inquisitorial procedure the aim of which is to establish certain categories
of information: who the deceased was, how, when and where the deceased
came by his death and the particulars required for the death to be registered'. He would not be allowed to express 'any opinion on questions of
criminal or civil liability'.

He did not, however, hold back in expressing his sympathy to the victims.
'As a consequence of the explosion 29 persons died,' he said in his opening
statement, 'including a 30-year-old woman who was about 34 weeks pregnant and expecting twin girls. The unborn twin girls also died as a result
of the bomb explosion. Who could deny that the true number of fatalities was in reality 31?† Over 300 people were injured, some very seriously.
Families were devastated. The horrific nature of the atrocity left many
people, not just the injured, deeply traumatised and some still require
professional help. I understand that for some the mental scars will never

---

* 'It has been said,' explained Leckey, 'that whilst an inquest is an inquiry in public into the
circumstances of an unnatural death, it is not a public inquiry. A public inquiry works to
terms of reference drafted specifically to address the particular issues under consideration.'
† The solicitor for eighteen-month-old Maura Monaghan and her mother, Avril, told the
inquest that 'the lack of recognition that has been afforded to the unborn twins has caused
upset to the father of the children and to the general family'. Although the Coroner was
sympathetic, an application to have the twins given the same status as the twenty-nine
dead under international human rights law had to be rejected on legal grounds.

heal. The true number of casualties – and the word "casualties" deserves to have a generous interpretation – from the Omagh bomb explosion is, without doubt, far in excess of the number killed and injured and the exact number may never be known . . . I am sure the media are conscious of the fact that each of the bereaved families has suffered a profound tragedy and will report the proceedings sensitively.'*

There were many horrors for the families during the following weeks. Some, like Stanley, could not bear to watch the three amateur video tapes of the minutes after the explosion; those from the Omagh group who did, watched on a screen in a family room and supported each other. Some footage showed bodies, some the faces of the injured. In the background of one tape a man with an Australian accent said over and over again: 'You just would not believe this. You would not believe what fucking happened. You would not fucking believe it. So much for the fucking peace process.'

There were many more distressing visual images on the huge screens: photographs of components of the bomb, of bodies wrapped in sheets, and diagrams and maps of where people had died. There was the pain of listening to tapes of the bomb warnings and the recordings of radio traffic between the RUC control room and the police on the streets herding crowds away from the courthouse and down Market Street. There was the graphic evidence from witnesses, many of whom were themselves visibly distressed, and the ghastly physical details presented by pathologists; several relatives had to answer questions regarding the movements of their loved ones or how they identified their corpses. For everyone involved, there was also the shock that the Coroner expressed towards the end of the inquest: 'there still are evil people out there, that is the dreadful thing. There have been two bomb hoax calls to Omagh since the inquest started . . . you really wonder what motivates someone to cause additional distress to all the distress that everyone in Omagh is undergoing at the present time.'

'Every night,' wrote the journalist Lindy McDowell, 'I see on television those two brave men Michael Gallagher and Stanley McCombe talk in their quiet voices about each day's proceedings. It is painful to watch them. God knows what it is like for them to go through that. They put

---

* Alan Radford's mother, Marion, would be one of the many bereaved who appreciated how Leckey did his job, asking her solicitor to thank him and his staff publicly 'for the compassionate and sympathetic way in which this inquest has been carried out'.

themselves through it because they are determined to get justice for an adored only son, a much loved wife.'

During the first few days, several members of the RUC, who were upset enough to start with, came under attack from two lawyers representing some of the deceased: Michael Mansfield, a flamboyant barrister from London, representing the next of kin of Libbi Rush, and Barry Fox, a solicitor from Omagh, who was representing those of the Monaghans and Esther Gibson.

At the beginning of 2000, in a furious attack on the Real IRA for appearing to blame the security forces, Laurence Rush had said: 'I would ask them, who built this weapon of death and destruction? Who transported this anti-personnel time bomb eighty miles to Omagh? Who set the timer? Who gave the false warnings resulting in this orgy of death?' Yet he was critical of the RUC too, and, at the November 1999 meeting between families and senior officers, he had been vociferous on the subject of police procedures. He could not bring himself to attend the inquest, but had appointed lawyers known for the enthusiasm with which they took on the state in high-profile cases.

Laurence's solicitor, Des Doherty, was acting for families at the Bloody Sunday inquiry; he would later become an adviser to the defence team of Saddam Hussein. Michael Mansfield was a colleague of his at the Bloody Sunday inquiry; among his controversial past clients were numbered the Angry Brigade, Marian and Dolours Price (whose bomb had destroyed his own car, parked outside the Old Bailey), the Guildford Four and the Birmingham Six. He had also appeared for the next of kin of Stephen Lawrence and would later represent Mohamed Fayed at the inquest into the deaths of Princess Diana and his son Dodi. If you wanted a barrister to challenge police procedures, Mansfield was the obvious choice.

Barry Fox was representing two very different clients: the Monaghans were as unshakably Catholic and nationalist as the Gibsons were religiously and politically Paisleyite. In intense cross-examination of low-ranking officers from the communications room and on the ground, Fox was extremely persistent, insisting that they should have realised that the two warnings about the bomb being in the main street related to Market Street. Mansfield concentrated on harrying junior officers and exposing deficiencies in areas such as guidelines, protocols, procedures and knowledge of codewords. At times the Coroner had to intervene to point out that junior officers were being asked questions to which they could not know the answers. As one lawyer put it later in a wrangle over the style of cross-examination, Constable William Hall, 'a police officer of twenty-six years' standing, of unimpugned integrity and who had given his evidence without evasion, without prevarication was, in our submission, quite unnecessarily, quite distastefully, reminded [by Fox] that he was under oath. The implication of that was clear: it was in fact reported in the national press the following day.' Hall was unable to go back to work for a long time after this.

These arguments were unfortunately being allowed to cloud the main issue. 'This should not turn into a trial of the RUC,' said Stanley at the end of the first day. 'The people who planted the bomb here should be facing questions.' There probably were deficiencies in police procedures, said Michael, and it was to be hoped that the inquest might help to bring about improvements, but attention should not be deflected from the people who carried out the attack.

The Police Federation in Belfast, which had not anticipated that its members would face aggressive questioning, hurriedly had to arrange for legal representation for individual police officers. It had been naïve not to realise that they might be vulnerable: some of the local officers could have told them that not all victims were well disposed to the police. There were bereaved and injured and suffering republicans whose instinct would always be to blame the police for failing to prevent a tragedy rather than terrorists who had made it happen.

The Provisional IRA had always categorised the police as legitimate targets* and republican propaganda had long represented them as the armed wing of unionism. During the 1990s, there had been such a concerted campaign of demonisation of the police that anyone who believed a tenth of what was alleged by the Sinn Féin leadership might have thought the RUC capable of deliberately letting civilians die purely in order to discredit republicans.

Stephen Ritchie, counsel for the Chief Constable, took on Fox and Mansfield, complaining that one of the lines of interrogation was 'to impugn the conduct of the police officers who dealt with this emergency'. Undaunted, Mansfield sought to widen the scope of the inquest – not, he insisted, in order to impugn individual officers, but to disclose information

---

* To put pressure on the new Labour government to negotiate with Sinn Féin, Constables Roland Graham and David Johnston, the last two RUC victims of the Provisional IRA, were shot in the head in Lurgan in June 1997 while on a morning foot patrol.

that might improve the arrangements for policing emergencies.* The objection to this, said Ritchie, was that Mansfield would be perceived to be accusing individuals: 'They will in effect be put on trial. That is certainly what people in general have picked up over the last week.' These policemen had come to the inquest to help the bereaved better understand how their relatives were murdered. 'Now what seems to be happening is that there is a close examination of the actions – with the benefit of hindsight, of course – the actions of certain officers that my learned friend has just named.'

It is the easiest thing in the world for barristers – and we do it every day, with the wisdom of hindsight which is much greater than the wisdom of the moment – to ask the question, 'If you reflected on that for a moment, do you think you might have done something slightly differently?' Whenever events are unrolling or developing over 30 minutes it is not always easy perhaps to make every decision correctly but it is easy for us to come in, having had a week or two to read the papers and have all the information at our fingertips, to ask questions which make us look good and make the witness look, perhaps, uncomfortable.

I am not suggesting for one minute that every decision that was made could not be open to some comment that maybe someone could have done something differently. As I say, this is not the place to air that.

Superintendent James Baxter clashed with Mansfield after more insistent questioning about contingency plans, trying to explain the difference between theory and practice and why officers on the ground had to be permitted to use their judgement. It was Baxter, too, who made an emotional defence of his men, his anger at the implicit criticism of them enhanced by his awareness of the guilt and trauma so many of them were going through. 'The only people that could have made any difference on 15th

---

* He wanted the 'how the deceased came by his death' question not to be limited to the immediate cause of death but extended to consider contributory factors: he cited in legal argument the precedent of the *Marchioness* disaster in 1989 where fifty-one people died; Mansfield was about to represent a group of bereaved relatives at the public inquiry which they had sought for years. In the event, after hours of debate among lawyers, the Coroner ruled that questions of a factual nature about police practice and procedure in Omagh on the day of the bomb would be allowed, but that 'what if?' follow-up questions would not.

August 1998 were those people who planted the bomb and those people who made the telephone calls in relation to it. They had within their power the ability to say that a car bomb was outside Kells's shop in Market Street. They had within their ability the power to say the colour and make of this car, the registration number of this car, but they did not do that.'

> My officers went into High Street expecting that a car bomb was parked there. They were still in High Street checking when the bomb exploded, and I can tell you, sir, that every one of those officers put their lives at risk to try and protect this community. Sadly, that was not to be, but that was because those who planted the bomb brought it in on a busy day, the busiest shopping day probably of the year.
>
> The person who planted that car bomb got out of it. He saw women and children walking on that street and he walked away. He did absolutely nothing to try and prevent people being murdered on the streets of Omagh.

After this he momentarily choked up with tears. Baxter would leave the police force soon afterwards: he never again spoke publicly about what happened at Omagh.

The treatment of individual police officers cast an acrimonious cloud over the whole inquest and would also bring to public attention the first signs of differences between families. On Monday 14th, Ken Duncan spoke for his clients Godfrey and Ann Wilson and Edith White when he said they would deplore it if 'any attempt be made in these proceedings to descend into any type of witch-hunt of the police which would allow the focus of these proceedings to shift from those who plotted and executed this act of mass murder to those, who to the best of their efforts, tried to prevent the destruction of life and property'.

The family of Mary Grimes, her daughter Avril, granddaughter Maura and the unborn twins had a different perspective; they reflected the viewpoint of Omagh victims who disliked the public rhetoric and actions of the self-help group. On 20 September, after the finding on these five deaths, a statement from the Grimes and Monaghan families was read out which thanked 'the hundreds and thousands of good people from near and far who in so many ways have done their utmost to help, comfort and sympathise with us in those first and dreadful days after the bombing', thanked all those who called to their homes, worked at the bomb site, at the morgue, at the Leisure Centre or who helped in any way.

They thanked, too, 'the good people, the firms, clubs, schools, churches, all of whom subscribed so generously to the Omagh Fund' and 'the small group who were given the unenviable task of distributing the funds to the bereaved and the injured'. But then came the explicit criticism of the OSSHG: 'We object to being misquoted in the press and said to have made statements at meetings when in fact we were not present, nor did we speak to a reporter. We further object to statements made by any group that claims, as we have read in the press, to speak for the families of the twenty-nine victims of the Omagh bombing, when in fact we never belonged to such a group.'

There was also an implicit criticism of the self-help group's calls for justice rather than acceptance. 'Finally, we feel sure that most people would agree that all who died were the most loving and the best loved people in our community and as such deserve to be remembered with affection and love. We feel sure that those of our families whom we have loved and lost would ask for nothing more than that we live on friendly terms with our neighbours and work together for peace and goodwill in our community throughout this land and over the whole world.' There was no specific mention of the police, but there was a plea to the bombers: 'We would ask, even beg, for an assurance from those who had any part in the bombing of Omagh to make sure that no such act would ever be contemplated again.'

Even if fissures were opening up between victims, there was, however, one viewpoint shared by all. 'What I want from this inquest,' said Marion Radford, 'is to know that my child didn't suffer and that he died outright.' All the relatives wanted reassurance about their loved ones and most also wanted to know where and when that person had died, though listening to the details was intensely painful.

At the conclusion of proceedings dealing with each individual, the Coroner would offer consolatory words to the family – especially those tormented by the possibility that their loved one might have been saved. In the case of Geraldine Breslin, for instance, who had lived for eight hours after the bomb, he reminded her family that the pathologist and the doctor had shown that surviving her life-threatening injuries had been a remote possibility. 'In fact Professor Crane has expressed the view that it was quite remarkable that she did survive for so long and he puts this down to the remarkable medical treatment she received . . . But that aside, I do get the impression that this was a woman who was fighting very much to live.'

Equally distressing were confusing conflicts of evidence, of which the most harrowing was the disagreement between two witnesses as to whether eighteen-month-old Maura Monaghan had died underneath her mother or been blown into the window of the Salad Bowl. The explanation for this was simple: bodies had been moved. But it was not until Sergeant Phil Marshall came to the witness stand on the final day that these confusions would be fully resolved. That he had seen a baby in the shop window he believed was his own daughter was a piece of particularly stark but conclusive evidence.

On 2 October 2000, the day before the Coroner presented his findings, Detective Chief Superintendent Eric Anderson, the Task Force Commander directing the criminal enquiry, gave evidence. Beforehand, Leckey reminded the lawyers yet again that this was a fact-finding exercise about how people died. 'I am not wearing some form of quality control hat to assess the investigation carried out by the police.' By then there had been interviews with 6,500 people, Anderson reported, '3,500 premises and homes visited, 2,700 statements recorded and 5,200 actions generated from the inquiry'.

Of overriding interest to his audience, of course, were the eighty-one arrests made by the gardaí and the RUC 'in an effort to apprehend the bombers and the godfathers who sent them out to do the bombing': fifty-eight south, and twenty-three north, of the border. Two individuals had been charged 'albeit loosely' in connection with Omagh: Colm Murphy and the alleged car thief. In answer to a question from the Coroner, Anderson agreed that he knew the identity of many of the godfathers: those 'who sat in the background and who organised and set up and gave instructions . . . those people who are not involved and who do not get their hands dirty'.

The Coroner had already issued a solemn warning in court that no one should mention a name of a person they believed to be responsible in any way for the bomb lest they prejudice criminal proceedings or even the police investigation: 'Nothing that happens at an inquest should affect proceedings that may take place subsequently in either the criminal or the civil courts.' This was intensely frustrating for everyone. Asked by Eoin McGonigal, counsel for Oran Doherty and Sean McLaughlin from Buncrana, if he believed all the people responsible lived in County Louth, Anderson could say only that in talking about eighty-one arrests he was indicating a northern as well as southern input into the bombing. When

Anderson was asked when there would be other arrests, Stephen Ritchie, the Chief Constable's counsel, had to intervene to say it was irrelevant to the scope of the inquest. 'Please let it be understood that if the police were in a position to give everyone all the details, they would do so. They cannot. In fact the Human Rights Act that came into effect today has a bearing on the rights of these people who may or may not be suspected.'

'In fact,' said an exasperated McGonigal, 'it is probably one of the most relevant questions not only for my own clients but for many others sitting behind us as to when and if other persons would be made accountable for it . . . After two years, it must be possible to give some class of responsible answer to the query.' But it was not.

Anderson did his best for the families by holding a private meeting with them afterwards. He was accompanied by Garda Detective Superintendent Tadhg Foley, to whom they were able to express their deep disappointment that the Garda Commissioner had refused to allow an officer to give evidence for fear of compromising Murphy's pending prosecution. That the Coroner had been unable to subpoena anyone outside his jurisdiction was a foretaste of future frustrations. Furthermore, the Coroner could not return the verdict of murder that his English or Welsh counterparts had the power to do: on 3 October, he could merely deliver the finding that each of the twenty-eight* deceased had died 'from injuries sustained as a result of a car bomb explosion in Market Street, Omagh, on the afternoon, 15th August 1998'.

'The Real IRA claim responsibility for the car bomb,' he said, 'though they sought to pass responsibility to the police for casualties. As far as I am concerned they were responsible for all that happened.' The end of the inquest might close a chapter in the story of the dreadful events of that day, 'but a criminal trial and convictions will be necessary to close the book'.

Afterwards, he addressed a question that he had been considering throughout much of the inquest. Some of the families had referred him to a coroner's rule† that entitled him to make a report to the Chief Constable and/or the Secretary of State if he felt – as they did – that police methods

---

* James Barker's inquest was the following day.

† 'A coroner who believes that action should be taken to prevent the occurrence of fatality similar to that in respect of which the inquest is being held may announce at the inquest that he is reporting the matter to the person or authority who may have power to take such action and report the matter accordingly.'

of evacuation and deployment were inadequate. He had occasionally, but rarely, felt compelled to make a report to the relevant authority, said Leckey, 'but the times when I have taken such a course is where the act or omission has been of a nature that I would describe as "gross"'. On this occasion, he felt there was no such basis. He felt sure, he said, that the Chief Constable of the RUC would be addressing the question of what lessons could be learned.

Leckey concluded his summing-up with a moving expression of sympathy to all involved, including the Omagh bereaved, families 'bereaved in other terrorist atrocities' to whom the inquest must have 'brought back painful memories', and the traumatised police and others who were at the scene that day. At the press conference after the inquest ended, gentle Marion Radford recorded her gratitude to the police for everything they had done. 'The inquest has done a lot of good for me,' she said, 'but it has been very painful.' Michael, however, said the harrowing inquest 'had achieved little other than carrying out the duty of the State: our dead weren't officially recognised as dead until today'. But he added that Garda Detective Superintendent Foley had been able to alleviate a lot of the self-help group's worries, there were still many issues to be pursued and that the fight for justice would go on. Stanley was more upbeat, saying the families had been reassured by their meeting with Anderson and Foley and had no doubt both police forces would eventually succeed in arresting the bombers.

Several of the families were back in court the next day to support Victor at the inquest into James Barker's death. 'My wife and I have read with great distress the transcripts concerning all the other deaths in Omagh on that dreadful day,' said Victor, 'and our thoughts and prayers have been with the other families even though we have not been able to be here with them.' Victor had done his homework well, and had been in touch with the Coroner weeks before, outlining whom he wanted to question and what he wanted to ask them. Principally, he wanted to know from the doctor and the pathologist concerned if his son could have been saved and if he had suffered. It was some consolation to learn how James had been treated in his last few hours and that he had almost certainly been unconscious throughout. What was hard to bear was the clear suggestion that, had there been more staff available, James might have been saved.

Victor was as generous as he was controlled in court, going out of his way to thank Dr Pinto for his efforts to save James and to record that he and Donna-Maria in no way blamed the bus driver who had directed his passengers to Market Street. 'I have met him on a number of occasions,' he told the Coroner, 'and he is struggling to come to terms with what happened.' The bus driver had not been able to give evidence at the inquest, said the Coroner. 'I think the whole affair has traumatised him completely,' answered Victor, 'which you can understand. They were young children, they were out on a trip having a good time. I do not blame anybody apart from the people who planted the bomb.'

This was yet another example, said the Coroner, after he had given his finding, 'that those affected by what happened in Omagh were not just the families of those who had family members killed, but the effects were like a pebble thrown into a pond: they have spread out and touched many people, not only in Northern Ireland but well beyond the boundaries of this troubled province. One of the features that has come out is how much support has been given to all concerned. I am aware that you are grateful for the support that you have received, and I am sure those who you think of when you make those remarks are very grateful that you are able to think of what they have done for you and your family at this time.'

The Coroner and his counsel and staff wrapped up the inquest, and Victor, flanked by several members of the self-help group, and displaying the poster of James used for protests, gave a lively press conference. He had already issued a statement on behalf of himself, Donna-Maria, Esther,* Estella and Oliver, which expressed unreserved gratitude to those who had helped James. He addressed head-on the issue dividing the families: 'I do not share, or associate myself with, some of the comments made during the Inquest, which seem to have impugned or criticised the acts of the Royal Ulster Constabulary, the hundreds of volunteer citizens and the innocent receivers of the bomb warnings. The sadness is that having been denied justice against those who are responsible for this outrage, some families will unwittingly turn attention to those who were simply forced to deal with the situation on the day.'

His own anger was directed first at Adams and McGuinness, whom he called on to condemn without reservation those responsible for the bombing and to encourage every republican with information to come forward. He had asked them, he told the media, to join him in Omagh, but had been told they were busy. Despite having called their press secretary ten or

---

* James's half-sister by Donna-Maria's first marriage: his second sister is Estella.

fifteen times over the preceding three months, 'they don't seem to want to meet me, for some reason. They were quite happy to come to my son's funeral.' But the government was under fire too, for 'their failure to grasp what was a real security alert situation in the days leading up to Omagh, in confining the Army to barracks as part of the peace settlement, and indeed their continued inaction in failing to give all the help and assistance to those who are investigating this outrage. I find it inexcusable that the Government of Great Britain has only chosen to give us pieties about the hunt for the Omagh bombers, and has singularly failed to deliver any form of justice to the innocent victims, especially the many innocent children whose lives and bodies were shattered, including my son James.

'I share the view that even if the RUC response to the bomb warnings in Omagh two years ago could be shown to have been inadequate, or ineffectual, there is a singular difference between security forces and terrorists, when bombs are planted. The security forces have to run towards them, the terrorists only have to run away. I remain steadfast in my opinion that right-minded people in this country, irrespective of religious persuasion or political beliefs, will ultimately unite with me in condemning the tunnel-vision barbarity which pervades the Real IRA, and their political wing, the 32 County Sovereignty Committee. I know that I share the views of many, who will continue to pursue those responsible with every means at their disposal to bring those who perpetrated this atrocity to justice, no matter how long it takes. The victims of Omagh have not gone away.'*

They certainly had not. The BBC had just announced that on the following Monday, in the John Ware film Victor had inspired, *Panorama* would be doing what nobody else had to date been willing or able to do by naming those they considered the main suspects for the Omagh bomb. And Victor had already signed up with the lawyer Henry Robinson had found for him, to sue the Real IRA.

---

* A deliberate allusion to a notorious comment made by Gerry Adams at a republican rally in August 1995. When a heckler shouted, 'Bring back the IRA', he responded: 'They haven't gone away, you know.'

CHAPTER ELEVEN

GOING TO LAW

'We let the police have a go,' said Paul Devine, 'and we are sure that they have done their best. Now we must do our best to get these people before a court. We can't let them just sit back in their comfortable safe home, thinking that they have got away with it.'

And Tracey adds: 'I want them to go to bed at night knowing that we haven't forgotten them' – the parents of Breda Devine, *Daily Mail*, 31 October 2000

Henry Robinson had been trying since March 2000 to find a lawyer to take on the Real IRA. He was turned down immediately by two legal firms in Northern Ireland, who would not even contemplate acting in what they thought of as a ludicrously dangerous case. But his young friend and solicitor, Stephen Taylor Heath, was enthusiastic and put some thought and research into the options. Ultimately, he reached the conclusion that a class action* might be a possibility and with Henry came to London to discuss the idea with Victor, Robert Cranborne and me. Stephen then sounded out his senior partners, who dismissed the idea out of hand.

Between the lawyers who said the idea was a non-starter and others who were terrified of taking on the Real IRA, as weeks and weeks went by Henry and Robert and I were beginning to lose hope. However, Victor was certainly not going to admit defeat.

Similarly, back in Omagh, Michael Gallagher was following Victor's occasional reports about developments in London with interest, as were several other families. As the months passed and still only Colm Murphy had been charged, they became increasingly despairing. Some were fatalistic; others angry. There was huge resentment at the refusal of the Sinn Féin leadership to ask their followers to give evidence. Sometimes they

---

* A lawsuit taken by a large group of people, class actions are increasingly popular in the US. In July 2000, a jury had ordered five tobacco companies to pay more than 500,000 people nearly $145 billion.

regretted that their own ethics prevented them from taking physical vengeance. At the height of sectarian violence, as a young man growing up in a loyalist housing estate, Godfrey Wilson had rejected invitations to join local paramilitaries. Nevertheless, 'I have often thought of taking the law into my own hands,' he said. 'I can't bear to have Lorraine's killers walking around not too many miles from here and maybe some of those involved or those who know something walking the streets of Omagh itself while my girl has been taken away from us.'

Then, in September, as the inquest was about to start, Henry decided to try the solicitor Jason McCue, whom we knew through Sean O'Callaghan – my other ex-terrorist friend.

In his teens, Sean, who came from a County Kerry IRA family, had joined the Provisional IRA with the intention of driving the British out of Northern Ireland. By the time he realised that his ignorance and bigotry had landed him squarely in the middle of a squalid sectarian war, he had robbed and murdered for the Provisional IRA, mainly in County Tyrone, where he was infamous. He left the organisation in 1974 and went to England, where he started a profitable business and married, but his conscience drove him to go back to Kerry and rejoin the Provisionals, this time working (unpaid) as an informer for the Irish gardaí; despite having a son, his marriage collapsed. Sean became a Sinn Féin councillor, a member of its National Executive, and, jointly with his old comrade Martin Ferris, was put in charge of what the Provisionals called Southern Command, i.e. the Republic of Ireland.

Sean's many successes – or treacheries, to republicans – included saving the lives of Prince Charles and Princess Diana by foiling an attempted assassination and helping to scupper a huge arms shipment in an operation that had the bonus of sending Ferris to jail for ten years. That a known former gun-runner like Ferris was later elected to the Irish parliament while Sean is unwelcome in Irish officialdom and still in danger from ex-colleagues poses obvious questions about the ambivalence of Irish voters and the Irish Establishment towards terrorism committed in the name of patriotism.

Sean fled Kerry with his new partner and baby daughter in December 1985, under suspicion of being an informer but pleading his innocence and claiming he just needed a break. After being debriefed by the British security forces at the request of the gardaí and then attempting to make a living in the dead-end jobs to which lying low condemned him, he gave himself

up in November 1988 for the crimes committed in his teens: his intention
was to turn supergrass against old colleagues.

Senior Provisionals including Adams had never believed Sean could be
an informer, so for more than three years in jail he continued successfully
to pretend to republican prisoners that he was a loyal member of the Provisionals, and thus was able to acquire useful information* to pass to the
police and the prison authorities. His cover was blown when he was placed
in the supergrass unit in Maghaberry high-security prison. To his intense
frustration, it became apparent that the peace process was inhibiting prosecution of leading members of Sinn Féin, so in 1993 Sean decided to go
public and told his story to the *Sunday Times*'s Liam Clarke. Then, because
the authorities were refusing to agree his early release on normal supergrass terms, he went on a hunger-and-thirst strike.

Although Henry Robinson had never met Sean, he knew of him, and,
alerted by a journalist, arrived with a colleague to visit him eleven and a
half days into the strike, when he was close to death, and helped persuade
him to settle for the offer of a review of his case. The following year,
Henry took me to Maghaberry, believing Sean could help me with my
anti-terrorism writing and campaigning. Having found Sean an invaluable political analyst, we spoke on the phone often and I visited him whenever I was in Northern Ireland. On one occasion I took an RUC friend
with me and listened with fascination as the policeman and the ex-terrorist
discussed the locality where the policeman lived and in which Sean had
spread fear, and compared notes on local republicans.

I was sitting in Robert Cranborne's grand office in the House of Lords
one evening, reporting Sean's views on the present state of republican
thinking, when I said, 'This is so frustrating. I wish you could talk to him
yourself.' Cabinet ministers, as a rule, do not chat privately to prisoners,

---

* Among those from whom he learned much that helped those trying to understand
republican strategy during the peace process were: Danny Morrison, who in 1981 had
argued for Sinn Féin's involvement in politics by asking if its members objected 'if, with
a ballot paper in one hand and an Armalite in the other hand, we take power in Ireland?';
Sid, or Seanna, Walsh, the most influential prisoner, who in 2005 was chosen to read to
the media the Provisionals' statement ending the 'armed struggle' and ordering decommissioning; and Marxist Brian Keenan, who masterminded Mountbatten's murder to
demonstrate the Provisionals' anti-imperialist credentials, ran the bombing campaigns in
England in the 1970s and as a senior member of the Army Council in 1996 would plan
the bombing of Canary Wharf.

particularly terrorist prisoners, but Robert makes his own rules. After a brief pause, he said, 'Do I dare?' And then he scribbled down a number and said, 'Tell him to ring me before 9.00 a.m. on a Saturday.'

When Sean telephoned him the first time, Robert said, 'Do you think the intelligence services are listening in?' 'Yes,' said Sean. 'Good,' said Robert, and they embarked on what was to become a firm and close anti-terrorist alliance. Sean was freed on Friday 6 December 1996 and came to London the following Tuesday; by prior arrangement I took him to meet Robert in the Lords. Sean had been splashed all over the *Sunday Times* that weekend and had declared himself an informer and proud of it, so the media were in hot pursuit. He needed to find a discreet phone for a radio interview with Vincent Browne of Radio Telefís Éireann, so Robert installed him in a colleague's office. The interview was intensely hostile, as Browne shared the erroneous but comforting view of many Irish nationalists that Sean was a fantasist and/or a British agent. It caused us much amusement that his interviewee was on this occasion physically located at the heart of the British Establishment.

Since Sean had become famous as an informer, and particularly after he published his autobiography,[1] many of his ex-colleagues had and have been keen to murder him, but he has insisted on living openly in London, trusting to luck, sensible precautions and the safe houses proffered by his numerous friends in all parts of the United Kingdom,* one of whom was Jason McCue, then of the law firm Henry Hepworth.

Jason is a buccaneer – as unorthodox a lawyer as Robert is a politician and Henry and Sean are ex-terrorists. He had visited Sean in jail in the early 1990s to seek his help on one of his cases and they had become friends. In May 1998 Jason was a solicitor on a case where Sean was a witness, appearing for the defence in a libel action that Thomas 'Slab' Murphy, Chief of Staff of the IRA, had taken against the *Sunday Times*, which had had the temerity to allege in print that he was an active and important member of the organisation he actually ran: he had lost the first round but had lodged an appeal that led to a retrial.

---

* Three other informers have been particularly high-profile targets because of going public with their stories: Eamon Collins (*Killing Rage*, 1997) was mutilated and murdered in South Armagh in 1999; Martin McGartland (*Fifty Dead Men Walking*, 1997), in hiding in England but indiscreet, survived five bullets from an assassin in 1999; Raymond Gilmour (*Dead Ground: Infiltrating the IRA*, 1998) has lived in Britain under an assumed identity for many years.

The libel laws in the Republic of Ireland are more favourable to plaintiffs even than those of the United Kingdom, and juries often award punitive damages, so libel writs often flew to newspapers and publishers from Northern Ireland republicans. 'If we lose the Murphy case,' Jason said at the time, 'it will all get worse: innumerable cases will follow.' In the event, the Dublin jury were unimpressed by Murphy's claim to be a simple farmer, not least because he had brought with him to court large numbers of arrogant, loud heavies from the Dundalk area.

Although the *Sunday Times* won against Murphy, Jason was involved in other Irish cases and had long been incensed that terrorists were using the civil law, and yet no one seemed inclined to use it against them – an argument that resonated with Henry's belief that somehow someone had to be able to sue a paramilitary organisation.

Jason is courageous to the point of recklessness: he was shocked but undeterred from pursuing similar cases even when one of his key witnesses from the libel case, Eamon Collins, was murdered in Murphy's fiefdom in January 1999.* Jason also has a big heart: we knew he would be sympathetic to the relatives. And along with his imagination and flair, he has boundless optimism and we needed someone who saw solutions rather than problems.

Jason had been the obvious lawyer to try in the first place, but Sean, who was in his office most days helping him on Irish cases, was unsure whether the Omagh case had any prospects and in any case had told Henry it was far more than Jason's small firm could take on, especially since the families had no money. But after months of disappointment and cul-de-sacs, Henry was beyond caring about anyone's opinion, and he gave Jason's number to Victor. The two of them went in to see him in his office in Holborn on 6 September 2000, the day Michael Gallagher and most of the self-help group had gathered in the Omagh Leisure Centre for the first day of the inquest.

Victor, who arrived bearing neat files, and who worked in a world of suits and respectability, was faced with a rather exotic and good-looking trio. It was not for nothing that – despite his metrosexual image – some

---

* It is generally believed that he was killed by the Provisionals; a less likely theory is that the Real IRA took revenge because he called for their internment after the Omagh bomb.

nicknamed Jason 'Indiana Jones'. With his appealing, mischievous face often designer-stubbled, he would sit in his smoke-filled office with his boots on his desk, his walls full of cartoons and photographs, and assorted other souvenirs of odd encounters in strange places, not least with members of the Provisional IRA. A favourite recreation was shooting, so one wall decoration was a target from Cambodia complete with bullet holes. There to take notes was his secretary, Davidaire Horsford, a willowy and striking West Indian who had been part of Jason's team in Dublin during the tense Murphy case. And then there was chain-smoking, mustachioed Sean, wearing jeans, boots and an open-neck shirt, whom Victor knew from Henry and me was a murderer for the Provisionals and an informer for the state: Sean had been skulking out of view upstairs, but Henry had persuaded him to come down.

Victor appealed to Jason's imagination and won his heart, though he did not yet entirely win Sean's head: after the meeting, Sean reiterated his warnings to Jason about the implications for the firm in terms of the over-stretching of limited resources. Jason, however, wanted a career-making case, and was so excited at the prospect of an extraordinary new adventure that he overrode the warnings. As he puts it: 'It was necessary to be judicious in sharing one's thoughts with partners on what this might entail, so as not to curb their keen enthusiasm to fight a good cause.' The firm at the time was in the midst of an acrimonious split: taking on an uncertain, dangerous and unprecedented case was likely to make everything worse.

'Thank you very much for coming in to see us on Wednesday and discussing what is clearly an extremely emotional and difficult topic,' Jason emailed Victor two days later. 'We were all touched and deeply moved by what we heard. We truly hope we can achieve something for you.

> We intend to spend the next week considering all the legal angles and which would be the best to suit your objectives. We had little time to fully consider the options in any detail prior to the meeting. What we do know, and would like to assure you of, is that if there is a will there is a way. We discussed 3 possible legal avenues to explore and I have no doubt there will be more. My mind is filled with ideas and possibilities. My initial views keep changing as does my approach to the subject. I do not think at this early stage that we should close our eyes to any option or fixate on one to

the exclusion of another. Analysis of procedure, law and evidence will be the key to unlocking the best legal route . . . you may ring my mobile night and day 7 days a week . . .

It was a pleasure to meet you as it will be a pleasure to represent you and the others.

Kind regards,

Jason

Now that he had his lawyer, Victor was busily trying to bring other families on board: the idea initially was to restrict whatever civil case was initiated to families of children under eighteen. Not that he was in any way curtailing his offensive against all his usual targets: 'I have not yet received all my files back,' he wrote to Jason after their meeting. 'If you could let me have them at some time I would appreciate it as I wish to keep tormenting the Secretary of State.' He was also keeping up with the transcripts of the Omagh inquests and liaising with John Ware about developments on the *Panorama* programme.

At Henry Hepworth, Jason was already on the move on the ground in Ireland, bolstered by an encouraging meeting with Robert Cranborne, who underwrote financially the early stages of the investigation. Having visited several of his contacts in the police north and south and having looked in on the inquest, he asked his young colleague Lucy Morgan to collect and collate preliminary research to put before Counsel. 'There were lots of "firsts" to consider,' remembered Lucy, 'not least the proposal that we should sue the Real IRA. Was it a legal entity that could be sued?'

> Our argument was that the law exists to protect those who agree to be bound by it – so why should it be used to protect members of a proscribed organisation (i.e. one whose objects were entirely unlawful and which did not wish to be bound by that law)? If judgment was held against the Real IRA, then (in theory) anyone convicted of membership of that organisation could be sued for damages caused (or claimed) by that organisation, even if they had nothing to do with the specific attack which caused the relevant damage. This would have serious consequences for membership of proscribed organisations in future – it could be expensive for members even if they themselves never took part in attacks.

As Jason adds: 'No one in the world, in any jurisdiction, had sued an alleged terrorist organisation in a civil court for a direct act of terror. We wondered how on earth would we serve the writs on them? Since this would not be a criminal case, we would not have a police force to effect an arrest.'

But it was a tempting prospect to use the civil law to effect social change. 'Most IRA members,' as Lucy put it, 'saw going to prison as part of the job, even cool. But the prospect of losing their homes/cars/widescreen tellies would be most unappealing. And not just to members, but, importantly, to their wives and families.'

With the help of information from John Ware provided weeks before his programme was transmitted, Lucy plunged in.

Along with Robert, whose bullishness about the case Jason found reassuring, the rest of us were trying to devise a strategy, not least how to raise what would obviously have to be vast sums of money. There was even the nightmarish possibility that, once writs were issued, the families would be exposed – if they lost the case – to the prospect of having to pay the Defendants' costs.

It was an extremely nerve-wracking time for those of us most closely involved, particularly Sean, who, as a result of long periods in solitary confinement, tends more than most to think things through and spot trouble around the corner. Even Jason began to have sleepless nights about what he had taken on so impulsively. 'I was approached,' he said to me one evening, 'to do this by Victor, a middle-class Englishman, who wanted to bring a case in Ireland – not the greatest thing for a Belfast court.'

> And who were the people around me? I had Sean, an ex-IRA terrorist who was hated by the IRA, I had Ruth Dudley Edwards, who was an attacker of all things republican and green, Henry Robinson, a Sticky* saint who was running a children's home and was also an ex-convict, Robert – a hate figure to all in Ireland where he was seen as Lord Establishment – and, you know, not a *Guardian* reader amongst them. Straight away, I was thinking, 'Guys, we've got to get something in the *Guardian*.'
> But it was very funny.

We did, however, have the BBC, in the shape of its most prestigious current affairs programme. John Ware, its presenter, was a highly experienced

---

* At Easter, Irish republicans wear a paper badge featuring a white lily with an orange stamen against a green background in remembrance of those killed in or executed after the 1916 rising; various branches of republicanism also commemorate their own dead heroes. After the IRA split in 1970, the Official IRA eschewed the traditional pin for an adhesive backing and earned the nickname 'Stickies'.

and fearless investigative reporter, whose investigations for *Panorama* had included human rights abuses in Saudi Arabia, price-fixing deals between car dealers and motor manufacturers and an attempt by paratroopers in Belfast to cover up their unlawful shooting of joyriders.

Ware's justification for making 'Who Bombed Omagh?', screened on 9 October 2000, expressed a view common to the journalists who have supported the families over the years. 'Omagh was so dreadful. Every terrorist murder is, and every family goes through what the families in Omagh went through, and are still going through. But the sheer scale of Omagh . . . We talked to lots and lots of relatives and these were broken people . . . I just thought this is such a bloody outrage, and so plainly wrong.'

With the help of material from Victor Barker and Detective Chief Superintendent Eric Anderson, Ware had put together a case against four men, based mainly on mobile phone evidence. Most of the self-help group supported him, and Michael Gallagher, Marion Radford and Kevin Skelton took part in the programme, but Laurence Rush feared it might prejudice future trials and applied unsuccessfully to the Belfast High Court to have it stopped. So, too, did the Northern Ireland Human Rights Commission, who also contended that it might put at risk the 'personal safety and right to life' of the men identified.* Their application was thrown out just ninety minutes before the programme was due to go on air, on the basis that the men named came from another jurisdiction.

The identities of two of the men named and door-stepped by Ware and his team were no great surprise: Colm Murphy was still awaiting trial and Liam Campbell had been charged on 4 October 2000 – the day before the inquest ended – with membership of an illegal organisation. Gardaí had raided Campbell's house and found incriminating evidence: in addition to an underground bunker, there were three walkie-talkies, disposable body suits, packets of white gloves and black insulating tape and small-bore tubing of a kind used to boost home-made explosive. But this was the first public mention of Seamus Daly and Oliver Traynor†, a businessman who

---

* It was a constant source of mystification to some of the relatives and supporters that human rights groups seemed so little concerned about the victims of the bomb and so protective of the alleged bombers. In November 2000, for instance, British–Irish Watch, whose sponsors included Michael Mansfield QC, accused the media and some politicians of waging a 'campaign of vilification' against the McKevitts; its report was sent to the UN special rapporteur on freedom of expression and opinion.

† No criminal charges were brought against Traynor, nor was he a defendant in the civil case.

sold plastic window frames and who Ware alleged in the documentary had lent a mobile to Campbell, who had it on him when he made the warning call from Newry. Ware's hope was that seeing these men on television might break 'the conspiracy of silence' and encourage others to come forward.* The Real IRA would later make clear their feelings about the *Panorama* programme: early in March 2001, they let off a car bomb outside BBC Television Centre in west London, which injured a passer-by and damaged the building.

The programme had four million viewers and was generally well received†, though Laurence denounced it as 'cheap' and an affront to justice. Despite some appalled criticisms left on the BBC website, the majority were enthusiastically on Ware's side, not least the author of the poignant entry I noticed years later:

> I would like to commend you on the excellent programme on Omagh that you showed last night. Maybe I am a little biased due to the fact that my little brother James was murdered by the Real IRA on the 15th August 1998, at the age of 12. I felt that the programme was informative and hopefully now the people who know even the smallest piece of information may come forward to the RUC or the Garda, and possibly someone can be finally brought to justice for the atrocity that has wrecked the lives of my family and hundreds of others in Omagh and surrounding areas. God bless to those who have suffered due to this stupidity of others.
>
> Erin-Esther Barker
>
> Weybridge

The programme caused much controversy. In Northern Ireland, Gerry Adams was 'against the naming of people involved . . . not least because those who were involved in the killings on Bloody Sunday are remaining anonymous in the courts', and David Trimble, a lawyer as well as First Minister, had 'very grave doubts' about its wisdom: 'I am not sure whether that programme was done out of a genuine desire to serve the public or for the sake of sensation.' The Secretary of State, Peter Mandelson, on

---

* The programme would win the Best Single Documentary Award of the Broadcasting Press Guild as an 'outstanding piece of journalistic investigation' and the Royal Television Society (RTS) Home Current Affairs Award as 'an immensely brave film that had required boldness on the part of its journalists and the managers in bringing it to air'. Described by the judges as 'a professional irritant in the very best journalistic tradition for many years', Ware was also RTS's 2001 Television Journalist of the Year.
† See, however, p. 199 and Murphy's contempt of court proceeding.

the other hand, described it as 'a very professional piece of work' that might attract witnesses. In the Republic, Bertie Ahern was furious about criticism of the government and the gardaí over their failure to prosecute anyone other than Colm Murphy and their failure to get informers to turn state's evidence because they would be difficult to protect.

Victor stirred the pot in the *Daily Telegraph* on 12 October with an article headlined 'DO THEY REALLY CARE AT ALL ABOUT MY MURDERED SON?', assailing the double standards tolerated in Northern Ireland: 'To use McGuinness-speak, "the reality of the situation" is that the terrorists know how to manipulate the system to their advantage: when arrested, to stare at the wall; take off their clothes; urinate on the floor while being questioned; and bang their heads against the wall alleging ill-treatment. After all, this is how the Green Book, the IRA's training document, helps to train them, and it tells them that, no matter how horrendous any act of violence may be, they must never inform on a "volunteer".

'The murdered IRA man Eamon Collins provided a clear example of what happens when a volunteer mutters even a word to the security forces. He ended up in a field with a stake through his head and his tongue ripped out. Where was his right to a fair trial? The fact remains that the police have to play by the rules, while the terrorists have their own system of summary justice and an altogether different rulebook.'

Pleading for witnesses to come forward, he tore into the Taoiseach: 'Let us hope that Bertie Ahern is not so keen to woo Sinn Féin into government in the south* that he, too, loses his appetite for justice because of political expediency. His criticism of the *Panorama* programme came as a surprise to me, and I ask him and his colleagues to steady the ship and continue the course that he promised me he would follow when I met him in Dublin last January.'

Ahern was already under great strain: another crisis was threatening to derail the peace process and he was now suffering a barrage of criticism in the media and the Dáil for having failed the victims of Omagh, with accusations that, to appease republicans, the government was interfering with the gardaí's investigation. Certainly the Real IRA believed there was foot-dragging, which had increased their contempt for the government.

---

* Victor was getting the wrong end of the political stick: Ahern was desperate to woo Sinn Féin into government in Northern Ireland but determined if possible to destroy them in the Republic; this he would finally manage to do in the 2007 general election.

McKevitt reported to a friend that in late September the Irish government had suggested negotiations; they had been told that negotiations 'needed to be with the Brits and not the Irish; he said that he also told them that it was not prisoners, or jobs or anything else on the agenda but Brit withdrawal was to be first, then the other issues'. McKevitt was convinced that politicians and Special Branch were terrified that if they used the new anti-terrorist legislation on a grand scale, Real IRA members would emulate ETA by killing police and politicians.[2] The arrest of Campbell on a minor charge was acceptable: his reported attitude was 'kind of shit happens, it is too bad but that is what happens', not least because Campbell was 'too trusting'. For instance, when the entire West Belfast Brigade had wanted to meet McKevitt, he was wary of informers, so would meet only the leader, whereas, he said, Campbell, who was less streetwise, would have met them all.[3]

Ahern took his anger out on the Real IRA the following Sunday at a peculiar annual event known as 'Bodenstown', which is the name of a churchyard in County Kildare where for more than a century republicans have gathered to commemorate Wolfe Tone, the most famous of the 1798 revolutionaries, who slit his throat to avoid being hanged. As well as the respectable Fianna Fáil – which calls itself 'the Republican Party' – various IRAs and their front associations also make pilgrimages and give orations at the graveside of Tone, each of them believing – to use Michael McKevitt's image of the relay race – that he was first to run with the republican baton and they are the last. As Bernadettte McKevitt's colleague Rory Dougan put it to a journalist apropos the Provisionals: 'If we were wrong now, then they were wrong for all them years: and if we are right now then they are wrong.'[4] Ahern lambasted the Real IRA, which was 'indelibly disgraced and should be dissolved'. It would not be allowed to ruin the lives of innocent citizens because – in its contempt for others – it was only capable of uniting Protestant, Catholic and Dissenter in death. Those responsible for the Omagh bombing had no right to describe themselves as republicans: they were defying the will of the sovereign people. Likewise, Republican Sinn Féin could not be taken seriously while there was 'continued involvement in armed struggle by the Continuity IRA in defiance of the clearly and freely expressed will of the Irish people in the referendums of May 1998'. But there was no promise of a crack-down.

The Ware programme had not worried the phlegmatic McKevitt. He saw it as an attempt by the British to keep Omagh in front of the public, but believed the public had lost interest. 'He says at the end of the day the program did OnE [Óglaigh na hÉireann] more good with the probable defenses of these guys by mentioning their names than it hurt us.'[5]

As he always did, McKevitt was underestimating the families. As Michael Gallagher had pointed out after the *Panorama* programme: 'Looking at the assets of the people named in the programme last night probably makes it more feasible that we will take civil prosecutions. We feel these people have to be held responsible in some manner.' Suing the Real IRA was no easy decision for many of the families, who were all too aware that its members dealt in murder and intimidation: I have held the hands of a terrified, weeping young woman who was convinced she would be killed but was nonetheless determined to put her name to a writ out of loyalty to her dead sibling. But apart from the effect of the programme, events had combined to harden the resolve of many of them. Just from August to October 2000, there had been the protest at Brennan's Bar, the news during the inquest of the bombing of MI6, press reports describing how the Real IRA had smuggled arms from Croatia and, four days after Bodenstown, there were photographs of six men and two women, in combat dress and balaclavas, in West Belfast, in full view of army helicopters, brazenly standing by the coffin of their murdered comrade Joe O'Connor as one of them fired a three-shot volley. Wearily used to the gardaí regularly making arrests that came to nothing, they were not mollified that Liam Campbell would go on trial for what was a minor charge. And then there was the news that Victor had found a lawyer. Victor, Michael and the more far-sighted of the families also realised that, as the sensational impact of the inquest and *Panorama* waned, it would be that much harder to reawaken interest from potential donors.

In London, we were trying not to panic. Without more money, the lawyers could not construct a case or instruct barristers to develop it, so we had to try to raise money before we even knew for sure if there was a viable case. Jason and his colleagues were prepared to take a gamble that their work might be unpaid, but the firm would be liable for any counsels' fees incurred, along with travel, accommodation and other such expenses. Yet no one would want to give money for a legal pipe-dream. Jason knew that as well as letting the families down, failure could seriously damage his reputation, and the rest of us knew that fundraising was sure to be nightmarishly time-consuming and we had livings to make. 'I wish that from the start,' said Jason once, 'I'd sat down and said: "Look, you guys, come back to me when you've got a Trust, you've got £2,000,000 and you've got a press team."'

'Our disorganisation was our strength,' said the ever-cheerful Henry later. 'More like chaos theory,' offered Jason when I told him this. 'After all, having no proper plan kept us necessarily flexible.' But it did not feel like that: the 'Keystone Cops' was how I frequently described our group, who found ourselves responsible for something we had neither the time, the skill nor the experience to do properly. Yet Henry is right in one sense: more organised and prudent people would never have become involved in the first place. Not even Victor Barker could have found a way to provide £2,000,000 and a press team, so nothing would have happened had Jason not been rash, had we not been over-optimistic and had we not all been driven by our commitment to help the desperate families.

Notwithstanding all the false starts and confusions, by late October there had been serious progress.

Jason had gone straight to his friend Heather Rodgers at Matrix Chambers, a brand new legal practice set up 'in anticipation of the complex challenges facing the law in the 21st century'. Immensely high-profile, not least because Tony Blair's wife Cherie was a member, it was particularly strong in human rights law and keen to push boundaries. Heather Rodgers, an expert in defamation, had suggested the barrister Danny Friedman, whose forte was criminal justice, and within a few weeks they had delivered a counsel's opinion that there was indeed the basis for a civil case, even if was still not clear whether such a case should be heard in Belfast, Dublin or London.

With the help of Victor's and John Ware's material and the informal police contacts on both sides of the border that Jason had put her in touch with, highly capable, focused Lucy Morgan, who had a gift for winning people's trust, had helped Jason to put together a preliminary brief.

Victor and Michael, meanwhile, were working as a team to persuade the families: 'I remember they came to the office,' recalls Lucy. 'Michael Gallagher big, quiet and sad; Victor short, animated and angry.' And the lawyers and families had had their first meeting at a hotel near Omagh to discuss the possible way ahead. For the families, there was a growing belief that at last they really could take some control of events.

Equally crucially, the fundraising had swung into action. There had been much heart-searching about which newspaper should be asked to take the lead. It had to be of the right: left-leaning media by and large would have been too worried about infringing the civil rights of alleged bombers. The

Daily Telegraph, which had backed the 'Defend the RUC' campaign, seemed an obvious choice, but ultimately the decision was to try for the *Daily Mail*.

The *Daily Mail* is seen either as a defender of the best of British values or a peddler of fear and loathing. For some, wrote the journalist Cristina Odone, its editor, Paul Dacre, 'is the last great Fleet Street editor, blessed with an unbeatable instinct for what his readers want to read, and how this should be presented; for others, he is a brutal taskmaster with an arrogant sense of destiny.' From our point of view, there were compelling reasons for going to Dacre: he had a very clear sense of good and evil, he was a passionate champion of family values, he had form in breaking the rules about naming names, he knew how to run a campaign, and he was absolute master of his newspaper.

To the amazement of his many liberal critics, it was the *Daily Mail* that in September 1997 had championed the parents of Stephen Lawrence when they saw the British legal system fail them in their search for justice for their dead son. Dacre is an emotional man, who became furious that the violent racists believed responsible for knifing a decent young man were unrepentant and unpunished. The front page headline over the photographs of the five suspects was uncompromising, purporting to identify the killers and then challenging them to sue if the paper was wrong.

While it was true that since legal aid is not granted for libel, the chances of such a lawsuit were slim, there are lawyers who might have taken the case out of antipathy to the *Mail*.* The paper was also running the risk of being found guilty of contempt of court. 'It is no light matter when a national newspaper condemns as murderers five men who have never been convicted in court,' said the *Mail*. 'But when the judicial system has failed so lamentably to deal with the killers of Stephen Lawrence, extraordinary measures are demanded.' There were indeed calls for Dacre to be jailed and the *Telegraph* was among his sternest critics, but the Attorney General cleared the paper of contempt of court and for the friends and family of Stephen Lawrence it was a major consolation that the lives of those thus accused were made more uncomfortable by this naming and shaming. When he was the castaway on Radio 4's *Desert Island Discs* in January 2004, Dacre chose Aaron Copland's 'Fanfare for the Common Man' as a tribute to the Lawrence family and Verdi's Requiem for the families of Omagh.

Jason could not get to Dacre, but he and Victor met the executive editor,

---

* 'No win, no fee' was not yet legal.

Jon Steafel, who got the go-ahead from his boss. Dacre knew well that anything to do with Irish politics is a turn-off for most English people and equally well that no one is enthusiastic about donating money for legal fees, but he believed that his readers would respond to the families' simple human stories of tragedy and courage. He was determined, too, to put pressure on politicians. The campaign – 'Justice for the Omagh Innocents' – kicked off within a few days. 'HOW *YOU* CAN WIN JUSTICE FOR THE BOMB CHILDREN' was the front-page headline on Saturday 28 October: inset was a photograph of little Breda Devine. 'The *Daily Mail* today launches a fighting fund to help the families of Omagh hit back at the terrorists who murdered their children' began the story by Michael Seamark, who would become the *Mail*'s link with the families.

Page 2 carried the headline 'SUSPECTS . . .', with photographs and brief details of Michael McKevitt, and the four men targeted by Ware – Campbell, Daly, Murphy and Traynor.* On the opposite page, under 'AND THE VICTIMS' were pictures and descriptions of James Barker, Breda Devine, Samantha McFarland and Lorraine Wilson, whose families had agreed to spearhead the campaign. There was a quote from Jason: 'We intend to use the people's court to hound and track down the culprits and seek appropriate legal remedies, to bring civil action by the people against the pariahs of society.'

A further two pages were devoted to an interview with Donna-Maria, who the writer, Angela Levin, reported was still taking James's favourite teddy bear to bed with her every night and was 'so wounded and raw with grief that you fear for her health'. Levin had interviewed her in Buncrana, where Donna-Maria had returned to spend half-term with her second daughter, Estella, still at boarding school in Northern Ireland: the giant picture of James was still dominating the living room. 'I feel such guilt for suggesting we move to Ireland,' she told the journalist. 'It's something I will have to live with for the rest of my life. I also feel guilty that I don't give enough to my other children. I've missed two years of their lives, but I just can't help it. At times I yearn for James so much I feel I am going off my head. Luckily I have a very strong husband who has coped with my wailing and crying. I'm so proud of Victor for not letting the politicians put what happened on the back burner.'

* On 31 July 2001, the *Mail* would settle a contempt action when it issued a statement that Murphy was 'entitled to be presumed innocent of the charges preferred against him unless or until proven guilty': that same presumption of innocence also applies to the other suspects named by the *Mail*.

The story was redolent with heart-rending detail. 'They gave me back his tuck box after he was killed and I've kept it with the half-eaten tube of Polos and the empty, straightened-out crisp packet.' In the midst of her weeping, Donna-Maria said, 'We all hurt so much – James's eighty-nine-year-old great-grandfather, his grandparents, Estella, who sleeps with James's T-shirt under her pillow, and Oliver, who hasn't been the same since his brother's death.' That there would be a civil action, she said, 'makes me feel lighter for the first time since his murder'.

'This paper', read the editorial, 'believes passionately in their fight – just as it backed efforts to get the killers of black teenager Stephen Lawrence onto the witness stand.'

A photograph of a happy Samantha McFarland and Lorraine Wilson with their arms around each other was on the front page on Monday, under the headline 'HOW CAN OUR LOVELY LORRAINE'S KILLERS GO FREE?' The lead article was more political. Godfrey Wilson accused the governments of putting politics before justice. 'Without justice, we cannot even start to think about getting on with the rest of our lives. What sort of democracy do we have if you have killers – and everyone knows who they are – walking our streets? Nothing can ever return Lorraine to us, but we can never rest when the men and women who killed 31 people are still out there walking about free.' That day's paper also featured an article by me, which I highlight because the conditions of writing it remind me forcibly of the sheer panic we were going through at the time.

I write crime fiction, and on the weekend the campaign was launched I was in Manchester for an authors-meeting-readers event and relaxation with good friends. I was thrilled by the Saturday *Daily Mail*, and particularly delighted to be able to show it to fellow-writer Simon Shaw, who had introduced me to Victor almost two years earlier, to prove that we were getting somewhere.

On Sunday morning, the *Daily Mail* features editor, for whom I sometimes wrote, rang me and said the campaign needed an article to boost it and would I provide it by that evening. Yes, I said, calculating that if I cancelled lunch, hid in a corner of the hotel lounge and kept my laptop plugged into the mains, I could write enough before I left for London to have enough battery power to finish the piece on the train and email it.

But I had forgotten my charger, so I had to write it by hand, something particularly difficult when you are writing to a pre-ordained length and have to keep counting words. In the surreal circumstances of a world where people wrote and/or read about fictional murder for entertainment, I began to write about the family of Breda Devine. 'Just imagine: your baby has been murdered, and murdered horribly. You see her tiny, broken, burned body. You carry the little white coffin to her grave.

'Two years on, you know the people who killed her and you know there simply isn't enough evidence to bring them to court – witnesses are holding back because of fear or misguided loyalty.

'You're told there can be no justice for your baby. The politicians who promised that the murderers would be hunted down are strangely silent. And the killers – the Real IRA – are planning more murders and priming more bombs. Whose child will be next?'

I was describing the frustrations of the families when the friends with whom I was travelling to London collected me. The weather was dreadful, we had to walk to the station through the rain, and I was so wet when I got to the crowded platform, packed with passengers awaiting delayed trains, that it was difficult to write without making everything soggy. Miraculously, I managed to grab a seat and finish the article, and I had enough power on the laptop to type it up. However, the signal was not strong enough to allow me to email the piece and then the battery packed up and I was thrown back on the manuscript, with all its crossings-out.

It was now coming up to early evening, and I was terrified that I was going to let down the families because of a combination of inefficiency, bad luck and technological collapse. I rang the *Mail* and they told me to dictate it. Outside was thunder and lightning and torrential rain lashing against the window. To dictate meant having to shout, so I left the carriage and hid in a lavatory yelling until an enraged banging on the door forced me to leave. I stood outside between compartments and, in the midst of a crowd of interested passengers, tried to communicate with a brilliant but challenged copytaker. Eight years on, I can still remember with a shudder – as well as a laugh – the difficulty of trying to communicate the sentence: 'Emboldened by the apparent impotence of the two governments, the evil men of the Real IRA were soon crawling out from under the stones where they had hidden after Omagh.' The biggest problem was with the word 'impotence'. My voice was going by now and by the time I had screamed the word four or five times, I could not look any of the people around me in the eye.

It was an enormous relief when, the following morning, I saw the printed article: the accompanying photograph of Breda Devine in her Babygro, bottle in hand, concentrating as she tried to stand up with the help of a steadying hand from behind, brought tears to my eyes. It still does.

Her parents, Paul and Tracey, were featured the next day, telling the story of how Breda died and of how her mother, uncle and his fiancée were terribly burned. Although Donna Marie Keyes still had to wear a face mask, she and Garry McGillion had married in March 1999. Tracey, too, was still in great pain and faced many more operations and skin grafts. During her six weeks of unconsciousness, said Paul, 'pieces of shrapnel were dropping from Tracey's body. Doctors couldn't remove them because of the extent of the burns. They had to wait for them to fall out naturally and the police gathered them for forensic tests.' Like the other parents, the Devines were helping with the campaign in the hope of saving other families from going through what they had suffered.

One week after the launch of the campaign, the *Mail* reported that readers had sent in £60,000. Ten days later it was up to £100,000. We were, of course, touched that so many people had been generous, but in truth we had hoped for much more. It was clear now that, on the fundraising front, we were in for a very, very long haul.

CHAPTER TWELVE

TAKING THE FIGHT
TO THE ENEMY

'They came knocking on our doors four years ago, and it's our time to go knocking on theirs. Perhaps now they will understand what it's like to be living under pressure' – Michael Gallagher

As well as the problems about the law and the money, we were pre-occupied with the political. The backdrop to the launch of the *Mail* campaign was yet another high noon at the Stormont seat of the devolved Northern Ireland government. Facing a revolt from his party ranks because of the IRA's refusal to start decommissioning, First Minister Trimble was threatening to exclude the two Sinn Féin ministers from statutory meetings with the Irish government. Adams's response had been that demands for decommissioning were 'stupid and unattainable'.

In my *Mail* article of 30 October 2000 I had touched on an issue that concerned three governments, had been preoccupying the Omagh group, its lawyers and supporters for months and about which Victor had written myriad letters. Sounding as angry as Victor, I recalled that, when in Omagh, Bill Clinton had 'promised the survivors and the bereaved that he would do everything in his power to help them:

> To date, he has not even put the Real IRA on the U.S. state department's list of terrorist organisations. So those Irish-Americans who think little Breda and children like her don't matter are free to go on funding her murderers without fear of interference from their government.
>
> There is, we are told by state department spokesmen, no policy against putting the Real IRA on the list; they just haven't got round to it.
>
> And it seems the Irish Government has also been resisting listing these terrorists on the flimsy excuse that it might give them the oxygen of publicity. Balderdash! This is appeasement.

In the last week of September 2000, Sean, Henry and I had gone to Washington to lobby on this very issue. Travelling to the United States with ex-convicts is a pain: both Sean and Henry had to apply for visas, provide a full itinerary and stick to it rigidly. I had been through all this with Sean in 1997, just a few weeks after he came out of jail. With the help of the *Sunday Times* and an old friend, the journalist John O'Sullivan, then editor of the New York *National Review*, I had set up for Sean a speaking and briefing tour which took us to Washington, New York, Boston, Chicago, Los Angeles, San Francisco and – improbably – Muncie, Indiana, where my close friend Kathryn Kennison organises events for Ball State University.

The purpose of the tour was to tell influential people about the brutal reality behind the romantic image so carefully cultivated by Sinn Féin and the Provisional IRA, so there were many radio and television interviews, and among those we met were Senator John McCain (who bonded with Sean discussing solitary confinement), the boards of several newspapers (including *Reader's Digest*), many prominent journalists, State Department officials and foreign policy experts: *National Review* also put on a debate with Sinn Féin's friend Congressman Peter King, who a year later would help Bernadette Sands-McKevitt find an audience on Capitol Hill. We asked to see the Irish Ambassador, Dermot Gallagher, whom I knew, more for mischief than anything else, and were curtly refused. My unhelpful criticism of paramilitaries in print and on radio and television had made me a *persona* so *non grata* that, on orders from Dublin, I had been dropped from the London Embassy party list: Sean O'Callaghan and his inconvenient truths about his old colleagues were the stuff of their nightmares.

We had made good contacts and friends and built on those relationships over the next few years. Now we sought to use our network to damage the Real IRA: the objective was to have them upgraded from being listed as terrorists in the State Department's *Patterns of Global Terrorism 1999* to being designated as an FTO (Foreign Terrorist Organisation), along with their front organisations. Designation would make it a crime under US law to provide funds, weapons or any kind of tangible support: it would also hinder fundraising by alerting Irish-America to the ugly activities of the 32 County Sovereignty Movement and the Irish Republican Prisoners' Welfare Association.

In 2000 we did not even bother to contact the new Irish Ambassador, Sean Ó hUigínn, who I believed had made his hostility to me clear and thought me unpatriotic because of my friendship with unionists, particularly David Trimble. As for Sean, Irish embassies were now welcoming former terrorists as guests of honour, but Sean O'Callaghan, who had worked for the Irish state, was shunned to placate the Provisionals in the perceived interest of the wider peace process. Some Irish diplomats privately thought this was a disgrace, but they did not include Ó hUigínn. Besides, we had reason to believe it was Ó hUigínn's influence that had caused the Irish government to resist having these organisations designated on the grounds that it would make them martyrs.

With a short detour to speak in Muncie, Indiana, the three of us spent a few days in Washington, DC, making the case privately, with the support of Robert Cranborne, who was there at the same time and had breakfast with us and a slew of influential sympathisers. I am not particularly disciplined, and, like Sean and Henry, have no sense of direction, but compared to them I am an organisational genius. 'How the hell did you two ever manage to rob banks, or whatever it was you did?' I have sometimes asked them through gritted teeth.

They are both, however, highly articulate and compelling, so, despite the disasters that included Sean losing the pad with all relevant names and phone numbers, our time in Washington bore fruit. It was clear from both the State Department and the FBI that they were putting the necessary wheels in motion. What was critical, though, was to ensure that neither the British nor the Irish government put spokes in them, so Victor and Michael continued to apply pressure.

Peter Mandelson, reported Michael Seamark, on the day the *Mail* launched its appeal, would that day be meeting representatives of the OSSHG. 'They will ask him to back the *Mail*'s appeal, and urge him to persuade the Irish government to back moves to put the Real IRA on the U.S. list of global terrorists.'

The families were by now disillusioned with politicians and did not expect much of Mandelson. They did not appreciate that, although in a world of New Labour pragmatists, he was genuinely repelled by terrorists. Answering a cantankerous letter of Victor's in June 2000, Mandelson had condemned the 'insensitivity' of Adams's letter refusing cooperation. In July, he wrote that the safety of the people of Northern Ireland was the government's top priority and that it 'had indeed been prepared to face considerable political pressure about the level of security in areas like South Armagh because of our recognition that dissident republicans still pose a potent threat'. What he did not say was that he was resisting pressure from Tony Blair and Jonathan Powell in Downing Street to give Sinn Féin more concessions on what was known as 'normalisation' and in practice meant the removal of observation posts that discommoded Slab Murphy and his criminal gang. On the police bill relating to the RUC's future, Mandelson told the *Guardian* later, 'No. 10 was always saying, "Give more, do more, concede more."'[1]

What Victor did not know, either, was that, where Mo Mowlam, the People's Minister, was rather cold of heart, Mandelson could be very warm. There had been gossip in the civil service when on an official visit he refused to revisit the Holocaust Museum in Israel because it had affected him so profoundly when he first went there.

Mandelson had visited Omagh before to meet local dignitaries. This time, he told me later, 'I asked to meet representatives of the Omagh victims' families who had been corresponding with me since I came into office. There was a slightly tense relationship, I felt, between them and the NIO [Northern Ireland Office], perhaps not surprisingly. The office had not been encouraging to me when I said that I wanted to meet them when I was in Omagh. But I thought it was for the best.'

Mandelson was right about the NIO, which had been encouraged by Mowlam to play down expectations of bringing the bombers to justice. Hence, civil servants feared that if their ministers did more than the necessary minimum with victims' families, this would give them the oxygen of publicity, with who knew what consequences. Blair and Powell would have agreed.

But Mandelson insisted. At the Bridge Centre he met grief counsellors, people from the trauma centre and other victims' support groups, and then he had a private lunch with Michael and Stanley. By then he was in turmoil. 'I had been invited to see the artwork that some of the victims' children had done in their bereavement therapy. I was completely unprepared emotionally for this. I can see it in my mind to this day. I was alone in the room. When I came out I didn't know what to do, I was so speechless. I was led into a dining area where everything was laid out for lunch by Michael and Stanley who closed the door and I just broke down. They were very understanding. I had come to offer them help, instead they comforted me. I don't remember what happened after but I stayed for some time.'

For the relatives, there was no doubt about Mandelson's sincerity. 'Peter

Mandelson is the nicest man, the best man,' recalled Stanley to me long afterwards. 'He is my man. Nobody better. I have all the time in the world for Peter Mandelson. He cried, he cried in there with Michael and me and he put everybody out of there, even his Private Secretary. All politicians want to do is look after themselves. They don't care about anything, but Peter Mandelson did care.'

The *Mail* got their photograph of Mandelson's grief-stricken face, and when Seamark asked him if he would back the civil action they also got from him a response that must have annoyed many of his colleagues and civil servants. 'When people act against people they suspect, using the law to do so, that is what separates us out as democrats from those who undertook this atrocity in the first place,' he said. 'I understand the frustration these families have and they have my profound sympathy. Anything that brings pressure on the bombers and invites people to make available the vital evidence and the vital information that we need to put a prosecution in place, I can't criticise.'

> I feel a sense of responsibility. I'm not a police investigator. I'm not a prosecutor. I'm not a judge. I am a politician, a minister who feels the sadness of the families. I feel a tremendous sense of loss every day I wake up and find yet another day has passed without these prosecutions we want taking place.

'This week I went once again to Omagh,' he went on to write days later in an otherwise standard we-must-all-support-the-Good-Friday-Agreement article. 'It was a visit I will quite simply never forget. Two years after the bomb when 29 people were blown up, feelings in the town are raw. Last month's inquest has brought the memories of what happened on that awful day back with a vengeance.

'Despite all the wonderful work by care workers, people are weary. Weary of having to cope with the enormity of the catastrophe, weary that they are known worldwide for only one thing. Weary, too, of waiting for the bombers to be tried and convicted.'

By then he had also met Victor, who bombarded him with specific questions which covered *inter alia* the foreign terrorist list, the attitude of the Irish government, problems with the gardaí, why Seamus Daly had not been arrested, the possible use of intercept evidence, the possibility of sending Marian Price back to jail for infringing her parole conditions by making incendiary speeches, Victor's desire to meet the head of MI5 and many more. Earlier that day a policeman in County Down had been badly injured by a Real IRA bomb: Mandelson promised Victor that he would fight to have them designated by the US. 'I know there is little I can do to assuage your pain or anger,' wrote Mandelson to him later, 'but I welcomed the chance to hear your views and, I hope, to address them.' And address them he did to the best of his ability. Victor and the Omagh group at last had at a real friend at court.

Trimble was sympathetic, too. This is the exchange in the House of Commons on 8 November 2000, when Mandelson had just congratulated whoever was about to be the President Elect of the United States.

> **Mr David Trimble (Upper Bann):** While endorsing the Secretary of State's comments on President Clinton and his successor, whoever that might be, can I urge him to make the strongest possible representations to the present and future incumbents of the White House on the failure of the State Department to list the so-called Real IRA as a terrorist organisation? In a week in which we have received a police warning that more Omaghs may be committed by that organisation, can he say to the American Administration that people throughout the British Isles cannot understand why the State Department is not classifying that organisation in the way that it should?

> **Mr Mandelson:** I am grateful to the Right Hon. Gentleman for raising that issue. We need constantly to bear down on the Real IRA and other dissident paramilitary groups, by all available means. When I was in the United States in September, I expressed the hope that the United States authorities would add the Real IRA to their list of designated terrorist organisations. I believe that that would frustrate the funding that the group receives from America and, crucially, assist us in carrying out any necessary prosecutions of that organisation in the United States. I am continuing to discuss that issue with my Irish opposite numbers because, clearly, the prospects of securing that outcome will be much enhanced if the British and Irish Governments act together in making a joint submission.

On this vitally important question, Mandelson was again out of line with Downing Street, who, it emerges from Jonathan Powell's memoirs, were relaxed about the Real IRA; they came up in negotiations only when Sinn Féin wanted to use them as a bogeyman to explain why they could not decommission or join the police board, for example.

The Omagh group were well on the case. Jason had organised a meeting with Michael J. Sullivan, the American Ambassador in Dublin, at the beginning of November – to which Davidaire Horsford had escorted several families – where it became clear that Sullivan was following the Irish government's line that designating the Real IRA could be counterproductive. He explained his position by letter to Michael, and had a learned and lengthy rebuttal from Jason. Briefing of the opposition in Dublin had led to a useful row in the Dáil, with the then Foreign Minister (now Taoiseach), Brian Cowen, expressing bitter resentment at the suggestion by the opposition leader, John Bruton, that there were 'undenied reports' that the government was lobbying US officials not to designate the Real IRA.

Other new allies of the Omagh group were strengthening their political arm. Gary Kent, a Labour Party researcher who had done much to educate his party on the realities of Northern Ireland, would effectively become an unpaid parliamentary lobbyist for the families. He had the sympathetic MP for whom he worked, Harry Barnes, put down a question asking the Secretary of State for Northern Ireland what assessment he had made of links between the 32 County Sovereignty Committee and the Real IRA. Adam Ingram replied for Mandelson by saying 'the Government believe that they are two sides of the same coin. The 32 County Sovereignty Committee is RIRA's political wing, and as such the two are inextricably linked.' We seized on that for a protest against the 32CSM three days later.

The group of activists within the OSSHG who were bent on legal action now called themselves 'the Omagh Victims' Legal Action Group' (OVLAG). Their target on 25 November 2000 was the Cock Tavern in Euston, where they had learned that the 32CSM were holding 'a function in aid of republican prisoners and their dependants', held in solidarity with the Turkish DHKC:* the entertainment included music, a raffle for prizes including crafts made by 'Irish political prisoners in Portlaoise Gaol' and speeches by republicans and representatives of the Cuba Solidarity Group and the Turkish-Kurdish Political Prisoner Committee, supporters of the PKK.† The event was timely. The previous day, the Irish government had

---

* Devrimci Halk Kurtulus Cephesi, the Revolutionary People's Liberation Front organisation, is the political wing of the DHKP-C (Devrimci Halk Kurtulus Partisi Cephesi), the Revolutionary People's Liberation Party Front.
† Partiya Karkerên Kurdistan, the Kurdistan Workers' Party.

finally caved in to the relentless lobbying and had issued a joint statement with the British calling for the US government to include the Real IRA on its list of 'foreign terrorist organisations': the DHKC and the PKK were already on that list.

To students of the Provisionals, it was no surprise to learn that the Real IRA should be keeping such company. It is another tradition of Irish Republican armies to make friends indiscriminately with any foreign organisations that will help them kill people at home. During the Second World War, for instance, the IRA were allies of the Nazis: the chief of staff, Sean Russell (still a Sinn Féin icon), died in 1940 from a burst ulcer on a U-boat taking him to Ireland from Germany, where he had been holding discussions on sabotage operations in Ireland and had undergone explosives training: he was Ireland's Quisling-designate. The Provisionals remain close to the Basque terrorists of ETA, and in the past – this organisation admired by many Irish-Americans – received money and help from Syria, East Germany, Libya and Soviet military intelligence. Even after the Provisional IRA ceasefire and the Good Friday Agreement, members of the Provisional IRA were training FARC – Colombian narco-terrorists – in the use of modern explosives, including car bombs.

That November evening, Sean was in a car with Henry down the street, briefing journalists on his phone, but keeping well away from the families, most of whom he had not yet met, and even further away from Real IRA supporters. I was in the background with Jason, Davidaire and Michael Seamark of the *Daily Mail*.

The Barkers, Michael Gallagher, Liz and Caroline Gibson, Stanley McCombe, Godfrey and Ann Wilson and their daughter Denise and her boyfriend Gary Kerrigan were there that night, initially holding a candlelit vigil outside the pub. Some carried placards with photographs of their dead; others held notices saying 'Attention. Real IRA fundraising in this pub. Purpose? Fundraising for murder.' Then, at 8.00 p.m., just as the function was due to have started, the families marched into the pub followed by journalists, photographers and camera crews. Michael handed to the woman behind the bar a letter which I had written for the group. 'In your public house tonight,' it said, 'money is being raised by supporters of terrorists.'

The Real IRA bombed Omagh on 15 August 1998 and murdered our loved ones. Their political front, the 32-County Sovereignty Committee – who the government confirm are inextricably linked to RIRA – have organised

a fundraising meeting here tonight. Among their speakers is a representative of the DHKC, classified by the US government as a 'Foreign Terrorist
Group'.

We cannot believe that you would knowingly condone money being
raised on your premises that could finance other RIRA attacks like Omagh,
or like the three that have already been launched in London this year.

For more than two years, we have worked for peace in Ireland. For the
sake of the dead, and to safeguard the living, please honour our vigil by
stopping this fundraising now.

We hope the people in the meeting will show us the respect that we are
prepared to show them. If there is any violent reaction from them we will
have to call the authorities.

The Omagh Victims' Legal Action Group

As the shocked woman read the letter, Liz Gibson pulled the plug out
from the juke box and Victor and Jason ran upstairs and tried to crash the
function. Barred by bouncers, they demanded to speak to a representative of the 32CSM and, to universal incredulity, Francie Mackey, their
Omagh hate-figure, emerged with two shaven-headed minders. Mackey
is hardened, but he was visibly shocked. Five times Victor asked him to
condemn the bombing, and five times Mackey refused. 'It is by your own
silence,' said Victor, 'that you are condemned.' Mackey's sheepish offer
to meet some of the families back in Omagh, 'to discuss my own political
analysis', was contemptuously dismissed.

The few people drinking downstairs were looking on in astonishment
when the emotional intensity was turned up by Donna-Maria Barker, who
climbed on a chair, waved the placard at them and tearfully shouted, 'These
people killed my beautiful boy. I feel so angry.' Liz Gibson sobbed as she
asked the pub landlord: 'Please will you throw them out?' It was moving
and dramatic and all transmitted live by Sky Television.

While the landlord and landlady made it clear they had known nothing
about the people using the room, and that they would not be letting
them come again, they did not feel able to try to throw out the undesir-
ables inside. Indeed, it was the families who were ejected when about
fifteen police in riot vans arrived and told them the rights of those
holding a private meeting had to be protected. Some officers made it
clear where their sympathies lay, but that was little consolation for the
relatives, who felt, once again, that the law was on the wrong side. Shocked

by the discovery of who had hired their room, the proprietor would write a heartfelt letter of apology to the families.

Outside the pub relatives took it in turn to address the cameras and give quotes to journalists. 'This group,' said Stanley McCombe, 'is openly meeting for a night of fun and fundraising in the very city where their friends have tried three times to bomb innocent people since Omagh.' 'It's very, very difficult to deal with,' said Michael Gallagher. 'There is no accountability for the money that is being raised tonight. In the past, money raised in America and elsewhere has ended up buying bullets and Semtex. I believe the 32 County Sovereignty Movement has an agenda to keep the bodybag in Irish politics.' 'We will not let them live Omagh down,' said Victor. 'We are here to challenge them until we get justice.' And Jason McCue spelled out that the result of this night's work, beamed across the world by Sky, CNN and Fox TV, was that the public would know 'that the 32 County Sovereignty Committee, who are inextricably linked with the Real IRA, are having a meeting here in the heart of London.' It would, too, put more pressure on the US government.

David Trimble was one of those delighted at the media coverage of the event. He publicly congratulated the families on their courage: 'The relatives of the dead and injured from Omagh are an inspiration to all of us who want to see an end to terrorist violence in these islands. Their fight to see the perpetrators of the bombing brought to justice and to stop their political wing growing deserves the support of everyone.' There were two distinct groups who were less than pleased. First, of course, there were the Real IRA supporters, horrified by footage and photographs of Mackey at bay and headlines like the *Sun*'s 'OMAGH SHOWDOWN "Real IRA" pub bash stormed by mums'.

Bernadette Sands-McKevitt issued a statement: true to the logic of Orwell's totalitarian ruler in *Nineteen Eighty-Four*, it defended the right of the 32CSM to freedom of political expression, and condemned Trimble: his 'active encouragement of those who attempted to thwart that right was irresponsible and questionable. Using the Omagh tragedy as a political tool to undermine opposition to the faltering Stormont Deal is an abuse of the victims' suffering.'

Less predictable, but no less important, were the decent people for whom Councillor Paddy McGowan spoke when he regretted that Omagh 'wouldn't be left alone and "left to rest for a while"': he would prefer to have the town seen in a positive light rather than experiencing so much negative publicity. 'The people should be allowed to grieve in peace.' Apart from those who embrace victimhood for political reasons, rural Ulster people have been prone to licking their wounds in private: it was becoming increasingly clear to members of the Omagh group that many of their neighbours resented their campaign. They were not, however, in any mood to take much notice.

In a highly emotional state, the relatives left around 9.30 p.m. with Jason and Davidaire to go to the bar in their hotel, and I followed with Sean, whom none except Victor had yet even seen and who was distinctly nervous about their likely response. There had been no problem with Victor. As far as he was concerned, Henry and Sean had paid their debts to society and he was grateful for their commitment, help and friendship. For the Omagh-based families, we knew it would be much more difficult. They themselves had had to park a great deal of baggage to become a unit: quite apart from their religious differences, they crossed a wide political spectrum, from dogged supporters of Ian Paisley, determined to stay in the United Kingdom, to constitutional nationalists of the SDLP who dreamed of a United Ireland. What bound them together was a hatred of terrorism, and we could not know how they would cope with the discovery that their core group of London supporters and fundraisers included two ex-paramilitaries.

Since the Brennan's Bar protest, they knew Henry, though only a few were aware of his past. Sean was a different matter. As a member of the ruthless East Tyrone brigade, it was in a pub in Omagh at the age of nineteen that, on the orders of a commanding officer, he had murdered face-to-face a decent policeman he wrongly believed was a torturer. His 1998 autobiography had been a bestseller, so there was no keeping his past a secret. On the positive side, the religious nature of Northern Irish society is such that the concept of redemption is widely understood and Sean had been atoning for his crimes for many years. Ian Paisley had shown that he lived up to his belief that a repentant sinner must be forgiven by meeting and talking to Sean, as had many Ulster Protestants including other unionist politicians and police. And Sean had become close to David Trimble, who was happy to be seen with him in the House of Commons and his First Minister's office in Stormont. But they were politicians, not victims.

Sean and I had found a corner away from where the families had gathered, and I left him there and found Victor. 'We'll do this by degrees,' he said. 'I'll tell Michael the story and bring him over. He'll be all right about

Sean.' And he did, and Michael was. Indeed, it was striking how warmly Michael greeted Sean. As far as he was concerned, the past was the past and anyone who wanted to help the families was a friend. Stanley McCombe saw it the same way, so we felt reasonably confident that in time Sean would be accepted. We moved away from our corner and joined the main group.

It was late November 2000, and we had begun to form a coherent, if eccentric, group of families and supporters. Now all we needed was a million or two.

CHAPTER THIRTEEN

FUNDING IT

'Think about it. We must have been mad. We were English lawyers trying to bring a case for which there was no case law, against the Real IRA who were bombing London, on behalf of victims who had no money, who had suspects that the police could not bring to criminal prosecution; we were basically running around raising money for lawyers, and everyone hates lawyers. Talk about "Carry on Campaigning"' – Jason McCue

The success of the London protest and the Irish government's capitulation on the issue of designating the Real IRA as a foreign terrorist organisation had given the families and their supporters so much heart and confidence as to induce a sense of premature euphoria, manifested in our belief that Bill Clinton could be persuaded to meet relatives on his visit to Ireland in December 2000, as his second term was about to end. But Clinton was on a lap of honour and wanted to be feted by large crowds, not required to sympathise with small groups: even letters to the US Embassy were unanswered.

The Omagh families who took their placards to Dundalk on 12 December in the hope of attracting Clinton's attention stood in cold rain for four hours, lost in a crowd of around 60,000. When the cavalcade arrived, they could see Gerry Adams step forward to kiss and hug Hillary. The speech was vintage Clinton, complete with poetry and sentiment and high ideals: 'To Unionists and Nationalists, native-born Irish and immigrants, to all of you, I say again, you cannot win by making your neighbour lose. Two years ago, after the horrid bombing in Omagh, you good people filled these streets. Young people came, not wanting to lose their dreams. Older people came because they wanted a chance to live in peace before they rest in peace. You stared violence in the face and said, "No more." You stood up for peace then, and I ask you, stand up for peace today, tomorrow and the rest of your lives.' And then, moist-eyed, he sang 'Danny Boy' along with the crowd and left, and the families trailed back to Omagh.

More discouragement had come that month from a wise man in Washington who Robert had suggested should be consulted about our plan for a January fundraising campaign in the US. 'What you are trying to do is very commendable,' wrote Robert's old friend Chet Nagle to Jason early in December, 'and certainly of great interest in the UK – where the issues are immediate and close to home for everyone. In the US, however, no one (with few exceptions) can even spell Omagh, or knows where it is, or cares to learn. The attention span of the US public is notoriously short in matters of foreign affairs, unless the interests of the Republic (or their individual economic well-being) are obviously threatened or injured.'

> An orchestrated national, regional, or city-wide campaign for *anything*, be it political, charitable, or commercial, is complicated and *expensive*. In my untutored opinion, such a campaign as yours, managed from the UK on a shoestring, is simply not going to succeed very much in any direction in the US. I am not happy to be so pessimistic, but the facts are the facts.
>
> The tragedy in Omagh, the suffering of the families, the political ramifications of it all, and in fact, the entire Irish question engender little or no interest in anyone except some specialised bureaucrats, certain politicians (mostly unfriendly to your cause) and some media people – but only on the day of the explosion, if there is enough blood and excitement. You are very close to the issue, and so it may be difficult for you, perhaps, to see these trees in the US forest.

Nagle's hardheaded and specific questions and suggestions were sobering, yet we nevertheless felt that a modified American visit had to go ahead. *Tonight with Trevor McDonald*, ITV's flagship current affairs programme, had promised to send its famous foreign correspondent Michael Nicholson to cover it, and for fundraising purposes we needed the publicity and we needed it as soon as possible. It would be a constant feature of the campaign that we had to devise stunts to keep the media interested, while rarely being able to plan them with anything like the necessary time and care. The writs had to be issued before the third anniversary of the bomb in August 2001, or proceedings would risk being statute-barred, there was an enormous amount of work to be done beforehand to decide whom to sue and on what basis, and all that ate up money. London solicitors are very expensive, the cost of London barristers makes one's eyes water, and the highly experienced investigator Barrie Penrose, who was helping to gather evidence, was not cheap. At Henry Hepworth alone, Jason, Lucy and Davidaire had been on the case almost full-time, with two others part-time, which left them unavailable for other, more lucrative, work. It was certainly surreal that Jason had to help raise money to pay himself, his colleagues and Matrix Chambers, and that, since his firm was struggling to cope with a case of this size and complexity, he had no option but to charge for the time he spent on political lobbying and relations with the press.

Putting together an American itinerary for early January 2001 which would include both private meetings with officials and public drama for the camera was a lot to undertake in mid-December. The process was not helped by Jason, Sean and Henry disappearing to a conference in Palermo on the UN Convention against Transnational Organised Crime. For Jason, the conference was an opportunity to interest the anti-terrorist world in his idea of using Omagh as a test case to develop the potential of civil law as a weapon against terrorism; Sean was already an occasional performer and networker on the international counter-terrorism circuit; and for Henry, Palermo was hallowed ground: his great hero for many years had been Giovanni Falcone, the Palermo magistrate who fearlessly and effectively cracked down on the Sicilian mafia by following the money trail and confiscating ill-gotten gains but was blown up in a revenge murder in 1992. For years afterwards, Henry had been haranguing his friends about the virtues of investigative magistrates. After a few days back in London, Jason left for whitewater rafting and Christmas in Costa Rica with friends, leaving Sean calling American contacts and – with Davidaire's help – trying in the few working days around Christmas and the New Year to sort out a sensible itinerary.

Victor, meanwhile, thought a woman should go instead of him, and there was simply not enough time to organise a visa for Sean. So, in the end, Davidaire travelled with Michael on 7 January to meet Jason in Washington. Sean and I sat anxiously at Heathrow briefing them on the people they would meet, who ranged from an official of the US Senate select committee on intelligence to a Real IRA sympathiser.

Those on Capitol Hill to whom Jason and Michael made their pitch for designating the Real IRA included staffers for the Foreign Relations Committee and from the offices of Ted Kennedy and John Kerry, presidential candidate-to-be: Michael was greatly moved to find that Richard Norland, the Director of European Affairs at the National Security Council who was an adviser on the peace process, had a photograph on his wall of Clinton and Blair in Omagh. There was a lunch with the influential *Reader's Digest* bureau chief William Schulz; John O'Sullivan, then Editor-in-Chief of the news agency United Press International, arranged a sympathetic in-depth interview which went out on the wires; my friend Janet McIver – who as an employee of the British Foreign Office had worked for years in New York and Washington combating Sinn Féin propaganda – introduced them to old colleagues; they even got to meet Ambassador Ó hUigínn; and for the benefit of the cameras they visited an Irish pub.

Davidaire, whose job was to fix timings, locations and transport, spent a lot of time trying to persuade uninterested New Yorkers to interview Michael. She was taken aback by the unthinking racism of the Radio Free Éireann contact:

> I was talking about the terrible tragedy of Omagh and he said to me, 'What's it got to do with you? Where do you come from?'
>
> 'I come from London,' I said. He said. 'You don't have a London accent.' I said. 'No, I live in London but I'm from the Caribbean, from Antigua.'
>
> 'Why don't you go and help look for the person who killed Damilola Taylor?'* he asked. 'Because this stuff is nothing to do with you. Leave Ireland for the Irish.'

When Irish-American republican sympathisers split over the Belfast Agreement, Radio Free Éireann had gone with the Continuity IRA and its appendages. Fluent though he was, Michael's broadcast interview with its founder, John McDonagh, probably won no converts, but his confrontation with the fifty-seven-year-old antique-dealer, fourth-generation-Irish Dorothy Robinson made good television for a programme that would be given the title 'Dorothy's Dollars'. She had been interviewed by Michael Nicholson in a New York hotel before being ambushed in the lobby by Michael Gallagher and the production team; reluctantly she agreed to speak before the cameras.

Robinson was typical of a kind of Irish-American cheerleader for violent republicanism that I knew all too well: ignorant of Ireland, carrying an anti-British ancestral grudge, adherents of the MOPE (Most Oppressed People Ever') narrative of Irish history, without any sense of perspective,

---

* Stabbed casually by black English children in a grim London housing estate in November 2000, ten-year-old Nigerian Damilola Taylor bled to death in a stairwell.

impervious to facts or logical argument, worshippers of a pantheon of republican heroes who had never been sullied by compromise, and unmoved by the suffering of anyone other than those whom they slavishly supported.

On my first encounter with a trio of such true believers – two cross women and an amiable man – I tried to stay civil when I found none had ever even visited Ireland; the most aggressive then snarled that I had not one drop of Irish blood in my veins, for in that world if your blood is thought to be insufficiently green, it is self-evidently not Irish. Fearful of losing my cool, I left. Despite greater provocation, Michael did much better with tunnel-visioned republicans. His natural skills as a communicator had been enhanced by his extensive experience of the media and although he sometimes lost his temper in private meetings with politicians, he had learned well how to keep it in public and how to simplify his message. Faced – probably for the first time – with a victim of republican brutality, Robinson, who admitted freely that she did not even recognise 'the Free State' government or acknowledge the gardaí as a legitimate police force, was embarrassed into condemning the Omagh bomb;* she denied she raised money for the Real IRA but made no apology for continuing to do so for its front groups.

Jason had listed the objectives of the visit as:

- To continue and intensify the campaign to get the RIRA on the FTO list
- To send a message to the terrorists and their supporters that victims too have a voice and will let it be heard
- To highlight the fundraising activity by the RIRA in the USA and to show their growing support both at home and in the USA
- To bring back to the forefront of the minds of Irish-Americans the devastation of the Omagh bomb which happened over two years ago
- To meet with other victim groups
- To highlight the global nature of terrorism
- To gain support for the civil action
- To raise funds.

---

* In a letter to the *Ulster Herald* she said that this was 'possibly an unpopular statement in Republican circles, but that's too bad', which gave some indication of the company she kept.

Jason and Michael proved persuasive, and in May 2001, to our delight and our enemies' consternation, the Real IRA would be designated by Secretary of State Colin Powell along with the 32CSM and the Irish Republican Prisoners' Welfare Association.* But, in truth, few of Jason's objectives were met: the visit confirmed how right Chet Nagle had been. It was eight months before 9/11, by and large Americans had little interest in terrorism and mainstream Irish-Americans were now dancing to the Sinn Féin tune, which precluded them from backing a campaign dismissed by Adams and his cohorts as unhelpful to the peace process. As for financing the case, we could forget about the US. Through a bank account set up for us by campaign supporter, the historian Joseph Skelly, we had an occasional gift of a few hundred dollars, but when it came to raising serious money we now knew we were on our own. The families' hopes were briefly raised in May 2001, when, on his way to what was to be the Clinton Peace Centre in Enniskillen, Clinton met members of the OSSHG and offered to help them raise money in the US, but nothing ever came of it. A message of support from President Bush a year later was encouraging, but equally had no practical effect.

2001 had begun with Michael and Patsy Gallagher and Victor and Donna-Maria Barker holding a vigil outside Downing Street on the evening of New Year's Day, where Ahern and Blair were discussing the latest crisis in the peace process. Sickened by a New Year message from the 32CSM that was both weasel-worded and bellicose, the families' press release said the assurances of the two prime ministers that the perpetrators of Omagh would be brought to justice and the Real IRA disbanded had 'proved hollow': instead, the organisation 'is flourishing. As recruits and funds increase, their effectiveness and arrogance grows. Only good luck has prevented further deaths.'

The month would end with the same little group in the same place, ignored by a series of embarrassed passers-by including the Deputy Prime Minister, John Prescott, Bertie Ahern and his Minister for Foreign Affairs, Brian Cowen. An OSSHG press release begged the British and Irish people to back the campaign.

* 'This action,' said the State Department, 'makes it illegal for persons in the United States, or subject to US jurisdiction, to provide material support to the Real IRA or any of its named aliases, requires US financial institutions to block assets of the designated groups and enables us to deny visas to representatives of the group.'

In the time between those two desperate bids for help there had been much activity. Colm Murphy's trial had been postponed for nine months because the Special Criminal Court was busy and his contempt of court proceedings against the *Daily Mail* and the BBC (over *Panorama*) had twice been adjourned.* Besides perpetrating various hoaxes, the Real IRA had planted a 1,100-pound landmine near Armagh city destined for but defused by the security forces, had narrowly missed killing two policemen with a bomb thrown at their car in Cookstown, County Tyrone, had planted a 100-pound bomb (defused) at the RUC station in the tragic little town of Claudy and had fired a mortar bomb packed with 200 pounds of home-made explosives over a security fence at Ebrington army barracks in Derry: it struck living quarters where thirty soldiers were sleeping, but failed to go off.

On the political front, there had been the shock resignation of Peter Mandelson on 24 January.† Within days Victor had written to the new Secretary of State, John Reid, asking for a meeting: 'As your predecessor will no doubt have warned you, there are many difficult, unpleasant and challenging tasks in your office, one of which is receiving correspondence from me!' Unknown to us, in his last few weeks in the job, Mandelson had been pressing hard for results on the investigation. He had not just been troubled, he wrote to me later, 'by the upset of the families and the sense of terrible loss. It was a feeling that not enough was happening to bring the perpetrators to trial. I had meetings with NIO security officials and at least twice with the Chief Constable. It was difficult. I was categorically assured that everything was being done to collect evidence against those suspected and that we had to be patient.'

He had raised the issue with the Irish authorities when he went to Dublin: 'I became agitated about the time it was taking and this became interpreted not only as impatience on my part but a belief on my part that people were not trying hard enough or that something was being covered up. I did not mean to give this impression, and I had no evidence for it.

* In January 2005 that with the BBC was settled when it said that, while it continued to deny contempt of court, it acknowledged that Murphy 'was fully entitled to maintain his innocence of the charges against him and to test the evidence against him at his trial'.
† Alleged to have used his influence to help an Indian billionaire obtain a British passport, Mandelson was forced out by a panicked response in Downing Street: he was later fully exonerated.

But I wanted to exert pressure and introduce some urgency.' And then he had to resign.

But while the loss of the campaign's only friend in Cabinet was a cause of distress, within a week he had given the self-help group a tremendous boost. At the end of his long article in the *Sunday Times* of 28 January explaining the sequence of innocent events that had led to his downfall, there was a note: 'A fee for this article will be donated to the campaign to prosecute the Omagh bombers': it was £10,000 and it brought us more publicity.

By now, we were in a desperate financial position. We had become aware early on that because £6 million had been donated to the Omagh Fund through concerts, sporting events, records and so on, the public felt they had made their contribution. Attempts by Victor and the OSSHG to persuade the Trustees of that Fund to help the legal case came to nothing: apart from anything else, their legal advice was that the funding of litigation was not a charitable purpose. The *Mail* appeal had generated around £150,000, which was not enough to pay outstanding bills let alone incur more. Chaos had ruled in the preceding few months. Henry Hepworth was in convulsions and there was no longer either a Henry or a Hepworth: it had been the bright idea of the ever-fashionable Jason to rename what was left of the firm H2O Law ('an essential element in your business'). In October I had arrived at Jason's office to be greeted by him and Sean begging me to provide them instantly with three volunteers to take legal responsibility for a trust to be called the Omagh Victims Legal Fund (OVLF), which would disburse the funds we raised: they were to come from Belfast, Dublin and London and include at least one Protestant and one Catholic.

London was easy. In my time writing about the Orange Order, my accountant and good friend Paul Le Druillenec, whose background was English and Anglican, had been my companion at a few parades, had come with me to Maghaberry jail to meet Sean, was well disposed towards the decent people of Northern Ireland and had helped with the 'Defend the RUC' campaign. Pedantic, idiosyncratic (he is the only person I know who refers to cabs as taximeter cabriolets) and kind, he worked mainly for satellite television companies and had a small firm. I knew him to be unconcerned with his physical safety, a prerequisite for being a Trustee. Fearless, too, was Dubliner Barbara Sweetman FitzGerald, a liberal Catholic who, as Secretary of the cross-border Irish

Association, did so much to encourage friendship between nationalists and unionists that she would eventually be awarded a CBE. It was Henry who suggested Sam McAughtry, a trades unionist from a Belfast Protestant background who became a distinguished writer and peace activist and had supported Henry's Families Against Intimidation and Terror: though he lived in Northern Ireland he had been appointed in 1996 to the Irish Senate.

There was malcommunication and muddle about the setting up of the Trust. With commendable calm, Paul wrote to Jason at the end of December 2000 to point out that just before Christmas the Trustees had received from H2O complex invoices (lawyers charge for each six minutes of their time) for fees and expenses of £75,000 during September and October, requesting urgent payment, along with 'engagement letters' for the three of them. 'I am not a lawyer, but my small knowledge tells me that we three Trustees are legally in charge of Trust Funds and personally liable if anything goes wrong with the actions taken in our name. It is also clear to me that I don't know what's going on and my fellow Trustees are relying on me to ensure that the Trust is properly administered.' He made suggestions for imposing some order. 'The Trustees will only proceed to authorise action to the extent that funds are available. If some action is undertaken which might involve losses in excess of funds available, then the Trustees will only authorise it if it is sponsored or the liabilities guaranteed by some substantial person or organisation. As in Jarndyce v. Jarndyce,* when the money runs out, the lawyers stop work.'

It would turn out that the 'engagement letters' – which were actually retainer letters – should have gone only to Victor, then the only client, and confusion was compounded by the same invoices going to Victor as had gone to the Trust. Jason's eight-page justification towards the end of January had the merit of explaining things clearly and being spattered with apologies, so Paul stayed on. An email from Jason to Paul, Henry, Davidaire and me on 25 January gives a flavour of the state we were in, how amateurish was the campaign, how dependent we were on volunteers and how much Jason despised capital letters:

* This fictional court case about a family inheritance featured in Charles Dickens's *Bleak House* dragged on for so many generations that almost the whole estate was swallowed up by legal costs.

all (inc. skip* and lc [Robert Cranborne])
many thanks for last night. to summarise:

all
- arrange fortnight meet. suggest a more private room.
- trust to employ fundraiser/media person.
- funding/campaign to be taken off h2o's hands.

h2o
- arrange omagh conference – counsel/trustees/clients
- draft foundation paper to be passed to lc/ruthy/p for input.

Paul
- to employ fundraiser – contract etc/trust rules

Henry
- client liaison manager with Davidaire
- visit families in near future – organise a coms. line/involve clients
- sell fundraiser to clients

Ruth
- help liaise with h2o/janet re foundations (please . . . I know it was not explicitly agreed at the meeting but . . .)
- fundraise/media/campaign

Sean
- fundraising/media/campaign
- dress code advice†

lc
- suggestions for fundraiser

if I have missed something important please remind me.

Once again, many thanks

---

* Skip was Sean. Since he was on the IRA hit list, as security sources kept reminding him, his friends devised nicknames for him to be used on the phone and in written communications. RUC friends referred to him as Sid, Jason and the lawyers called him Skip (because sometimes he did), Skips and Skippy, others called him Rose (as in Rose of Tralee), Minstrel (as in Wandering Minstrel, because he disappeared at times), the Reverend, Tellytubby (because he was skinny), Ambrose Golightly, the Brigadier, Red Eagle, Lord Tout, His Nibs, our mutual friend or Big Republican (as opposed to Baby Republican, who was Henry).
† This referred to the porters at the Reform, which has a strict dress code, having to provide Sean with a jacket and a tie.

The two Irish-based Trustees rapidly concluded that it would be impossible to sort out at long distance what was clearly a shambles and had the potential to cost them their houses; there was no acrimony when they resigned. They were replaced by two of my close friends in London. Máirín Carter, an apolitical Irish speaker from an Irish Catholic background, was events manager of the Institute of Mechanical Engineers in London. She had an emotional involvement with Omagh, as the bombing had happened on her fortieth birthday. 'It's easy to feel a bit sorry for yourself on a day like that,' she recalled, 'so the news from Northern Ireland was a bit of a reality check.' I had worked for John Lippitt, CB,* who is from a Church of England background, when I was a civil servant and he a number two at the Department of Industry; he now ran a consultancy. Máirín and John knew Paul, Sean and Henry and therefore had some idea what they were getting into.

There are several people without whom the Omagh case would never have come to trial, and Paul, Máirín and John were three of them. Paul's meticulous administrative ability was important, but so too was his courage in giving his office address for use in public appeals for the OVLF. Máirín is convivial and down to earth and would prove invaluable as the Trustees' main link with families, fundraisers and lawyers. She also has an unusual ability to cut to the heart of any issue, as has John, who is a risk-taker. At times of crisis and panic, John, who is extremely forceful, would propel Paul, who is cautious, and Máirín, who is risk-averse, into taking the perilous rather than the prudent decision. As Jason put it once: 'You've got to have someone who is just going to be a dogmatic pain in the arse and say "Fuck it, this is what we're doing." And that's what John did.' This would cause Máirín sleepless nights.

Peter Mandelson was also utterly central. In February 2001, Sean O'Callaghan's fertile imagination developed a plan for a Commons launch of a £1 million fundraising campaign for the Omagh Victims Legal Fund to be spearheaded by Mandelson and as many as possible of his predecessors as Secretary of State. Sean wanted to organise this himself, but there was a problem: although his behind-the-scenes political activity mostly involved seeking media support for David Trimble, he was also known to be no fan of New Labour, and Mandelson distrusted him. The solution was simple: in all Sean's phone conversations with Mandelson's office, he claimed to be Henry Robinson.

* Companion of the Bath.

Mandelson agreed readily to launch the legal fund publicly in mid-March 2001; he was already making its case at Question Time in the Commons. Having congratulated his successor John Reid on an excellent start, he continued: 'May I draw his attention to the financial appeal launched by victims and bereaved families in Omagh in pursuit of the civil action that they seek to take against the perpetrators of the bombing in 1998? I will not ask him to commit himself to that course of action, but will he take the opportunity to reaffirm the Government's good will towards the Omagh support group and the bereaved families? Will he reaffirm also the Government's determination to do everything in their power to bring the perpetrators of that atrocity to justice at the earliest possible time?'

> **Dr Reid:** Yes. I very much appreciate the fact that my Right Hon. Friend is here today . . . On the specific issue that he raised, I know that shortly after leaving office, he literally put his money where his mouth had been – his pocket had previously been sealed because he was a member of the Cabinet. I very much agree with the sentiments that he expressed, and we are examining ways in which we can further assist and support the victims of that terrible tragedy.

After much behind-the-scenes activity by Mandelson, Robert Cranborne, Gary Kent and others, an invitation had gone out to every MP and peer inviting them to meet bereaved relatives and ex-Secretaries of State for Northern Ireland on 14 March 2001 at an event hosted by three MPs* from different parties: if they could not attend, they were asked to sign the invitation to indicate public support and return it to Victor. The politicians' response was better than we could have hoped, not least because the Real IRA was back in the consciousness of Londoners. There had been the bombing of the BBC's White City offices on 4 March in revenge for the *Panorama* programme, and, much worse, the torch-bomb outside the Territorial Army barracks in White City on 21 February. Michael McKevitt had once bragged to a friend that he had invented the idea of filling a flashlight with plastic explosives and leaving it at a checkpoint: 'He said the Brit walked up and switched it on to see if it worked, bang, arm gone.'[2] This was the device that blew off the left hand and left ear of

---

* The English Dominic Grieve (Conservative and later Shadow Home Secretary), the Northern Irish Lembit Öpik (Liberal Democrat) and the Scots Malcolm Savidge (Labour).

fourteen-year-old army cadet Stephen Menary, ripped open his chest and stomach and left him blind and partially deaf.*

For the 14th, Sean had booked the Atrium, a restaurant across the road from the Houses of Parliament in a building which houses BBC, ITV and Sky studios. As arranged, Mandelson arrived outside the building promptly at midday to meet and pose with a line-up of relatives carrying placards. There was a tremendous turnout of cameras and journalists, an impromptu press conference on Palace Green nearby and several radio and television interviews. At lunch, journalists mingled with the families and many accompanied them to the meeting at the Commons where there was a good attendance of parliamentarians.

I had been dragooned by Sean into chairing the launch, of which my main memory is having to shut up the Reverend Ian Paisley – who never contributed a penny to the campaign – as he tried to hijack it. Mandelson described the Real IRA as having 'no shame, no conscience and no inhibition in carrying on their murderous activities', and was photographed with two Conservative predecessors, Peter Brooke and Tom King, and Labour's Lord Merlyn-Rees, signing a message of support;† several others – particularly Sir Patrick Mayhew and Lord Hurd – had lent their enthusiastic backing and most had contributed financially, albeit much more modestly than Mandelson.

The relatives were superb that day. By now, the self-help group had become what Henry Robinson, a connoisseur, judged probably the best

---

* He did not receive compensation until 2008; for total blindness he would have got £110,000, but half was docked by the Criminal Injuries Compensation Authority because he had lost his right eye to cancer as a baby.

† 'We, the undersigned ex-Secretaries of State for Northern Ireland, express our solidarity with the victims and bereaved families who were, in the words of Dr John Reid, our successor, left "bereft and distraught" by the terrible bombing of Omagh on 15 August 1998. Like Dr Reid, we deeply regret that despite the best efforts of the RUC and the Irish Gardaí, it has not yet been possible to bring the perpetrators of this atrocity to justice.

We applaud the courage of those families who are seeking to take a civil action against a number of suspects. In standing up to the Real IRA, they are standing up to a vicious group of murderers, who are still continuing their deadly work in Northern Ireland and London. In doing so they are doing us all a signal service and we owe them gratitude and help. Today, we publicly wish them every success, hereby pledge our financial and moral support and urge our fellow-citizens to contribute generously to their fund-raising appeal.'

community anti-terrorist group he had ever encountered. Unlike peace groups, which have a tendency to hold vigils and parade somewhat aimlessly with candles, this group knew exactly what it was about. His own organisation, Families Against Intimidation and Terror, retrospectively he thought had been too diffuse in its objectives, while the OSSHG was single issue: it networked but it did not take on others' baggage. What was more, while the leaders of most such groups tend to give up or move on, Michael Gallagher and the same core of allies had remained. And the Omagh Victims Legal Group was even more focused; its members were prepared to do anything legal in pursuit of justice.

The press coverage was generous and the money started to roll in. Paul's staff, his brother Simon and Sylvia Kalisch, were in their little mews office when the first Royal Mail van drew up outside and delivered a whole sack of mail, 'full', remembered Sylvia, 'of cheques, money, postal orders, letters and the occasional totally off-the-wall ranting. Can you remember our favourite guy who proclaimed to be a Catholic priest or some such and sent missives filled with hate and obscure theological justifications for those rants?' 'We have literally been inundated with cheques, cash and even gift vouchers,' wrote a euphoric Jason, whose office at times was an alternative address. 'The typical amount is £25, which is often accompanied by a letter apologising that they could not send more – some explain problems of their own. All in all it is all very touching and (not to be repeated) making me feel sentimental.' Most of us in London were writing pleading letters or emails to the potentially sympathetic: 'I don't usually touch my friends for my causes,' began mine, before trying to do just that.

The Trustees paid Sean expenses for those long periods when he gave all his time to corralling the media and hired Hugo Plowden – the son of a friend who wanted part-time work – to open the envelopes, bank the money, keep records and research relevant financial foundations and other possible sources to tap, and help me write mission statements, briefings, letters and press releases. 'It was learning on the job,' he wrote to me later. 'I once remember getting a banner made up somewhere in Tottenham, and them making it upside down (pole holes) but I only realised at the last minute and had to botch things up with scissors and a stapler.' After much frustration, he and Paul's team managed to set up a credit card hotline. Sylvia's favourite memory of the period is when the fund's bank insisted it must explain to the Trustees how to use telephone and internet banking. John Lippitt's default position on modern technology is hostility: 'I cannot think of one person and one cause less suited to each other,' recalled Sylvia, 'even though he liked trying to chat up the pretty bank official. In my mind, all I can hear is "Bollocks to that. Why do I have to remember a password? What is a PIN? I thought they are for sewing clothes with rather than stitching up honest money-generating bank customers. Go and speak to my secretary about this, I am about to be busy having lunch."'

Much of Hugo's work involved finding the contact details of likely rich Irish and English sympathisers. 'If my memory serves me correctly,' he wrote to me, 'you and I composed a letter to them asking for £1,000 from each, signed by Victor and Michael. I also remember the media packs I put together for the press launches – essentially photocopied articles, but the folder they were in was fairly captivating: completely black but with a list in white type of all the people who had been killed by the bomb.

> There were, of course, frequent meetings in H2O's office in Doughty Street where tactics would be discussed under the cloud of Jason's and Sean's cigarette smoke and I would take minutes that I'm not sure if anybody ever read!

Robert Cranborne has spent a lot of his time over many years hustling for money for good causes and he, meanwhile, knew donations from the public would not raise the amounts we needed. Even as he sent off the first of many rounds of begging letters, several of which brought in four-figure sums, he warned us that raising money for the Omagh civil case would be much harder than we expected: 'Terror terrifies,' he said bleakly. Even so, we were staggered to discover how many people were so scared of terrorists that they would not even contemplate contributing money. And we had very little luck in attracting experienced fundraisers to steer our amateur efforts.

Robert's old friend Lady Janie Dawnay, who had been brought up in Fermanagh on the estate of her father, the Duke of Westminster, was for thirteen years the Duchess of Roxburgh, and later married Robert's oldest friend, was a striking exception. As 'a local girl', she cared passionately about Omagh. When Robert put me in touch with her in February, she gave me great confidence. She was, she said, laughing, a dab hand at extracting large sums of money for good causes from the rich of Northern Ireland.

She was a marvellous recruit, who greatly enjoyed the bizarre mix of people in the Omagh support group, particularly Henry, who would even-tually buy one of her racehorses. But her optimism was soon tempered by disappointment and she began gloomily reporting to meetings what was by now all too familiar – that likely donors seemed convinced that the Real IRA would track them down and murder them in their beds. Even large corporations with armies of lawyers and wealthy individuals with off-shore accounts were convinced that terrorists would somehow find the source of an anonymous donation. Fearless herself, Janie was utterly bewildered by the extent of friends' cowardice. But then many people – when you ask them for money to help victims of terrorism – become terrified that those same terrorists will wreak vengeance on their families; the argument that members of the Real IRA were mostly stupid, tunnel-visioned provincials who would not know a bank draft from a cowpat rarely worked: 'I can't,' they would say. 'I can't put my family at risk.' Janie's charm, tenacity and ruthless emotional blackmailing of friends and relations did make a crucial difference, but it was a long, hard struggle. There were weeks when she visited or gave lunch to several different people and extracted nothing from them.

By early May 2001 we had raised around £220,000. MPs and peers had donated about £7,500, £5,000 of which had been given by David Trimble, cheques in response to begging letters were trickling in and the public were still responding, but as John Lippitt pointed out at our fundraising meeting on 2 May, if we were to get the writs issued in August, we needed another £100,000–150,000. Some of the action points from that meeting give a sense of our desperation: Sean was to try to get the editorial boards of all major newspapers and magazines to meet Michael and Victor face to face; Jason's father was to make contact with the Freemasons, whom Janie would coordinate; Hugo was to prepare a flyer to circulate to army regiments; and Victor was to write to 1,500 golf clubs.

What made Victor's continued prodigious fundraising efforts so extraordinary was that he had already resigned as a client. He and Jason rarely saw eye to eye and their personalities clashed. 'Whilst for some reason I always seem to be the "client" when bills are delivered,' he had complained in a spurt of anger on 24 March 2001, 'I am *never* consulted about the work undertaken (and what work is to be charged for) and my wishes are often ignored. Jason seems to now regard me with a degree of contempt because I have the audacity even to question what he does and my honest opinion (for what it is worth) is that his firm is not good value for money . . . I believe that the relationship between Jason and myself has broken down irretrievably and I no longer wish to be involved with either the litigation or the legal side, though I will of course lend my support as best I can to the fund-raising efforts and all the other activities.'

He was right and he was wrong. Certainly, H2O's fees seemed incredibly high to a solicitor practising in Surrey, but they were lower than many London firms'. And as Jason frequently bewailed, H2O gave substantial discounts and often gave their time for nothing, and not only at weekends and in the evenings. It was true, too, that Jason was wilful and that taking instruction was not his strong point, but the same was true of Victor. And while Jason was often chaotic – especially when it came to administration – his chaos was creative: you would not choose him to do your conveyancing, but then suing the Real IRA required different talents. Also, though Jason might appear cavalier in his treatment of others, he was risking his whole reputation on the Omagh project.

It helped that David Greenhalgh became involved with the case in 2001. He was pleased to be joining a team that included his old and close friend Jason, whom he had met at Queen Mary College, London, as well as Davidaire, whom he had met when as a student he worked part-time at a call centre and whom he had persuaded Jason to take on as his legal secretary. He was attracted too by the legal challenge and had an emotional interest in the case. 'I had spent a lot of time in Omagh years before when I dated a lass from there. Also, like Jase, I am a Warrington lad and from near Manchester so the bombings were something I felt strongly about.'[*]

'I remember the first time in Paul's flat that we met Jason and Greenie,'[†] recalled Máirín. 'First impressions: Greenie was the lawyer and Jason saw himself as Indiana Jones. Never had any reason to change that. Jason kept saying things like, "But we have told the families we won't pursue them for the money if they haven't got it." I found it all a bit naïve – how would he keep himself in Birkenstocks?' Yet to Lucy Morgan, a calm, wise young woman who worked with Jason for five years: 'As a lawyer, Jason is technically brilliant and mostly importantly intuitive – he really thinks outside the box. As a colleague he was fun and commanded respect despite his mateyness. He was a great boss. One of the great things about him is his

[*] In 1993 an IRA bomb in Warrington injured many and killed two boys who now have a peace foundation named after them.

[†] Jason is incapable of sticking to anyone's given name, e.g. David was Greenie, Davidaire was Dee, he was J, I was Ruthy or Mother Superior: the Omagh relatives were known as 'the rellies'.

ability to put together a great team – he attracts people who complement his skills. Diligent and thorough, funny and sympathetic, Greenie was a great team member. Davidaire – glamorous, ambitious and hard working – she looked after us.' Jason's tribute to Lucy is that she was 'a pleasure who added humour to our lives and was a great legal sounding board who never refused to take anything on'.

It helped, too, that despite all the financial and legal uncertainties, Jason had persuaded Lord Brennan QC to be the lead barrister. A member of the bar in England, Ireland and Northern Ireland, and Chairman of the Bar Council of England and Wales in 1999, he was voted Lawyer of the Year in 2000, when he also became a peer. Dan Brennan had a career of great distinction nationally and internationally, as well as an outstanding record of bringing multi-party actions by ordinary people devastated by extraordinary events; he had, for instance, acted for haemophiliacs contaminated with HIV who sued the British government. Combative, adventurous and mischievous as well as brilliant and dogged, Dan enjoys going where no one has gone before, so Jason had made a perfect choice. It was Lucy Morgan who reported that when Dan Brennan had left their office after agreeing to take on the case, she and Jason danced all around the hall. Not so, says Greenie: the whole legal team danced.

In the meantime, the other families who had come on board as clients had no idea how to determine if their lawyers were charging reasonably or doing a good job. Indeed, so dire was Jason at administration that there was little on the record concerning much of the time he had spent in the library, Westminster or visiting County Tyrone. The volunteers took as much of the fundraising burden off H2O as they could and the Trustees agreed to have Jason answer to them, to scrutinise the invoices on behalf of the families and – subject to checking with designated family members – to take all financial decisions.

The fundraising meetings were often enjoyable as well as doom-laden; I remember particularly the evenings in my club, the Reform, which would begin with a Trustees' meeting. 'Fairly short and to the point,' remembers Máirín. 'They usually lasted for ten minutes before the fundraising meeting and involved a bit of cheque-signing. Paul was punctilious, John was impatient and I really remember very little of what was discussed, other than John saying "How much do we need now?" and then nodding calmly when told anything between £50 and £500,000.' John would then demand wine – for which he would pay – his ebullience would raise morale, the fundraising group would arrive and we would address the financial black hole once again. Many of us shared a similar sense of humour* and we laughed at each other a lot. A smattering of Trustees, lawyers and other volunteers often ended up drowning our sorrows afterwards in wine bars.

Máirín also enjoyed the discomfiture of our newest recruit, the ferociously clever, hardworking and disciplined Old Etonian George Bridges, a friend of Robert's, who had worked for Prime Minister John Major at Number 10 Downing Street and was now with a media operation: 'Robert asked me while I was shooting at Cranborne one weekend. He knew that I like these kinds of things.' 'I remember,' said Máirín, 'lots of meetings in H2O's offices in Holborn. Henry and Sean coming up with wild schemes, George Bridges's face comical in its agony when he realised that there was behind them no planning, no strategy, just a few tactics and plenty of flash bang yabbadab-badoo Barney.† How do you get the message out when you have no phones? That kinda thing.' George's recollections are benign. 'I think the overriding sense I had of it was that it was wonderfully English – which is ironic, I know – in the sense of the peculiar mix of people; the freelance, "up and at 'em" approach; the amateur nature of it (obviously J [Jason] and Lord B [Brennan] aside); and the way we didn't wallow in the horror of the bombing – we talked about the bomb, but I cannot recall any meeting or conversation descending into an Oprah Winfrey style weepie.

As for the people, rarely have I come across quite such an eclectic mix. As they say (cliché alert) truth is stranger than fiction. Take a scion of the British aristocracy, add a sprinkling of London types, a slug of Irish and a twist of IRA terrorist – and what have you got? An entertaining team, for whom meetings were more of an art form than a means of deciding on next steps. The only thing we had in common was that we wanted to see the bastards behind the bomb in court, and paying for it.

As for the meetings, memories always revolve around Swan Walk,‡ and Robert sitting in his armchair, in a Delphic pose; Sean smoking incessantly, tearing off the filters of his fags as he said "Hold on a minute" (another minute); Jason ruminating on the latest twist in the tale; Máirín wisely pointing out that all this was very well, but where is the money coming from and we don't have much left.

---

* When he was a child, Robert's great-grandmother taught him the useful principle that one should learn to laugh at nothing, as there's usually nothing to laugh at.
† A reference to *The Flintstones*.
‡ Robert's London house.

Enough money came in to take the lawyers through to the issuing of a writ of summons on Friday 10 August 2001 in the Belfast High Court notifying five men (Liam Campbell, Seamus Daly, Seamus McKenna, Michael McKevitt and Colm Murphy) and the Real IRA that proceedings would be taken against them. On Saturday, Pete St John, best known as the composer of the hugely popular folk-ballad 'The Fields of Athenry', went to Michael Gallagher's house to play for the families his 'Song for Omagh', the rights to which he had given the campaign. And the day after, the Sunday nearest the anniversary of the bomb, relatives gathered to commemorate their dead. Greenie remembers the planning of 'a Carry On press launch with me, Jase and Skip [Sean] in a Portakabin in Mike Gallagher's garden and us trying to hide Skips from the journos.* We set up a stand in the main street and it poured down – Jason's speech got soaked and ran – we also got shouted at by local tramp.' Jason was asked to write a diary of his week for the *Independent*[3], which amused his friends by inadvertently exposing the hypochondria which sits rather endearingly beside his daring.

Sunday

Today I get together in Omagh town with the families of the Omagh bomb victims. We stand in the market-place not far from where the bomb went off three years ago. I've spent a week organising this press conference, and it's been an exhausting process. I stand in front of the press with one family member [Laurence Rush] at 3.06 p.m. – the time the bomb went off.[†] It's a difficult speech, not only because of the emotion, but because it's pouring with rain. I have to take off my glasses, and then my notes run. We finish around 5 p.m.

Afterwards, I go back with the families for a drink to relax and celebrate. It is very emotional, because this is the first time that a terrorist organisation has been sued. It's a great stand: the families want to do their talking in court so that they can have judgement and closure. I'm completely knackered and very wet by the time we get back to the hotel. They buy me whiskeys and I have just drunk them when Sky and Channel 4 call at 6 p.m. to ask me to do a live interview. I proceed to drink a great deal of coffee, and my metabolism is all over the place. A total nightmare. The interviews are fine, but I'm so tired that I fall asleep and everyone else goes out to celebrate without me.

---

* While Sean was close to journalists in London, he had to be very careful in Northern Ireland, where there were some who were hostile; he organised the media by phone.
† Should have been 3.04.

Monday

   I go to say goodbye to the families, and then it's back to the UK. When
I arrive in London, I find I'm locked out of my home. Fantastic. Back in
the office, I realise I've caught a cold, probably from standing out in the
rain so much.

The rest of the week involved the death of his grandfather, press and TV
interviews, discussions with people in the music business about the Omagh
song, writing a chapter of his thriller because he couldn't sleep, work on
a case concerning the Yemen, 'boring admin', numerous conversations
with the families before they're interviewed by the press, dinner with an
ex-girlfriend, taking the Omagh team for a drink, laughing at the
Warrington Guardian ('After my 15 minutes of fame with the world press,
I'm put on page nine in a "Warrington boy takes on Real IRA" type of
story. I share a page with a plea to find homes for two dogs called Charlie
and Rex. Humbling.'), being 'really shattered' so taking off on Thursday
afternoon to recuperate in Cardiff with friends before a Saturday stag
party.

   Press coverage of the issuing of the writs helped to take donations up
to close on half a million pounds by the end of 2001. We tried another
protest in London that we hoped would attract the media and raise the
campaign profile. Having heard that the London branch of the 32 County
Sovereignty Movement were to demonstrate on 1 December outside the
Irish Embassy about the treatment of dissent republicans in Irish prisons,
we brought several relatives over for a counter-protest. There were as
many of us as of them, they kept very quiet, and, despite Sean's best
efforts, there was hardly any media interest.

   We were weary from money-grubbing, yet letting down the families
and the donors (and, indeed, ourselves) was unthinkable, and the brutal-
ities of the Real IRA at home and the destruction of the Twin Towers on
9/11 strengthened our resolve: Greenie was actually in the Silver Birches
Hotel in Omagh taking statements from the families about their psychiatric injuries when the planes struck the towers; already in the distressed
state these meetings reduced him to, he watched the ensuing horror on
the television in the bar. But the costs of developing the case swallowed
up every penny: as Máirín put it, 'it was like Groundhog Day – no matter
how much money was found, we always needed more'. As the case slowly
moved forward it was clear that it was much larger and more complex

than anyone had expected and there was a need for far more time and money than had been anticipated to be spent on legal analysis, investigation, research and involvement with the families. Increasingly, too, we had to think of the public relations aspects of everything we did and to put more emphasis on political lobbying.

We needed another relaunch, we realised, and it had to be carefully coordinated for maximum effect. Our new deadline was August 2002, when the families would have the straightforward choice of giving up the case or committing themselves to having the writs that had been issued the previous year actually served on the Defendants; this would put them at risk, if they lost, of having to pay the other side's costs.

A meeting was arranged at which Paul Dacre of the *Mail*, who up to now had left the campaign to his executive editor, would encounter Michael Gallagher and Liz Gibson. For Liz the occasion was a great strain, for she found herself suffering one of her frequent attacks of survivor guilt: what was she doing in Kensington in an imposing office with cream panelling, a thick carpet, comfortable sofas and antiques when Esther was lying in her grave? She had difficulty maintaining her composure but she managed it and left the talking to Michael. 'I was very moved by this dignified man's dreadful story,' Dacre told me, 'and I felt so angry that there was no justice for his son or the other victims that I decided we would go with it.' He was also visibly moved, reported Sean, who was there, when Liz said she was going through with it because 'My Mammy would never forgive us if we didn't.' Jason's job was to suppress his fears and doubts and assure Dacre with total confidence that the case had an excellent chance of success. 'I talked it up,' he recalled. 'What else could I do?'

Robert Cranborne once said of Paul Dacre and the then *Telegraph* editor Charles Moore that they were both moralists, but Dacre's moralism came from the gut and Moore's from the intellect. On 2 February, the gut moralist wrote an outraged full-page editorial, and took the unprecedented step of putting the words 'The Editor' at the bottom of it: illustrated with photographs of the dead, it was followed by a two-page interview with Michael. Headlined 'Today I am asking you, our wonderful readers, to help a group of quietly magnificent people shamefully betrayed by British justice', Dacre complained angrily that, although the government were spending enormous sums on the Bloody Sunday Inquiry and billions on eliminating al-Qaeda, 'the realpolitik of the Ulster peace process means that neither Whitehall nor Westminster wants to know the Omagh victims' relatives'. The Omagh families were exhausted, he said, but their courage was unfaltering. 'No longer are ordinary people willing to cower before the bombers and the gunmen. No longer can these swaggering killers exploit the criminal law through intimidation and fear. This is an opportunity to strike a blow for civilized values. I urge you to be as generous as you can.'

Assorted politicians and celebrities and most of the British and Irish media were lined up to give the campaign legs.

Barry White, who worked for the Ulster Unionist Party, had been busy with Roy Beggs, a UUP MP, organising an Early Day Motion* signed by one hundred MPs. Beggs used it in the Commons on 7 February as a pretext to demand that the government provide matching funding for all money raised privately. Though no one really thought this a runner, several politicians made themselves available to the media in support.

And then, a few days later, Bob Geldof came fully on board. For a long time he had been the celebrity we most wanted because of the passion he had shown on *The Late Late Show* in Ireland not long after the Omagh bomb. Unfortunately, since he is a businessman and a musician, spends a great deal of time trying to save Africa and is always in demand by charities, he was a difficult man to reach, let alone recruit. We knew he was already doing some fundraising of his own for the families: when he had concerts, buckets were passed around and in interviews he often mentioned Omagh. Fortuitously, on a trekking holiday in Nepal towards the end of 2001, Jason had fallen in love with the broadcaster Mariella Frostrup who, it turned out, knew everyone. She and Geldof had a mutual friend, so we were able to get a phone number.

Apart from watching the Live Aid concert and reading about him in the press, I had once observed personally how Geldof operated as I stood in a patient queue in the Irish Embassy in London waiting my turn to give my coat to the cloakroom attendants. Geldof came through the front door,

---

* These are formal motions submitted by MPs which go on the record but are rarely debated. This one read: *That this House remembers with deep sadness the Omagh bombing of 15th August 1998 in which 31 people – including seven children* [they counted sixteen- and seventeen-year-olds as adults] *and two unborn babies – were murdered by the Real IRA; commends the courage of the families of the victims of this bombing in launching an unprecedented civil legal case against five named individuals, suspected of planting the bomb, and the Real IRA; congratulates the families on their persistence in attempting to seek justice; and urges the public to show their support for the families' legal action in whatever way they can.*

cast a cursory look at the queue, threw his coat across the foyer into a corner and marched upstairs to the party. Essentially, I concluded, he did what he liked and despised convention; fortunately, one of the things he likes is following the dictates of his big heart.

His terms were made clear from the beginning. He wanted no involvement with committees and a bare minimum of meetings, but he would front the campaign. It was he who – in the interstices of giving interviews upstairs about Africa – took the lead on 20 February at an event at the Irish Club in London where, once again, the families showed their placards and told their stories and Hugo Plowden, with difficulty, tried to keep the home-made upside-down banner the right way up. Messages of support were read out from well-known names that included the novelist Maeve Binchy, U2's Bono, the left-wing mayor of London, Ken Livingstone, and Margaret Thatcher's authorised biographer and then editor of the *Daily Telegraph*, Charles Moore. Flanked by Peter Mandelson, David Trimble, Mark Durkan, the leader of the SDLP, and the former world featherweight boxing champion Barry McGuigan, Geldof told the audience that the Omagh bombing 'was our September 11. These people should not be allowed to get away with it. America went after the people who attacked it – we should do the same.'

Newspapers mostly hate each other and they do not run joint campaigns, but Sean had taken some of the relatives to meet senior editors and almost the entire British media was in support. The following day Omagh-appeal donor forms or articles appeared in most tabloids and broadsheets: the public were urged to raise another million pounds for legal costs and a contingency fund to cover the families should they lose the case. Editors and journalists would mostly remain deeply sympathetic to the cause and continue to give it as much coverage and support as they could. In some cases – like the *Sunday Times* and *The Business* – they ran free advertisements, which Jason enjoyed drafting. But as Sean kept reminding us, newspapers cannot afford to bore their readers, so requests to donate could be made only rarely and in response to an anniversary, a particularly affecting interview or a dramatic event.

Perhaps because we tried to buoy up the families rather than whinge to them, we could appear unduly optimistic and competent. There was a minor panic in London when the *Sunday Times* – to which a euphoric Michael had been speaking unguardedly – reported that the campaign organisers were planning in Omagh, with Geldof's help, 'a huge Live

Aid-style concert'. The comment from a tactful spokesman for Geldof was that he would need to discuss this first: 'Bob is committed to helping the relatives as much as possible, and when he did his own gigs on either side of the border he asked for contributions for the fund.'

Fundraising would go on for another eighteen months. There would be joyful periods, when thousands of envelopes arrived at Paul's office, to be opened by Hugo and Sylvia and Paul's brother Simon – both of whom also often came to fundraising meetings. Sometimes Alison Bowles, an occasional employee of John Lippitt's, would help out, or Sylvia would recruit some tiny young women from the Chinese channel where Paul was Company Secretary.

While, of course, money came mostly from the United Kingdom and the Republic of Ireland, contributions also came from Australia, Austria, Bahrain, the Canary Islands, France, Germany, Gibraltar, Greece, Jamaica, South Africa, Spain, Switzerland and the US. The London group, like the families, would be sustained by the warmth of the messages of support from ordinary people. 'I read the *Daily Mail* article and cried my eyes out. I hope this little bit helps. It makes my problems seem so insignificant' (£25); 'From an unemployed Limerickman living in London – Good luck' (£1); 'My husband and I were married on the afternoon of 15th August 1998 and I hope this donation will go a little way to appease some of the guilt I feel remembering the day as the happiest of my life yet knowing it brought such devastating sadness to so many families' (£30); 'Never forget, the silent majority does care and won't forget either' (£25); 'When governments fail us the people have to stand together' (£20); 'I hope my contribution will in some small way help you to raise the million pounds needed to bring R.I.R.A. to justice. From Alex (15)' (£3). 'So sorry I could not afford more. I am an 83-year-old WWII veteran, profoundly moved by this appalling business. I hope with all my heart that you have great success in the courts' (£10); 'I enclose my second donation. It's a widow's mite from an O.A.P. who feels very deeply about this issue' (£10). An octogenarian 'who has witnessed the evil humans are capable of, and despaired at the failure to eradicate the guilty', wrote for the families a poem called 'The Assassins of Omagh' and accompanied it with a cheque for £500. Accompanied by a cheque for £10, one of the most moving letters was addressed to Michael by a woman called Julie. Praising his dignity, courage and humanity, she wrote: 'To lose a child must be the worst kind of loss, and having never had children I cannot pretend to know the depth of pain you must feel. However, I would like you to know that out there there are thousands like myself; who view with outrage what has happened, and extend an invisible hand across the miles for you to grasp. We are with you in emotion, spirit and hope.' Jason's favourite, about which he still becomes emotional, was an old lady who sent a little money and a promise that she would pray at Knock shrine for two weeks for everyone involved with the case.

Should anyone ever doubt the worth of sending a tiny donation to such a cause, let me reassure them that, in terms of morale, the support of the man and woman in the street is worth its weight in platinum. 'It was crucial to the lawyers,' says Jason, 'in encouraging us to go the extra mile.'

The famous and the rich were generous, too. The Northern Irish racing driver Eddie Irvine, who, like Barry McGuigan, is noted for his loathing of sectarianism, gave £100,000; and, following the lead of Robert and Janie, several of their friends gave £5,000, as did some charitable trusts and businesses, some of them – like many individuals – anonymously. Among the names we recognised who gave substantial sums were Maeve Binchy, Frederick Forsyth and Martin McDonagh, a playwright famous for a vicious satire on terrorism, who sent £1,000 with his love to Victor and Michael. Generous businessmen included the newspaper proprietor Conrad Black, and the communications entrepreneur Denis O'Brien, and, as a result of my chance meeting with my warm acquaintance, the then Chairman of the Rowntree Trust, Lord Smith, we received enough to keep us going for a crucial few weeks.

Then the envelopes would stop arriving and we would sit around morosely, trying to think of another publicity drive. One such event was a fundraising dinner on 17 May 2002 in Warrington, Jason's and Greenie's home town, organised by Jason's godfather, Norman Banner, and held under our new slogan: 'PEOPLE AGAINST TERRORISM'. Mariella Frostrup was Master of Ceremonies, the speakers were Geldof, Mandelson, Robert Cranborne, Jason, Daphne Trimble (standing in at short notice for her husband, Northern Ireland First Minister David) and Esther Gibson's sister Caroline Martin (substituting for Michael Gallagher). Geldof, who was not known for natty dressing, was greeted by Donna-Maria Barker: 'You're a disgrace to the Irish, Bob, with your clothes and hair in such a state. I should take you upstairs for a haircut.' More alarmed than anyone had seen him before, he shouted, 'Keep this woman away from me.'

Caroline was completely overcome by the emotional strain of the occasion and had to be comforted by both Geldof and Janie Dawnay, but her tearful speech was moving. The dinner raised about £16,000 and heightened the Trust's profile, but the amount of organisation involved at the Warrington end and the time required from busy people made us realise that we were wholly unequipped to take on organising such events.

Victor had embarked on another solo money-raising effort. He wrote about it in April 2002 in a letter to the *Spectator* responding to an article which put forward a common view, that, 'as a matter of principle, victims' families should not have recourse to civil proceedings. It should be for the state to prosecute – with all its resources – in such matters.' (We were less than thrilled that the *Spectator* had run such an article, since the previous week Sean had taken Jason to meet the editor, Boris Johnson, and as they left he had raised a clenched fist and said 'Right on, comrades!' Presumably he could not bring himself to break the news that a critical article had already been accepted.)

Sir: I read Fenton Bresler's article ('Don't privatise justice', 13 April) with some interest. I agree to some extent with what he says, but after two years of correspondence with various secretaries of state and with the Prime Minister – as well as with the office of the incompetent so-called Minister of Justice Equality and Law Reform in Dublin – it was made abundantly clear to us as the families of the Omagh victims that the likelihood of a criminal prosecution was very slight.

In such circumstances, how are we to seek justice? How do I stand up and fight for my 12-year-old son murdered among the 28 others?

This week, at 45 years of age, I ran the London Marathon for the first time, with my right leg covered in bandages from plastic surgery, and finished in 4 hours 43 minutes. For the last five miles I carried a flag: 'The Omagh Victims Legal Trust – the real Irish Freedom fighters.'*

At least we do not plant bombs in busy shopping centres and then scurry over the border to safety – we stand up and fight for justice, and that is what we will continue to do.

Victor Barker

---

* Greenie points out that this large flag has been occupying a lot of space in his office ever since.

He raised £16,000 in sponsorship and would continue running the marathon for James every year until a leg packed in.

Behind the scenes Paul Dacre had been addressing one of the families' major stumbling blocks: the fear that if they lost the case, the Defendants would go after them for costs. In February 2002 a firm of solicitors acting for an anonymous client began talks with Jason and Dan Brennan. For weeks before the day when the families had to decide whether or not to go ahead, Máirín 'was waking up in the middle of the night, worrying about these poor people proceeding with the case, seeking justice and peace of mind, then being left with a million pound legal bill – for the other side . . . I was growing an ulcer.' At the last moment, the affirming call came to the Trustees and they were able to reassure the families that there would be enough money to proceed with the case and sureties against any costs or damages they might have awarded against them.

The writs were served at the end of July: the *Daily Mail* ran with a front-page headline: 'A GIANT STEP FOR JUSTICE', with photographs of the five Defendants. How they were served will be described later, but the drama involved and the enormous press coverage gave a fresh impetus and brought more money rolling in. But by the beginning of 2003 we were despairing again. It appeared the Defendants were likely to fight the case, and for legal reasons there was no chance that – as we had expected – it would come to court in 2003. Costs were piling up and we were beginning to run out of fundraising road. Paradoxically, the only hopeful development was the news in January 2003 that Campbell and McKevitt had been granted legal aid by the Northern Ireland Legal Aid Department: this inspired another Early Day Motion in the House of Commons, a media storm and another round of appeals for money in the press. Optimists believed the government might feel obliged to provide legal aid to the families, but realists knew there was no such possibility.

Geldof was one of the optimists. Following a plea from Henry, he had agreed reluctantly to meet him, Victor, Sean and John, who were to persuade him to do even more on the fundraising front: the theory was that he would be moved by Victor's passion, Sean's persuasiveness, Henry's messianism and John's forcefulness. One afternoon the four of them sat in the Picasso Café on the King's Road, Geldof's choice of venue, waiting and waiting. But there was no Geldof.

As an organiser, Henry's chief failing is that he never uses a diary and persists in trusting his imperfect memory for arrangements. 'I bet you've screwed up the date,' said Sean gloomily. 'Nonsense,' said Henry. 'It was definitely Wednesday.' But he went outside and phoned. 'Henry Robinson here, Bob. We're waiting in the café.' 'What do you mean you're fucking waiting in the café? I waited there for you for a fucking hour-and-a-fucking-half last fucking week.'

Henry grovelled rather than argued and then asked if Geldof could come now. 'I've just had fucking root canal surgery and you want me to come to a fucking meeting that's a week fucking late?' He came, but he was impatient and kept insisting that there was little more he could do on the fundraising front and the government would have to fund it.

Then came what we feared was the *coup de grâce*: it was delivered by John Ware, whose *Panorama* programme had been central to getting the case off the ground.

Ware would later express regret and explain that what had inspired him to investigate where the money had gone sprang from his default position that lawyers are a greedy bunch. He knew Jason only slightly and Dan Brennan not at all, and had decided that H2O and Matrix were exploiting the families for financial gain. The *Sunday Telegraph* of 9 March 2003 gave his article the headline 'They raised £1.2 million to bring the Omagh bombers to justice. Now most of it is gone'. Why had the costs doubled since the initial estimate? asked Ware. Though both solicitors and barristers were charging at a discounted rate, combined fees could amount to £1.6 million to take to court what was a speculative case. *Panorama* had provided H2O with the skeleton of a case. How could it have cost £1 million for H2O to put legal flesh on it? Jason, he noted, now lived with Mariella Frostrup in a house in one of the most expensive parts of London.

Like the excellent investigative journalist he is, Ware was equipped with material not in the public domain: he knew that Victor – of whom there was a large photograph – had been expressing his concerns about costs before coming off the writ in March 2001; he had got hold of estimates of H2O's costs for trial as well as an invoice for August 2002, the month when Jason served writs in a blaze of publicity, which he quoted to prove Jason sometimes charged for items that were not strictly to do with the law, like organising press conferences. 'None of the families we contacted wished to comment publicly,' said Ware. 'They are concerned that the legal fees may exhaust the goodwill of a generous public. Privately they hope the Trustees will subject future bills to professional legal scrutiny.' John Lippitt had told Ware that the Trustees had indeed 'scrutinised these expenses carefully and they are all valid expenses in the interest of the families. We have also questioned the size of the fees and are satisfied that they have been heavily discounted for the public good', but while Ware did not doubt John's word, his mind was not changed.

A week previously Ware had asked H2O for answers to innumerable questions about where the money was going. Although H2O provided a thorough explanation which satisfied the Trustees and Michael Gallagher, on counsel's advice they were unable to produce a detailed explanation to Ware for fear of waiving privilege in the case files, which could have not only been the thin end of the wedge but could have prejudiced the action. This, of course, made Ware think they had something to hide.

Jason, whose heart and soul were in the case, was in a state of mingled rage and disgust. For H2O as a whole, who had risked all and put themselves on the line, this personal attack caused them bitter upset, frustrated further by their knowing that no one would care about lawyers' hurt feelings. Their involvement in Omagh imbalanced the tiny firm: although the employment department run by Greenie and Paul Fox's media and defamation work was profitable and subsidised Omagh, the firm was owed a great deal of money and there was a real fear that the *Sunday Telegraph* article could cause the collapse of both the firm and the case.

If the money runs out, Ware asked rhetorically, will the lawyers abandon the case? Would they work on unpaid? He quoted from an interview Jason had given *The Times*: "'This is one of the few cases genuinely about principle. Money isn't the objective – justice is the objective." Perhaps. But whatever happens, it is difficult for those who are not lawyers to believe that the only way to achieve justice for the relatives of those murdered by the Omagh bomb is to pay £1.6 million to lawyers.'

The ever-loyal Victor came in immediately to tell the press: 'I am 100 per cent behind the trustees, the legal team and the fundraising committee. You cannot expect people in this day and age to work for nothing unless it's a huge legal practice that can afford to underwrite something like this. These are the charges you get from London lawyers, but I have placed my complete faith in the hands of the trustees to examine the costs and make sure they are fair.'

In London we held an emergency meeting. The fallout on the fundraising front might not be as terminal as we had initially feared, pointed out some wise heads: not everyone reads the *Sunday Telegraph*, and other papers had not picked up the story. But of course the article had deeply unsettled the families and Michael had signalled that we needed to send a team to Omagh to reassure them both that the lawyers and trustees were doing a good job and that the money would be found to go on. Since we were still about £800,000 short of the latest estimate, that was a wildly optimistic message.

The support group agreed that both lawyers and trustees should be kept out of the firing line, which left few others to choose from. I knew the families best, and Sean, who had been involved in myriad negotiations with Ware and the *Telegraph* that had toned down the article somewhat, knew the ins and outs of the accusations and how to rebut them. Ideally, we needed a reassuring figure like Robert or Janie to go with us, but only Henry could go at such short notice. Yet the pasts of Sean and Henry made them an object of suspicion and resentment to several of the relatives.

Regardless, the two ex-terrorists and I went in dread to Omagh, sat in the Portakabin among worried, suspicious people and tried to explain why lawyers could charge per hour what most of them might earn in a week. I gently tried to describe to people who book holidays six months in advance why Jason, whose plans inevitably changed at short notice, needed more expensive, flexible tickets. And so on. Michael, Mark Breslin, Stanley McCombe, Godfrey and Ann Wilson and Esther Gibson's sister Wilma were among the majority who backed our argument strongly and we returned to London with the families still on board to go back into discussions about what to do next. Janie and Sean spent an enormous amount of time trying to organise a £1,000-a-head dinner at Claridge's and had only five takers by the time they had to pull the plug.

On 28 April 2003 I was at an ill-attended meeting where the Trustees told the three H2O partners – Jason, Greenie and Paul Fox – that the Fund did not have the money to pay the backlog of their fees. 'The solicitors', say the notes, 'agreed that they were fully informed of the financial position but did not want the Trustees to call a halt to proceedings while there was a chance of finding more funds.' All sources seemed to have dried up, but the Trustees agreed anyway 'not to stand down H2O on the strict understanding that no one subsequently claimed that they were not aware of the financial position'. In effect, the lawyers agreed to bankroll the families' case.

The next day I had a call from Dan Brennan asking me to see him.

Dan is compelling and his message was simple: he believed in the case and he did not want the fundraisers to give up. He suggested I introduce him to Peter Mandelson. A few days later we went together to meet him and Dan explained why he believed the case could succeed. In answer to a question from me, Mandelson was adamant that there were no rich people in his world for the fundraisers to tap, but he hinted he was trying to convince the government to award the families legal aid. 'I was lobbying the Prime Minister hard on this,' he wrote to me later, 'and made myself a thorough nuisance.' He told Dan that he would write to two specific ministers on the issue: the following morning photocopies of handwritten, persuasive letters landed on Dan's desk.

On 15 July 2003, we had what George Bridges described as 'that hysterical breakfast meeting at the Reform' to discuss how to put pressure on the government. John Lippitt was in the chair and those around the table included Mandelson, Geldof and Andrew Neil, the broadcaster and journalist, who, as Editor-in-Chief of the *Scotsman* and *Sunday Business* had been immensely supportive. The meeting was dominated by Mandelson and Geldof, who began by making fun of each other's clothes, but whose single-mindedness, decisiveness, wit and ability to cut to the chase impressed everyone, even John, who still had only the slimmest grasp of why Geldof was famous and was having to overcome a deep antipathy to New Labour in general and Mandelson in particular. 'If needs be, Bob,' said Mandelson at one stage, 'we'll go to see the Secretary of State together. He'll see us because I once had his job and you're famous.' Andrew Neil made it clear that his papers would lean heavily on the government. As Messrs Geldof, Mandelson and Neil rushed off, it was one of those rare moments when I thought we really could win this. 'What interesting friends you have, Dr Edwards,' observed the hall porter as I left.

Geldof and Mandelson never had to mount a joint assault. The new Lord Chancellor, Charlie Falconer, 'overcame the official advice and resistance and made the decision to give legal aid to the families,' says Peter Mandelson. It was announced on 8 August 2003 by the latest Northern Ireland Secretary of State, Paul Murphy. 'While I recognise the legal constraints and complexities,' he said, 'I have always believed that this is an exceptional case and the vast majority of people in Northern Ireland and beyond want to see the families bring it to court. The magnificent scale of the financial donations from the public to date supports that view.'

'It is fantastic, unbelievable news,' Michael told the press. 'I think it will go a long way towards giving the families justice. It takes an enormous burden off our shoulders.'

When I had rung Robert to tell him the news he said, 'Had I still been a minister, I would have advised against it.' 'And had I still been a civil servant,' I said, 'so would I.' And so would ex-civil servant John Lippitt and political analyst Sean, for it set a worrying precedent. But we had been too committed to care. All of us had lobbied for legal aid for the families and all of us were absolutely delighted with the result. For H2O, it meant the firm was safe.

Only Henry, Máirín, Paul, Greenie and I could get together that night to drink to Peter Mandelson, the fundraisers and donors who had got us so far and to everyone else who had helped, but we did so with great enthusiasm.

CHAPTER FOURTEEN
GOING TO COURT

'This appeal has been characterised by the inclusion of every conceivable technical objection to the judge's order. The case generally has spawned much interlocutory litigation where, again, every possible ground on which the action might be frustrated has been canvassed. There has been satellite litigation challenging the grant of funds to the respondents for the legal costs of the action. The time has now arrived for this case to proceed with all dispatch' – Lord Chief Justice Kerr, Lord Justice Campbell and Lord Justice Higgins, HM Court of Appeal, Belfast, 15 March 2007[*]

Where *did* the money go?

It went, first, on paying lawyers and an investigator to determine who could be sued, on what basis, where and by whom; on developing an unprecedented case; on raising the money to pay for it; and on handling myriad complexities, delays and what often seemed like deliberate obstruction by governments and agencies of Ireland and the United Kingdom. The families' (Plaintiffs') lawyers needed help from the police, the security services and the justice system in Britain, Northern Ireland and the Republic of Ireland and also from the US State Department and the FBI; yet most people in authority saw the civil case as a pointless nuisance which might jeopardise criminal trials and in any case would get nowhere. Because some of the men on the writ were also being tried for unrelated terrorist offences in Dublin, and as any found guilty would immediately appeal, there were always reasons for delays. There was also the geography: the Plaintiffs mostly lived in Omagh, their lawyers were based in London, the relevant courts were in Belfast and Dublin, and a vital witness was hidden by a witness protection scheme in the US. Additionally, the Defendants had thorough and indefatigable lawyers who explored every avenue that could kill off or delay the case against their clients.

In September 2000, after meeting Victor, Jason had a client and a

---

[*] See the legal timeline at Appendix B, which lists most of the hearings connected with the civil case and also criminal proceedings against the Defendants.

few thousand in seed-corn money provided by Robert Cranborne; blithely, he had set counsel straight to work on developing a case and had begun roaming around Northern Ireland making contacts and picking up information about what evidence there was and about whom. One of his primary jobs was to sell the idea to other potential clients: at a meeting in Omagh on 21 October to which all bereaved families had been invited, he made much of his Irish (Protestant) and Polish (Catholic) background and sought to clarify what he was about in layman's terms. 'Law is the cement of society,' read his notes, 'and the essential medium for change. That is what we learnt at law school. When I worked on a building site I learnt there were hundreds of types of cement. Geographic and climatic factors determined the best type of cement for the job.'

> The rain cloud brought over n.i. by these new dissident terrorists has placed limitations on the effectiveness of the criminal law cement. In order for a change we need to look at using different legal mixes of cement. We are going to try a new civil law mix to see if we can lay a sound foundation for the families to build some justice for their loved ones.

Enough families showed interest to justify the feverish activity going on elsewhere. Having built up the broad picture, Jason despatched Lucy Morgan to Northern Ireland to collect evidence, having great faith in her not least because of her adventurous temperament. After university, Lucy had travelled around Europe with a Belgian circus, specialising in stilt-walking, fire-breathing and the Hungarian bullwhip dance and had then qualified as a commercial litigator with media experience: she had joined Henry Hepworth as Jason's assistant in August 1998, coincidentally the month of the Omagh bomb.

It was Lucy who processed the information passed on by John Ware and who amplified it steadily. Ex-Detective Chief Superintendent Eric Anderson, who had taken early retirement in disgust at what he considered the subversion by the Patten Commission of the RUC, had made it clear both in private and in public that he would give any assistance he could to those wishing to expose the bombers, and was an important source for Ware and of great help to Lucy.

From February 2001, as the evidence began to come together and Jason began to construct a framework for the case; he had a key helper in David Greenhalgh. Jason had trained in media and libel in the glamorous firm Mishcon de Reya. Greenie was a perfect complement: he had specialised in employment, family and criminal law; in acting for big casinos, he had been involved in recovering hidden assets world-wide; on personal injury claims, he had worked closely with fragile clients; and as well as his expertise on damages, he offered administra-tive competence. 'I got the Omagh case shipshape and running in terms of practicalities of structure,' Greenie recalled. In contrast to Jason, he loved systems.*

In pursuing the Omagh case, Jason had decided to focus on tort, a negligent or intentional act that injures someone, who may then sue for damages. Danny Friedman, a human rights specialist who knew the terri-tory, Heather Rodgers, who was strong on drafting claims, and Simeon Thrower, described by Jason as 'an elder statesman', were asked to advise; they would conclude that there was a valid course of action based on a combination of statute law, common law and tort. Although tort allows a period of up to six years to elapse between the act and the summons, with personal injury this falls to only three, so since the case involved both, counsel advised that to issue the writ after 15 August 2001 would be to risk the whole case.

In March Simeon Thrower produced a lengthy document putting together the work done by H2O and the barristers, which showed not just that the lawyers had been very busy indeed but that there was an enor-mous amount of work still to be done even to establish that there was a case. In the words of George Bernard Shaw, 'all professions are a conspiracy against the laity'. Part of that conspiracy is to devise arcane terminology to add mystique and exclude laymen; even the most informal of lawyers are trapped by linguistic convention. 'IN THE MATTER OF PROPOSED PROCEEDINGS BETWEEN THE FAMILIES OF CERTAIN VICTIMS OF THE OMAGH BOMBING and THE OMAGH BOMBING TEAM THE REAL IRA ("RIRA") THE 32 COUNTY SOVEREIGNTY MOVEMENT ("32CSM"): INSTRUCTIONS TO COUNSEL TO ADVISE ON MERITS, QUANTUM,† JURISDICTION AND EVIDENCE IN CONFERENCE AND THEREAFTER IN WRITING' was no exception.

---

* Greenie also set up what would become a top-ranking employment department that – together with the media department run by their colleague Paul Fox and other work brought in by Jason – helped keep the firm going at times when Omagh funds had dried up.

† The total amount of compensation or damages the claim is worth.

The documentation provided included profiles prepared by H2O of minors killed, adults killed and of twelve potential Defendants. Relevant certificates of conviction, documentation regarding business interests, police witness evidence and material relating to the projected trials of Murphy and Campbell were appended. Background information included a dossier of press cuttings concerning the bombing and the action, an H2O report on the 32CSM and information from their website, the *Panorama* video with a transcript along with unshown material, and the transcripts of the inquest.

'Evidence research' included analysis and documentation relating to Real IRA members and prisoners; information on every relevant telephone call and caller in the relevant geographical area from 12 to 15 August 1998, on calls between suspects pre-15 August, on car theft-related calls and on who on 15 August was using which main suspect phone and when; police interview information; notes on the supply of registration plates and explosives, on bomb making, on the storage of the bomb car and identification evidence relating to the drivers; a blast-range report; details of warning calls; related Real IRA bombings and a report on dissident terrorist attacks; investigative reports from Barrie Penrose; John Ware's information; and information gleaned from police on both sides of the border.

Previous instructions to, and advice from, counsel were appended, along with an immense amount of documentation on case law and statutes relating to personal injury and death, conspiracy, pre-action discovery, limitation periods, limitation period extensions, the effect of refusal to testify and silence in civil cases, admissibility of recorded information, criminal injuries compensation, deceit, categorisation of personal injury claims, and the many uses of the Human Rights Act 1998. And there were draft letters to the heads of the RUC and the Garda, to British Telecommunications plc, Vodaphone, Eircell and Colm Murphy seeking relevant documentation on the potential plaintiffs.

The 'current client families' were relatives of James Barker, toddler Breda Devine, Samantha McFarland and her friend Lorraine Wilson, Aiden Gallagher, Ann McCombe and her friend Geraldine Breslin, Alan Radford and Esther Gibson. Their aims were defined:

a) To obtain justice by obtaining judgements against as many as possible of the proposed Defendants. The current client families do not however

wish to commence actions which are likely to be struck out* at any
early stage.

b) To seek the maximum damages available against the proposed
Defendants.

c) To defend the victims and everyone else's future right to life.

d) To cause the proposed Defendants as many difficulties as possible.

e) To question the proposed Defendants, in court, and at preliminary stages
(i.e. witness statements/Further and Better particulars†) as to their
movements on the day of the bombing.

Counsel were asked to note 'that achievement of the current client
families' objectives does not necessarily depend upon final victory at
trial'.

The main causes of action would arise from the planting and detonation of the bomb and the misleading warning calls, but H2O wanted
counsel's advice on several possible legal routes. These are a few questions typical of the many dozens asked.

In a tort of unlawful killing, what burden of proof was likely to be
applied? Was there any difference between a claim for unlawful killing
in the Republic of Ireland and Northern Ireland? Could the leaders
of the Real IRA be joined as co-conspirators because they led an
organisation which had claimed responsibility for the illegal act? Would
the families be able to recover their own losses and not just those
suffered by the deceased? Would families who at the inquest watched
the video of the aftermath be able to claim for nervous shock? Could
those responsible for the bombing be injuncted‡ from carrying out
further acts of violence? In the case of the warning calls, could the tort
of deceit be committed when a Defendant knowingly or recklessly
makes a false statement of fact intending that it should be acted on by
the receiver of the warning, the receiver acts on the false statement,
and a third party thereby suffers damage? Would the Plaintiffs have to
prove that the victims acted on the warnings by moving into the bomb
zone?

---

* A judge could strike out a case, i.e. order that it be dropped, because of, for instance,
lack of evidence or of a reasonable basis in law.

† Additional information.

‡ Ordered by the court.

What was the most appropriate jurisdiction or combination of jurisdictions to bring these actions and could proceedings issued in Northern
Ireland be served on Defendants living in the Republic? Would families
who had received compensation be prevented from seeking damages on
the basis of double recovery?

There were many issues raised about differences in civil procedures and
rules in Northern Ireland and the Republic concerning, for example,
discovery, limitation, jury trial and hearsay evidence. There was discussion
of likely police and other witnesses and a query as to whether criminal-
interview material could be adduced in civil proceedings and, if so, how?
Could police be subpoenaed and, if so, would they be able to claim public
interest immunity? Would material relating to Defendants' silence or lying
in police interviews be admissible? What were the implications of failure to
defend the action or attend court? What were the arguments likely to be
made by the Defendants under the Human Rights Act and how could they
be countered? Did the nature of the funding of the case have to be disclosed?
Since the public might donate further when an action had begun, when could
the identities of the Defendants be put in the public domain?

What information would H2O be able to obtain from the RUC and
Garda investigation files? Could reports of evidence be subpoenaed from
the police authorities? Could evidence collected by the police relating to
the telephone calls be obtained under subpoena, thus saving the Plaintiffs
from having to pay substantial costs to the phone companies for supplying
the same information?

Should this be a multi-party action, or was there an argument for a
different Plaintiff taking actions against different Defendants? And this is
where, in a mind-numbing but crucial document, the ordinary people
taking this case swam back into view: 'Counsel is asked to advise whether
current client families should be further split into those victims who died
instantaneously, victims who survived for a short period before death, and
victims who were providing financial support to their families.'

The legal term for a collection of papers, large or small, is a 'bundle'.
On 15 May 2001, three months before a writ of summons would have to be
issued, an enormous bundle was sent to Dan Brennan asking him 'to advise
in writing on potential defendants on evidence, potential causes of action,
the likelihood of success, forum* and consequential procedural points'.

* Appropriate court.

As if constructing and financing a case were not difficult enough, there were the serious potential legal problems about liability: the Trustees had had to consult independent lawyers to consider the possibility that if the funds were insufficient and the case were lost, they and the families could be personally liable for any outstanding invoices and the Defendants' costs. The Trustees accepted Jason's assurance that H2O would never pursue either clients or Trustees if invoices could not be paid, and having been advised in March 2001 that it was 'most unlikely' a court would make an order for costs against them, they were brave enough to stay in post. The families were reassured that the case would not be irrevocably launched unless there was enough money to pay putative costs; this then required lawyers, trustees and fundraisers to have convoluted hypothetical discussions about whether any leftover money should be returned to donors pro-rata or given to charity.

There was also what to laymen seemed incredible – a real fear that donors could be liable for costs. Neil Hamilton, a Conservative minister who effectively lost his parliamentary seat because of allegations by Mohamed Fayed that he had been paid to ask questions in the Commons, had taken an unsuccessful libel case against Fayed with the help of about £400,000 from sympathisers: he lost an appeal in December 2000. Although Fayed had to pay his costs, Hamilton was unable to pay his own, which now amounted to around £3 million; the court ruled that anyone who had contributed more than £5,000 could be identified and pursued for costs. So, in March 2001, the Omagh Trustees needed a legal opinion on the liability of donors. The conclusion was that the law was uncertain but there was 'little risk', yet even a little risk proved enough further to discourage prospective major donors. Another complication was Paul Le Druillenec's valiant efforts to have the trust converted into a charity. This would have been financially very advantageous, but it took a long time and was beginning to look promising just as fundraising ceased.

Dan Brennan gave his advice in early June 2001: 'Clearly this will be a novel claim. Research thus far has not identified any other similar civil claim against a terrorist group or its members. But that is not a barrier, rather a challenge. Intuition suggests the law surely provides civil remedies for the commission of criminal acts.' His advice was that 'there are reasonable prospects of establishing civil liability in tort against the Real IRA and in the named individuals Murphy, Daly and McKenna.'

Dan took on a case that he expected would come to court within a couple of years but which took almost seven. In addition to being the lead barrister, he would play the same vital role as had Robert Cranborne and John Lippitt: he had authority, he had nerve and he steadied troops when they looked like panicking. Although, like all successful barristers, Dan sometimes fought cases on behalf of people he despised, there were many he took on out of interest or sympathy, and with Omagh his heart was engaged as well as his head. Being on top of his subject, he has the priceless attribute of being able to *explain*, and from the beginning he offered to go to Omagh and tell the families in straightforward language what they would be taking on.

The law might still have been mysterious to the families, but, like their supporters and lawyers, they were all too aware that the Real IRA was resurgent and dangerous, that bombs were being planted regularly in Northern Ireland and London, and that while the security forces north and south were having considerable success in damage limitation, the organisation was still alive, well and angry. Since Colm Murphy was but a name to most of McKevitt's followers, his arrest in 1999 and his tortoise-like progression through the Irish legal system on a charge of conspiracy to cause an explosion was not of great significance. But the charging of Liam Campbell and Michael McKevitt was a different matter and, in the minds of many Real IRA followers, the Omagh families were to blame for their incarceration.

Campbell had been arrested on 4 October 2000, the day before the inquest ended and several months after the PSNI had asked that he should be, and was in prison awaiting trial on a charge of membership of an illegal organisation. McKevitt and his wife Bernadette had been arrested on 29 March under anti-terrorist legislation and, although she was released, he was now facing the same charge as Campbell along with the infinitely more serious accusation of directing the activities of an unlawful organisation between August 1999 and October 2000. True, neither was charged with involvement with the Omagh bomb, but McKevitt faced the possibility of life imprisonment. What was more, it had emerged that the chief witness against him would be David Rupert, an American who had moved in the highest echelons of the movement both in Northern Ireland and the US, while an agent of the FBI and MI5. To McKevitt, who had trusted Rupert implicitly, this was a terrible blow: to his followers, reading in the press that Rupert had been privy to details of how the dissident network operated, the revelation of betrayal by an informer and the gullibility of their boss caused both fear and rage.

Against a background of crisis in the peace process over the issue of decommissioning, and rumours that the US was about to disrupt its fundraising by designating it as a foreign terrorist organisation, the Real IRA's response was defiance. On Easter Thursday, 12 April, a fully primed mortar bomb packed with 200 pounds of explosives in a van with a hole cut in its roof was found in a forest ten miles from Omagh after an anonymous tip-off; it would take three days to defuse. On the following Saturday night, a small bomb was exploded in a postal sorting office in north London: journalists were not slow to spot the symbolic significance of republicans bombing a post office at Easter.

The Real IRA leadership spelled things out with their Easter messages: 'British manipulation,' they declared, 'coupled with treachery on the part of others, has led to and has upheld the partition of Ireland. Partition has failed and those who attempt to uphold it will fail. As for Republicans, we will continue to attack the problem at its root and make no apology for undertaking this necessary task. We will continue our struggle until the 32 county socialist republic has been achieved.'

The Real IRA leadership was 'trapped in a time capsule,' responded Michael Gallagher. 'The statement is just like something the men of 1916 would have produced. But they are all dead and dead men can't change their minds. But we can change our outlook and can move on. Ireland is a different place to 1916.'

Gerry Adams was making the same point from a different perspective – and also needling the Real IRA – when at an Easter Rising commemorative speech in County Donegal he invoked a famous remark of Bobby Sands: 'Everyone, Republican or otherwise, has their own particular part to play.' 'You have to accept that you have a role to play in this struggle,' said Adams. 'You do not have to emulate the men and women of 1916, you do not have to emulate the hunger strikers, you do not have to emulate the people who have died in our struggle.' This 'do-as-we-say-not-as-we-did' message was not one which appealed to dissidents.

Simultaneously, Sands's sister, along with Marian Price and Francie Mackey, was leading the 32CSM ceremonies in Dublin. At Arbour Hill cemetery, where the executed of 1916 are buried, Mackey pointed out to two hundred supporters that 'the stance they took then was met with demonisation and vilification to discredit the legitimacy of their position, and although small in numbers, they have proven to be correct'. Among his targets were 'those who have lost their nerve and have compromised the republican position by accepting an agreement which is contrary to the wish of the vast majority'.

Whether they recognised it or not, the particular role the dissidents were playing in the wider political picture was to strengthen Adams and his colleagues. Every dissident bomb enabled them to frighten the two governments with warnings that, without further concessions to republicans, support for the irreconcilables would grow. Yet such concessions in no way mollified the dissidents: like Sinn Féin/IRA before them, they were seeking to outrage politicians and security forces into overreaction.

While it was alarming and distressing enough for the Omagh families that dissident violence was increasing, what really hit them hard was the vandalising of the memorial garden. Festering hatred was manifest when the garden dedicated to the dead of Omagh was wrecked: the ten heavy wooden benches were overturned, as were cast-iron flowerpots out of which the flowers were pulled and trampled; and the candles were pulled out of the red lanterns of remembrance. Most painful for the families was the disappearance of the remembrance plaque in the centre of the garden calling on everybody 'to honour and remember' the twenty-nine people who lost their lives in the bombing.* 'This was a frenzied, meticulous attack on a place that is sacred to so many people in this town,' said Michael Gallagher. 'In fact, many of the relatives were in tears this morning.' Francie Mackey, opposing plans to protect the garden with a closed-circuit television camera, put the damage down to anti-social elements who flourished because the nationalist population had no confidence in the police. Liz Gibson articulated the more mainstream view that the attack was linked to the extensive coverage of the projected civil case. For the families who were contemplating putting their names on a writ, it was the starkest of reminders about the viciousness of the people they were up against.

Those of us who lived in London were often asked if we were not afraid the Real IRA would come after us because of our involvement with the families. Mostly we were not, though some of us were concerned about the vulnerable Sean, and about H_2O, which was housed in an easily

---

* The dishonouring of symbols of the grief of others is not uncommon in Northern Ireland. In March 2009, supporters of dissident republicans destroyed flowers left in honour of Stephen Carroll, the first policeman to have been murdered in over a decade.

accessible building. Having tried, and failed, to get some protection from the Metropolitan Police, Jason shrugged and carried on.*

On Saturday 14 July 2001, there was an expedition from London to Omagh. All except one of the families who had lost a relative in the bombing had been invited.† As well as Dan Brennan, there were Jason, Greenie and Davidaire from H2O, the Trustees were represented by Máirín, and the rest of the London group by Janie Dawnay, Henry, me, and Hugo, our administrator. Sean came too, but did not appear until the families he did not know had left. Although he was crucial to what was going on in London, both as an analyst and conduit to the media, in Ireland, where his past made him both an object of suspicion and a target for the IRA, he necessarily kept in the shadows.

We had given a lot of thought to the choreography of the meeting, since the issues for the families were as immense as they were complicated and some of them knew little of what had been going on behind the scenes. First, Henry gave the background to the case and spoke about the protests and lobbying in the UK, the Republic of Ireland and the US against the Real IRA and its offshoots. Then came Dan, who had a very difficult role, because he was asking people to try to understand the alien, arcane world that was the law, tell them honestly something of the constraints, illogicalities and frustrations that went with the territory and give them encouragement to proceed while allowing the opportunity to drop out without embarrassment.

I would see many of Dan's future court performances, but the memory of him winning the confidence of the small, bereaved group for whom he was the last and only hope sticks with me above all. He displayed

---

* One of Jason's wall decorations was a letter from a friend quoting Jim Malone, the American-Irish cop in *The Untouchables*, who tells Elliot Ness: 'You wanna get Capone? Here's how you get him. He pulls a knife, you pull a gun. He sends one of yours to the hospital, you send one of his to the morgue. That's the Chicago way, and that's how you get Capone.' (Malone ended up dead: Ness got his man.) The friend had added underneath: 'You wanna get RIRA? Here's how you get them. They pull a knife, you pull a writ. They send one of yours to hospital, you send one of them to court. That's the civil law way. And that's how you get RIRA.'

† The exception was the family of Michael Grimes (who had lost wife Mary, daughter Avril, granddaughter Maura and the unborn twin girls), who had rebuked the Omagh Support and Self Help Group at the end of the inquest. He had walked out of the October 2000 meeting where Jason told the families of a potential civil case, and later sent a legal letter saying his family did not want to be contacted.

gravitas, but he also showed the humanity that has driven so much of his legal work. For the families, Lord Brennan and his beautifully cut suits, his fabulous shock of expensively coiffed white hair, his gravelly voice and his formal choice of words (in public, that is: in private he is salty) seemed like the epitome of the Establishment. Yet his message was that, although he had to remain objective and professional, he had a history of challenging the powerful on behalf of the powerless. One difficult but successful case he told them about was where haemophiliac children had been denied compensation by the government because they had contracted HIV from infected blood plasma.

Dan painstakingly went through the options under civil law and their implications. The main advantage of a civil case was that hearsay evidence was admissible, and in theory that there was a lower standard of proof, though in practice the gravity of the charge meant there would have to be strong evidence. He recommended the families pursue punitive exemplary damages, normally awarded in the case of negligence or abuse of power, but which should, he believed, apply to those committing acts of terrorism. The claims would be based on a combination of principles: intentionally causing injury, conspiracy and intentionally doing something which indirectly causes injury.

Could the Real IRA be sued as a group? he asked. Why not? Had they not admitted their responsibility for the bomb? Huntingdon Life Sciences, beleaguered by violent protesters, were already setting a precedent by suing a nebulous animal liberation group. Whether the Real IRA alone or the Real IRA and the 32CSM should be the target was under consideration, as was the choice of whom to sue.

'Why pursue the action?' is a heading in the notes of that meeting. 'From a legal point of view, the objectives are:

- This has never happened before. It is the first ever claim against a terrorist group in a civil court. The victims are claiming against the terrorists. The claim is brought with a distinct purpose – damages.

What effect might it have?

- The threat of recovery is very damaging [to the Defendants].
- It has morale-damaging potential, which is reassuring for the families.

- The publicity would have an enormous effect. It would demonstrate that there are ways to counter terrorist attacks by ordinary people. It would be an historic example.'

Then, step-by-step, Dan described to the families what would be involved if they decided to go ahead. He explained how the Plaintiffs – those taking the case – would have their names alphabetically on the writ that would trigger proceedings, as would those chosen as Defendants; how a writ was served; what would happen when proceedings began; what could go right and what could go wrong. Warning the families that if they went ahead, they would have to cooperate fully with H2O and keep all sensitive material in total confidence, Dan predicted a 65 per cent chance of success. 'Why not 100%?

- At the moment there isn't enough evidence
- Uncharted legal territory
- Can't predict what might come out of the woodwork on the other side.'

Knowing that Colm Murphy, for one, had already by 2004 transferred substantial assets to his family, there were questions about how the Defendants could be made to pay. It might not be possible, answered Dan, though if the families won the law might be changed.

While the families did not qualify for legal aid, Dan had explained, all costs would be met by the trust funds. It was Máirín's job to put that in context and apply the brakes to any undue optimism. She introduced herself, explained it was the Trustees' job to control the spending of money and told the group where the money had gone and what was still needed just to issue the writ in August. Deliberately low-key, cautious, practical and realistic, she was reassuring about how the writ could be discontinued if financial pressure was too great. There would be a year's grace after the lodging of the writs in the High Court before the point of no return – the actual serving of the writs on the Defendants.

Janie had been saved for last. While some of the families never quite understood where the London group was coming from, they could all relate to Janie. Although the daughter of a duke, she had been brought up locally, loved the countryside of Fermanagh and Tyrone, could chat learnedly about horses with Gerry McFarland and Stanley McCombe and had obvious personal reasons for being devastated by Omagh. She is also sunny and effervescent, gave the families hope and made them feel part of the fundraising effort. 'The meeting was fascinating in a horrible way,' said Máirín afterwards. 'They were all completely different people and had only their experience in common. Almost everyone was in a rage and those that weren't were just sad, sad, sad. But Godfrey and Ann [Wilson] I found the saddest of all. Decent, good people. The story Ann told me about Lorraine and her wedding dress was the most poignant thing I had heard all weekend – probably all year.'

Just a few events from the twenty-seven days between this meeting and the lodging of the writs give an idea of the extraordinarily complex and shifting background against which the families would be single-mindedly pursuing justice. On the 14th, inter-party and inter-government talks to rescue the peace process broke down and the 32CSM trumpeted their expansion in England and Ireland; on the 17th, President Bush called upon the IRA to disarm to save the stalled peace process and the media reported vicious infighting within the Real IRA over suspected informers; on the 19th and 20th there was a bomb and an arms find; on the 22nd, a tabloid Sunday newspaper had an 'exclusive' story from Michael ('OMAGH BOMB SUSPECTS FACE CIVIL ACTION: Plea for cash to help fund £1 m legal costs') in which he said: 'We believe we have got the best team we could have and we are going to see this through'; Michael was in the *Irish News* on the 24th, confirming the writ would be lodged by the cut-off date; on the 26th, it was reported that anonymous senior security sources had 'admitted it was unlikely that the Real IRA unit responsible would ever be charged with the 1998 murders'; on the 28th, gardaí arrested four men at a Real IRA meeting at a County Meath hotel – including Liam Campbell, then out on bail; on the 29th, there was uproar when the *Sunday People* ran an allegation that a former double agent known as Kevin Fulton* had tipped off his RUC Special Branch handlers three days before Omagh that the Real IRA was preparing an enormous bomb but that to protect a mole nothing was done; it was also alleged that though gardaí had been tipped off by

---

* His real name was later publicly revealed to be Peter Keeley, who for years had been fighting to force the government to provide him with a new identity, relocation and a pension from the British government that he claimed he had been promised in his years as a double agent.

another informant about the details of the Vauxhall that would transport the bomb, they had lost track of it; on the 30th it was reported that
the gardaí refused to comment but the RUC vehemently denied the
allegations, which Michael described as being 'very, very serious' and
in need of being 'fully and independently investigated'; that same day
Campbell and three associates, who had been found with a stun gun,
were charged with membership of an illegal organisation and were
remanded in custody; on Tuesday the 31st the families had a two-hour
meeting with John Reid, Peter Mandelson's successor as Secretary of
State.

Afterwards Michael said little about the encounter except that they had
been assured that the Omagh investigation was 'very live and active' and
there would be no let-up. Laurence Rush was less diplomatic, dismissing
Reid as yet another minister doing nothing, showing no commitment and
'papering the walls'. Godfrey Wilson was even angrier. 'We're just victims
and as far as I can see the system would wish us – what has been happening
for the past 30 years – to go away . . . it's just bury our dead and just go
away.' More and more, disappointed victims were voicing their disillusion
with the justice system and the political establishment.

Back in London, where lawyers and fundraisers were furiously at work,
the violence came close to home. On Thursday 2 August, some friends
were at my house in South Ealing, west London. A few seconds after
midnight, several of us were dancing when the journalist Dean Godson
– then writing a biography of Trimble, and one of our main allies in the
media – who was gazing at us sardonically, suddenly said, 'I've heard a
gunshot.'

'Nonsense,' said Sean. 'Just a car backfiring.' And some of the rest of us
so-called experts on terrorism mocked Dean for his overactive imagination. What he had heard was, in fact, a 100-pound car bomb which the
Real IRA had set off up the road in Ealing Broadway. By a miracle, for
hundreds of young people were leaving clubs and pubs at that time, no
one had been killed and only seven injured. Several businesses were
destroyed and debris was flung more than 200 yards, but Ealing had been
lucky.* While we were appalled when the news came through, we had to
laugh. Had they parked near my house, they could have taken out people

---

* In April 2003, John Hannan (19), Aiden Hulme (25) and his brother Robert (23), Noel
Maguire (34) and James McCormack (34) were found guilty of this bombing campaign.

at the heart of the campaign against them. Henry, Máirín or I could have been done without, but the eradication of Sean or Jason would have finished off the case. 'Sean,' Jason said to me once, 'was the common linchpin with everyone and the only person who understood how tough I found it being everyone's fall guy internally and publicly. As far as I was concerned, I think of all those times I thought we were going to go bust, Greenie or Paul had had enough, I thought I'd lost everything including the law firm and Sean would convince me something was going to come up and made me want to believe it.' 'Jason's at his best when his back's to the wall,' Sean has said of him. 'That's when he really focuses and comes up with something no one else could think of.'

On Sunday, Henry, Jason, Sean and I were among those in the grave-yard of a Surrey school as a priest blessed James Barker's gravestone. In the media, that same day, Michael was further drawn into the Kevin Fulton imbroglio, backing the suggestion that the Police Ombudsman should investigate his allegations and, on television, Sir Ronnie Flanagan warned that Real IRA capacity was approaching the level of the Provisionals. That was a message which annoyed the Irish government, which had been briefing for weeks that not only was the Real IRA fatally compromised by infiltrators and garda raids, but that McKevitt's arrest signalled its demise. The following day Dublin reported that the Criminal Assets Bureau was now investigating Real IRA suspects including those suspected of being behind the bomb. The Continuity IRA, clearly feeling left out, complained on the 7th that two of their prisoners were on hunger strike in Portlaoise prison in protest against bullying by the INLA; they were demanding segregated facilities and political status. And on Thursday, in response to the news that Slovakia looked likely to extradite three Irishmen alleged to have been procuring weapons for the Real IRA, the 32CSM issued a statement warning darkly of the sinister agenda of those trying to save the 'failing peace process' and promising a campaign to force the men's release. The following day, 10 August, with the filing of the writ at the High Court, attention was firmly back on the victims of Omagh as well as the alleged bombers.

Nine families – twenty-two individuals – representing ten victims, went on the writ of summons filed with the Northern Ireland High Court of Justice on 10 August. Geraldine Breslin's widower Mark headed the list, followed by Aiden Gallagher's parents Michael and Patsy and sister Cathy, Esther Gibson's father William, brothers Eddie and Robert and sisters

Audrey, Caroline, Liz and Wilma, Ann McCombe's widower Stanley, Samantha McFarland's father Gerry, Alan Radford's mother Marion and brother Paul, Libbi Rush's widower Laurence, Edith White, widow of Fred and mother of Bryan, and Lorraine Wilson's parents Ann and Godfrey and brothers Colin and Garry and sister Denise.

There were a few names missing from among those who had backed the case early on and had told their stories to help with fundraising. Victor Barker had already pulled out for professional reasons, as he was a lawyer himself: although he would continue being supportive to the end, he knew he was more useful as a fundraiser, media spokesman and harasser of authority than as a client who would be forever second-guessing H2O. Breda Devine's mother Tracey still faced years of pain and skin grafts and, with three young children, she and Paul decided they could not cope with the strain of the case on top of everything else and detached themselves from the campaign. Philomena Skelton's widower Kevin had gone to pieces under the strain of trying to cope with his grief and his four motherless children. Having given up his job and his football refereeing and turned to drink, he fell apart for a time. 'It was pure hell,' he told a journalist years later. At his lowest point, 'I had a double-barrelled gun under my chin with my fingers on the two triggers.' He would rally magnificently by throwing himself into fundraising for Romanian orphans and be a stalwart in the OSSHG and a great friend to Michael.

There had been much agonising about who should be named as Defendants: H2O wanted more than counsel thought sensible. Yet the only relevant issue was whether the lawyers had enough evidence, so – with a promise that if circumstances allowed, more would be added – reluctantly the list of possibles was reduced to the Real IRA and five men: Seamus McKenna (43), of Silverbridge, Newry, County Down; John Michael Henry McKevitt (50), of Blackrock, Dundalk, County Louth; Liam Campbell (37), of Mount Pleasant, Dundalk, County Louth; Michael Colm Murphy (48), of Ravensdale, Dundalk, County Louth; and Seamus Daly (30), of Culloville, near Castleblaney, County Monaghan. Four out of five lived in the Irish Republic.

Morale was boosted by the media coverage and the cheques that followed, but there were troubles ahead. Kevin Fulton's allegations would exacerbate differences between members of the group and Laurence Rush's interventions about the RUC during the Omagh meeting had caused Dan

Brennan concerns, which Jason had relayed to the families before the issuing of the writ. 'Lord Brennan clarified the nature and focus of this action: the RIRA. He stated that your strength is that you and the other families have no political agenda and that you are all motivated by the loss of your loved ones and a search for justice . . .'

> I appreciate that there are many views on where the fault may lie for this tragedy but our only focus in this action is on those responsible for planning, planting and detonating the bomb. Should anyone feel aggrieved at any other third parties then that grievance should be addressed through other means. Any departure from our focus will damage not only your own claim but also the claims of the other families which are pursuing this particular avenue of justice.

Yet Fulton's widely publicised accusations were threatening this focus. In mid-August, on the third anniversary of the bomb, Laurence interrupted a joint press conference called by the gardaí and the RUC to appeal for witnesses. 'My dear sir,' he said, 'this is a conspiracy . . . by the British government and by everyone involved in the administration. This is an example of administrative terrorism. Why did Sinn Féin close their office the day before the bomb? Why was the army confined to barracks? Why, sir, did the RUC have only three men on the streets of Omagh and twenty-four men out in the surrounding areas?'

Peter Mandelson, former Secretary of State, defended the police: 'While they have very strong intelligence, they have been able to identify who they think is responsible, they know who they want to bring to court, the problem is converting intelligence into evidence that will stack up in court.' He called for the laws preventing the use of intelligence material in court to be changed. But the next day, Fulton's claims were given new respectability by an enormous spread in the *Guardian*: 'REVEALED: THE EVIDENCE THAT FORCED A NEW OMAGH INQUIRY'.

David Sharrock, the *Telegraph*'s veteran Northern Ireland correspondent, coolly analysed the latest developments. The newspapers 'both tell of murky goings-on in the intelligence world, alleging that the Royal Ulster Constabulary ignored a warning given by an IRA informer before the bombing that might have prevented the carnage. The allegations, if true, are horrendous. If false, they are spectacularly cruel, not only to the detectives investigating the bombing, but also to the families of the victims who still hope that the killers who robbed them of their loved ones will be caught and convicted.' Yet, as Sharrock pointed out, Fulton had been for years making allegations to the media about security forces being party to killings to preserve intelligence sources, he had appeared on television and had for £50,000 sold a story to the *Mail on Sunday*, which they had not published. He had also visited Victor Barker, who had been unimpressed. Sharrock also quoted a letter from Chief Constable Sir Ronnie Flanagan to the editor of the *Sunday People*. 'You should be aware that the so-called informant behind this story is known to the RUC and to the investigation team headed by Sir John Stevens [the Metropolitan Commissioner who is investigating allegations of collusion between the security forces in Northern Ireland and terrorists].' At his own request, Fulton had been interviewed by Stevens's team 'and at no stage made mention to them of the Omagh outrage'. And retrospective information given to the RUC about Omagh was 'without any foundation whatsoever'.

Flanagan's letter concluded angrily: 'Your publication can only have caused further untold and needless distress to the victims of this terrible atrocity, who have already suffered and continue to suffer so much.' Pointing out that what was preventing the police from charging those they believed were the bombers was 'the Irish republican omerta code – the code of silence', Sharrock ended with a quote from Flanagan – given after he had attended the memorial service – welcoming the news that the Ombudsman was launching an investigation. 'I am sure that it will show that these claims are nonsense.'

Yet at the beginning of December, the media were in a state of great excitement arising from leaks suggesting Nuala O'Loan's report would be excoriating Special Branch. The timing was terrible. A month previously, and almost eighty years after its foundation, the Royal Ulster Constabulary GC* had been renamed the Police Service of Northern Ireland, further

---

* In November 1999, at the instigation of Peter Mandelson, the RUC was collectively awarded the George Cross for gallantry. The citation was: 'For the past 30 years, the Royal Ulster Constabulary has been the bulwark against, and the main target of, a sustained and brutal terrorism campaign. The Force has suffered heavily in protecting both sides of the community from danger – 302 officers have been killed in the line of duty and thousands more injured, many seriously. Many officers have been ostracised by their own community and others have been forced to leave their homes in the face of threats to them and their families. As Northern Ireland reaches a turning point in its political development this award is made to recognise the collective courage and dedication to duty of all of those who have served in the Royal Ulster Constabulary and who have accepted the danger and stress this has brought to them and to their families.'

demoralising many police who believed politicians had sacrificed them to appease republican sensibilities. Now, gleefully, republicans were exploiting the leaks further to belabour Special Branch, conspiracy theories about police sacrificing innocents to protect informers were rampant and many of the families were consequently in a state of heightened distress. At the thought that Aiden might have survived had warnings been acted upon, Patsy Gallagher – a rock of strength – took to her bed in despair.

In London, lawyers and supporters alike were fearful that the fundraising effort would be damaged as the focus moved from the bombers on to the police, and Henry and I were despatched to Omagh to talk to Michael about steadying the ship. He was calm and thoughtful, but he and other members of the OSSHG had met Fulton and, unlike Victor, Jason and others who had met him in London, mostly they believed him. Michael was suspending judgement pending the report.

Henry and I sent messages to Flanagan urging that he reassure the families urgently, but he was pre-empted by Mrs O'Loan, who spent four hours in Omagh presenting her report to victims immediately before making it public. Among her allegations were: Fulton's evidence was credible and should have been acted upon; an anonymous warning on 4 August of an 'unspecified' attack on Omagh had not been passed on to the Omagh police commander; the investigation was riddled with errors;* and 'the judgment and leadership of the chief constable has been seriously flawed'. Sympathetic, lucid and supremely self-assured, she gave a strong impression of someone fearlessly taking on the Establishment. One of the serving police present commented to me later: 'She almost convinced us that our colleagues were Keystone Kops and that Special Branch feeds its own babies to the wolves.' Some of the families immediately called for Flanagan's resignation.

In the view of Flanagan at a press conference later that day, O'Loan and her team had reached 'erroneous conclusions in advance' and then conducted 'a desperate search' to find the facts that supported her theory. Her mostly English detectives were ignorant of the area they were investigating: 'I am astounded by their ignorance of terrorist operations.' The report was gross 'in terms of its basic unfairness' and its 'sweeping

---

* Much of the criticism came directly from the unpublished internal Omagh Bomb Review Report of November 2000 by Detective Chief Superintendent Brian McVicker. (See Chapter 7.)

conclusions about myself and about other colleagues without any of us being spoken to'. In a 'denial of natural justice', the Ombudsman had refused to give him adequate time to refute the report's findings before publication. Flanagan then completely lost his cool and declared that if the Ombudsman's conclusion about defective leadership had been reached 'as a result of a rigorous, fair investigation, I would not only resign. I would go on to publicly commit suicide.' The media were ecstatic.

Among those horrified at the turn of events was Senator Maurice Hayes, who as a member of the Patten Commission had written the report that led to the setting up of the office of Police Ombudsman. O'Loan had, he wrote, gone beyond the terms of her job, which was 'not about the efficiency of police operations'. Coupled with her 'trenchant and uncom- promising' language, he feared she might 'well have made it impossible for her office to maintain any constructive relationship with the police'. Peter Mandelson – who, as Secretary of State, had refused DUP demands that he replace O'Loan because she was married to a nationalist politician – told the BBC, meanwhile, that the report was 'a very poor piece of work' and 'displayed a certain lack of experience and possibly some gullibility'. In *The Times*, he deplored her failure to understand that 'the achievements of Special Branch and those associated with them far outweigh their deficiencies' and described it as 'wrong and offensive' to 'pit the "testimony" of a self-confessed liar against the reputation of a Chief Constable of Flanagan's integrity and courage'.

The Real IRA nevertheless saw an opportunity, and issued a statement that they knew of two 'agent provocateurs' handled by MI5 who were 'instru- mental in the planning and implementation of the bombing that occurred that day' and that 'a senior government representative, as well as a cleric' could confirm the Real IRA's 'minimal involvement in the bombing'.*

The PSNI's detailed eighty-seven-page rebuttal of O'Loan's 'signifi- cant factual inaccuracies, misunderstandings, material omissions and

---

* This was a reference to the 1998 meetings with Martin Mansergh and Father Alec Reid. In November 2002, in response to media allegations that a deal had been done between government and the Real IRA post-Omagh, Bertie Ahern said that the government had had no contact whatever with the Real IRA 'after Omagh or at any other time'. In October 2003, Ahern was embarrassed when the truth about the Mansergh meetings emerged, courtesy of a journalist. Michael Gallagher's comment was that revelation was all the more reason for a full judicial public enquiry to be held into the Omagh bombing. 'We have been told mis-truths, after mis-truths.'

unwarranted assumptions' and the bruised and angry Flanagan's subsequent five-hour meeting with the families did not repair the damage. What he was desperate to communicate was his belief that, even if the police had responded differently, they still could not have prevented the bombing. The trouble was that the Ombudsman's intervention had accentuated the families' growing distrust of those in authority. 'I feel we are being used,' said Kevin Skelton, 'by would-be politicians such as Gerry Adams and Sammy Wilson [of the DUP] to score points. The whole emphasis has turned into a slanging match between the chief constable and Nuala O'Loan. There has to be a public inquiry.'

Laurence Rush came off the writ in February 2002 and initiated a civil case of his own against the police and the government. With the exception of Patsy Gallagher (who continued in support), the others stayed on, but the strain on them told as they became more and more cynical about politicians, police and the criminal justice systems north and south of the border and murkier and murkier allegations surfaced.*

To many of the families it seemed an outrage that Ronnie Flanagan resigned not because of Omagh but in order to take up a job in Her Majesty's Inspectorate of Constabulary. There were also mixed feelings about what was happening to the Defendants in the Republic of Ireland, where three were in jail. Liam Campbell was serving five years for membership of an illegal organisation; Colm Murphy had been given fourteen years in January 2002 for conspiring to cause an explosion; and McKevitt had been charged in March 2001 with directing an illegal organisation and was on remand. Seamus Daly was charged in February 2002 with membership of an illegal organisation and was on bail. The general view among the families was that, as a result of their public persistence, the police had come under political pressure to make a special effort to get those on the writ behind bars.

What mattered to the families was that Murphy alone had been charged in relation to Omagh. What mattered too was that the Real IRA were continuing on their murderous path, but that the authorities still soothingly insisted they were under control and little attention was paid by the media unless someone actually died. Kevin Myers was an exception. He wrote a haunting piece in March 2002 in the *Irish Times* about

---

* Conspiracy theorists were now convinced that the two governments had allowed Omagh to happen in order to help the peace process; some believed they had organised the bombing.

25 JANUARY 2003

the times
magazine

77 HOURS
The trapped
American miners
tell their story

PLUS
LISA STANSFIELD
STEVEN SPIELBERG
KATE MUIR
ROBERT CRAMPTON

The
Enforcers
The lawyers taking on the Omagh bombers

Lucy Morgan, David Greenhalgh, Jason McCue, Paul Fox
and Rose Alexander of H2O, September 2002

Robert Cranborne tidying Jason McCue at a fundraiser, Warrington, May 2002

Peter Mandelson, Donna-Maria Barker, Daphne Trimble, Victor Barker, Jason McCue, Caroline Martin, Bob Geldof and Mariella Frostrup

Caroline Martin, Barry McGuigan, Claire Radford, Bob Geldof, Carol Radford and Ann Wilson, February 2002

Godfrey Wilson, Stanley McCombe, Patsy Gallagher, Ann Wilson, Michael Gallagher, Kevin Skelton and Carol Radford after a meeting with the Irish Justice Minister, May 2004

Marion Radford, Claire Radford, Michael Gallagher, Stanley McCombe, Caroline Martin, Ann Wilson, Mark Breslin, Carol Radford and Godfrey Wilson outside court in Belfast after the first procedural hearing, 23rd April 2004

Jason McCue, Godfrey Wilson, David Greenhalgh, Lady Janie Dawnay, Ruth Dudley Edwards, Victor Barker, Edith White and Carol Radford, Whitehall, November 2005

Dan Brennan QC

Tony McGleenan, Brett Lockhart QC and Dan Brennan QC outside Court No. 2

Jason McCue,
John Ware and
Charlie Mitchell
on the steps of
the court

Matthew Jury and Beverley Wong in Bittles

Paul Dacre, editor of the *Daily Mail*. The *Mail*'s fundraising campaign gained widespread public support for the families

Stanley McCombe, Michael Gallagher, Godfrey and Colin Wilson, Mark Breslin, Ann Wilson and Denise Kerrigan addressing the media outside the High Court in Belfast, 7th April 2008

Godfrey Wilson, Victor Barker, Ann Wilson, Stanley McCombe, Michael and Patsy Gallagher, and Marion and Carol Radford outside 10 Downing Street, after meeting Prime Minister Gordon Brown, 11th February 2009

Lesley-Anne Henry, Mark Breslin, Peter Kelly, Godfrey Wilson, Jason McCue and Michael Gallagher after the victory

Daily Mail

TUESDAY, JUNE 9, 2009   www.dailymail.co.uk   50p

HALLELUJAH FOR JUSTICE

Our day of reckoning: A victorious Michael Gallagher, centre left, and fellow Omagh campaigners outside Belfast High Court after yesterday's judgment

For 11 years – backed by a Mail campaign – they refused to give up. Yesterday these Omagh families won a historic court case against the Real IRA bombers who slaughtered their loved ones . . . proving ordinary people CAN take on the terrorists

SPECIAL REPORTS AND ANALYSIS — PAGES 4-7

Peter Mason. 'In his mid-forties, he has been banished to a world in which there is no light, no sound, no dignity, no independence.'

> This abominable fate was not caused by some freakish accident, but by the deliberate deed of wicked people. Peter, a civilian security guard with the British army, lost his eyes, his ears, his arms, after he picked up a flask on the ground near Magilligan Strand, Co. Derry, on February 8th. He turned it over to examine it. It had a tilt-switch which was triggered by this move-ment, detonating the explosives concealed within, instantly ending his life – not with death, but by an exile to a silent, lightless, touchless hell, one made by the Real IRA.
>
> The Real IRA: they haven't gone away, you know. And why should they? In essence, they got away with the Omagh bombing, and they have got away with much since; worse, they are growing. And any broad measure to sweep these heathen savages into the confinement they deserve will be denounced as a threat to the peace process by their rivals for ownership of the republican conscience, Sinn Féin–IRA.

If the Real IRA leadership read this, it did not trouble them: in August, David Caldwell, a builder, was killed by a booby-trapped lunchbox at a Derry Territorial Army base.

Scepticism grew, fuelled further by Nuala O'Loan. In March she presented to the Irish Minister for Foreign Affairs a report concerning allegations made to her by a serving garda officer that gardaí had with-held from the RUC information which might have prevented the bombing; she requested that the Irish government initiate an investigation. The Irish government were unhappy, not least since they knew the unnamed officer to be John White, a sergeant who had been arrested on corruption charges in March 2000.* On 9 May it was announced that a three-man-group† was investigating his claims.

That was the same day Michael, Victor, Kevin and Billy Jameson (whose

---

* Although he was cleared in two trials in 2005, after White was found by the Morris tribunal investigating garda corruption in County Donegal to have been implicated in 'farcial' and 'inappropriate' policing, planting evidence to make wrongful arrests and making false statements, he was dismissed from the force.

† Eamon Barnes, former Director of Public Prosecutions; Joe Brosnan, former Secre-tary of the Department of Justice; Dermot Nally, former Secretary to the Government. White's claim was that an informant had told him that the week before Omagh he was asked to supply two cars to dissident republicans.

wife and son had been injured in the bomb) met the Home Secretary, David Blunkett. 'You could see that he was moved by what we had to say,' said Michael afterwards, outside the Home Office, 'but he didn't comment in any way.' Victor, who still distrusted Fulton, had been stunned by the allegation from the still-unidentified Sergeant White. Officials had continually insisted that there was no specific intelligence and that police either side of the border were cooperating, he said to the television cameras: 'We now believe this was a lie and we in the communities, North and South, have been deceived. Significant action and leadership is now required from both governments if we are ever to have the belief that a full, transparent, joint investigation is to take place where politics and religion play no part in the search for the evidence that will bring these evil people to justice.' Billy Jameson, Presbyterian and hitherto loyal Ulsterman, spoke for many members of the Omagh group when he later told a journalist: 'I am never going to vote again in my life. I wouldn't talk to a politician because they are nothing but liars.'

In the midst of all the gloom, there was the euphoria of Friday 26 July, when the writs were actually served. Much planning by Jason and Sean had gone into this to ensure maximum media coverage. Selected members of the press had been told to rendezvous at a hotel in Dundalk, to dress casually, not to have anything that identified them as journalists, not to assemble in groups but to carry a copy of the *Daily Telegraph* – a very unusual paper to be reading in Dundalk. Jason – sporting designer stubble, a baseball cap and glasses – introduced himself and produced a frisson of excitement by telling them that he would be risking a good beating if anyone recognised him. He had reason to disguise himself, being already a familiar face on television, and his association with Mariella Frostrup had really got the press excited. 'MARIELLA'S MAN TAKES ON THE REAL IRA' said the *Daily Telegraph* two months before the serving of the writs: he 'appears unfazed by the attention paid to his more recognisable girlfriend at film premiers and fashionable restaurants,' wrote the legal editor, but 'defeating the Real IRA in court would make Mr McCue a national hero. Before long, he may be the one the photographers want to see.'

Seven cars set off from Dundalk police station at 5.30 a.m. under a grey sky, some with journalists and some with gardaí, and pulled up at Seamus Daly's scruffy, red-brick house in County Monaghan, where his white van had been seen the night before. Four gardaí – two in flak jackets – watched as Jason knocked repeatedly at the front door. The curtains were drawn and the windows were open but no one answered, so Jason put the writ through the letter box and the convoy proceeded to Daly's parents' farm, five minutes down the road. As dogs barked and Jason knocked, the television cameras struck lucky. A curtain was pulled back by Daly's elderly father, and Jason passed a copy of the writ through the window saying, 'This is a writ to your son on behalf of the families of the Omagh victims. Could you pass it on to him?' 'Get out, youse fuckers,' shouted Daly and shovelled the writ back out of the window. Seamus Daly's father cannot have been pleased either that his encounter with Jason was transmitted on television as a lead story or that there were dramatic press photographs complete with an elderly woman crouching by his side.

Jason had to be content with posting Seamus McKenna's writ through his letter box, and then others from H2O took over. In the afternoon, journalists waited outside Portlaoise prison, about seventy miles from Dublin, where Campbell, Murphy and McKevitt were then residing. Davidaire asked to serve the writs, and now that she was a trainee lawyer, Jason and Greenie agreed. Campbell and McKevitt would accept the writs, she was told, but Murphy had refused. A 'very very nervous' Davidaire was taken by a female prison officer into a waiting room, stood with the writs in her hand and the officer brought in Campbell and McKevitt. The Ireland of that time, north and south, was almost exclusively white, so, whatever they were expecting, it wasn't a tall, thirty something, stylishly dressed black woman wearing dark glasses. They were a bit shocked, she remembered. 'It kind of took the wind out of their sails.' What struck her most was how different they were. 'McKevitt was really up for an argument but Campbell was totally different. He was very, very cold, staring at me fixedly, trying to stare me down like a hard man.'

Campbell did not address a word to her in the ten minutes the three of them were together, but McKevitt talked. 'I know why you're here,' he said, when she had begun explaining that she was serving writs on them. 'I'm telling you now, I never murdered anybody in Omagh and there are people out there who know who killed these people in Omagh and nobody said anything about it.' 'So who do you think killed the people in Omagh?' she asked. 'And he said, "You don't expect me to answer that, do you?"' So she repeated the explanation of why she was there and gave them the writs. Murphy's writ was handed to him later by the prison authorities.

'NO ESCAPE' was the *Daily Mail* front-page headline, with a quote from Michael: 'It is three years, 11 months and 11 days since the terrorists came knocking on our doors . . . now it's our turn to go knocking on theirs.'

After all that heady excitement, to Jason's and Greenie's horror it emerged on Saturday that, because of a technical error at the Belfast end, the writs were invalid. Thus it was that, armed with replacements, Jason made from Dublin late at night a shamefaced call to Charlie Mitchell, who had been a key but anonymous player in the saga of the civil case. I had been introduced to Charlie in the mid-1990s by Henry Reid – with whom he had been at school – and in turn introduced him to London friends. What Charlie did for a living in County Tyrone in army intelligence was to save lives – which involved repeatedly putting himself in danger. A legendary networker, he liaised with other security agencies to become an expert on the psyche, habits, strengths and weaknesses of the local paramilitaries: his circle called him 'Oracle'; one of his innumerable friends, the Duke of Abercorn, who lives in Tyrone, nicknamed him 'Long grass', for Charlie knows how to watch and wait (or 'skulk', as Abercorn put it). If an attack was expected, Charlie told me, 'I would pass up the food-chain to the decision-makers and covert agencies the best possible information for the purpose of planning an operation to thwart an attack, or, if there was no other option, a return-serve!'

Up against the fearsome Tyrone brigade of the Provisional IRA, Charlie's network was itself to become an awesomely efficient intelligence operation, with around 80 per cent of operations planned by republican or loyalist terrorists somehow frustrated or disrupted. When I asked Charlie more about it, he responded with a shiver. 'I was speaking with an old friend a few weeks ago, and he was recounting the number of lives saved and the number warned they were about to meet their maker . . . I tell you this, it was bloody scary – literally dead men walking! The great thing is: few ever knew how close they were, nor do they ever need to.' One person Charlie had not been able to protect was Michael Gallagher's brother Hugh, whom he warned just twenty-four hours before he was murdered in 1984 not to drive his taxi in the local area. Hugh simply shrugged fatalistically, saying he had to support his family; he died a few hours later near Omagh riddled with bullets.

Charlie did not confine himself to his job. Warm-hearted and munificent with his time, money and hospitality, he became close to those he called 'the posse', which included Jason, Henry, Sean, me and anyone else he thought was doing something useful for Northern Ireland and whom he could help. There was a particularly strong bond with Sean: they shared the mutual respect of old enemies. Charlie would turn up in the most unexpected places: in Dublin during the Slab Murphy trial; at Hatfield House, then the home of Robert Cranborne's father, during a unionist conference organised by Sean; at events at the Commons. He could always be relied on to pick up Sean at Belfast airport when he was making a clandestine visit, or to ferry a lawyer or two or any of the posse if he thought we needed protecting. In return, we might find ourselves giving after-dinner talks about politics to the officers' mess.

Charlie assured Jason that he'd look after things and called a senior garda friend. Jason drove from Dublin, arriving at Charlie's house in the middle of the night, and the writs were successfully served again that morning on the Daly and McKenna households with only Charlie and a couple of gardaí present. This time Jason was physically attacked by a brother of Seamus Daly and though not averse to a scrap, he did not fight back but ran and bore the bruising as a badge of honour. The onlookers did not interfere: a punch-up involving a family of rabid republicans, a London lawyer, a British spy and two gardaí was not part of the plan. By order of the High Court, the other writs were considered served by post and newspaper advertisements.

There were few highs for anyone during the almost six-years saga before the case came to court. One such was in February 2003, when the families subpoenaed Gerry Adams, Pat Doherty, Martin McGuinness, Brian Gillen and Brian Keenan, whom they alleged to have been members of the IRA Army Council at the time of McKevitt's walkout. This caused terrific media excitement, especially when Adams declared darkly that there must be an ulterior motive and elicited a threat from H2O to sue him for slander.* In time, there was the overwhelming relief for the fundraisers of being put out of business when, in 2003, Peter Mandelson had managed to secure the families legal aid. But since there were

---

* Six years later, when the case came to court, this initiative had long been abandoned: there was no likelihood that anyone would be forthcoming and the inevitable media circus threatened to be counter-productive.

outstanding bills to be paid and legal aid was not retrospective, it would take many begging letters from the Trust to previous donors to extricate ourselves fully. The London group stayed on call if needed; the Trust stayed in existence to deal with technical or financial crises, Sean and George Bridges helped out with the media and Robert Cranborne was always available as a source of advice and encouragement when anyone despaired at the latest setback.

Various of us would show up in support of the families when we thought we could raise morale: there would always be someone to greet Victor when he crossed a marathon finishing line. And there was Henry's involvement with Victor and Michael in campaigning to have vicious pro-Real IRA websites closed down. Essentially, the support group was off-duty but available when needed.

One memorable occasion was on 29 November 2005 when, after five years of lobbying, an OSSHG delegation came to London to meet Tony Blair to ask for a cross-border judicial enquiry. It was during another period of intense frustration: in August, McKevitt's lawyers had succeeded in securing a High Court ruling that the Lord Chancellor had no legal power to order the Legal Services Commission – which dispensed legal aid – to fund the Omagh relatives. Although the Lord Chancellor's lawyers had made it clear that a way would be found to provide the money even if it required a change in the law, H2O's source of income had abruptly stopped: with invoices outstanding and no means of paying counsel, they had no option but to suspend work on the case during the six months it took to resolve the matter.

Jason and I and a few other supporters had lunch with the relatives. Janie Dawney and I left early to join Victor, whose requests to meet the prime minister had again been rebuffed but who had come up from Surrey to stand outside the gates of Downing Street with a placard reading '31 dead, still no justice – remember Omagh?' In doing so he was acting illegally: infuriated by Brian Haw, who had been protesting loudly in 2001 from his unsightly one-man peace camp in Parliament Square, the government had recently banned all unlicensed protests within half a mile.*

Janie and I arrived to find Victor, flanked by a silent Sean, arguing

---

* There was public outrage in October 2005 when Maya Evans was charged under the new act for standing at the Cenotaph reading out names of British soldiers killed in Iraq.

with police who had first moved him across the road and were now telling him that he would be arrested if he stayed there. Jason joined us just when Janie and I – outraged that Victor of all people should be the victim of oppressive legislation and heavy-handed policing – had decided we would be arrested rather than move. It was shaping up to be an interesting afternoon when a woman officer took over and was so reasonable and conciliatory that we compromised. But just as the Omagh families arrived, Ken Reid of Ulster Television recognised Victor and told him to follow him into Downing Street. So the power of the media prevailed and Victor got to talk to Tony Blair again. At the press conference after the forty-five-minute meeting, Victor reported that the Prime Minister had promised that no one connected with the Omagh bomb would be granted an amnesty. Michael believed they had been given a fair hearing, but that Blair had said no enquiry could be held until after criminal and civil cases: 'We are weary after seven years of campaigning but will go on. I feel that some of the people close to the prime minister have been a bit naïve in how they have handled the Omagh bomb and they have underestimated the Omagh families' determination to get to the truth.'

I was also wearying, as I had become locked into the case by agreeing to write a book and there seemed no end in sight. It was Sean's fault. He suggested I do it and eventually wore down my resistance through emotional blackmail: knowing the true story, how would I feel if an outsider did a bad and unfair job? The publishers of my previous book were keen, were unafraid of the Real IRA and were relaxed about the impossibility of predicting when the case would end and the book could be published, so in December 2003 I signed a contract, thinking the case would be over and the book out by 2005.

The families were good to me. I had got to know them as individuals over the years in strange, often highly charged, circumstances, had watched with fascination and admiration how they coped with extraordinary challenges and always appreciated their openness in talking about their tragedies and their lives. From all of them I learned enough about grief to share their anger at how facile can be those who have no knowledge of deep suffering but who lecture those who have. I interviewed each of them independently, but my most valuable insights often came from listening to their reactions after big events. But as I spent more time with them, I became ever more aware of the strain the case was putting on them and on their relationships with each other and with the outside world. Although the group had quietened down after Laurence Rush went his own way, there was a great deal of tension. While they were proud of the extent to which they had transcended politics and religion, there was, of course, residual cultural baggage. For some, Michael's high profile was a cause of resentment since it inevitably made his son more prominent than other victims. 'Of course no one died except Aiden Gallagher' was one remark that took me back to my childhood. My republican grandmother had occasionally gone to tea with the widow of Tom Clark, one of the executed of 1916, and would always return saying: 'Mrs Tom Clark says the Pearses* think they own 1916.'

It is human nature to want those you love to be given the honour they deserve, but there was little Michael could do about his public prominence. No one else had the ability – nor indeed the desire – to be chairman of the OSSHG. Articulate and accessible, Michael was the face and voice of Omagh, so it was no surprise that he became the central figure of a film.

Paul Greengrass had written and directed *Bloody Sunday*, a well-made 2002 film of which I had been highly critical because of what I saw as its remorseless anti-state bias.† My comments in the *Daily Mail* attracted a libel writ from Don Mullan, who described himself as a 'co-producer and source writer', and a row on RTE radio with the lead actor, James Nesbitt.

Before they had even finished *Bloody Sunday*, Greengrass and Mullan were in touch with Michael about the possibility of a film. For Greengrass, 'Omagh and Bloody Sunday are for me two events that bookend the Troubles,' he told the *Observer* in May 2004. 'There were many terrible and meaningful events in between, but Bloody Sunday was the moment at which the tide towards conflict became inevitable. It seemed to sum up several generations of injustice in one afternoon . . . And Omagh was the point at which that was reversed, when the tide to settle became irreversible.'

---

* The mother of the executed Patrick and Willie was dead by then but one sister published a book about the family and another remained a Fianna Fáil Senator until her death at the age of ninety.

† I did not know until much later that Greengrass's long-standing interest in the more shadowy activities of the British security forces had taken him in the early 1980s to Australia, where he co-wrote with Peter Wright the notorious *Spycatcher: The Candid Autobiography of a Senior Intelligence Officer*.

Mullan liaised with the families and was a co-producer; Greengrass co-wrote and co-produced but did not direct *Omagh*, as he took off to Hollywood to direct a blockbuster spy movie, *The Bourne Supremacy*. *Omagh* was first shown to around fifty victims' relatives in Belfast, where the pre-bomb scenes of innocents enjoying themselves were, as Godfrey Wilson put it, 'heartbreaking and almost unbearable', and the graphic scene where the bomb explodes caused one survivor to throw herself screaming and convulsing on to the cinema floor. 'I hope the film will open the eyes of millions of people to the pain we're still going through,' a sobbing Caroline Martin said to the *Irish Times*. 'We're hurting with pain, day in, day out.' Along with some of the London group, a few of the relatives and Kevin Fulton, I saw *Omagh* in May 2004. Essentially the story of the Gallagher family, Michael was superbly played by the Omagh-born actor Gerard McSorley, who depicted him as he had found him: 'very quiet and unassuming, but also very forthright, with an air of quiet authority'. It had addressed honestly the tensions caused by what his family sometimes thought was Michael's obsession with justice. 'There are a lot of times,' he told the *Daily Mail*, 'my wife's said: "Look, we've done what we've done. Maybe we should get on with our lives while we've still got some left to live."'

I found much of it very moving, but I was disturbed by what I considered its one-sidedness. Fulton and John White appeared as credible witnesses, Sir Ronnie Flanagan came across as patronising and mendacious, while Nuala O'Loan, played by the Oscar-winning Brenda Fricker, was a heroine who bravely told the families that the police had failed them comprehensively.* Yes, as Greengrass had wished, it did suggest that 'out of tragedy the families of the Omagh Support and Self Help Group have

---

* Five years later I saw *Five Minutes of Heaven*, a film that I thought far better than *Omagh* showed something of the true agony of victims and what they suffer from the uncomprehending. Based on a true story, it stars James Nesbitt as Joe Griffin, who is consumed with anger at Liam Neeson's Alastair Little, who had ruined his life. Not only had Griffin – as a child – the horror of watching his brother's murder, but his mother had always irrationally blamed him for not stopping the gunman. His fury intensifies as the well-meaning try to push him to forgive. It was brilliantly scripted by Guy Hibbert, who had co-written *Omagh*, and who comes from the town. 'I first started out thinking this would be about truth and reconciliation and all those rather cliched thoughts,' said Hibbert. 'I had a quite a simplistic view, I suppose, although I had done *Omagh*. But I learned through the process that it's a lot more complicated than those awful simplistic words like "closure" and "forgiveness". It's incredibly tough.'

pursued a campaign for justice that symbolizes hope for us all', and it would go on to win prizes, but I regretted the emphasis on conspiracy. While I knew the police had made mistakes and that governments were dissimulating and fudging and covering up errors in the way governments do, I distrusted Fulton* and John White,† and in the ensuing years believed myself vindicated. Michael and I did not discuss such issues: we understood where we disagreed and we agreed to differ; he knew how committed I was to the families, trusted me to write the book fairly and gave me all the help he possibly could. Similarly, when Victor decided that Sir Ronnie Flanagan should resign because he bore the ultimate responsibility for the botched aspects of the investigation and criticised him harshly in public, he knew I thought he was being unfair but it never affected our friendship.

I had some conversations about the film with other relatives, but not about the thrust of the film. All had found it very painful to watch, though Patsy Gallagher laughed at being portrayed by someone young and glamorous, as Victor chuckled at the nerdy Englishman who popped up from time to time suggesting a civil case and taking a remorselessly rational line against the emotional Laurence Rush. Yet, though Stanley, the Wilsons, Marion Radford and some others of Michael's close allies had no problem with his domination of the film, others did. 'So James had no mother,' said Donna-Maria Barker at the showing. And for the Gibson sisters in particular there was a deep hurt that their story had been virtually ignored. I defended to them the filmmakers' focus on the Gallaghers as a necessary dramatic device, but I could see why it caused pain and exacerbated divisions among bereaved people who were emotionally exhausted from

* I kept an open mind about Fulton, read and checked out his various allegations and finally met his ex-handler from Special Branch, Ivan Sterritt, who took me through the twists and turns of Fulton's career as an informer – from reliable to erratic to untrustworthy to Walter Mitty. I decided to leave Fulton's theories to those more inclined than me to believe in conspiracies rather than cock-ups.

† I have no illusions about the Establishment's propensity to conceal and whitewash, but, having followed the various investigations into White's allegations, I do not find him a credible witness. Even allowing for my scepticism about the Establishment, I know and trust Dermot Nally, whose report said White voiced no concerns about Omagh until March 2000, when he was arrested, and Michael McDowell, the then Minister for Justice, with whom I had a helpful conversation about White. Yet in the view of the OSSHG, expressed forcibly when a fifteen-strong delegation met the Taoiseach in March 2004, the Nally report was incompetent. Chief Superintendent Norman Baxter, who at first took his allegations seriously, eventually dismissed them.

disappointment, frustration and pressure from outsiders to drop a case that many doubted would ever get to court.

It is easy to forget how courageous were those who took the case, for in addition to their fear of the Real IRA all knew that locally it was unpopular. For those who wanted the town to return to normal, it was an embarrassment to keep talking about the bomb and well-wishers thought them obsessive and urged them to give up and move on. Their insistence on keeping Omagh in the public view annoyed many who had lost loved ones in equally tragic circumstances: for some of the bereaved of Enniskillen, only twelve miles from Omagh, it seems as if the eleven murdered at the cenotaph on Remembrance Day 1987 were unimportant by comparison because they were all Protestants. What was so special about the Omagh victims that entitled them to the justice that had been denied so many?

Likewise, some nationalists passionately committed to the peace process resented the embarrassment to Sinn Féin every time Michael or Victor pointed out that Adams and McGuinness still refused to ask witnesses to come forward: in *Omagh* there was a fictional meeting with Adams which portrayed him as cold and evasive. There were unionists who resented the criticism of the police and there were Establishment representatives in Belfast, Dublin and London who found the OSSHG a confounded nuisance. They were, however, indefatigable in seeking to meet anyone they thought might help and, as they became more and more aware of the prevarication of authority, they became more and more confrontational. Bertie Ahern was stung when he came to Omagh the day before the fifth anniversary service and the OSSHG refused to meet him because he had never before agreed to their requests for a meeting and was now offering only a few minutes. He met them in Dublin the following March and had to put up with strong criticism about the limitations of the Nally report. A friend in Irish officialdom told me of an occasion when an OSSHG delegation came to Dublin to meet a senior minister: 'We were all on their side until they arrived, but they were so suspicious and angry that by the time they left we never wanted to see them again.' At a meeting with the Irish Minister for Justice, Michael McDowell, Godfrey lost his temper and told him that politicians 'were lying through their teeth'.

Mistrust and anger had become a feature of OSSHG meetings even before *Omagh* but the rows forced some to realise that they had to make the organisation more professional and more focused on all the victims of Omagh. 'None of those in charge had a clue how to structure an organisation or run meetings,' Kevin Skelton told me once. And funding was hand-to-mouth: in August 2003, Michael told a journalist that the group had received only £4,000 in official funding in five years. Henry had given the group £10,000, the full proceeds of a successful libel action ('It comes with admiration, affection and best wishes to you all from Henry,' wrote his solicitors), and I contributed £5,000 from my book advance. But while sums like that made it possible for the families to travel to meetings, they were still in a prefab and had no administrative help.

Yet at the AGM in June 2005 Michael was able to report remarkable progress: consultants had helped create a three-year plan which had secured funding, there was a full-time coordinator, and a management committee training weekend had taught the participants a great deal. The OSSHG now had clear objectives: 'Our mission is to promote, advocate, and address where possible, the needs of victims of the conflict in Ireland in order to achieve health, peace of mind, security and the foundations for personal growth. We are committed to addressing the real and practical needs of those bereaved and injured as a result of terrorist activity, and ensuring that victims are afforded the respect and consideration they deserve.'

Michael's chairman's report spoke of 'the turbulent time' the group had gone through in mid-2004, the culmination of a long period of strain and divided opinion. Samantha McFarland's father, Gerry, who had been Treasurer and the main link on legal issues with the Trustees and H2O, and Liz Gibson, who had been Secretary, were at loggerheads with Michael, and, by extension, with his close allies; this breach had been exacerbated by *Omagh* and ended with their departure from the group along with all the Gibson family except Eddie. They would come off the writ in July 2007, citing the disagreements, the intolerable delays and their belief that there was an Establishment conspiracy which would preclude justice. Edith White, exhausted by delays, frustrations and disapproval from people she knew, had come off too, although she continued as Assistant Secretary to the group and a fierce supporter of a public inquiry. Those left on the writ were down from nine to six families, from twenty-two to twelve individuals representing six victims: Mark Breslin, Michael and his daughter Cathy, Eddie Gibson, Stanley McCombe, Marion and Paul Radford and the Wilson family.

The wonder was not that several of the relatives came off the writ: it was that any stayed on at all. What they, the Plaintiffs, wanted, was a smooth path to an early trial. What the Defendants wanted was to drag proceedings out for as long as possible in the hope of breaking the spirit of their accusers. The weapons they used were legal technicalities and appeals – the more time-wasting the better. And they were assisted by the lack of urgency in the legal system – particularly in the Irish Republic – and the reluctance of police to help the civil case if they felt that it might in any way jeopardise any of the criminal cases grinding their way through the courts. All began at the Special Criminal Court, where three judges, sitting without a jury, try cases involving subversive and organised crime.

The saga of Colm Murphy, the first of the five men on the writ to be charged, continues to the time of writing. He was charged with 'conspiracy to cause an explosion likely to endanger life or cause injury' and bailed in February 1999; his trial began in October 2001 and was halted for a time by a judge's illness; he was convicted in January 2002 and sentenced to four-teen years;* in April 2004, appealing against the rejection of his application to the Special Criminal Court for legal aid to appeal, he was granted it 'reluctantly' by the Court of Criminal Appeal on the grounds that, having given his house to his estranged wife and his money to a trust fund for his children, he was without assets; his conviction was overturned in January 2005 over an allegation that two gardaí had altered interview notes, a new trial was ordered and he was bailed; in October 2005 the gardaí were found not guilty of perjury; in May 2007 judgement on a judicial review at the High Court was reserved after the argument that the retrial should not go ahead because delays had prejudiced Murphy's right to a fair trial, and his capacity to defend himself was prejudiced by the short-term memory loss he had sustained after a head injury in 1988; in October 2007 the High Court ordered that the retrial go ahead; in October 2008 the Supreme Court heard his appeal against that refusal to halt his retrial, and at the time of writing, the Supreme Court's judgement on that appeal has still not been handed down.

Campbell was next. Having been charged with Real IRA membership in October 2000 and bailed, arrested and charged with the same offence in July 2001 and held on remand, he was jailed in October 2002 for five years; the Criminal Assets Bureau seized almost €1 million of his assets because there was no obvious source for his substantial wealth, and in January 2003 ordered him to pay an €820,000 tax bill; his conviction was

---

* In Portlaoise prison, he took up residence in the wing of the Real rather than Continuity IRA.

quashed in December 2003 by the Court of Criminal Appeal because of irregularities in evidence, but in May 2004, described as 'the former director of operations of the Real IRA', he was convicted on two separate counts of Real IRA membership and given two four-year sentences to run consecutively, with the final eighteen months suspended. The court took into account his previous good record, his commitment to his family and the fact that he had not contested the evidence, which it said would be equivalent to guilty pleas. That same week a High Court judge in Belfast acquitted four men found in possession of a rocket launcher of Real IRA membership on the grounds that the organisation was not proscribed;* 'this is the degree of incompetence and indifference I have dealt with over the past five years,' said Michael; in February 2005 Campbell's appeal on the grounds that the Real IRA was not a proscribed organisation in the Irish Republic was dismissed by the Supreme Court.

Having taken a statement from David Rupert about Michael McKevitt's Real IRA activities, in March 2001 gardaí had stormed the McKevitt family home and charged him with 'membership of an illegal organisation' and 'directing terrorism', i.e. being a Real IRA godfather; his trial ran from June to August 2003, when he was sentenced to twenty years; his appeal to the Court of Criminal Appeal was rejected in December 2005; in July 2006 he was given leave to appeal to the Supreme Court; his appeal was rejected in July 2008; in March 2009, in rejecting his application for a fresh hearing of his appeal on the grounds of an admitted factual error in the 2008 hearing, the Chief Justice said the five-judge court considered McKevitt's application 'unmeritorious and opportunistic'.

McKevitt was desperate to get out of jail and was prepared to make concessions to do so, but since Campbell, as ever, would brook no compromise that might make some deal with government possible, there was a vicious split between them and their supporters inside and outside prison. In October 2002, McKevitt's faction – five Real IRA prisoners in England and thirty-six of the thirty-nine in Portlaoise – issued a statement 'calling the Army Council to stand down with ignominy' and denouncing 'this Army leadership' as criminals who had forfeited all moral authority; their targets believed the authors were looking for lighter sentences. An

---

* Specifically, that it was not listed in a legal schedule of banned organisations appended to the Terrorism Act 2000, which named the Irish Republican Army and the Continuity Army Council. The Northern Ireland Court of Appeal overruling of that judgement was upheld by the House of Lords.

accompanying briefing document said the Omagh bomb had irreparably damaged the Irish republican struggle. 'It represented an enormous tactical blunder on our behalf and it graphically pointed to the monumental dangers that flow from any unauthorised co-operation with any other republican organisations.' There was no prospect of military activity yielding any political advantage: 'When it becomes apparent that the continuation of armed operations is futile, it is the moral responsibility of the republican leadership to call a halt to such a campaign.' Campbell and two allies, now moved for their own protection to the INLA wing as 'guests', opposed any ceasefire and remained in alliance with the outside leadership. To Real IRA critics, by implicitly pointing a finger at the Continuity IRA, McKevitt was committing the unforgivable sin of 'squealing on a sister organisation' and it was 'business as usual against the Brits': he and his supporters were expelled by the outside leadership, who stayed loyal to Campbell.

When Daly was served with an arrest warrant in February 2002, he maintained family tradition by ripping it up. Charged with membership of the Real IRA between April 1998 and November 2000, he was granted bail against gardaí objections, not least because searches at and near Daly's home had found number plates for a car with the same markings and colour as that used in Omagh, as well as sugar bags and gloves containing nitrates.* Daly pleaded guilty in March 2004 to the very much reduced charge of membership on one specific day – 20 November 2000 – which took him out of the frame for Omagh – and was sentenced to imprisonment for three and a half years, half the maximum, as he had a clean record. 'Sentences like the one today and the way these people have been treated are a further blow to us,' said Michael, perplexed as to why the charge against Daly relating to membership in 1998 had been dropped. 'It seems all the authorities, including the government, are happy to be [dealing with these people] outside the period of Omagh because it is easy.' What made it worse was that PSNI sources claimed that at the time the gardaí had arrested him, officers north of the border had been waiting for him to go drinking in Northern Ireland so they could interrogate him over Omagh.

Seamus McKenna, found in a farmyard in County Louth in June 2002 mixing more than 1,200 pounds of home-made explosives, was charged

---

* Icing sugar and ammonium nitrates can be used in bomb making.

with unlawfully and maliciously possessing an explosive substance with intent to endanger life; he pleaded guilty in December 2004 and was sentenced to six years. In July 2006, the Director of Public Prosecutions failed in his bid to have sentences increased on McKenna and his accomplice, Joe Fee,* who had pleaded not guilty and been sentenced to ten years.

Of the five, McKevitt's was the trial that provided high drama. There was the sight of Omagh families sitting in the public gallery only a few feet away from Bernadette Sands-McKevitt and her mother; there was the occasional outburst from Laurence Rush, who shouted 'what about Omagh?' as the charges were being read or 'scum' when evidence was particularly painful; and above all, there was the improbable six-foot-seven-inch figure of fifty-one-year-old David Rupert, who arrived under heavy American and Irish security and with difficulty squeezed his twenty-stone frame into the Special Criminal Court witness box, where he would calmly deal with fifteen days of often gruelling cross-examination. Of Mohawk Indian and German descent, he had been nicknamed 'The Big Yank' and 'The Mohawk Mole' by the republicans he would betray to his FBI and MI5 employers.

Rupert was already a hate figure. It had emerged at Woolwich Crown Court in London in May 2002 that he had provided the information about McKevitt's search for sponsorship from a rogue state which had enabled MI5 to set up an elaborate sting featuring an agent posing as an Iraqi arms dealer. Declan Rafferty, Michael McDonald and Fintan O'Farrell had been charged with conspiracy to cause explosions and Rupert was in London to give evidence that would implicate McKevitt, the real target of the sting, when, to save their boss, the defendants pleaded guilty; they were each sentenced to thirty years in jail.

So Dublin was Rupert's debut outing in person. It emerged early in the proceedings that he had had what was politely described as a 'colourful' past, which included spells in haulage, insurance, construction and catering, three bankruptcies and four marriages. His connection with Ireland had begun in 1992 when, while on holiday with an Irish-American activist girlfriend, he got to know members of the Continuity IRA and became a

---

* Joe Fee was a key figure in the Continuity IRA, but cooperated with the Real IRA. An engineer known by Irish intelligence to be part of the Continuity IRA, Fee had returned to Ireland in 1997 from Bosnia after working for eight months for the unwitting Department of Foreign Affairs' Irish Aid organisation.

frequent visitor; in 1994, he accepted an offer from the FBI – who had been tipped off by Garda Special Branch – to finance his trips to Ireland in exchange for information and in 1997 he agreed a contract to work as a well-paid agent; he would soon also work for MI5. 'He described himself as a whore,' said the prosecuting counsel, pre-empting what McKevitt's defence might pick up on, 'saying whoever would pay him he would work for.' Rupert would later dismiss this as a joke: his morals might have been lax, but he disapproved of murder. Rupert proved to be a natural: he had courage, was cool under pressure, inspired trust, was streetwise, a good judge of people and a keen listener and had an excellent memory for names and numbers that made the more than two thousand detailed e-mails he sent his FBI and MI5 handlers invaluable: he earned his $1.25 million.

His cover was that of a prosperous, affable, republican sympathiser. In June 1999, McKevitt set up an umbrella group called Óglaigh na hÉireann* that included members of the Provisional and Continuity IRAs and INLA along with the post-Omagh rump of the Real IRA; in August, Rupert was taken to a recruitment meeting and introduced to McKevitt; and the following month he had a proper meeting with him and Seamus McGrane.

In the Dublin court, short, stocky, balding McKevitt watched Rupert closely through his gold-rimmed spectacles and took copious notes: the baseball cap and windcheater of his usual public appearances had been replaced for his trial by outfits more befitting a small-time businessman; he had gone, wrote the journalist David McKittrick, 'from the dramatic to the dapper . . . from the sinister to the clerical'. 'The meeting went real smooth,' said Rupert. 'I liked Mr McKevitt. He seemed pretty personable. I felt the feeling was mutual.' Rupert would meet him twenty times, become a close colleague and confidant, his IT consultant and occasional provider of technology and dollars, and his representative in the labyrinthine politics of republican Irish-America. He gave evidence that his instructions from McKevitt were to report to him 'number one, to Liam Campbell number two and to Bernadette McKevitt number three'.

McKevitt, said Rupert in evidence, had told him that the Real IRA was 20 per cent, and the Continuity IRA 80 per cent, responsible for Omagh, as the Continuity had chosen the target. When they found the parking place intended for the bomb was inaccessible, 'he said the boys should have just driven it out to the country but they drove it down the road and

---

* Volunteers of Ireland: see p. 1 footnote.

parked it and created the Omagh atrocity', which had made McKevitt 'horribly upset'. While the Real IRA had claimed responsibility, the Continuity had remained silent and Ruairí Ó Bradaigh, President of its political wing, had denounced the bomb: 'it left the Real IRA in a hot spot,' said Rupert. Yet, regrouped as Óglaigh na hÉireann, the Real IRA had been responsible for the June 2000 bombs on Hammersmith Bridge and the September 2000 rocket attack on MI6 headquarters. Car bombs 'were out' because of Omagh.

In December 2000 the FBI had asked Rupert to testify against McKevitt, but he had refused because he feared he would be murdered. They asked him to take one more night to think about it, and that evening he switched the television to a 'random channel' which was showing a documentary about two Omagh survivors – a blinded girl and a boy who had lost his shoulder blades – that moved him to change his mind.* But he wanted to be sure that, if he testified, it would not be 'a minor arrest', but one that 'put this terrorist organisation out of business'. He agreed a new contract that would pay him and his wife $12,000 a month until they were no longer deemed at risk. Only when, at the end of his cross-examination by the prosecution, he was asked to identify McKevitt, did their eyes momentarily meet.

Apart from innumerable arguments before various courts about which documents could and could not be disclosed, McKevitt's defence had put a great deal of time and money into researching Rupert's background with a view to discrediting him as a fraud, a criminal, a tax evader, a smuggler, a liar, a perjurer and much else: there was questioning about shady deals, swindling creditors, dodgy associates, plans for offshore gambling, a period when he tried to become a professional wrestler and the transporting of an underage girl across state boundaries. He was quizzed too about a period working in an undercover FBI drugs operation, a job which he said he took on to get out of the house as 'my first wife was a bit of a bitch'. Eventually, Hugh Hartnett, the defence counsel, making much of occasional inconsistencies, put it to Rupert that he had 'concocted and invented a tissue of lies', his evidence had been 'serial deceit' and he had never met McKevitt. 'That's foolishness,' said Rupert. Gardaí later testified to having seen the two men together.

Then, sensationally, McKevitt first applied for the trial to be halted

---

* *Omagh the Legacy: Claire and Stephen's Story* was first broadcast in 1999.

because of late disclosure of a document which showed that Rupert had made a mistake in a date, and, when he failed, sacked his legal team. His address to the court ended sonorously with 'I will not participate any further in this political show trial and I now withdraw with my dignity intact.' He refused to reappear in court so the trial went on without him and on 6 August the judges declared him guilty of both charges: the court considered Rupert 'a very truthful witness' with 'considerable knowledge of the facts to which he testified'. McKevitt was not there to hear that, nor, the following day, to hear Presiding Judge Richard Johnson sentence him to twenty years; he pointed out that McKevitt was fifty-three and married with a young family, and that the relevant offences took place after the Omagh bombing and the court 'must not be seen to seek revenge for the atrocity'. Subsequently, his wife Bernadette stood outside Portlaoise prison reading a statement from him which concluded: 'From the outset I never expected to find justice in the Special Criminal Court. Since its inception the Special Criminal Court has shown itself to be a discredited house of law and devoid of justice. In this regard my expectations were confirmed, as I was systematically denied a fair trial throughout the past six weeks. However, I am determined to take my case before another court in an attempt to overturn this flawed judgement and to attain justice.'*

After the verdict, standing outside the court, the Omagh relatives told the press that this result bolstered their determination to see through the civil action. Victor homed in on McKevitt's defence of the Real IRA's role in Omagh: 'There can be no percentage of responsibility. If you stole the car or mixed the bomb, you are 100% responsible.'† And then he said goodbye and went off to meet a representative of the Real IRA. Again.

There had been no diminution of Victor's determination to pursue justice for James by any means he believed reasonable: acting besides as part of a team when he could be useful, he had continued to hoe his own row. Sinn Féin, like everyone else of significance, was badgered mercilessly. It

---

* www.michaelmckevitt.com has this statement, the address he made to the court and the full text of 'The Framing of Michael McKevitt', a 'political hostage', which 'outlines the gratuitous suffering imposed on the McKevitt family culminating in the framing of Michael' and was written by his sister-in-law Marcella Sands.

† A week later, the Continuity IRA condemned the 'political show trial in the Stalinist style' and denied it had cooperated with the Omagh bomb: 'We wish to totally refute these absurd lies uttered by this mercenary.'

was Victor – not Michael, as portrayed in *Omagh* – who had the unsatisfactory meeting with Gerry Adams, also attended by Pat Doherty and Martin McGuinness, with whom Victor had a curious relationship. While Adams appeared completely cold, McGuinness seemed to have a human streak and was vulnerable to Victor's goading, particularly to what became the anniversary text message. This exchange was typical:

15 Aug 2007: 'Martin 9 years today since oglaigh na h'Eireann murdered my 12 year old son and still no justice. Isn't it now time 4 u 2 come clean and tell me the truth? Victor Barker

16 Aug 2007: Victor, in my last text 2 u I said I would meet with u the next time I am across there. I will keep my word on that, V. I kno 2day is another very sad anniversary for u all, but 2 credit me with knowledge I just do not have is most unfair. Other than the perpet'ors, both govts and their agencies kno more about Omagh than anyone. Best wishes, M

Unknown to any of us, for he had promised secrecy, Victor had begun hounding the Real IRA in 2002 for a meeting, using as an intermediary the journalist John Mooney, who was writing a book on the Real IRA and who, like so many who made friends with Victor, had found himself conscripted to James's cause. Eventually, Victor wore down the Real IRA and flew over to meet them with Mooney, in a hotel in Swords, north Dublin, in December 2002, when the schism within the organisation was raging. He was greeted by Francie Mackey, who stressed that he was there on behalf of the 32CSM: 'Surely you don't expect me to believe that?' asked Victor, and Mackey repeated his position. Of Mackey and the two men there who admitted to being of the Real IRA, Victor asked what good had come of murdering James and other innocents. They spoke for three hours, much of it, predictably, about Irish history and the merits or otherwise of the Good Friday Agreement before Victor demanded they tell him if the Real IRA was still committed to violence. 'Mr Barker,' said one, 'there is a feeling among some sections of Óglaigh na hÉireann that armed insurgency is now counter-productive. But you have to understand that we find ourselves in a sensitive position. Nothing is simple.'

It wasn't much of a concession, but Victor drew some comfort from it, as he had from the pre-arranged meeting he had later the same day with Bertie Ahern. Having given his word not to speak of the Real IRA meeting, he instead asked Ahern if he should meet them were it to prove possible.

According to Mooney, who was present, Ahern answered: 'If you think something good can be achieved, then work away. You certainly won't be doing any harm and you might get through to someone.'

So it was that eight months later, on the day McKevitt was convicted, Victor went back to the Swords hotel with Mooney to meet a Real IRA contact, this time asking if the new Army Council would agree to meet him face-to-face. It was out of the question, said his interlocutor, and there was the same predictable argument about history and violence. Before Victor left for London, he asked if McKevitt's conviction would stop the Real IRA: 'Victor, it's a storm in a tea-cup. McKevitt will be forgotten about in two weeks' time. The army, be it the Provos or the Real IRA, will always be there. That's just the way it is.'*

Back in Omagh, approaching the fifth anniversary, it was another period when the relatives were on an emotional roller coaster. On Wednesday 6 August McKevitt was convicted; on Thursday he was sentenced; on Friday, it was announced that the British government would back the civil case financially; and on Saturday, in an *Irish Times* article about Omagh five years after the bomb, Michael, Laurence and Gerry spoke of the importance of justice, while Esther Gibson's Uncle Oliver, still a DUP councillor, expressed forthrightly his objection to the case her family were taking. 'I fear it [the civil case] could be a waste of time and money and the outcome could be a disappointment to the people of Omagh who have already suffered so much. We should concentrate on improving life for those left behind. The bombers have to live with their consciences. It's better leaving these things to God and providence. I want Omagh famous for something other than the bomb. We need a forward-looking society, not one with a chip on its shoulder.'

Now an Assembly member for West Tyrone, he pointed out that ninety-seven other people had died in West Tyrone during the Troubles. 'Their relatives haven't been as vocal as some Omagh bomb families. They have coped with their grief with dignity, far away from the cameras. They feel

---

* When news of the meetings was leaked in October, Victor was defiant. 'By meeting them I was not in any way legitimising the Real IRA's campaign. I went there to help them understand what they did to James and other victims and to urge them to choose a path away from violence . . . This is a path that I chose to pursue. I would meet them again.' Mooney would give an account of Victor's meetings with the Real IRA in *Black Operations*, which was published a few months later, in December 2003; Victor provided an introduction.

some Omagh families seek special status, while they are relegated to being second- or third-class victims. That's felt in other parts of Northern Ireland too. When Omagh bomb spokesmen come on television, there is a feeling, "here we go again".'

Yet on the Sunday came reports that David Rupert might testify against McKevitt in the civil case, a development welcomed by Jason, who was getting nowhere in trying to persuade any security forces to provide either witnesses or documentation. On the following Wednesday, the Irish Department of Justice compounded the frustrations of families and lawyers by saying it did not have the power to provide the families with any relevant court transcripts.

After the first heady days, once the writs had been served, H2O had had to face years of a regime that had infinitely more drudgery than drama. Not that the media had that impression, for, courtesy of Omagh and Mariella Frostrup, Jason had become a celebrity lawyer, a role he claimed to hate but really loved. His conversation became sprinkled with names like 'Mick' (Jagger) and 'George' (Clooney), people from Mariella's circle with whom he had bonded: 'George embraced Jason as a long-lost pal from the minute we started going out,' Mariella told a newspaper. 'I'd pay not to spend time with them, Jas,' I told him meanly one day as he related highlights of his night in the Groucho Club with 'Damien' (Hirst, the frontman of the conceptual Britart movement I despised) and Bono (whose dark glasses and peace babble set my teeth on edge).

Jason was loyal to his old friends, although we mocked him relentlessly. The Saturday morning in January 2003 when he and his colleagues were on the cover of *The Times* magazine, clad in black and glowering to fit in with the 'Enforcers' theme of the lead article, Máirín and I sobbed with laughter over the phone, before sending Jason rude texts. 'If you were casting a television series about a young, idealistic law firm you couldn't better it,' read Paul Mungo's report. 'It's as if the producer said, "Let's include a tall, striking black woman [Davidaire], a former actress [Lucy], an Englishman [Greenie] and an Irishman [Jason, who is actually only second-generation half-Irish]." The mix – although the black woman, Davidaire Horsford, has now left the firm* – is serendipitous: all

---

* Davidaire left when she qualified as the firm could not afford another qualified solicitor. By the time the article appeared, Lucy had handed over to Richard Devall, a university friend of Greenie's, and had moved to Cornwall.

volunteered to work with McCue on the case.'* It was an article that raised money for the case, but had the unfortunate side effect of helping convince the BBC's John Ware that Jason and H2O were charlatans.

One of my most incongruous memories is of a meeting in an Omagh hotel in June 2004 where I was telling the families about the book and asking them to allow me access to the information about them held at H2O. Caroline Martin delightedly brandished a magazine featuring George Clooney serving champagne on his Lake Como motor launch to guests who included two of his co-stars in *Ocean's Twelve*, Matt Damon and Brad Pitt, Pitt's then wife Jennifer Aniston and 'pregnant Mariella Frostrup and her lawyer husband Jason McCue'. The middle-aged men present appeared to have heard of none of them.

At the coalface there was little glamour. Brett Lockhart QC, the Northern Ireland counsel who joined the team in 2002 and became a hero of the case – not least because in pre-legal aid days he charged nominal fees when he charged any at all, subsidising his generosity by his lucrative commercial practice – had laughed at London's hopes of a case beginning in mid-2003. It was Brett who predicted myriad problems and who persuaded H2O to write, in September 2002, to the Senior Queen's Bench Judge, Queen's Bench Division, asking that the case be assigned to a specific judge for regular review. The action was unique, entailed 'arguments as to novel principles of law and the application of recognised principles in new situations', involved a vast body of evidence and 'a large number of procedural and interlocutory matters are likely to arise'. 'We are advised by counsel, and believe, that this action is far removed from the normal personal injury litigation. It is respectfully submitted that this is an action that may benefit from the supervision, from an early date, of

---

* Paul Fox (English), who supported the firm's involvement in the case even when its financial survival was threatened and helped keep it going though reputation management of clients like John Leslie (wrongly accused of rape) and Jade Goody (in trouble for beating up her boyfriend), was not part of the fantasy television series; nor was Rose Alexander (English), a barrister who had joined in March 2002 to track investigations and court procedures north and south. In fact the interviewer had missed a trick by failing to pick up that Greenie was in a gay relationship. He would soon, with Nichola Carter, a lesbian, establish H2O as pioneering lawyers in the field of gay rights; later, he would enter a civil partnership and successfully adopt before the case finished, which caused some hilarity as Dan Brennan and Brett were devout Roman Catholics opposed to same-sex adoption.

a learned judge who may give directions, hear applications and supervise this action generally.'

Mr Justice Higgins (Sir Malachy) was assigned to the case in October 2002 and in the autumn of 2004 was replaced by Mr Justice Morgan (Sir Declan), who would see it through to the end. The Statement of Claim – essentially the Plaintiffs' case – was filed with the High Court in October 2002, but the first procedural hearing did not take place until 23 April 2004. 'This is an historic case,' Dan told the court. 'It is the first time in British jurisdiction that a civil claim has been brought against a terrorist organisation.' Mr Justice Higgins fixed a provisional date of 17 January 2005 for the start of the trial. 'Now the end is clearly in our sights,' Michael told the media. It would in fact take just under four years and around seventy-nine hearings before the High Court and Court of Appeal in Belfast, and the High Court, Court of Appeal, Court of Criminal Appeal, Supreme Court and Special Criminal Court in Dublin, before the case actually began, in April 2008. H2O's Rose Alexander spent a great deal of time in airports: on occasion she would fly to Dublin for a hearing, only to have it adjourned after five minutes to suit a judge or a Defendant's lawyer.

It would be impossible to write for non-lawyers an interesting chronological account of what went on over the six years from serving the writs to beginning the case. There were innumerable pre-trial issues that ate up money, time and hope. Take, for example, the attempts to get hold of the evidence compiled by the prosecution in the Woolwich case in the autumn of 2002 when H2O were desperately trying to put together the statement of claim. In a lengthy letter in May 2004, Rose Alexander reminded the Treasury Solicitor that on 7 August 2000 H2O had sent a five-page, detailed request to Sir David Spedding, the head of the Secret Intelligence Services of the British government, the Head of the Security Service, New Scotland Yard and the Director of Public Prosecutions; on 22 August, 'you indicated that you were instructed on behalf of the Government Agencies' but on 4 October indicated 'you were not willing to assist', not least because the agencies were 'not minded' to allocate the necessary resources or to be involved in any 'wasted effort'; to a detailed response from H2O on 18 November the Treasury Solicitor had replied on 11 December that the Agencies 'felt unable to consider our request at that stage in the proceedings'.

Then there was Dublin. An extract from one of the schedules of correspondence shows during that same frantic period – between early September and mid-December 2002 – the following exchanges with the garda: 'GS letter of acknowledgement re request for interviews with officers; H2O acknowledgement fax to GS; GS letter – still awaiting the advice of Counsel; H2O letter – re possible meeting; GS letter – still awaiting the advice of Counsel; GS letter re possible meeting; H2O letters to GS re meeting and confirming that as discussed, H2O expecting statements within a week; H2O letter to GS chasing statements; H2O letter to GS re not giving statements; GS letter refusing to give prepared statements and suggesting that we apply for depositions.'

During the same period, correspondence with the PSNI ran along very similar frustrating lines.

Sometimes, over the years, the authorities in London, Dublin, Belfast and Omagh were helpful, sometimes they were obstructive and most often their priorities were simply different from those of the families. London was preoccupied with precedent and security, Dublin with the endless trials, appeals and retrials and Northern Ireland with securing a successful criminal prosecution. It did not help that relations between the two police forces were often poor or that Jason had a serious personality clash with Detective Superintendent Norman Baxter, who took over the Omagh investigation in May 2002. Baxter believed H2O were exploiting the families and the case had no chance; Jason thought Baxter rigid and unhelpful. Neither could see the other's strengths and talking to either of them about the virtues of the other proved to be a waste of time. Yet both were driven by a passionate anxiety to win some kind of justice for the families; their means just differed and Baxter was genuinely terrified that the civil case could undermine his developing case against the man he believed to be the Real IRA's bomb maker.

The appended legal timeline gives some impression of the complexity, aggravation and sheer tedium of the actual legal proceedings. From the beginning, for instance, it was not even clear which of the Defendants would fight the case, not least because their status with regard to legal aid kept changing as appeals against its rejection succeeded: Daly and Murphy were still refusing to accept correspondence two years after the writs had been served. Ultimately, all except Campbell, who had nothing more to do with the case ('he sits in the pub and says, Fuck 'em', Charlie's sources reported), were granted legal aid. From a legal point of view, the loss of Campbell was disappointing, since his defence was promisingly bizarre, including denials that any of the Plaintiffs had suffered any personal injury, that he had anything to do with the Real IRA or that the Real IRA had anything to do with the bomb. Still, it was bad enough having three separate sets of solicitors and barristers to help the Defendants spin proceedings out by making sequential appeals about the same issues.

The Plaintiffs' legal aid was another nightmare. It was promised in August 2003, subject to the case plans and costings Greenie then spent weeks drawing up. In February 2004 it was formally granted by the Legal Service Commission (LSC), but in April 2005 McKevitt applied to challenge the decision by means of a judicial review and in August the Northern Ireland High Court ruled it *ultra vires* (beyond its powers). This meant there was no money to go on with the case until, in February 2006, the law having been tweaked, the Plaintiffs were awarded new funding. This was challenged in June by Murphy and Daly and it was not until June 2007 that it was dismissed, though they promptly lodged an appeal that got nowhere.

There were also countless legal wrangles about what is technically known as 'Plaintiffs' application for discovery', essentially a request to the Defendants for copies of the transcripts and books of evidence relating to their criminal trials at the Special Criminal Court. The first request was made in November 2004, but between Defendants' challenges[*] and buck-passing in the Irish courts, the issue was not finally resolved until March 2008, despite the Court of Appeal having delivered a blistering condemnation of the Defendants' time-wasting tactics. The high point of madness was arguably reached when at one stage the Defendants were demanding from the Plaintiffs the very material being sought from them.

Then there was the issue of David Rupert, the Plaintiffs' most important witness, since he could testify against Campbell, McKevitt, Murphy and the Real IRA. Dan, Jason and Richard Devall visited him in the US, where he lived under the witness protection scheme, as Dan needed to assess the scope and value of his evidence. They liked and were impressed by him and embarked on the procedure necessary to have him give evidence by

---

[*] A classic was Murphy's and Daly's appeal on the grounds that production of these documents would be a breach of Article 6 of the European Convention on Human Rights in that it would amount to a shifting of the burden of proof as well as a breach of the Defendants' privilege against self-incrimination; also – contrary to evidence – they claimed that Irish law prohibited them from producing the material requested.

video link. In April 2004, the US Department of Justice wrote to the judge explaining that Rupert and the FBI had concluded he would not be able to travel to Northern Ireland to appear in court. In Ireland in 2003 he had been 'under elaborate security measures that involved enormous financial and law enforcement personnel resources. Even under those circumstances, the stress Mr Rupert experienced adversely affected his health in no small way.' Death threats had been made during the Woolwich and McKevitt proceedings, there was evidence he was being searched for on the net by persons unknown and the risk was still acute, so a video link was the only option. The Plaintiffs' application for him to be heard via video link, first made in June 2004, was brought before the High Court twelve times and finally resolved in their favour in November 2006, long after it had become clear that the FBI would not allow Rupert even to do this – refusing to say if it was for financial or health reasons. The Defendants' delaying tactics had worked. It would have been one thing for Rupert's face to be plastered over the newspapers within months of the exposure in the McKevitt case, but if he wanted ultimately to lose himself in America and lead a normal life and the FBI wanted to save money, it would have been folly to allow that three or more years later, even if Rupert could have borne the stress of another savage cross-examination. Jason fell into despair (his other reactive moods were euphoria, mischievousness and petulance) but, as usual, emerged from it cursing a new enemy – in this case the FBI – and trudging on.*

I went to one typical hearing in the Belfast High Court of Justice in March 2007. Apart from court officials, there was no one present except me, a friend whose loyalty I was sorely testing and eight lawyers: on our side were Dan Brennan and Brett Lockhart, with H2O represented by Jason and Matthew Jury, the latest young lawyer to become excitedly involved in a famous case only to spend months toiling away at minutiae

---

* Possibly the most frivolous delaying tactic was the application to have the writ invalidated because it came from the wrong address. When it came to issuing a writ for proceedings to be held at the High Court in Belfast, H2O consulted the Northern Ireland authorities and were advised to use a Belfast address, which was provided by a friendly solicitor whose name could not be used for security reasons. In June 2005 Murphy and Daly applied to have the Plaintiffs' claims struck out because 'the use of H2O Northern Ireland to sign the writ violated Order 6 Rule 4 of the Rules of the Supreme Court' and so the proceedings were a nullity. These applications were finally thrown out in January 2008.

and learning to cope with intense frustration.* There were four Defendants' barristers, with solicitors for one Defendant or another coming or going, but I had no idea who was representing whom, since the legal protocol is to refer to them as First Defendant, Second Defendant and so on rather than by their names. Nor did I understand anything they were talking about – not surprisingly, since it concerned mysterious applications and pleadings and listings.

My friend fell asleep and I sat in a state of near catatonia, relieved only by the occasional smile from the legal team and Dan calling me out in order to tell me that one of the opposition counsel was driving him insane. Úna and I were ecstatic when it was over and we could go out to lunch with Jason and have him point out that at last I had a glimmer of how mind-numbingly awful the law was and how much he suffered.

Matthew would later give me a snapshot of what life was like for an H2O junior lawyer in a particularly busy year for the civil action. 'When Rose left in January 2007, I took over the day-to-day running of the case,† which largely meant fire-fighting the Defendants' "numerous and vexacious" applications, and becoming H2O's almost-weekly envoy to the High Court of Northern Ireland.' Highlights of his year included the preparation of a forty-five-page review of the conduct of the trial to date and working with two counsel† from the Republic of Ireland to acquire eventually, after ten or so hearings, the long sought-after transcripts and books of evidence from the Defendants' criminal trials. It was tough and often nerve-wracking: 'Fortunately, I always had Dan and Brett to rely on in addition to Jason.'

During those years of hearings so dreary that not even the most committed of the families could bear to attend, lawyers came and went, relatives came off the writ, supporters drifted away to get on with their lives, Jason had two children and Dan almost died. He would look back on his heart attack with much appreciation for the comedy of the occasion.

As President of the Catholic Union of Britain – an association of the

---

* English by birth and education, Matthew had worked on death row in South Carolina for a group of non-profit defenders and was admitted in New York as an attorney-at-law. As he was not qualified in the UK, when he came home he started at the bottom in H2O in April 2006 as a paralegal (trainee lawyer).
† Richard Devall retained dealings with the FBI and Rupert until he left in October, by which time Matthew was Jason's main assistant.

Catholic laity – Dan was much involved in public debate about reproductive ethics. On the night of 19 November 2007 he made a speech in the House of Lords debate on the Human Fertilisation and Embryology Bill, calling for the creation of a national bioethics commission. Baroness Paisley, wife of the Reverend Ian, followed him, speaking against the bill in terms that would have warmed the Pope's heart. 'I trust your Lordships' House will take these words to heart today and reject the proposals in this iniquitous and immoral Bill,' she was saying, when Dan collapsed and the sitting was suspended.*

The Health Minister, Lord Darzi, a leading surgeon, was among the doctors who gave him the heart massage that kept him alive. 'I woke,' Dan told me later, 'looking up at that ornate gilded ceiling and surrounded by praying bishops and thought I was in paradise. Then I realised I couldn't be because they were Anglicans.'

When he came back two weeks later to speak on the same bill, he began with his thanks to those who had saved him and those who had sent him messages in hospital. 'I thank God for the opportunity to return to the love of my family and to continue to serve in this House,' he added, before beginning a demand for clarification from the government on human reproductive cloning. Halfway through a sentence he stopped, said, 'I shall not continue my speech', and fell back in his seat. His new pacemaker had malfunctioned and he had to be taken back to hospital.

We never even speculated on what would have happened to the case without Dan because the thought was too terrible. Year in, year out, he travelled back and forth to Belfast and Dublin for meetings and hearings that taxed his very limited patience, and regularly he went to Omagh to explain, yet again, why the law was being such an ass. That he stuck it out was down to a combination of professional honour, dedication to the families, a refusal to let the bad people win and his chemistry with Jason, who made him laugh.

'Jason McCue', Jason had written to Dan in his first letter in May 2001, briefing him on H2O, 'is arguably the "weakest link" in the legal team. I see my role as being the eternal optimist.' As a lawyer that was one of his distinguishing characteristics, along with the reputation Omagh had brought him of going where more sensible lawyers feared to tread. In 2005, Jane Amestoy, who was desperately trying to stop her boyfriend John Packwood

---

* Hansard simply records: '[*The Sitting was suspended from 7.36 to 8.30 pm.*]', after which one of their lordships asked that the debate be adjourned.

from being extradited to Morocco on a preposterous charge,* was recommended to try Jason. At H2O, she said, 'everyone seemed very young and energetic, yet laid-back at the same time. When Jason himself came striding out to greet us I was immediately struck by his charisma. As he led us into his office I noticed he wasn't wearing a suit, just a shirt, jeans and boots. He was unshaven and puffing on a large smelly cigar as he listened to our story – not the usual lawyer type.'' In the two-and-a-half-hour conversation she was struck by his confidence and quickness. 'He didn't ask any of the dumb questions we had been asked a hundred times before. He seemed to understand and be completely certain that he could get Johnny back. In fact he seemed to be champing at the bit to start on the case.'

He went to Spain and, wrote Packwood later, 'bowled into the prison like a breath of fresh air. "I can get you out of this," he said, "but it will cost you." "Whatever it takes, mate," I said. "But what happens when my savings run out?" "John," he said, "I will stick with you to the end, even if I have to do this in my own free time."' Jason failed to stop the extradition and was in Morocco to see the local lawyer fail to halt the trial. But with all obvious routes exhausted, he learned that the King of Morocco was a fan of George Clooney, who duly wrote a diplomatic letter that produced a royal pardon. The overconfidence, excess optimism, panic followed by the flash of inspiration that saved the day, were all very characteristic.

The legal work Jason enjoyed was the exotic, the adventurous and the boundary pushing, especially if it included standing up for victims. He was thrilled, for instance, at becoming the UK arm of a multi-billion-dollar lawsuit brought against Arab Bank – which is accused of helping finance Palestinian militants – by seven hundred victims of Palestinian terrorism, though it was Greenie – who loves exotic cases, too – who had to spend weeks in Israel listening to the victims. There was the class action on behalf of victims bereaved or injured by IRA explosives provided by Libya, which drags on and on and has involved much political lobbying. An underlying theme was Jason's belief that terrorism should be fought by giving legal redress to victims rather than by eroding civil rights, and that publicising the suffering of victims might show potential terrorists that their bombs hurt people rather than governments. 'Maybe one mother in the Middle East sees our campaign,' he told a magazine in May 2005,

---

* A vast consignment of drugs had been found on a boat he had three months previously helped deliver from Southampton to Agadir, where it had been thoroughly searched.

'and when her son says, "I'm going to be a *shahid* [martyr]" she says: "No you're not, sunshine. You're coming with me, shopping."'

The optimism and thirst for excitement showed themselves too in unpaid campaign work, which gave him the opportunity to spread his celebrity net. Mariella's friendship with Gordon Brown's wife, Sarah, brought Jason into the ambit of Downing Street, where he began to talk to Brown about the horrors of Darfur, which were much on his mind. Visiting H2O one afternoon I was told I'd find Jason in the pub, where he introduced me to a youth called Marlon and a vaguely familiar thirty-something called Alex. The talk was of a song for the suffering displaced of Darfur, which Marlon was to write and Mick Jagger was to finance. I finally clocked that Alex was the erstwhile hellraising member of Blur, Alex James, latterly a teetotal Cotswolds sheep farmer and cheese maker. I left them to it, but Darfur would continue as a backdrop to the Omagh case which provided ever more impressive reasons why Jason couldn't attend this or that: 'Sorry, I'm going to China with George to talk about Darfur'; 'No, can't do it. Have a Darfur meeting at No. 10 with Gordon.'

Jason needed distractions from the frequently unendurable frustrations of the Omagh case. Even when the trial date was set for April 2008, the PSNI and the gardaí continued to refuse to produce vital evidence, or to agree to give evidence in a Northern Ireland court, and legal wrangles about transcripts and books of evidence dragged on. There was, however, the fascination of the criminal case that had been grinding on in the background since September 2003, when more than two hundred police officers and soldiers raided the house of Sean Gerard Hoey, Colm Murphy's nephew, and charged him with possession of explosives and a timer for use in an explosive weapon. Held in custody for more than four years, there would be fifty-eight charges against him, including twenty-nine of murder in relation to Omagh, as well as five counts of conspiracy to murder, four of conspiracy to cause an explosion, six of causing an explosion and twelve of possession of explosive devices. In addition to the Omagh bomb, he was charged with thirteen bomb and mortar attacks.

The case came to court in Belfast on 6 September 2006, was suspended because of the sickness of defence lawyer, Orlando Pownall, restarted on 25 September and lasted fifty-six days spread over ten months. The police investigation had cost in the region of £16 million: defence lawyers came to £2.5 million. There were no witnesses – intercept evidence cannot be used in court – and so the prosecution case against Hoey as a bomb maker rested mainly on scientific evidence, applying a new forensic technique called Low Copy Number DNA, which uses microscopic particles to obtain a DNA profile, to fragments of material gathered at the scenes of bomb attacks.

It was admitted in court – even by a prosecution expert – that there was still 'a lot of confusion' about the science, which was as yet relatively untested and used in very few countries. It was also clear that, for LCN analysis, exhibits had to be handled with particular care in case they were contaminated with other people's DNA; since LCN was not known to NI police and forensic scientists in 1998 they had taken inadequate precautions. Anyone who watched Pownall in action, and the remorseless way in which he discredited much of the evidence, agreed that he was well worth his money.

Initially full of hope, many of the relatives watched on a video link to Omagh, but, as Pownall got to work, some soon lost faith. Kevin Skelton was the most forthright. While the judge was considering his judgement, Kevin told the press: 'I watched the first two weeks of it through a video link in Omagh and I had to stop – it was a shambles. It's a show trial. I wouldn't convict him [Hoey] on the evidence that was presented to the court. The police witnesses were a disaster, it was all over the place. The people who should be in court are the government.'

The police, of course, did not see it that way. Norman Baxter was certain that Hoey would be found guilty and that at least one other successful criminal case would follow that would be jeopardised by the civil case, so he continued obdurate about withholding evidence crucial to the civil case against Daly, McKenna and Murphy. In June 2007 an application was made to the judge for a split trial, with the case against Campbell, McKevitt and the Real IRA to go ahead at the earliest opportunity; it was turned down in September, which increased the pressure on the lawyers. There were tensions between H2O, who wanted to plough on regardless, and some of the London supporters, who thought Baxter's view that the case should be stayed pending developments on the criminal front should at least be considered seriously.

All that changed after the Hoey verdict. In the High Court public gallery on 20 December 2007 there were two factions – families of the Omagh dead and a group of relatives and supporters of Sean Hoey that included Colm Murphy – sitting uneasily side-by-side to hear the judgement. In the course of his delivery, Mr Justice Reg Weir showed what was described as 'thinly veiled judicial anger' that two police witnesses had been guilty of 'deliberate and calculated deception in which others concerned in the investigation and preparation of this case for trial beyond these two witnesses may also have played a part.'* He also slammed the 'slapdash approach' to collecting and storing the material to which LCN DNA was applied.†

'I am acutely aware,' he ended, 'that the stricken people of Omagh and every other right-thinking member of the Northern Ireland community would very much wish to see whoever was responsible for the outrageous events of August 1998 and the other serious crimes in this series of terrorist incidents convicted and punished for their crimes according to law. But I also bear firmly in mind the cardinal principle of the criminal law [that] justice "according to law" demands proper evidence. By that we mean not merely evidence which might be true and to a considerable extent probably is true, but . . . "evidence which is so convincing in truth and manifestly reliable that it reaches the standard of proof beyond reasonable doubt." The evidence against the accused in this case did not reach that immutable standard. Accordingly I find Mr Hoey not guilty on each of the remaining counts on the indictment.'

Delivered as he looked directly at the defendant, this was hardly a ringing endorsement from Mr Justice Weir, but there was raucous applause, clapping and even cat-calling from some Hoey supporters and tears from some of the devastated Omagh relatives. Even Kevin Skelton had thought Hoey would be found guilty on some counts. 'I'm flabbergasted, dumbfounded,' said Stanley McCombe. 'All the resources over the last nine-and-a-half years have not got us anywhere.' Alan Radford's sister, Carol, said she had lost all hope anyone would ever be brought to justice. 'We were told the prosecution had a strong case but I watched as day by day it fell apart in front of my eyes. As families, we feel hugely let down.'

Victor was taking a different tack when he marched out of court, and with Donna-Maria and their son Oliver – a tall thirteen-year-old unrecognisable from the little boy who had followed his brother's coffin – stood shoulder-to-shoulder with Norman Baxter, now the target of ire from many of the Omagh families. 'It is the appalling inefficiency of Sir Ronnie Flanagan that has meant Chief Superintendent Baxter has not been able to secure a

---

* Much later it would emerge that evidence that contradicted this had not been drawn to the judge's attention and the police were cleared by the Ombudsman.
† Weir's questioning of the reliability of LCN DNA profiling in criminal trials even when forensic samples are properly handled caused a suspension of the technique in the UK which was lifted in mid-January 2008 following a review by the Crown Prosecution Service.

conviction,' he told the cameras. 'He said he would fall on his sword if anything was wrong with this investigation. I will give him the sword.'* He accepted that the legal system was there to protect the human rights of such as Hoey, but 'it is only a great shame that my son and 31 people who died in Omagh had no human rights at all'. In any case, he said, 'It is my view that Sean Hoey is one of the conspirators who was involved in the Omagh bomb.'† When he found a spare moment, he sent a text to Martin McGuinness reporting that some of Hoey's supporters had 'called me fucking British scum. Are you prepared to do anything to give us assistance? I think not.'

Michael felt 'utterly betrayed'. There was overwhelming evidence that the security forces on both sides of the border withheld vital evidence that could have led to the bombers' arrest, he alleged to the media. 'The RUC had Kevin Fulton working as an agent, the FBI had David Rupert and Garda sergeant John White has already confirmed that the Irish authorities had informers within that Real IRA gang as well. At every level all the key intelligence agencies knew who was responsible for Omagh but did nothing. They can no longer refuse to give the families an inquiry. This case has been a disgrace by any standards.'

In London, I watched television with mingled emotions of incredulity and rage. To Norman Baxter, with whom I had developed a rather strained relationship over what I thought some of his black and white attitudes, I sent a text expressing sympathy. 'Unbelievable,' he responded. 'Very sorry for the families.' Like the rest of us, he retired to lick his wounds. On Christmas Day Victor disseminated a quotation from Alexander Solzhenitsyn's *The Gulag Archipelago*: 'the line between good and evil does not run through states, nor between classes, nor between political parties either, but right through every human heart'.

In the New Year, the long-standing obstruction from the PSNI was replaced by cooperation: accompanied by the barrister Danny Friedman,

---

* In late January 2008, Flanagan went to Victor's office for a private meeting and was ambushed by a Channel 4 journalist. On TV he apologised to the Omagh families 'without reservation' and 'wholeheartedly'. The retired Brian McVicar, who in 2000 had written the critical report of the investigation on which the Ombudsman's report had been based, said publicly that it was unfair for Flanagan to take the rap rather than the senior officers just below him 'who are just as much to blame as he is and they've escaped all the abuse and criticism Sir Ronnie is having to take'. Victor was unmoved.

† Kevin R. Winters, the solicitors Hoey shared with McKevitt, warned that Hoey might sue Victor, but nothing came of it. Instead, Hoey joined the call for a public inquiry and had in any event been acquitted.

Matthew walked out of Omagh police station in February 2008 with around ten boxes of material and the seeds of what would be a new relationship between the Omagh investigation team and the Plaintiffs' lawyers.

In the Republic, the gardaí made it clear that although they still refused to give evidence in a foreign court, they were genuinely anxious to help. It was the judge, Sir Declan Morgan, who solved the problem by finding a hitherto unused EU directive that required the judicial authorities in a member state to facilitate the taking of evidence in a local court. If they would not come to him, he would go to them. Of course there were procedural wrangles, which involved Matthew in a letter-writing war of attrition with the Irish Ministry of Justice, but they were eventually resolved, though it required help from the Fine Gael leader, Enda Kenny, and other opposition parties, the families and the Irish media to defeat official foot-dragging.

Otherwise, the first three months of 2008 ran true to form with crises, last-minute appeals and other unexpected hitches as the Defendants' lawyers strove doggedly to prevent the disclosure of the documents without which the Plaintiffs would have no case. But Mr Justice Morgan, who had been extraordinarily patient over more than three years, dug his heels in and refused to countenance any further postponement. The case would begin on Monday 7 April regardless.

The week before was nerve-wracking. On Monday, the judge dismissed an application by Colm Murphy's lawyers to have the trial adjourned lest his criminal retrial be prejudiced; he also dismissed the consequent application for a ban on any publicity in the civil case. But it was not until Friday afternoon that the Republic of Ireland Supreme Court ruled that H2O could have the books of evidence and transcripts of the Defendants' criminal trials and it was not until Jason rang to tell me this that I believed the case would actually happen. He then settled to writing an e-mail to colleagues. 'It's not for publication, but to show you I can feel emotion,' he wrote when he forwarded it to me. I had to lean on him later to remove the ban.

Dear all,

I will no doubt regret this outburst. I cringe at the idea of a rallying eliza-bethan* speech to the generals and the soldiers about to do battle – not least because the analogy is not apt in many ways (but that's never stopped

* A rather mystifying comparison with Elizabeth I's speech at Tilbury where she allegedly said: 'I know I have the body but of a weak and feeble woman, but I have the heart and stomach of a king.' I suspect he was thinking of Henry V at Agincourt.

me before in this case) but also because I know it is not needed. However, I had to say something after all these years and you will just have to put up with me on this one occasion on the working day eve of this trial. It's a passionate case so excuse my indulgence.

Just a quick note simply to say thank you to everyone in the legal team for getting us to this point. The moral victory has been won and the defendants know that. You have done a marvellous job, which has been more than difficult at times. Credit to all – those that have been the distance and the new blood that has worked so hard to get to terms with the material.

7 years ago, the families came to us and asked could we get them a day in court. You have got them 8 weeks. Detractors at the outset said it was not possible and the team has proved them wrong. Our problems are waning whereas the other side faces difficulties for the first time as they face the glare of the evidence.

It will be a historic case, I suspect in more ways than we appreciate. Although we can only do our best at trial, we must keep our heads and dignity for the families whatever is thrown at us – and it will be thrown – we must expect the unexpected. So, for the families, let us for the final time roll up our sleeves and be prepared for one last scrap. If we fight as a team and are prepared to fall as a team, we will win. Let's encourage and support everyone in the team and leave recriminations and frustrations for the other side.

Dan from now on will be calling all the shots. We all have supreme confidence in dan, brett and tony* – we could not have picked a better or more passionate counsel. Let's support them all we can.

Good luck everyone.

Thanks for everything, particularly to your families who have had to endure this case and will have to put up with us a little while longer whilst we put an end to the lack of justice the omagh families have had over the last 10 years.

See you in court on monday.

A mildly emotional Jason

---

* Tony McGleenan, an academic lawyer-turned-barrister, had come on board as Northern Ireland junior counsel.

CHAPTER FIFTEEN

THE CASE

'I said there was a society of men among us, bred up from their youth in the art of proving by words multiplied for the purpose, that white is black, and black is white, according as they are paid – Jonathan Swift, *Gulliver's Travels*

The lawyers and I were to meet Michael Seamark from the *Daily Mail* in Belfast on the evening of Sunday 6 April, the day before the case opened. I lived near Heathrow, but had mistakenly booked to fly from Gatwick, a nightmarish journey requiring two tubes and a train, which is truly irritating when you are lugging a suitcase, a tote bag containing a handbag, a laptop, a tape recorder, tapes, notebooks, newspapers and books. Before I left, Henry's response to Jason's e-mail came through: 'If I had known you were making an eve of battle speech I would have brought the tank up front. Now that you have fired the starting pistol I echo your words, with '"everyone to their stations".' The snow I had admired from the train had caused chaos in Gatwick; after reading in a queue for two hours, I was offered an 8.55 flight the following morning, which would have had me late for the trial.

Henry, the problem-solver, told me to book myself forthwith to join him on the first flight from Stansted. So I did, and duly got up at 3.30. At the airport I bought the *Mail* and reread what I'd written that weekend. 'Whatever the verdict, the Omagh bombing trial is a triumph for courage' was the headline over an article as emotional as Jason's e-mail. 'Please say a prayer for,' it began, 'or drink a toast to a group of brave, tenacious people who against all the odds are in Belfast High Court today for the beginning of their civil action against the Real IRA and men they believe were among the bombers of Omagh.

And do the same for the supporters who helped them get there, including the thousands of *Daily Mail* readers who gave money to what so many said was a hopeless cause.

I have been a part of this campaign since it began, as a journalist, an anti-terrorist campaigner, an amateur fundraiser and a friend.

As I write, like many others who have been closely involved, I am filled with a mixture of sadness, euphoria, exhaustion and apprehension.

The sadness at the suffering of the bereaved and the injured is a constant; the euphoria is caused by joy that, after years and years of financial and legal setbacks, the families have actually got to court; the exhaustion has been cumulative over years of frustration, and in my case comes also from reliving it all in the book I have been writing about the case; and the apprehension is lest, after the 50 legal hearings it has taken to get to this point, there might yet be hidden legal landmines.

Yet it is the euphoria that should be predominant today.

Whatever happens, we must celebrate ordinary people who have stood up to terrorism, called the Real IRA to account in a court of law and done so against terrible odds.

At Belfast City Airport, Henry and I waited for Victor; he had not intended to come until the end of the trial but had been bullied by us into being there at the beginning on the basis that he had started all this in February 2000 and should be there for the first day of a trial most people thought would never take place.

'Be careful what you say in the cab,' hissed Henry, as we stood in the queue; his years of living under death threats have left him what he calls careful and I call paranoid. This caution not to show our hand to a potential dissident-supporting taxi driver was somewhat spoiled when Victor gave a long telephone interview to RTE's *Morning Ireland*. Practised interviewee that he had become, he explained the history crisply and then said: 'It should be up to the state to prosecute people – not for the families to pursue civil claims. But if that's the only chance of justice then that's what we've got to do.' Asked about the prospect of a public inquiry, he said that, while he sympathised with his fellow victims who sought one, he could not see either government agreeing.

Then we caught up with progress on Victor's most recent initiatives. One was his application to be Northern Ireland's Victims' Commissioner. After a long history of trouble and disagreement over this appointment, First Minister Ian Paisley and Deputy First Minister Martin McGuinness ordered, in October 2007, that the post be readvertised; the short-listed candidates would be invited to make a presentation to them personally.

Already enjoying the thought of what they would say in their presentations, Victor and Henry had decided to apply. To my chagrin but not my surprise, Henry missed the deadline: Victor did not make the short list.

Naturally, he had demanded to know why: the range of consultative bodies was one reason given, and lack of organisational experience – of which he has plenty – another. He was unlikely to have been told what he knew was the truth – that a boat-rocker like him would have been anathema as much to officialdom as to ministers and that he would have been a troublesome and embarrassing interviewee.

We called by my host's house. Professor Liam Kennedy of Queen's University Belfast is a mild-mannered economics historian who looks as if he could be blown away by a puff of wind, but in his spare time he has been an inveterate public critic of all paramilitaries, particularly in their brutal treatment of the vulnerable in their own communities. Despairing that most established human rights groups concentrate on state rather than paramilitary violence, he founded the Northern Ireland Human Rights Association and stood twice against Gerry Adams for Westminster to draw attention to the beating, shooting and mutilation of children in his constituency.

It was coming up to nine o'clock when the four of us arrived at the court. Victor's phone rang again as he got out of the cab: 'Hello, Martin.' It couldn't be, I thought. But it was. Victor had sent a text to McGuinness the previous day to ask if he was coming to court to cheer the families on; the Deputy First Minister was calling from abroad to apologise for not being there and to wish the case well. Since McGuinness still refused to call on republicans to give evidence about the bombing, the sentiments he was expressing appeared absurd, but it was further proof that Victor had found in him some spark of humanity.

As we strolled towards the court I saw a familiar figure sitting on a low stone bench smoking a cigarette. 'It's a down-and-out,' I said loudly, and Liam looked sympathetically at this unshaven, hunched, creature in a battered trench coat. He had never met Jason before, dresses like an indigent student himself, did not recognise designer stubble or retro fashion when he saw them and could not know that this sad specimen was exhausted because the lawyers' hotel was located beside a club from which happy clubbers had been exiting long into the night. Matthew had been serenaded from the next bedroom at 3.00 a.m. with the song 'Sisters Are Doin' It For Themselves'.

The company cheered Jason up and there were emotional encounters for all of us, families, lawyers and supporters alike, including Michael Seamark, who had by now known the families for more than eight years. There was intense interest from the media, with television cameras across the road from the court and alert reporters swooping on relatives and any other well-known faces. Michael Gallagher had already told RTE that the families 'really see this as the last step in the Omagh process because we are not aware of any pending proceedings, either civil or criminal . . . it is going to be difficult coming so soon after the trial of Sean Hoey, but we are confident in our legal team and we put our trust in the courts.' Flanked by his loyal allies, he gave interviews in the street, one of which deliberately echoed a phrase of Gerry Adams's: 'I would say to the people that bombed Omagh, we certainly haven't gone away – and we will not go away.' Next morning's Irish edition of the *Sun* would lead with a photograph of Michael under the lead headline 'WE HAVEN'T GONE AWAY'.

Victor had already sent grateful text messages to those supporters whose numbers he had or could extract from the rest of us. Typical was that to Janie Dawnay: 'The case begins on Monday in Belfast and it would not have been possible without the help and support of my many friends. Thank you all so much and God bless, James, Victor.' 'You do know you are the hero of our times,' she responded. 'I have in front of my desk the photograph of James. Please keep in touch, these are momentous times.' True to form, Robert Salisbury replied with self-deprecating regret that he had been able to do so little. Later on, Máirín, coming out of a tough meeting, was overwhelmed by Victor's thoughtfulness.

'So look who's not here,' observed an unsurprised Liam Kennedy, surveying the courtroom that day. 'We have a huge human rights industry – Committee on the Administration of Justice, Children's Law Centre, British–Irish Rights Watch, the Pat Finucane Centre, the Northern Ireland Human Rights Commission. Where are they?'

In court, from the press box, I was watching those of the families that I knew best, those with whom I had talked and eaten and drunk and protested and begged and celebrated and despaired and sometimes cried and sometimes laughed during almost eight years: Victor Barker, Mark Breslin, Michael and Patsy Gallagher, Marion Radford, Stanley McCombe, Godfrey and Ann Wilson. Their faces bore signs of years of grief and frustration, but also of that steadfast, single-minded sense of purpose that had brought them finally to the High Court.

Court Number 2 is tiny and windowless – apart from those in the roof that are too opaque to offer much natural light and serve mainly to drown out speech during a thunderstorm. Apart from a gallery tucked away at the back and very high up, it has only three rows of wooden seats for the public: it was dominated by large TV screens on either side of the judge and by shelves and shelves of lever arch files beside both sets of lawyers and the judge: the consignment sent from London to Belfast by H2O had weighed more than three tonnes. I sat with the press in what would normally be a jury box.

With the help of a prison officer in Portlaoise prison, a technician had established that the expensive link installed for Michael McKevitt was working properly. It soon emerged, however, that McKevitt had decided not to participate, just to watch. So there were no Defendants to be seen in court, just their phalanx of lawyers. Only Liam Campbell and the Real IRA were not represented.*

Formal proceedings began at 9.30, when Mr Justice Morgan addressed himself to various technicalities. He impressed me as a man who intended to manage his case efficiently and give both sides a fair hearing, but who would not be trifled with. Nor did he seem awed by an unprecedented case with far-reaching legal implications.

He dealt briskly with the attempt of Dermot Fee QC, acting for Daly and Murphy, to raise the issue of what the standard of proof was: 'Unless there is some change of law I am not aware of then I intend to follow the House of Lords since it is binding on me.' The standard of proof to apply in the case was to be the civil standard of 'on the balance of probability'. A major issue was when the books of evidence and transcripts would be

---

* Seamus McKenna: Tara Walsh Solicitors; counsel, Brian Fee QC and Patrick Connolly. Michael McKevitt: Kevin R. Winters & Co.; counsel, Michael O'Higgins SC (Senior Counsel) and Kieran Vaughan. Seamus Daly and Colm Murphy: Higgins, Hollywood & Deazley Solicitors; Dermot Fee QC, Mary Higgins QC and, after a few weeks, Laura McMahon. Although usually Jason and occasionally Greenie were in attendance, throughout the trial Matthew Jury and his accompanying paralegal (Beverley Wong initially) were the constant presence, taking notes, finding documents and handling the complex administration; counsel, Lord Brennan QC, Brett Lockhart QC and Dr Tony McGleenan (Danny Friedman, who had been with the case from the outset, was tied up with another case).

made available: not to provide documents would prejudice the Plaintiffs' – the families' – right to a fair trial, the judge pointed out. McKevitt, Daly and Murphy had their copies, Brian Fee QC explained, but his client McKenna had destroyed his, so he would have to approach the Director of Public Prosecutions for copies. 'I will draw inference from the steps [to delay proceedings] taken by the Defendants,' said the judge, and adjourned the discussion until the following morning to give time for consultation with clients.

In essence, the Plaintiffs' case was that the Real IRA had run a terrorist campaign which included planting the Omagh bomb, that Michael McKevitt was the leader of the Real IRA and Liam Campbell its Director of Operations, which made both responsible, that McKenna and Daly were involved in driving the bomb to Omagh, using mobile phones lent them by Murphy, that Campbell had made one of the warning calls and that the families should be awarded exemplary damages. The job of the defence barristers was to challenge the evidence adduced by the Plaintiffs and also to deny the justification for exemplary damages; even though Campbell and the Real IRA were not represented, they could only benefit from any undermining of the case against the others.

Dan Brennan's opening speech on behalf of the families began at 10.30 and described at length what had happened at Omagh, the grounds for the case and in considerable detail the 'solid and wide-ranging' evidence he would be drawing on, including telephone data, forensics, the British secret service's anti-Real IRA sting operation, testimony from the FBI's mole, David Rupert, the PSNI, British police and secret services and from gardaí. Delivered in what one journalist called 'a soft growl', his style was low key but the words were eloquent. To his delight, it would be described in the *Irish News* as a 'powerful oration'.

Describing the bombing as 'a massacre of innocents', Dan depicted the scene graphically. This was the first of many moments which inevitably brought terrible pain to the families. He quoted the Omagh consultant surgeon's description of the scene in the hospital being 'of battlefield proportions', and spoke of 'dead bodies, broken bodies, walking wounded and blood everywhere': when I first read the inquest reports my nightmares were so terrible that I had had to go to a psycho-analyst. For me the worst came when there flashed up on the screen the now familiar photograph of the Spaniards – a child sitting on the shoulders of a man – posing in front of the bomb car only minutes before it went off: I saw the agony on Victor's face and wished I had not pressed him to be there.

This was 'a civil claim unprecedented, certainly in the UK and probably around the world,' said Dan. 'For the first time the victims of terrorism are confronting the alleged perpetrators. For the first time, private citizens are confronting terrorists in our courts.' The case would 'expose the Real IRA and their lies'.

The Real IRA and its members, 'in which we include McKevitt, Campbell, Daly, McKenna and Murphy, could never have contemplated families could bring civil actions against terrorists to a court in this country. For them it was never part of the scheme of things. It is now.' It being the Plaintiffs' belief that 'the defendants were responsible for cowardice and inhumanity'*, that would 'merit very special condemnation and exemplary damages'. And such damages would be enforced 'relentlessly' against the Defendants, including the Real IRA 'and its lackey organisations', the 32 County Sovereignty Committee and the Irish Republican Prisoners Welfare Organisation. 'If successful, and damages are pursued, the result will be that every terrorist and the woman of every terrorist will have to live in fear that their essential belongings, their house, their car and other valued possessions will be taken from them.'

Dan spoke for hours, with interruptions from the defence. Dermot Fee objected to his having referred to Defendants' convictions in a foreign courts (Daly's in the Republic of Ireland; Murphy's in the United States), but the judge ruled that it was up to Dan to adduce in his opening statement whatever evidence he chose; it was a matter for Dan to take the consequences if later applications resulted in evidence being ruled inadmissible, said the judge.

This caused much protest. Michael O'Higgins, for McKevitt, shared the concerns of his learned friends and found Dan's remarks 'utterly prejudicial': since David Rupert would not be in court, his evidence should not be adduced. The court had been told that certain gardaí would be giving opinions about his client, but he had not seen what those opinions would be, so they should not be mentioned in the opening statement.

---

* Dan quoted the condemnation in the 1916 Proclamation of the Republic – read by Patrick Pearse outside the General Post Office as hostilities began – of 'any dishonour brought about by cowardice and inhumanity'. This was a clever allusion to the document that is Holy Writ for all republicans.

Everything said in Dan Brennan's address would be 'reported in collo-quial terms by the ladies and gentlemen of press', which would have an impact on his client's name. And, what was more, he strongly objected to McKevitt being described by the 'pejorative' term of terrorist, which might be taken as being factual, or having his conviction mentioned. Brian Fee, for McKenna, agreed fully.

Dan took them on robustly. It was my first experience of how combative he can be in court. Sadly, I had missed the hearing where, I am told, he became so furious with the Defendants' resistance to obeying court rulings that he pulled off his wig and cried 'Comply or die'. This was a civil not a criminal case, he retorted, and he was reciting what was publicly known about the Defendants: 'That is what I have done and will continue to do.' There had already been some forty interlocu-tory applications in this case, and now his learned friends were making a ludicrous attempt to disrupt his opening. As an ex-chairman of the Bar Council of England, he said haughtily, he did not need lectures on what was appropriate in opening a case. Dan, I was learning, did not give a damn about alienating the opposition. 'My attacks may be full-blooded but they are also usually full frontal,' he observed truly on another occasion.

The judge closed down the argument. This was an opening state-ment: nothing in it was necessarily evidence or fact. So Dan was largely left to get on with it. He ended with a fine peroration: 'The time has come for the Plaintiffs to present their evidence in this claim. They do so willingly. They know this Court will give this case objective, fair and dignified consideration ensuring that justice is done and seen to be done. This trial will find its place in Irish history because it represents the first judicial determination of claims by citizens against terrorists arising from an appalling atrocity.' ('No pressure on the judge, then,' I thought.) On behalf of the Plaintiffs, many witnesses and thousands of pages of documents had been amassed. 'We have done our best to meet all the Court's requirements as to provision of state-ments, witness lists and the case management issues in this trial.' Yet there was still no word as to whether any Defendant would give evidence, no defence witness lists, no disclosure of any expert witness evidence upon which the defence intended to rely, no documents disclosed and no evidence had been sought from the PSNI about any risk to the Defendants that might explain why the four at liberty had not turned up to court. 'The Omagh bombing has already assured its place in Irish history. The Real IRA and any of these Defendants as are found liable know they will never be forgotten by the people of this island for what they did. In such circumstances the failure of those at liberty to attend their trial to defend themselves in person is damning.' It would subsequently emerge that McKevitt had decided not even to follow the proceedings: the video link would be used only to consult with his lawyers.

I have sat through trials on jury service, but never one in which I was closely involved or one remotely as complicated. For the first time I understood why judges rarely sit for more than four days a week. It requires formidable concentration to note every detail of importance, take in the points of law being made, find your way around the documents, deal with the legal challenges, make good decisions, ensure that counsel are not wasting the court's time and manage the practical issues like the timetable. All this Mr Justice Morgan did without showiness or fuss, and with only the very occasional indication of irritation. In the many weeks I spent observing him in court, as he assiduously noted every point made, I never once saw his concentration slip. And, though sorely taxed, his temper held.

Nor do solicitors and barristers have it easy. As well as organising the graphics, being sufficiently on top of the files to provide counsel with whatever they needed, Beverley had the nerve-wracking job of taking down a record of proceedings on which counsel could rely – a job that within a few weeks gave Bev repetitive strain injury. Jason was moved to compete by reminding us of his bad back.* It was easy to see how a performance like Dan's would be intellectually and emotionally taxing, but, watching Brett Lockhart, I realised how important is barristers' teamwork. Tony McGleenan mostly sat silent in court, but in the law library achieved much to underpin the Plaintiffs' legal arguments: 'Dr McGleenan has justified his doctorate,' said Dan one morning, when Tony had produced extra authorities for an argument. As for the opposition, fighting the case of people who had been stalling for years and refused to turn up in court, I could only marvel at their ingenuity and chutzpah, and, in the case of Dermot Fee and his colleague Mary Higgins, their stubborn determination to fight every inch of even the

---

* 'I think of Jason as John Wayne with hypochondria,' observed Dan.

most unpromising legal terrain, even when they were driving everyone mad.

Victor had left after lunch and was back at his desk in Surrey by six o'clock, sending grateful e-mails. The most moving was to Peter Mandelson and included the paragraph: 'When we first met your perception of me was that of a very angry and hostile man with a myopic vision of justice. However, your humanity and kindness towards me even at that time will not be forgotten – of all the ministers with whom I have had contact over the years, it was you that showed his human face and offered personal support to us all.' 'I was, indeed, thinking of you all yesterday and sent a text message to Michael Gallagher (I hope he got it) wishing the families well,' responded Mandelson. 'Yes, you were angry but you had every reason to be.'

By the time the court rose, Michael Seamark had disappeared to write his story on the trial, Liam Kennedy went back to his office and the Omagh relatives went home, but not before I had met Stanley McCombe's two accompanying sisters, one of whom was Rosemary Ingram, the traffic warden who had been so badly injured and had felt humiliated by lawyers when claiming compensation. Jason took off for London to have dinner with George Clooney and take him to Downing Street to talk to Gordon Brown about Darfur,* and the other lawyers had been whisked away by the posse's friend Charlie Mitchell, who, with his colleague Larry Morrow – retired from RUC Special Branch – would look after their safety and wellbeing throughout the case and ferry documents back and forth to Dublin. After leaving army intelligence, Charlie had gone into the security business, first in Iraq – from which he returned with jokes so black I could hardly bear them – then Uzbekistan and latterly the United Kingdom and Ireland. At awful, mind-numbing moments in court, I would escape to Charlie and Larry for emotional and intellectual sustenance. Charlie's injunction on the worst excesses of lawyers – 'Let's all join hands and contact the living' – or Larry's sardonic comments on pretty well everything kept me going.

Later, Henry and I and a great friend of ours, Jim McDowell of the

---

* 'Day one! 40 to go. Went well?' he e-mailed me from the airport. 'How did families feel?' 'Families very happy,' I responded. 'So are we. I'm feeling so benign and proud of you I'll overlook you consorting with Gordo in Downing Street.'

Sunday World (for whom Henry used to write the paramilitary-baiting columns), had joined a few of the lawyers for a long, gossipy session in a bar, dominated by a sense of mild hysteria and sheer relief. Dan, who gets easily bored by respectable society, quickly took to enormous, shaven-headed Jim, with his generous heart and his hilarious foul-mouthed anecdotes about the many criminals of his acquaintance and the numerous libel suits which kept bringing him before 'wankers in wigs'. The feeling was reciprocated and Jim, who was fascinated by Dan's hoarse voice, did him the honour of nicknaming him Shirley Bassey.

The following morning, weighed down by all the national and local newspapers, I walked across Belfast to the 9.30 management session. This morning, on behalf of Daly and Murphy, Mary Higgins asked that the issues surrounding the bomb should be limited to 'causation and liability': in other words, that graphic details about types of injury, loss of limbs and so on were 'inappropriate': 'We have accepted that 29 people were killed and that should be sufficient,' she said. But this evidence was relevant to liability, countered Brett Lockhart, and, in any case, the other Defendants had not made even such an admission. 'It is not an admission. It's not a formal admission,' she answered. All they had said was: '"We formally admit that the bomb was carried out by the Real IRA." This is not an admission by our Defendants.'

He would not be limiting the scope of the Plaintiffs' evidence, said the judge, although he wanted to avoid duplication of witness. He was considering how Defendants could have a means of communication with the court for consultation purposes. 'Have any of you written to the PSNI to ask whether any of the Defendants would be subject to detention if they returned to Northern Ireland?' he enquired. 'I think I know the answer but has anyone been brave enough to make that request?' There was silence. He ruled that McKevitt's video link should be kept in place, in case he changed his mind and wished to give evidence.

Before the case proper resumed, I had time to have coffee with a journalist and go through the papers, which were full of photographs of the bomb scene and quotes about blood and bodies from Dan's statement. Incredibly, and quite coincidentally, in a *Daily Telegraph* article headed 'Fear of Islam is ruining our chance for peace', the novelist Andrew O'Hagan asked if the bombings of Enniskillen and Omagh are the result 'of the mad actions of a generally blood-thirsty people who craved a United

Ireland' or rather 'the desperate acts of some parts of that community hounded into extremism by the British State's consistent abuse'.*

At 10.00 the trial resumed with the showing of the three amateur videos taken on the day of the bomb. The bizarre details that struck me in the middle of all that agony were the sunniness of the day and the brightness of the clothes worn by so many people on whom actual and metaphorical darkness had descended in an instant. I was very glad none of the relatives was there to watch those scenes and sounds of terror, death, mutilation and destruction, or to listen to the police evidence which followed. There were just four police officers in the witness box: Sergeant Wesley McCracken, Constable Louise Stewart,† Constable Geoffrey Eakin and Constable Alan Palmer,‡ all of whom had given evidence at the inquest and with whose testimony I was painfully familiar. Brett is sympathetic both in manner and in heart and it was his job to guide them as humanely as possible through their dreadful stories, causing them the least strain while extracting the horrible truth. I was not surprised when, after the third witness, he made way for his colleague Tony McGleenan.

Two quotations stand out as particularly terrible: one was from the woman Wesley McCracken remembered crying out to the police from among the casualties: 'you drove us into the bomb, the police drove us into the bomb'. The other was from Geoffrey Eakin, describing the three bodies he had been given care of: 'The first woman, I was quite taken aback by it because she had been completely decapitated. There was no head on the corpse at all. Just taken clean off. The second woman, the top half of her head had been removed by the force of the explosion. In contrast, the body of the small child appeared to be totally intact.'

Veering from the disarming, through insistence and sometimes to

---

* Later that day I wrote an enraged letter to the editor which concluded: 'I am writing a book about the bereaved families who have taken a case against the alleged bombers of Omagh. Their relatives were murdered by a tiny group of blood-thirsty republican fundamentalists who crave a United Ireland, represent no one but themselves and have so far got away with their terrible crime. The Real IRA leadership, who are mostly based in the Republic of Ireland, will no doubt take comfort from Mr O'Hagan's implication that they might have been driven beyond endurance by British abuse to put a carbomb on a crowded street on a Saturday afternoon. The families whose lives they destroyed will be sickened.'
† See Chapter 3.
‡ Ditto.

near-aggression, the defence barristers' questioning of the officers seemed designed to show police failings meant that a bomb not intended to hurt anyone had instead caused carnage. These exchanges were followed by hours of reading from statements by civilians and police who had received or dealt with bomb warnings and witnesses on the Omagh streets before and after the bomb, as well as the Omagh hospital surgeon, Dominic Pinto. Thereafter Dan was on his feet to get stuck into procedural arguments, most of which centred on what evidence would be admissible, how its validity would be formally proved and what weight should be given it. Now that the early novelty had worn off, I was already finding legal debate increasingly tedious. There would be many more months of it.

What would always be interesting, however, was the combative nature of the two barristers from outside the Northern Ireland jurisdiction: Dan from London and Michael O'Higgins from Dublin. One thing they agreed on was the adversarial nature of justice. O'Higgins, once a tough investigative journalist, had achieved notoriety at the Bar when he successfully defended the drug dealer John Gilligan on the charge of murdering Veronica Guerin by a painstaking and ruthless demolition of the key witnesses. He had on occasion acted for Colm Murphy and McKevitt and now was trying every possible tactic to stop David Rupert's e-mails being accepted as evidence. O'Higgins looks rather like a middle-aged Victorian cherub, especially when his curls peep out from under his wig, and he affects a rather nineteenth-century eloquence ('In my respectful submission' and 'I put it to you' feature frequently), but he is as tough and self-confident as Dan and their underlying competitiveness would add some entertainment to proceedings. Not, however, on this occasion. As so many of these wearisome wrangles ended, the judge instructed both sides to provide him the following week with submissions relating to their arguments, pending which he would hear whatever evidence was offered by the Plaintiffs. Over the duration of the case he must have had to consider hundreds, maybe thousands, of pages of skeleton arguments and submissions.

The next two days were scheduled for technical evidence concerning bomb making presented by forensic scientists, followed by the reading into the record of related statements, so I had decided to go back to London. At the airport I saw in the *Daily Mail* one photograph of a happy George Clooney gazing at a radiant Mariella Frostrup and another of him looking sombre beside a grinning Gordon Brown.

The case was expected to take eight weeks and to finish in June or July 2008. In the event it took 76 days, spread over 25 weeks; just 12 days short of a year. To allow time for the assessment of evidence expected the following week, court generally sat for only four days, usually from 10.30 to 4.00 with a one-hour break for lunch, though there were many procedural sittings from 9.30. The endless delays and postponements and timetable changes were bad enough for the local lawyers, including the judge, trying to juggle other cases. For Michael O'Higgins from Dublin it was much more wearing: for the London lawyers, it was always debilitating and infuriating. And for Dan, who had long-standing engagements abroad, it was particularly hard. On one occasion he left Dublin on a Thursday, flew to London for an unexpected meeting, to Frankfurt to make a speech and back to London on Friday, from where he went to Cambridge, to Norfolk on Saturday for a wedding, home on Sunday, to Belfast on Monday morning for erudite wrangles and in the afternoon to the US to engagements in Minneapolis, Washington and New York. Around the same time, after a weekend at Chequers with Gordon Brown, Jason told me he would be going to Cannes to talk Darfur with Kofi Annan, former Secretary General of the UN. 'So how was Cannes and how was Kofi?' I enquired the next week. 'I didn't go in the end. I was in Como with George and it wasn't logistically possible to get to lunch with Kofi, so I had to apologise.' 'I want to be a celebrity: get me in here,' commented Charlie.

Rescheduling when a witness was ill or – as often happened – lawyers overran by hours the time they had predicted for a cross-examination, led to lengthy horse-trading between the busy judge and various barristers. And finding days that suited the Irish court was another complication.

Some weeks court sat only one or two days, not necessarily consecutively, and life was dominated by endless hassles about planes and hotels and bag-packing. At least the lawyers could take flights that suited them, and had Charlie and Larry, their security detail, to drive them to and from airports, look after documents and generally mother them, but I was on cheap flights, so had far too many 5.30 a.m.s for Luton or Stansted and much killing of time in Belfast before catching the last flight out. Yet, my various Belfast and Dublin hosts and friends and visitors to the case like Henry or Janie Dawnay enlivened our social life. Bittles pub, where Jason, Matthew and I and various paralegals went to lunch most days, and where

I could plug in my mobile and laptop, became my office, refuge and main meeting place.

It was clear that no one had predicted how complex it would be dealing with four separate defences: during one session, Brian Fee was cross-examining a policeman about his interview with Seamus McKenna's wife; O'Higgins was demanding that the security services be required to disclose all their information on David Rupert in the hope it would undermine him, and Daly's and Murphy's lawyers were seeking to change dates and times because they insisted that they must read through all the Dublin material that they had spent years trying to block before it could be given to the Plaintiffs.

'We need to know who compiled this report,' intervened Dermot Fee one afternoon, as Brett was reading out reports used by the United States to designate the Real IRA as a terrorist organisation. 'Who compiled this report in the Northern Ireland Office, who is involved in the RUC and the security services etc?' 'As far as I understand it this information doesn't affect your client at all,' said the judge. 'Ah,' said Fee, 'the accusation is that all defendants are involved with the RIRA, therefore allegations against the Real IRA are relevant to the totality of the trial.' This report was admissible, said the judge, 'and it is up to me to decide on the issue of weight'. Brett resumed reading. Fee intervened to wonder 'in terms of an unrepresented defendant how this is dealt with?' 'If an unrepresented defendant chooses not to attend court then this is his responsibility,' said the judge. At which stage O'Higgins protested that the material was based to a considerable extent on Rupert's evidence, and since the admissibility of that was in doubt, no more of it should be read for now. So everyone went home at 3.15.

To use David Rupert's statements and e-mails without him being present was classified as hearsay, permissible under civil law in certain circumstances and fiercely resisted by O'Higgins, and ending with Jason unexpectedly being called into the witness box to be cross-examined about his affidavit explaining why Rupert was not giving evidence in person. Had he kept notes of his conversations with the FBI, he was asked, which raised a smile with Jason's colleagues, who know his antipathy to note-taking. We had feared that Jason might become too chatty in the witness box, but he was mostly laconic. 'Rupert is fond of money,' observed O'Higgins. 'Like us all,' responded Jason genially.

And so the logical sequence of events the Plaintiffs' lawyers had planned for steadily became a pipe dream. It was awe-inspiring to see how time evaporated.

What was more, one counsel or another insisted at various times that almost every piece of evidence had to be read aloud into the record – often for hours at a time – rather than being lodged in writing. The judge was sympathetic to this: 'This is a public trial,' he said early on. 'And I need to make sure it doesn't turn into a private trial.' Nor could anyone have predicted the hours of procedural wrangling. Or the innumerable adjournments while counsel consulted solicitors and each other, or the overstretched resources of the Belfast courts had to be used to photocopy more reams of material for each set of lawyers and the judge. Had the Real IRA and Liam Campbell also been represented, the case would be running still.

The law in Northern Ireland is a more leisurely business than in London, so Dan was frequently irritated at the unavailability of familiar short cuts and what he saw as the old-fashioned approach of the Northern Ireland bar. The judge was always polite when Dan made suggestions designed to chop off an opposition argument at the knees, but he rarely budged. 'You may have a view as to how I should deal with this, Lord Brennan,' he would say, 'but it's my view that I shouldn't deal with it in this way.' Dan also showed his annoyance at what he thought of as provincial cosiness and old-fashioned procedures. After being told that a particular course of action was not followed in the Northern Ireland jurisdiction, he retorted: 'Things can always change for the better' and Morgan – who defused anger – responded smilingly: 'I'm sure you will take much back from here to yours'. Brett would remark later that it had been very good for the Northern Ireland bar to experience Dan and Orlando Pownall, who kept coming back to take on other controversial cases: 'we should learn instead of being such a tightly-knit small club.' After a series of exchanges between Dermot Fee and the judge, Dan intervened with a sardonic reference to the 'duet', and went on to promise to be 'as pedestrian as the law requires'. 'I may be accused of being "pedantic",' observed Dermot, who was demanding a level of proof for the origin of a source that the judge thought inimical to an expeditious hearing. 'It is particularly ungracious for me to make my learned friend feel pedantic,' snarled Dan. 'The term is relentless.' Sometimes Dan reached boiling point. Delays over producing documentation had him fuming about 'brazen indifference to the court's function and powers' and openly amazed that the judge didn't clap those concerned in irons. He called me over one day to report this was the first time he had used the word 'barmy' in one of his submissions. 'It's all right for Dan,' Brett Lockhart would say, 'but I have to live here.'

Although our lawyers were forever moaning that the judge should have clamped down on what they saw as the opposition's time-wasting, it was clear that his tolerance was motivated by a determination to give no one any possible cause for crying foul play or putting his final verdict at risk in the Court of Appeal. He also had a scholarly fascination with teasing out points of law, as, for instance, in an elaborate, lengthy and often learned exchange between him and O'Higgins on what constituted fairness under Article 6 of the European Court of Human Rights.

After sitting for fourteen days in April (albeit some of them partial), the case had not progressed very far and now there was to be the excitement of the move to Dublin on 12 May to hear evidence from the gardaí. Here a local judge would preside and Mr Justice Morgan would attend in plain clothes. On 1 May, a day dominated by hours of arguments about hearsay and privacy and human rights and adversarial procedures, in which Dan laid about him ruthlessly with most of the weapons in his well-stocked intellectual arsenal, there was also discussion about what material had to be taken to Dublin, and about procedures, but also about etiquette, with due attention to necessary solemnities. There was conflicting sartorial advice: court would be sitting in an out-of-term week, explained O'Higgins, the font of local knowledge, during which counsel traditionally do not robe, yet the judge had been told by the local court official that the Dublin judge would be robed.

In the event, District Justice Conal Gibbons was indeed robed, and, though not wearing a wig he had a splendid white bob that fell almost to his shoulders and reminded me of the older Franz Liszt. Mr Justice Morgan, wearing a suit, sat beside him. After Belfast, it was a pleasure to have some space and three big windows. Michael and Patsy Gallagher and Godfrey, Ann and Colin Wilson, a courteous young man who went to court to keep his parents company, sat in public benches and a long row of gardaí sat at the back of the court, waiting to be called to give evidence. As in Belfast, I sat in a jury box allocated to the press. A bizarre effect of that was that, out of habit, Michael O'Higgins was often staring directly at me as he scored a point off a witness. In Belfast, I was usually alone except for the court reporter, Alan Erwin, who raced in and out, and, sometimes, Lesley-Anne Henry from the *Belfast Telegraph*; after the first day, all other reporters had to all intents and purposes disappeared. On the first day Dublin was a media scrum and the families posed for the usual photographs and gave the usual interviews, but afterwards I was usually one of two or three.

This was the first occasion on which a judge from the United Kingdom had sat in the Irish jurisdiction and the procedural waters were uncharted. Indeed, explained Judge Gibbons, the legal architecture not being in place because of different legal systems, he had not finalised the rules of engagement for what was technically a hearing, not a trial, until the previous week. In theory, Judge Gibbons was in charge and Declan Morgan merely there as an observer: indeed, there would be much argument from Dermot Fee in Belfast afterwards that Judge Morgan should not be able to use any of the notes he took in Dublin as he wasn't a judge at the time. Had there been a clash of judicial egos there could have been a problem, but instead Morgan was humble about his lack of status and Gibbons courteously and regularly consulted him. As he explained to the court, he asked Declan Morgan's opinion as 'he is a judicial authority and recognised. But he has no direct role. I am the presiding judge.' 'What a trial it will be for me,' said Morgan, introducing lawyer's humour, 'to speak only when asked to.' As the legal argument intensified, Gibbons made legal history again by ruling that to settle an admissibility argument without everyone having to go back to Belfast, he would the following morning allow Morgan to sit in his court as if it were the Northern Ireland High Court. And as the days progressed, although they went through the formal motions, Gibbons largely adopted the role of host and Morgan that of judge in all but name.

It was frustrating for the London and Belfast contingent that Dublin hours created even more delays: 11.00ish to 3.30 with ninety minutes for lunch and lengthy adjournments seemed to be the accepted norm, though Morgan's influence gradually had us starting earlier, ending later and enjoying less leisurely lunches. Despite the representations of defence counsel, Detective Sergeant Thomas Finbarr Healy, a member of the National Surveillance Unit, was called to the witness box on the second morning as the first garda witness, to give evidence of seeing Rupert and McKevitt together. 'What was McKevitt wearing?' asked junior counsel, Kieran Vaughan. 'Trousers,' said Healy, to chortles from the court. And another garda, asked if he was sure he recognised David

Rupert, pointed out that Rupert was one of the largest individuals in Ireland.

This was the first of many examples of how confident the gardaí seemed compared to the PSNI. The gardaí seemed to expect to be believed; the battered PSNI assume they will not be. Many police in both jurisdictions thoroughly dislike lawyers and believe the law has little to do with justice. The gardaí had clearly been well-trained to avoid eye contact with barristers and directed their answers to the judge rather than their questioners. A particularly disenchanted uniformed garda on security duty downstairs summed up his attitude: 'What has ye all hanging about?' he asked me one day when the court had been adjourned. 'A technical issue of some kind,' I said. 'You mean they're milking the case for all it's worth,' he said. His colleague chipped in. 'These aren't courts of law. They're courts of lies.' And he paused to deliver what was obviously a favourite observation: 'There are more honest people coming through here in chains than in wigs.' Another pregnant pause.'You're not here looking for the truth, are you?'

Frustrated though I often was, I could not subscribe to the garda's jaundiced views. I believed we already had the truth: we were looking for justice and Brett Lockhart was becoming seriously optimistic: 'What a scrapper Dan is,' he said. 'And this case has everything for him. Tremendous challenge and plenty of legal points. This case will not be replicated. Dan and Jason are heroes. It'll be legendary.' Yet, as the families and I agreed at lunchtimes in the Legal Eagle, the pub across the road from the Four Courts, the case might be legendary but that did not stop it being mostly unbelievably boring for the layman.

Yes, there was interesting evidence about the Defendants from the dozens of gardaí called, but for those familiar with the details of the case it was all old news. I drew what entertainment I could from the jousting. There were good moments, for instance, in the hours of O'Higgins' cross-examination of Detective Superintendent Diarmuid O'Sullivan, who had a face like granite and nerves to match. 'Doesn't this memorandum sound to you like a cheap James Bond novel?' asked O'Higgins. 'I don't know, Judge,' said O'Sullivan with a slight smile. 'I haven't read James Bond in a long time.' 'Are you under pressure here, Detective Superintendent O'Sullivan?' asked O'Higgins after one long onslaught. 'Not in the slightest, Judge.' O'Higgins could not be faulted for persistence, and for a fine performance as an injured innocent, but he got nowhere in his attempts to force an admission from O'Sullivan that Rupert, whom he described as a brothel keeper and a child smuggler, could not be trusted. It was the irresistible force up against the immovable rock.

That stint in court lasted from 12 to 15 May, with only seven of the planned twenty-nine officers having been examined. We were back in windy, rainy Dublin from the 27th to the 29th, this time in a small court with the families squashed in a corner. I did a head count on the first day: only sixteen gardaí now in the back row, but a total of nine barristers and seven solicitors. Judge Morgan made a desperate plea 'to respect the court's timescale and use our time fruitfully', but that did not prevent Dermot Fee questioning officers critically and at length about procedures and note-taking: 'Sometimes it's not feasible to take notes,' said one irritated garda. 'Like when you're driving a car.' For distraction, I would study Dan's profile. 'Sometimes you look like an outraged owl,' I told him, 'but you have really perfected that look of disdain.' 'And that's only for his own side,' said Jason.

Who would be a policeman? I thought, not for the first time. At one moment an aggressive counsel was affecting incredulity that they could not remember something from ten years ago: at another, he would be asking, 'Are you seriously suggesting that seven years on you remember this?' Being accused of lying and dereliction of duty was absolutely routine, yet most of the gardaí seemed unaffected. One barrister involved in a separate case explained his defence strategy in a tricky case to some of us at a dinner party: 'I don't want any evidence coming out because it's all bad for my client, so I roar and shout and object all the time.'

Of course, proceedings overran in Dublin, but they had to be interrupted as the following week in Belfast was the hearing of evidence about the effects on the Plaintiffs of the bomb, and evidence from Dr Cooling, the psychiatrist who had interviewed them and evaluated their condition. The families were demanding exemplary damages, which have the purpose of punishing and deterring, and are usually associated with cases of state wrongdoing and institutional corruption. 'When it comes to terrorists they think they can do what they please and the law does not think, as yet, in this context they should be subject to this kind of remedy. The ordinary person would find this an utterly unacceptable state of affairs,' Dan submitted. He also informed the judge that if necessary, on this the Plaintiffs would appeal all the way to Europe via the House of Lords.

It was Brett's job to make the damages case.* 'We've been caught up in technical argument,' he announced. 'Now we're back to reality'. This really was the families' day in court that they had so long sought; it was to be both desperately painful and cathartic. Those on the writ had to describe what had happened to them; those not, to explain how their relatives had been affected.

Mark Breslin was first. Although he is neither confrontational nor aggressive, there is steely determination and quiet courage. He told me once it gave him great satisfaction that the writs and associated documentation that Michael McKevitt saw began: 'Breslin and Others v. McKenna and others.' It was Brett's job to ask the questions that would bring back to the consciousness of the court the horror of that day and its aftermath and Mark did not flinch in answering. Asked how did Geraldine look when he saw her first after the bomb, he answered of his lively, attractive, fashion-conscious wife: 'As I went towards her there were bandages on her face and a patch over one eye. Some of her teeth were missing. As I put my head over so she could see me her eye that wasn't covered was kind of rolling around looking at the ceiling. But as I looked over she fixed her eye on me and realised who I was. Briefly she raised the energy to say a few words.' Asked what they were, and close to breaking down, Mark replied, "I'm sorry." He was then questioned about his mental state afterwards and his erratic work record ever since and ended: 'I have got more stable – I would like to think so.'

The defence barristers were wary of cross-examining victims, but O'Higgins tried. Beginning with an acknowledgement of the horror and sadness, he began to ask questions about evacuation procedures in Omagh that day, something he knew Mark had studied closely. The objective appeared to be to establish that the police had been in some way negligent, but Mark courteously but confidently rejected his allegations, including that it had been wrong to decide that the warning of a bomb in 'Main Street' meant 'High Street' rather than Market Street. Mark's brother Liam wept, as he told how outgoing Geraldine had brought happiness to

---

* The necessary pre-conditions to qualify for damages are: (i) the claimant must have had a close tie of love and affection with the primary victim; (ii) the claimant must be close in time and space to the event caused by the defendant's breach; (iii) the claimant must have had a sudden appreciation by sound of the horrifying event or its immediate aftermath; (iv) the claimant must not be a person abnormally susceptible to psychiatric illness.

his shy brother and her death anger and stress. Still preoccupied with the bomb, Mark now had a girlfriend, 'which means he can have some interest in life. She's a former friend of Geraldine. It all goes back to Geraldine.'

Lorraine Wilson's sister Denise cried too, and it was hard not to join in when she described the destruction of a happy family, with a father who had changed from being family-oriented and fun-loving into being angry, bitter, argumentative and loud: he talked of nothing but politics and 'everything's a lecture'. Denise's husband spoke of what depression, drink and rage had done to his bubbly, sociable fiancée.

And so all day the terrible stories went on. Mark Breslin had his head in his hands during the testimony of Marion Radford, now a prey to poor health, loneliness and depression: 'I see my children suffering as well and it'll go through the next generation too.' The evident anger and distress of her children Paul and Carol confirmed what she had said. Paul suffered insomnia, moodiness, nightmares and guilt – confirmed in a written statement by his wife, Samantha – and Carol spoke of the deterioration in both her mother and brother. She had moved to another neighbourhood when 'IRA' had been painted on her walls, a republican flag put on Marion's roof and no one seemed to want to help.

Stanley McCombe broke down as he told his story of how the life of a happy-go-lucky friend had become angry and arid. He had feared his sons might want to get even with the bombers in the wrong way: through the civil case, 'All I want is to get even, get even in the proper way. Fighting for justice and what Ann meant to me is what will keep going until the day I die.' Shaking and crying afterwards, Stanley was hugged by his son Clive. Among the families there was a great sense of mutual support and pride. Victor had rung and sent them love.

Grim and straight-talking, but crying through most of it, Godfrey Wilson gave evidence next morning. He mentioned an interviewer who had asked Ann: 'Do you think your husband a wimp for crying all the time?' He talked of the good times, of getting married 'to have a happy, healthy family. I thought that was what life was about', and of all the outdoor activities the family went in for. 'I liked wains to go out and do things.' He and Ann had coped with the death of their baby son Gavin and their beloved Colin's learning difficulties, but Lorraine's murder had destroyed the family, finished him at work and had made him and two of his children suicidal. Godfrey described unflinchingly how Colin woke him up one night calling him to the garage, where Garry had 'put a rope around the beam' and on being stopped from hanging himself, Garry had run into the river. Godfrey talked too of how Ann needed alcohol to sleep and managed a joke: 'Is Ann's prescription ready?' he would ask in the off-licence when buying her wine. Ann could not face giving evidence, but she told in her written statement of how Colin had become and remained paranoid, traumatised and fearful. And in statements, Garry and Colin gave their own stories and Garry's wife, Lesley, wrote about him.

And then there were the Gallaghers. Cathy, who was also on the writ, gave evidence about how her brother's death had stunted her career and caused her to take a drug overdose; Michael spoke of the horrors of that day in Omagh and how he had never since then been able to work. Like many of the others giving evidence, he described counselling as irrelevant and explained why meeting other victims was the only effective therapy. Patsy, not on the writ, had the job of explaining what had happened to her husband and younger daughter. Michael, she said, had recovered from his brother's murder after about five years – a period that had made them more independent of the world as a family since so many people had turned against them on learning that Hugh had been in the security forces. Michael was by now a considerable figure internationally and an honoured and eloquent speaker at international victims' conferences, but he had to listen as his wife unflinchingly told bewigged strangers how he had become bad-tempered, demanding, aggressive and obsessive: 'not a father any more or a husband any more'.

Edmund, the only Gibson left on the writ, was also too fragile to give evidence in person, but provided a statement, as did his wife, who spoke of how a sociable man who had never had a day off work in ten years, despite witnessing terrible death and destruction, had been so damaged by being on duty in Omagh the day Esther was killed that he had to retire and now had barely any interest in life.

Liam Kennedy was so moved by Patsy that he wrote an article called 'On the Road of Tears'. 'She is a mother-like figure in the witness box, a little plump, by times composed and solicitous, at other times overcome by grief. In a soft voice she relates that her daughter Cathy returned to Magee University College in Derry following the family tragedy but never really settled back into her studies.

A sudden phone call from Derry, day or evening, and Patsy would be on the road from Omagh to bring her student daughter back home. The phone calls were frequent. Cathy's trauma was easily triggered: by the glimpse of a young man with Aiden's hair colouring or the sight of a sweater that he might have worn. On the way home, crouched in the front seats of the car, the two women, mother and daughter, would keen uncontrollably for the son and brother forever lost to them. Between them, they christened the road from Derry to Omagh: The Road of Tears.

Liam wrote too of Patsy overhearing Michael 'crying hysterically' in the disused garage: 'this is the personal grief because ultimately each man or woman really is an island', echoing John Donne's words.* Yet in that meditation on life and death, said Liam, Donne also 'laid bare a further truth: the interconnectedness of all in a particular community and within the wider human family. There is the terrible and additional pain of seeing and hearing spouses, children, siblings, friends overwhelmed by grief, sobbing in their bedrooms, in the garden, or in public places like the supermarket. Astonishingly, there is also the hate.'

That was a brilliant summary of what the case was all about, but we were shortly back to business as usual. The families' evidence had been given according to schedule, not least because after Michael O'Higgins' disappointment with Mark Breslin no defence barristers cross-examined anyone, but it was open season on the psychiatric expert, Dr Cooling. After he had given evidence with Brett's help about the various mental illnesses of those on the writ, and how they had been exacerbated by the belief that the deaths were intentional and 'have slipped into such deep depression, they will probably never make a full recovery', he was questioned on his protocols and use of medical notes and records. Aspects of his past were held up to close scrutiny: it was implied that he was exaggerating the seriousness of the condition of various clients, that he had been asking leading questions of Plaintiffs about whether their distress was exacerbated by intentionality – believing the bombers intended to kill – and it was suggested that Edmund Gibson's condition was more the fault of the police service for which he worked than of those who left the bomb in Omagh.

We were back in Dublin for more interminable cross-examination of gardaí from 9 to 12 June: Morgan's reminder that 'time is a scarce commodity in this court' had no discernible effect on the defence, engaged

* *Meditation XVII.*

as they were in endless wrangles. Dan's profile, I noted, now resembled that of a homicidal owl. During a break I threatened Dermot Fee that I would sue him under the human rights act for cruel and unusual punishment, but he blamed the gardaí. 'There is no end,' he said. 'There'll never be an end of it.' And later, to a witness, 'If you don't answer my question we'll be here till September.' Inevitably, things dragged on so long that several witnesses had to be postponed until after the summer vacation.

Back in Belfast for eight more days in June, there was the usual round of legal arguments, reading evidence into the record, rigorous examination of PSNI officers and telephone experts and pleas from the judge to give him accurate predictions of how long everything would take. 'I admit I'm a very bad predictor,' offered Dermot Fee disarmingly. 'Thirty years hasn't taught me anything.' I noted that barristers sit in court being bored and irritated by each other, but having to be alert. Dan often took refuge in hauteur. 'You stayed out of it today,' I said to him one evening. 'Do you think I would lower myself to the depth of such advocacy by participating?' he asked. He would sometimes tell me how he believed a particular cross-examination should have been conducted. 'Only ask questions you know the answer to', was one piece of advice. 'The whole art of cross-examination is to demonstrate to the court that the witness is devious,' was another. 'Not to accuse him of it.'

Most of us at times fought off hysteria. Possibly the most memorable reaction came when Jason took his frustrations out on his rather grand hotel, which had left him a pompous letter saying his room had to be 'deep cleaned' because he had been illegally smoking. Their failure to answer his angry response put him in a filthy mood after dinner. Prowling the grounds resentfully, he saw the full-size plastic stags that masqueraded as bronze, picked one up and put it on the back of another, in full view of the CCTV cameras. He was rebuked the following morning, I reported to my friend, the literary critic Eamonn Hughes, on the grounds that this simulation of rutting would shock children. 'The cry of the unimaginative down the ages,' observed Eamonn judiciously.

'Jason is a rock-and-roll lawyer,' remarked Jim and Lindy McDowell's son Jamie one evening. 'In fact you'd never guess he was a lawyer at all.' I have never seen Jason more pleased with a compliment. Yet he *was* a lawyer and he had to stick with a case that even Dermot Fee admitted to me was 99 per cent boring. It was a strange aspect of a ground-breaking case with huge implications for the law that even the families and those who had given years of passionate commitment could hardly keep our eyes open in court. Tempers were fraying. Nostrils flaring, Dan was telling the judge that we 'want a fair and expeditious conclusion.' 'Your Lordship has been an exemplar of fairness throughout, but there comes a time to say "enough",' Dan rasped. O'Higgins retaliated by calling Dan unhelpful and even Brett lost his temper and denounced one defence manoeuvre as 'a wild application thrashing out in the hope it might hit something'. Occasionally, I would think of a line from Patrick Pearse, the Real IRA's great hero, himself a non-practising barrister: 'The dragonfly among insects is in fact as the tiger among beasts and the hawk among birds, as the lawyer among men, as England among the nations. It is the destroyer, the eater-up, the cannibal.'

There were two memorable happenings before court broke up for the summer on 26 June. The first came in the context of the constant criticisms and queries I met in Belfast, Dublin and London from friends and acquaintances who could not understand why I had spent years on this case: 'Michael Gallagher is an obsessive'; 'Why don't these people give up and move on?'; 'They're making life worse for other victims'; 'Why are you wasting your life?' and so on. I never once doubted that the case was worth it all. My long-standing preoccupation with terrorism, and the stories I heard from Charlie and Larry and others about the reality of violence in Northern Ireland, kept me in touch with the nature of the enemy the families were confronting. Yet, the grind could sometimes get one down, as could the Real IRA apologists.

Taxi drivers usually asked what I was doing in Belfast. In the same week in June I had encountered two very different responses. A devout Muslim cab driver told me the bomb was a misunderstanding, that the police had got the street wrong and the bombers had no intention of killing anyone. 'So why was the bomb parked at 3.00 p.m. rather than 3.00 a.m.?' I asked so testily that he shut up. Yet that same week a BBC driver who turned out to be an ex-policeman said, 'I have nothing but admiration for the Omagh people.' Walter was taking me on a long drive to participate in *Let's Talk*, the local version of *Question Time*, and he had time to tell me about Sergeant Stephen Buttle and what the ripple effect of the Omagh bomb did to him.

Later I tracked down Sean, one of Stephen's colleagues in the RUC BRIT (Body Recovery and Identification Team), who told me the full story. After Lockerbie, the Home Office wanted dedicated teams geared mainly to major air disasters and Sean and Stevie were among the volunteers for the RUC BRIT. They received about two weeks' training, hearing from people with experience of disasters like Lockerbie and Zeebrugge.

Omagh was the first time the RUC BRIT team was used: up to then they had practised on mock car crashes. They were put into the makeshift morgue that Saturday evening. Sean, an Englishman who had married a local, was there first, at about 7.00; the others came from Belfast. 'We were just told to get on with it,' he said. 'You do it because someone has to do it. You step up to the plate. But people should have been better prepared.'

His first shift lasted twenty-four hours. Sean had had seen many, many awful scenes, but Omagh was unique because of the range of people: 'everyone there could see the vulnerability of a child, a sibling, a parent, a wife: something for everyone's nightmares'. A particularly bad thing was that, although in principle they were just to work with bodies, they had to deal with families as well. 'You don't want to see the impact on the relatives. It's bad to have that cross-over. You should have responsibility for either the dead or the living.' And because there was no team-debriefing before dissolving, there was a sense that the experience was left half finished.

'Omagh tested the resolve of everyone,' said Sean. 'After such happenings, people re-evaluate their lives, jobs and families. You can't share your experience and you try to protect others from it. That's why so often families break down and people just leave their jobs. It's why there are so many RUC suicides. And personality and values change and tolerance levels decrease. The troubles of others seem minor: "Is that all you're worried about?"'

Sean's BRIT colleague Stevie Buttle was a tall, strong man, but he was so affected by Omagh that he functioned badly at work afterwards and both his work and domestic relationships deteriorated. 'So when it got too much for Stevie, he got hold of a body bag, put himself into it and shot himself in the head. He didn't want anyone else to have to deal with it.'

It was only a few minutes after I heard Walter's shorter version of this story that I met the MP Clare Short, who was on the same programme. 'What are you doing now?' she asked, so I told her about Omagh. She looked at me with what seemed like a mixture of impatience and pity: 'Why pick at the scabs?'

The second memorable event was the arrival of John Ware, who in 2000 had made the *Panorama* programme that was so crucial to the families, who had generously helped with the development of the case and then in 2003 almost scuppered the fundraising, and throughout had taken a keen interest in all that was going on. He was making another Omagh programme for *Panorama* and he and Jason were now on good terms.

Over lunch in Bittles John discussed the debacle of 2003. He had been influenced at the time by his cynicism about lawyers in general. Later he wrote to me that, in hindsight, 'the piece 'exposing' how donations were being used was indeed unjust to Jason because it didn't fairly reflect the man's clear commitment and courage in pursuing this case. I am full of admiration for the way he has persevered against all the odds. The record will show that when victory comes he's been the man of the match.' Yet it was true that some relatives had complained to him that so much money 'had been raised and spent for – apparently – little gain at the time', and he had felt responsible since the fundraising had been kicked off by *Panorama*. 'The point that tipped it for me was the projected costs of the barristers. The documents I had projected counsel fees at nearly half a million quid for a 20-day hearing. When I read that I nearly fell off my stool.' Now he appreciated the huge amount of work that had been undertaken and knew Dan – who was 'self-evidently deeply committed to the case' – he said he had changed his mind and was happy to put the record straight.

John Ware was with a cameraman in Omagh on Sunday 17 August for the families' tenth anniversary service, but not for the official service on Friday 15th awash with dignitaries from Dublin and Belfast and which unveiled a complex artwork. There had been general incredulity in the world outside that the Omagh Support and Self Help Group had refused to amalgamate their commemoration – held every year on the Sunday nearest 15 August – with the main memorial event organised by the council at which Terry Waite would make a speech about reconciliation before the unveiling of an enlarged memorial garden, now to be known as the Garden of Light. It was dominated by a lake and thirty-one heliostatic mirrors on stilts which tracked the sun and reflected light on to a heart-shaped crystal in a fifteen-foot glass obelisk on the bomb site. Was this not the time for standing together as a community? For inclusiveness? Why were these people so difficult?

True, many of the families disliked the memorial: as Laurence Rush put it to me, 'we had a little garden where we could sit and be melancholy;

what's there now is a tourist attraction'. But the main reason the OSSHG had problems with the council was that ten of its 21 members, including the chairman, were Sinn Féin. The previous year, when work began on extending the garden, the council had removed the OSSHG plaque which read – 'To honour and remember 31 people murdered and hundreds injured from three nations by a dissident republican terrorist car bomb'.

A team of facilitators was brought in to determine what should be 'the narrative' for the garden. After 80 meetings, the compromise was that the memorial at the bomb site would mention 'an act of terror'; that on the street wall at the garden would refer to the bomb; four of the five sections within the garden would say nothing contentious; and the fifth would include the OSSHG's wording but attribute it to the group. However the group still had no intention of attending the council ceremony: the garden was to be opened by the council chairman, who – with Martin McGuinness – would lay wreaths to the bomb victims.

Henry Reid and I went to the council event on Friday. Sheltering before-hand from the driving rain in a coffee shop above the Salad Bowl, where Marion Radford had been about to pay when the bomb went off, we met Roy Kells, proprietor of the drapery S.D. Kells that had seen such carnage. Unable to go to the families' event on Sunday as he would be in Edinburgh for the world pipe band championships – where he had been in 1998 – he recalled what it had been like coming back to a traumatised staff and introduced us to his shop manager and an assistant, neither of whom had ever really talked of what happened that day but felt the need to commemorate it.

The council had expected 10,000: there were perhaps 1,000, of whom Henry told me at least 100 were council employees. Quite a few republicans also boycotted the ceremony because there were police on the platform. The excuse for the poor turn-out was that the weather was atrocious and it was a weekday, but it was much more to do with the Sinn Féin connection. The Irish Taoiseach and Shaun Woodward, the Secretary of State for Northern Ireland, were there; there was a lot of ersatz Celticy peace stuff and some good poetry and bible readings, but essentially the ceremony was damp. And a squib. Two events moved me. One was seeing Father Kevin Mullan, whom I had seen weeping on television the night before, alone behind the platform, clearly praying. The other was the scattering by children of red petals: it had not been planned this way, but because of the rain, Market Street again ran with red water.

On Sunday, a sunny day, the families were there in force among a crowd of 800 or 900, of whom everyone, as Michael said, 'was there because they wanted to be there'. They included victims of other terrorist bombings like Enniskillen, Shankill and Claudy, with whom the OSSHG had forged close links. There were prayers, poems, hymns and readings in English, Irish, Spanish and Hebrew and a speech from Michael that warmed journalists' hearts by thanking the media for all their support over the years. It was a generous and thoughtful speech, written with the help of Peter Kelly, a London-based teacher and part-time journalist who over the years had been a devoted supporter of the families and had become a close friend of Michael's. Dan and Matthew, were there, driven by Charlie, having flown in from London for the afternoon, as was Jason, who had come by car and ferry from Scotland.

September brought much more of the same as well as a new drama. Reunited in Dublin on 9 September, we were back in a familiar world of procedural wrangles and duels between gardaí and lawyers, including a continuation of the stand-off between the irresistible force and immovable object. 'My clients are listening to this with frank incomprehension,' said Dan at one stage, during an elaborate minuet about a document that was physically in court but the Defendants' lawyers maintained should not be in court and the fate of which must therefore be addressed in yet another set of submissions at a later date, which necessitated another postponement and a further return to Dublin. A journalist who looked in for a few minutes shook his head at me as he left and said, 'Groundhog Day'. Dan's Spanish wife Pilar came to a wet and windy Dublin to see what was taking so much more of her husband's time than had been expected. She was so enraged about what she had seen in court that Jason and I realised how institutionalised we had become. Whereas we were shrugging about predictable frustrations, she was seriously angry about the slowness, the delays and the sheer waste of time she had observed in only a couple of hours.

There was a new distraction, however. On Monday 15th the BBC was to transmit John Ware's latest exposé on Omagh and there were meetings about how families and lawyers should react. The arrangement was that the families would be shown it two nights beforehand and would say nothing about it until a press conference in Belfast on Tuesday morning.

John Ware's programme, 'What The Police Were Never Told',

revealed that GCHQ in the UK had been monitoring conversations on a mobile phone which was used in the Omagh bombing, both in the weeks leading up to the bombing and – crucially – in the hours after the bomb exploded. The programme stated that this intelligence had not been passed on to the RUC Special Branch until three days after the bombing and as a result, information which might possibly have had crucial value to the early stages of the investigation – the 'golden hours' as they were called by one contributor to the programme – including the use of the phrase 'the bricks are in the wall' to signify that the bomb was ready, had not been available to the RUC Special Branch in the early stages of the investigation.

The statement Michael read to the press conference – where he was supported by more than a dozen relatives and many supportive journalists – asked Special Branch and the security services if they confirmed or denied the *Panorama* allegations; if the bomb team's calls during delivery of the bomb were recorded, was anyone listening in real time and if not, why not? Was this key intelligence given to police and if not, why not? 'Evidence of the fact of the phone calls is a current live issue in the trial . . . we implore those in the intelligence community to search their souls and voluntarily provide this material in our civil action.' 'Our capacity to talk about Omagh,' John Ware had said to me that morning, 'is not equalled by the ability of others to listen.' Yet the liveliness of the discussion suggested there were some journalists left who still were engaged. 'Intelligence people want to keep secrets secret,' said Michael. 'Let us have the truth. We dealt with what happened on the 15th August 1998. Nothing could be more painful.' The media took off for Belfast, where Gordon Brown was visiting briefly; his press conference was dominated by embarrassing questions about Omagh.

Jason was in his element, threatening all means of action against GCHQ if it did not come up with the goods and organising methods of putting pressure on the Prime Minister, who had quite separately also just refused to follow the example of the US and demand compensation from Libya for IRA victims who were Jason's clients. The Prime Minister, however, kicked the issue into touch by asking Sir Peter Gibson, the Intelligence Services Commissioner, to examine all intercept material and see how it was shared; he gave him a deadline of three months. This became yet another bone of contention to be gnawed in court without providing nourishment to anyone, affording much opportunity for arguments about whether in the unlikely event of the material being made available it would be admissible.

Over the next days and weeks many MPs, peers and other influential figures called in vain for the release of the intelligence, with little sign that any attention was being paid to them: 'Wait for Sir Peter Gibson' was the mantra. The best hope came from an unexpected quarter: after fifteen years of bitter enmity, in early October Gordon Brown brought Peter Mandelson back from Brussels and into his cabinet. I sent Mandelson an e-mail: 'Congratulations, Peter. You have an infinite capacity to surprise . . . I will continue to follow your career with interest and, for what it's worth, you are a hero in *Aftermath: the Omagh bombing and the families' pursuit of justice*, which will be published shortly after this case ends.' I had no ulterior motive, but he replied within half an hour asking if I could bring him up to date with the Omagh trial. 'Is there any issue in the government I can help on at all?'

What was urgently needed, I told him, were full details of GCHQ recordings and the relevant transcripts and a guarantee that public servants who help the lawyers and/or give evidence in court would not suffer prosecution or persecution. Mandelson promised to pursue the matter, and he did. He called occasionally to report what he had found out, but, as he warned, as Business Secretary he had no standing with the security services.

Gibson interviewed John Ware in such a hostile way that it was no surprise to any of us when in January he produced what we regarded as a whitewash report that condemned the *Panorama* film. But while he asked whether the bombing could have been prevented if the intercepting was being done live – which Ware had not alleged was the case – he never addressed the key issue of why detectives hunting the bombers were not told immediately about the intelligence that GCHQ had gathered which could have allowed them to make early arrests. When in May Gibson appeared before the Northern Ireland Select Committee it would emerge that his terms of reference had been set so narrowly that they did not allow him to look at that issue; it would also emerge that it was the Prime Minister who had refused to have more than a quarter of the report made available to anyone, even the Chairman of the Select Committee.

What Mandelson did achieve in the end was to arrange for the families to meet Gordon Brown, who had previously turned them down. By now it was February, and if anything was going to be provided for the case, now was the time. Victor asked me to go with him as a friend.

I was not among the optimists who thought the Prime Minister might cut through all the bureaucratic obstacles, rush through the necessary legislation and present the GCHQ evidence to the judge wrapped in a pink ribbon. Yet even for me this episode was a particularly shabby example of how Whitehall protects itself at all costs. First there was the call to Victor the day before the visit to Downing Street from the Northern Ireland Office to say that while they would not ban me, it might distress the other families to know that, because I was a journalist, my presence would inevitably ensure the Prime Minister would be less frank. So of course I dropped out. Number 10 staff went through no such niceties with Jason, who was simply told he would not be admitted. What questions did they think we would ask that the families would not, he wondered? What were they afraid of?

Number 10 had chosen February 11th, an excellent day to try to bury Omagh: the media were preoccupied with a visit by hated bankers to the House of Commons and there was little press interest. Mandelson had certainly achieved a good turn-out: he was there along with Gordon Brown, Shaun Woodward, the Northern Ireland Secretary, Sir Hugh Orde, Assistant Chief Constable Drew Harris and a Number 10 official. The Prime Minister assured the families that he had personally viewed all the intercept evidence, but that there was nothing there of any use. Mandelson concurred. John Ware, it was said, although a good journalist, had made mistakes. Hugh Orde volunteered that he would not blame the families for being angry about the serious flaws in the first investigation. The general line was that GCHQ were in the clear and any failings were to be blamed on the pre-Orde RUC.

The message, said Donna McCauley, the OSSHG Coordinator, was: 'We hear you, but we can't do anything. Intelligence is not evidence.' Godfrey Wilson's defence of Ware was shot down; Patsy Gallagher asked the Prime Minister why he paid for MI5 if they didn't pass on information and when Brown showed her out, told him, 'You only want rid of me.' 'What do you do? Where do you go?' asked Stanley afterwards. 'It's a brick wall.' 'It was a Dear John meeting to close us down,' said Carol Radford. 'They closed ranks,' said Godfrey. There was a sense of helplessness about the group, a belief they had been stitched up, yet they still had no intention of giving in. Michael drew comfort from Brown not having actually refused a public inquiry, and, as he said often, 'We will continue, whatever it takes, however long it takes, and how much embarrassment we cause governments.'

On his way home, Victor rang to say he had believed the statement that the material was useless to the case, but only because Mandelson had said so. In the families' view, Mandelson had done and would do anything he could for the families short of embarrassing the government. Jason, however, was fuming: what did the Prime Minister or any of them know about the civil case that qualified them to say what evidence was or was not relevant? They were not lawyers and knew nothing of the specific, detailed legal proceedings. The material should have gone to the judge.

The case would go on until March 25, with the caravanserai having occasional forays to Dublin. There were good moments. One was on October 2nd. I was keeping Jason company while he smoked on the court steps when Matthew emerged to announce that a retired Metropolitan policeman had just arrived to give evidence carrying a tape of phone calls linking McKevitt to the Woolwich Three arms-dealing sting. Admissible as evidence because the conversations were recorded, not intercepted, he had got them by the simple means of ringing up an ex-colleague and asking for the Met's copy of the tape. When we had stopped rejoicing, Jason said, 'When this is over, I'm going to write to people like the Treasury Solicitor who for six fucking years has been saying we can't have the McKevitt tape and say "Nyaaa nyaaa nyaaa nyaaa"'. 'I will go to church with renewed enthusiasm on Sunday,' said Dan.

Of course, the tape could not be played until hours of legal arguments had been endured. What with other pre-arranged witnesses and a visit to Dublin intervening, it was not until the 30th that I actually got to listen to the flat voice with a Louth accent who claimed to be called Karl, making arrangements in a foreign city to meet someone near a Burger King. It was fascinating but rather anti-climactic and inevitably called to mind Hannah Arendt's description of 'the banality of evil'.

I had a moment with Michael O'Higgins, whom I liked, that gave me great satisfaction. Back in Dublin in mid-October, I had listened to him trying and failing to get Assistant Commissioner Dermot Jennings to agree that since David Rupert had described himself as a whore, he was therefore himself untrustworthy. The morning had provided some enjoyable cabaret. Before the court sat again after lunch, I observed to Michael that I had read about a disgraceful figure he had just taken on as a client. 'I just take the brief,' he said. 'So you're a whore,' I said. He got the joke. 'It all becomes a game for criminal lawyers,' said Paul Bennett of the PSNI later, and told me of a conversation he had had with a lawyer about the lawyer's paedophile client; the lawyer explained, 'It's our profession. It's what we do.' The day five extra barristers appeared in court to represent various authorities I went home to Liam Kennedy and said: 'I keep searching vainly for the right collective noun for lawyers.' Without a pause, he suggested: 'A fleece.'

My notes show increasing desperation as the arguments became more and more detached from reality, the dates went on slipping, left-over witnesses were scheduled here and there, and the peripatetic existence got us all down. 'Behind every silver lining, there's a big, dark bugger of a cloud,' proffered Larry. 'What's the difference between farce and fiasco?' I asked Tony McGleenan once. 'Is it that you have control over a farce but are helpless in a fiasco?' 'It's disaster without any hint of levity,' offered Tony. Tony had cause to understand such concepts. During our case he was sometimes involved at the expense of the British taxpayer in a separate case, trying to secure legal aid for a prisoner who – according to the Prison Service – had neglected his budgie and permitted it to be a health and safety hazard and, now that it was dead, wanted a new one.

I had been the only one of our group pessimistic enough to predict the case would go on until Christmas: by December, bets were being placed on Easter. Dermot Fee and I occasionally amused ourselves by trying to teach Brett how to pronounce phrases like 'A chara' or 'Óglaigh na hÉireann'. Defence lawyers tried to restrict what the judge could hear or see, including *Panorama*, while themselves demanding full disclosure from both *Panorama* and Ware. Not to be outdone, the Plaintiffs were demanding tapes from the security services and a wide range of individuals who might have heard them. We were all bored and tired. The seasons changed and so did the good-looking and exotic H2O paralegals who tapped away all day on their laptops trying to make sense of what was going on. Beverley Wong was much missed when she moved to another job in H2O, but Marina Themistocleous, Anna Wakeling, Zubin Irani, Ramesh Patel and Stephanie Lawson provided an occasional lift in our jaded routine.

Whether Sean O'Callaghan could give evidence that Michael McKevitt had been in the IRA became a big issue from November. The defence's insistence that there be full disclosure of all PSNI and garda documents on Sean added several weeks to the case and ensured no sittings at all in January. Eventually, in March, the judge decided he should not be called: since little PSNI and almost no garda documentation was forthcoming, and Sean, as a spy, was by definition 'a practised deceiver', it would be necessary to test his evidence against what he had said to the police north and south and that was not possible. The Plaintiffs could have appealed, but no one had the appetite for more months of this. This was a great relief to Charlie and Larry, who were not looking forward to the security problems of protecting an IRA informer in a Belfast court.

Two soldiers were murdered by dissident republicans on 7 March and a policeman on the 9th. Martin McGuinness called on republicans to give information to the PSNI. Victor is still waiting for a reply to his question as to why this should not also apply to Omagh. In his closing submission on 20 March, Dan put in a spirited performance. 'How was it?' he asked me afterwards. 'Excellent,' I said. 'Though maybe you patronised the judge once too often.' On 25 March, the defence submissions just seemed to peter out.

'Has the case just ended with a whimper?' I asked Matthew. 'With a sigh,' he said.

EPILOGUE

'The basics of British justice belong to the people of Britain: they are not just dependent on the legal system. Today, because of the courage of the Omagh families, it has been proved that justice works' – Dan Brennan QC

The considerate Mr Justice Morgan told the court on 25 March that he would let us know in mid-May if he could not deliver his judgement during the summer term. In the event, he gave two weeks' notice that it would come on Monday 8 June at 11.30. This was the first occasion in eight years that the legal system moved faster than expected.

On the eve of the judgement some of the posse gathered and we brought each other up to date on the Omagh Defendants. Michael McKevitt had reached the end of the legal road in the Republic of Ireland, having had his appeal for a fresh appeal turned down by the Supreme Court the day after the Omagh civil case ended; Colm Murphy had not yet had a decision from the Supreme Court on his appeal against a retrial; for some unknown reason, Seamus Daly had recently landed in hospital having been beaten up by several men in Carrickmacross. In mid-May Liam Campbell – on bail in the Republic of Ireland as Lithuania sought to extradite him on arms-smuggling charges – had been nominated as public relations officer of the Community Alert scheme in his County Louth village of Faughart. However, a couple of weeks later he had foolishly given his wife a lift to her job in Northern Ireland, had his car rammed by the PSNI and been arrested. His brother, Michael, alleged to have been smuggling cigarettes and arms, had been residing in a Lithuanian jail for a year and Liam was reluctant to join him in what their sympathisers call the 'Baltic Guantanamo'. Still held on remand in Northern Ireland, pending resolution of extradition proceedings to Lithuania, his lawyers were trying to have him returned to the Republic.

Dan, Greenie and Matt arrived the next morning, along with Victor, but not Henry, who had taken the wrong documents to the airport and been turned away. Jason was giving interviews, after which he went over to the court and, for old times' sake, smoked a cigarette sitting on the stone bench where we had found him on the first day of the trial.

It was sunny, and outside the court the media were in full pursuit of the families who had arrived by mini-bus from Omagh. Everyone on the writ was there except Garry Wilson, who had emigrated to Australia to try to escape the legacy of the bomb. With them too were several of their relatives, along with Edith White, who had come off the writ in 2006.

We were in a larger court this time, the press box and the public gallery packed with journalists and the public benches almost full. The judge was prompt; he explained he would read only the key parts of his judgement and that afterwards a summary and the full judgement* would be handed out by court officials afterwards.

Dan Brennan's final 180-page submission had been designed to 'assist the judicial task of ordered analysis governed by intellectual discipline in assessing the evidence', and it had indeed given the case a helpful coherence. Mr Justice Morgan's judgement reflected that in its clear narrative structure, simple language, the calm, measured way it dealt with contentious legal issues and its avoidance of any kind of ambiguity. Dan, who is sparse with compliments, spoke of it afterwards as the product of a first-class mind. It also reflected the common sense that had seemed so often missing during legal wrangles. It was not his job, said the judge, to determine whether any criminal offence had been committed, but to establish whether the Plaintiffs had demonstrated that the Defendants were responsible for causing them harm and, if so, decide on what damages were payable.

Having reviewed the evidence on the location of the car bomb, the telephone warnings and the bomb components, including the timer device, he concluded that the bombers were so keen that the bomb should explode without detection, that 'the safety of those members of the public in Omagh town centre was a best a secondary consideration'. He concluded 'that those involved in the planning, preparation, planting and detonation of the bomb recognised the likelihood of serious injury or death from its detonation but decided to take the risk'.

From the telephone evidence, he concluded that there was an 'irresistible inference' that a phone registered to Colm Murphy and another lent to him by the unwitting Terence Morgan had been used in the bomb run.

---

* Available at www.courtsni.gov.uk.

He dismissed the case against Seamus McKenna, the First Defendant, as it was dependant on the unreliable evidence of his estranged wife.

The critical issue with the Second Defendant, the Real IRA, was that in law it is an unincorporated association which cannot therefore be made a defendant in its own right. But, said the judge, 'those who were members of the Army Council of the Real IRA in August 1998 bear responsibility for directing the Omagh bomb as part of the campaign that was being waged at that time and are therefore liable'. He specified Liam Campbell as having been proved to have been on the Army Council at the time, but emphasised that all other members of the Army Council of the Real IRA on the date of the bombing were also liable for damages.

Despite the efforts of the Third Defendant, Michael McKevitt, to deny the credibility of David Rupert, the judge 'was satisfied to a very high standard of probability' that the 2,293 pages of e-mails 'represented actual traffic' occurring between Rupert and his handlers: 'the extraordinary level of detail' and the references to many other people was 'compelling evidence that these accounts represent an attempt to provide an accurate and comprehensive record of actual meetings'. Rupert's hearsay evidence was the 'sole or decisive' evidence against McKevitt, who, concluded the judge, 'has always held a significant leadership role within the Real IRA', and was undoubtedly responsible for encouraging the bombing campaign in 1998 which culminated in Omagh and in 'aiding, counselling and directing the commission of the tort [the wrongdoing]'. His failure to give evidence in court was 'inexplicable and makes the case against him overwhelming'.

Rupert and telephone evidence sank Liam Campbell, the Fourth Defendant, whom the judge was overwhelmingly satisfied had an important leadership position in the Real IRA, had received calls from the Murphy mobile and made warning calls about the bomb which demonstrated his involvement in directing and participating in the operation. It was inexplicable, said the judge, that he should not have answered this case if he had an answer to it.

The Fifth Defendant, Colm Murphy, appeared several times in Rupert's e-mails as a member of the Continuity IRA; the judge found 'significant and cogent evidence' that Murphy was 'a dedicated terrorist who has been an active participant in carrying on terrorist attacks over a long period.' Judge Morgan was satisfied that there was evidence Murphy had provided the two mobiles for the bomb attack – which he found was a joint operation between the Real IRA and the Continuity IRA – 'knowing full well the nature of the attack which was going to be conducted'. Murphy's counsel had claimed he could not give evidence as he was still to face a criminal prosecution in the Republic, but though the judge had offered to make 'stringent arrangements to protect the evidence about him from publicity or disclosure in advance of this prosecution', Murphy did not take up the offer.

The case against Seamus Daly relied primarily on his having made a call on Colm Murphy's phone on the afternoon of 15 August to someone who had no involvement with the bomb but was able to identify Daly as his caller. Additionally, his failure to give evidence further supported the case against him.

As he had already concluded in an earlier ruling on the case, it was not legally open to him to award exemplary (punitive) damages in this case, said the judge, but he considered aggravated (taking account of psychological suffering) damages fully justified. Although he was not satisfied that there was a specific intention to cause massive death and injury, 'I recognise that the likelihood of injury or death occurring was plain in circumstances where a fully loaded car bomb was placed in the centre of a busy market town on a Saturday afternoon'; there was also the matter of the deficient warnings, which 'contributed to the sense of distress felt by the victims'. From the reports he had read and evidence given in court by the plaintiffs it was clear 'that the senseless and indiscriminate nature of this appalling outrage has deeply affected each of them,' and he would include damages for emotional distress also. He would not rehearse the accounts he had heard or read of the 'enormous difficulties a number of those involved had in coping with the consequences of this bomb. For many the effects are catastrophic and their lives will never be the same.'

Working under legal guidelines for damages assessment, he awarded general damages to everyone on the writ: Mark Breslin, £60,000; Marion Radford, £100,000; Paul Radford, £75,000; Stanley McCombe, £75,000; Michael Gallagher, £75,000; Cathy Gallagher, £50,000; Edmund Gibson, £60,000; Godfrey Wilson, £75,000; Garry Wilson, £50,000; Colin Wilson, £40,000; Ann Wilson, £100,000; Denise Kerrigan £75,000. Everyone was awarded an extra £30,000 in aggravated damages and three plaintiffs also received awards of special damages in respect of loss of income attributable to the deaths of their loved ones.

Reading the judgement took about an hour and fifty minutes. About twenty minutes before the end his decisions on certain key evidence made me at last certain he would find in the families' favour. Tiny changes in the expressions on our lawyers' faces confirmed my optimism, and one could see that the more legally sophisticated of the families were daring to hope. I almost never cry, but I could not hold back tears, unprofessional as it was for a journalist in a press box. When he finished, the judge said something crisp about addressing outstanding issues in two weeks and, as Dan rose to thank him, Morgan stood up, bowed, and left. He is to be the new Chief Justice of Northern Ireland and he has made an auspicious and brave start. There were no shouts of triumph: these families and supporters had been dignified and showed respect to the court at all times. But as the recognition dawned on us that we had crossed the finishing-line, lawyers, families and some journalists hugged each other indiscriminately as we left the room.

The first person I spoke to as I came out of court was Larry. In the middle of rejoicing crowds he gave me his customary quizzical look and enquired: 'When's the appeal?'

We were all enveloped in a sense of simple joy and intense relief. Some of us said amicable goodbyes to the opposition lawyers, and then the families, their lawyers and supporters abandoned the media for a few minutes for a final valedictory gathering in an upstairs room so tiny that people were spilling out of the open door. An exultant Dan spoke of a famous victory that would resonate around the world, give terrorists cause to worry and give other victims hope. Liam Kennedy, who so often has seen the good people suffer at the hands of the bad, cried along with many of us. There were grateful hugs all round. And then the families went out and faced together, as they had done so often before, the ranks of cameras and reporters. As I was leaving, a court official said: 'We're all delighted here. Every day you see bad people getting off scot-free and you realise that the law and justice have nothing to do with each other. But today was different.'

Encircled by cameras and microphones, these by-now practised interviewees were revelling in the novelty of giving happy interviews to mark the moment when – for the first time in British law, and as far as anyone knows anywhere in the world – victims of terrorism had taken on in court those they held responsible and won. 'This was the day of reckoning, the day of truth', said Godfrey. 'I hope against hope that there is a heaven up there and Lorraine is looking down and rejoicing with us.' 'It's a result we hoped for but didn't expect,' said Stanley. 'We've been let down so many times before. It was never about money. We can stand up and say that these guys are responsible for Omagh. That's what we wanted.'

That theme of naming and shaming was picked up by Victor. 'This is about identifying people responsible, identifying them in their own community and saying: "these people should be rejected; they are not part of a decent society and they should be regarded by everyone as pariahs." It is time to look at these people and to say, "We don't want you in this country. We don't want you fighting for Irish freedom on our behalf. Let the people of Northern Ireland decide what they want by voting."'

Michael was bullish: 'We have sent out a message to terrorists 'that from now on you don't only have to worry about the authorities – the families of your victims will come after you. It's also a message to governments that if you don't do it, then we will. We have also sent a message to victims of terrorism around the world. You now have a way of challenging those who murder your loved ones.'

Beyond the significance of the verdict, everyone was asking about the next step. 'We can apply for attachment of earnings against individuals and go to courts in the Republic to enforce the judgement,' said Jason. 'Even if they've got rid of their assets, we can go after their cars and their tvs, said Dan. 'We will chase these people every way that we can,' said Michael.

Victor went home, and among the people he wrote to was Peter Mandelson. 'Just a brief note to convey my very grateful thanks to you for all your support since we first met all those years ago. Despite our differences and my dark moods at the time – you offered me friendship and counsel – and have always tried to support us. Both James and I will be forever in your debt.' 'You were entitled to your dark moods' was the response. 'I am so thrilled by the result for you and James, and all the families. Peter.'

Families and lawyers went to Bittles pub to celebrate together, and I settled in a corner to write a triumphant article for the *Daily Mail* which all those years ago had begun the fund-raising, while also keeping half an ear to what was going on around me. 'Can you do another telephone interview, Michael?' called his friend Peter Kelly, who was acting as his go-between. 'Who is it?' 'Al Jazeera.' Michael was tired, but as Lindy McDowell, who joined us, wrote the next day: 'In the ten years I've known him it was the first time I can say I saw Michael Gallagher truly smile. Smile not just with his lips but in a way that lit up his eyes and his whole being. For once that terrible pain that you always saw in Michael's face was – temporarily at least – gone. It was the same for all the families.' For all of us, it was astonishing to see this joy written all over the faces that for years had been marked by grief. Even the news that McKevitt had told his solicitors to appeal could not dent spirits. Lindy and Dan were beside me as I typed. 'What does it feel like?' she asked him. 'In law, winning, well, that's just life,' he said. 'But winning something you truly care about – there is no feeling like it.'

Janie went to the airport and the joyous families left for Omagh early afternoon. Before he left, the ever-professional Michael gave me a quote for my article. 'We are full of gratitude to all those people who helped us. I hope that everyone who gave us support of any kind knows how much it meant to us. It has been a day we've worked for all these years and yet never believed would come. I will sleep well tonight.' Victor slept well that night too. 'I think I can get on with my life now,' he told me the next morning.

There would be practical decisions to be made about what to do next on the legal front, but no one wanted to think about that on Monday night. We had dinner together and rejoiced. Jason kept rushing in and out to take calls and answer texts and would come back showing messages from Clooney, Bono, Geldof and the prime minister's wife, Sarah Brown, but, rather more movingly for me, from counsel and solicitors from the past, all of them delighted that their project had finally succeeded: Heather Rodgers, Danny Friedman, Lucy Morgan, Rose Alexander and Richard Devall. Impromptu speeches were made. Michael Seamark, from the *Daily Mail*, said that when Jason had first turned up at the office, they thought he was mad, but they were proud to have taken the risk of backing him. Brett Lockhart had been initially sceptical of Jason, but even though none of his colleagues on the criminal side had believed the case could succeed, he had taken the plunge because he thought it right; Dan was the best barrister he had ever worked with and it was his confidence and the crucial calls he had made that had brought victory. After more than four decades in the law, Dan wanted us to know how rare it was to see justice done and how important was this result. Matt, who clings on to the idealism that had him helping those on death row, spoke of being over-joyed to have been part of a case that performed a public service and Greenie spoke of his pride in the team. Liam talked of the families, and of Cathy and Patsy Gallagher on the road of tears between Omagh and Derry, and Lindy spoke of their triumph. Jim McDowell and Jason's father Terry told everyone how wonderful they were and Charlie refused to speak because of the constraints of the Official Secrets Act. I proposed a toast to some of the absent friends who had been so vital to the case: Henry Robinson, Robert Salisbury, Paul Dacre, Janie Dawnay, Sean O'Callaghan, Paul Le Druillenec, Máirín Carter, John Lippitt, Peter Mandelson and the rest of the team, and all those others who had offered financial and moral support through the grim years. Jason asked that we remember everyone involved in the case for what they had done in bringing a smile to faces that had not smiled for a long time. And then he proposed a toast to David Rupert, a six-foot-seven-inch American with a chequered past now living under witness protection, who through intelligence, industry, courage and a belief that it was wrong to kill, helped bring about this famous victory.

ACKNOWLEDGEMENTS

First, I must thank the bereaved families of the Omagh bomb for trusting me to write their story. It has been an honour to be involved with these indomitable people: when I saw their faces after the verdict I had one of the moments of greatest joy I have ever experienced. As in the case of lawyers and campaigners, I feel it acutely that so many people who did so much are given little recognition here, but the story is complex and space was limited.

I have wonderful friends, several of whom played crucial parts in this campaign and also provided information and reminiscences for the book, as did others who kindly gave me interviews or communicated by email – their contribution will be clear – and Martyn Frampton, an expert on dissident republicanism, who gave invaluable help on the chronology. Key people in preventing me from succumbing to despair were this time, in London, Máirín Carter, Sean O'Callaghan, Henry Robinson, Robert Salisbury, David Trimble and Nina Clarke, an inexhaustible source of kindness and support, in Dublin Úna O'Donoghue, who died in 2008 and whom I miss every day, James McGuire and Barbara Sweetman FitzGerald, in Northern Ireland Paul Bew, Eamonn Hughes, Brian Kennaway, Liam Kennedy, Jim and Lindy McDowell and Henry and Lorraine Reid, many of whom, along with Jasper and Caroline de Montmorency Wright, were most generous hosts, and in farther-flung parts, Kathryn Kennison, Neasa MacErlean and Janet McIver. Thanks are due also to all those who read and commented on the book in typescript, including Máirín, Nina, Sean, Victor Barker, Robert, my brother Owen, and Carol Scott, who for almost two decades has been my prized and much-loved assistant.

H2O have asked me to say that they owe a debt of gratitude to those people who helped the legal case on its way: apparently they will know who they are, as will many people – including serving and retired police officers – who were of great assistance to me both on and off the record: their involvement will be clear from the book.

My thanks to all at H2O, to my dear friends Jason, Greenie and Matt – whose hard work as my official nit-picker was invaluable – whose companionship I so much enjoyed along our rocky path, to Elizabeth Barton for many kindnesses, and to Beverley Wong, Marina Themistocleous, Anna Wakeling, Zubin Irani, Ramesh Patel and Stephanie Lawson for their help and their company. Dan Brennan and Brett Lockhart unstintingly helped me understand something of the foreign culture that is the law and were inspirational and great fun too. And Charlie Mitchell and Larry Morrow made the last year bearable.

No one can ever have owed their publishers as much gratitude as I owe mine. Encouraged by my agent, Peter Robinson, that marvellous Harvill Secker team of Geoff Mulligan and Stuart Williams took on the book in 2003, expecting it to be ready in 2005: because of the vagaries of the law, it was delayed until June 2009. For their calmness, encouragement, their brilliance as editors, their astonishingly high level of emotional intelligence and their unquenchable sense of humour, I will be eternally thankful: it grieves me that Geoff was not still there to see *Aftermath* through to the end. Because the book could not be finished until after the judgement on 8 June, Stuart was faced with publishing it in three weeks. Hats off to Ellie Steel and the other colleagues, including Vanessa Milton, Penny Liechti, Simon Rhodes and Louise Rhind-Tutt, and Andrea Martin of Eugene F. Collins Solicitors, who helped him beat that impossible deadline.

I may be the only person in 2009 to say a good word about a bank, but with real sincerity I thank Kevin Peirson and HSBC for helping me through a tough time.

NOTES

Chapter 2
1. John Mooney and Michael O'Toole, *Black Operations* (2003).
2. Eamon Collins, *Killing Rage* (1997).
3. Richard O'Rawe, *Blanketmen: An Untold Story of the H-Block Hunger Strike* (2005).
4. Evidence of David Rupert.
5. Much of this background evidence comes from evidence given by David Rupert at McKevitt's trial.
6. Quoted in Kevin Rafter, *Martin Mansergh* (2002), p. 261.
7. The account of this meeting is based on interviews recorded in Mooney and O'Toole, *Black Operations*, pp. 114–15.

Chapter 3
Unless otherwise stated, quotes here are from the inquest.
1. In addition to Phil Marshall's evidence to the inquest, I have drawn on an interview he gave the *Tyrone Constitution* on 27 August 1998 and another he gave me in April 2007.
2. Interview with RDE.
3. Deposition of Tara McBurney at inquest; she was too mentally scarred by her experiences to appear as a witness.
4. Interview with RDE.
5. Interview with RDE.

Chapter 5
1. At the inquest.

Chapter 6
1. Thought for the Day, BBC Radio 4, 17 August 1998.
2. Mooney and O'Toole, *Black Operations*, p. 170.
3. Ibid. p. 172.

Chapter 7

1. Toby Harnden, *Bandit Country* (2000), p. 156.
2. Mooney and O'Toole, *Black Operations*, p. 187.

Chapter 9

1. 30 November 1988.
2. 'We Will Remember Them', April 1998.
3. Ruth Dudley Edwards, *The Faithful Tribe* (1999).
4. David Rupert evidence.

Chapter 11

1. *The Informer* (1998).
2. David Rupert evidence.
3. Ibid.
4. *Scotland on Sunday*, 11 March 2001.
5. David Rupert evidence.

Chapter 12

1. Interview, *Guardian*, 14 March 2007.

Chapter 13

1. In 'Out of History: Ireland, That "Most Distressful Country"' (an essay in his *Colonialism, Religion and Nationalism in Ireland*, 1996), the economic historian Liam Kennedy examined the claim of victimhood-embracing Irish nationalists to be the most oppressed people ever. Comparing Ireland with other countries from such standpoints as location, climate, land occupancy, political and religious rights, economic welfare and violence, he established that the Irish experience was no worse that the average European experience and in many respects much better.
2. David Rupert evidence.
3. 18 August 2001.

Chapter 14

1. John Packwood and Jane Amestoy, *Extradited!* (2007).

CHRONOLOGY:
POLITICS AND TERROR

(Apart from a few key incidents affecting the political process that are specifically attributed to the Provisional IRA and loyalist paramilitaries, all the terrorist incidents listed in this chronology are the work of dissident republican terrorists. Since sometimes no specific terrorist group claimed responsibility, at other times members of CIRA and RIRA and Óglaigh na hÉireann did – sometimes assisted by freelancing members of INLA and PIRA – and for a long periods the Real IRA chose to attribute its activities to the Continuity IRA, I do not differentiate between them.)

Places: NI (Northern Ireland); RoI (Republic of Ireland); US (United States)

Parties: DUP (Democratic Unionist Party); PUP (Progressive Unionist Party); RSF (Republican Sinn Féin); SDLP (Social and Democratic Labour Party); SF (Sinn Féin); UDP (Ulster Democratic Party); UKUP (United Kingdom Unionist Party); UUP (Ulster Unionist Party); 32CSM (32 County Sovereignty Movement)

Paramilitaries: CIRA (Continuity IRA); INLA (Irish National Liberation Army); LVF (Loyalist Volunteer Force); Óglaigh na hÉireann (ÓnH); PIRA (Provisional IRA); RIRA (Real IRA); UDA (Ulster Defence Association); UFF (Ulster Freedom Fighters); UVF (Ulster Volunteer Force)

Titles: FM (First Minister); DFM (Deputy First Minister); IMC (Independent Monitoring Commission); MLA (Member of the Legislative Assembly); MP (Member of Parliament); PM (Prime Minister)

1993
15 December Conservative PM John Major and Fianna Fáil Taoiseach Albert Reynolds issue the Joint Declaration on Peace (aka the Downing Street Declaration), which *inter alia* says it is for the people of NI to decide whether to stay in the United Kingdom or become part of a united Ireland, and promises that the two governments will work for an agreement between all the people of Ireland and towards the end of paramilitary violence

1994

31 August   PIRA declare 'a cessation of military operations'

1 September   UDA/UFF murder Catholic civilian

10 November Postal worker killed by PIRA during robbery in Newry; PIRA blame breakdown in chain of command

15 December Albert Reynolds succeeded by John Bruton of Fine Gael

1995

22 February   Governments publish Framework Documents, outlining an NI Assembly and north/south institutions

8 September   David Trimble becomes leader of UUP

28 November Joint communiqué by governments outlines a 'twin-track' process to make progress in parallel on all-party negotiations and the decommissioning of paramilitary weapons (with the help of US Senator George Mitchell)

30 November On a visit to NI, President Bill Clinton shakes Gerry Adams's hand

1996

24 January   Mitchell report on decommissioning sets out the 'Mitchell Principles', acceptance of which will entitle parties to join all-party talks, during which decommissioning should take place; it is accepted by governments, Alliance Party and SDLP as well as UDP and SF, linked respectively to the paramilitary UDA and PIRA; UUP have reservations and DUP reject it

29 January   Twin-track talks begin with SDLP, PUP and UDP

9 February   On the day before Major is to meet SF, PIRA, alleging bad faith from British government and unionists, end their 'cessation' and explode a bomb in London's Docklands, killing two, injuring forty and causing £150 million worth of damage

30 May   110 delegates elected to a Forum to decide who will participate in all-party negotiations: UUP 30, DUP 24, SDLP 21, SF 17, Alliance 7, UKUP 3, PUP 2, UDP 2, NI Women's Coalition 2, Labour 2

7 June   PIRA members kill Garda McCabe in RoI during armed robbery

10 June   All-party negotiations begin at Stormont: SF excluded

14 June   Forum meets in Belfast; boycotted by SF as partitionist

15 June   3,000-pound PIRA bomb in Manchester: two hundred injured; city centre devastated

7 July   Portadown Orangemen prevented from parading from Drumcree Church down Garvaghy Road; widespread unionist protests and loyalist rioting

11 July   Parade permitted: widespread nationalist protests and republican rioting

13 July   1,200-pound car bomb in Killyhevlin Hotel, Enniskillen, County Fermanagh, injures seventeen

6 September   SDLP and SF boycott Forum

29 September   250-pound car bomb abandoned in Belfast; army hold controlled explosion

7 October   Two PIRA bombs at Thiepval Barracks, Lisburn, County Antrim, kill one, injure thirty-one

21 November   600-pound bomb fails to explode in Derry

1997

12 February   PIRA kill Lance Bombardier Stephen Restorick, at army checkpoint in Bessbrook, County Armagh

5 April   PIRA bomb threats cause postponement of Grand National in Liverpool

1 May   UK general election produces Labour landslide: Tony Blair PM. NI MPs: UUP 10, SDLP 3, DUP 2, SF 2, UKUP 1

16 May   Blair endorses Framework Documents, Mitchell Report on decommissioning and the criteria for inclusion in all-party talks and authorises talks between officials and SF

3 June   Stormont talks resume without SF

6 June   RoI general election: Bertie Ahern becomes Taoiseach; SF win first seat since abandoning abstentionism in 1986

16 June   Two policemen shot dead in Lurgan, County Armagh, by the PIRA

25 June   Governments state that if PIRA call ceasefire within five weeks SF will be allowed into talks after six

6 July   Orange parade down Garvaghy Road permitted; widespread republican rioting

16 July   DUP and UKUP leave talks in protest at lack of clarification on decommissioning

19 July   PIRA call cessation

31 July   500-pound bomb near Lisbellaw, County Fermanagh, defused by army

9 August   Hoax van bomb planted on Craigavon Bridge, Derry, prior to Apprentice Boys' parade

26 August   Three-man Independent International Commission on Decommissioning appointed

29 August   Mo Mowlam, Secretary of State for NI, invites SF into talks

9 September   SF pledges to abide by the Mitchell Principles

11 September	PIRA say they would have problems with some of Mitchell Principles but that what SF do is up to them
15 September	SF joins talks
16 September	400-pound bomb causes extensive damage in Markethill, County Armagh
7 October	Beginning of substantive talks; all parties involved except DUP and UKUP
10 October	Michael McKevitt and eight supporters walk out of PIRA convention in Falcarragh, County Donegal
13 October	Gerry Adams and Martin McGuinness meet Blair
30 October	Holdall bomb left in Derry government building fails to detonate
9 November	UVF murder Raymond McCord
20 November	Small bomb at Belfast City Hall
27 December	INLA kill Billy Wright, leader of LVF, in Maze prison

1998

7 January	500-pound car bomb in Banbridge, County Down defused
24 January	Car bomb explodes in Enniskillen: nightclub badly damaged
26 January	UDP expelled from multi-party talks over UFF's involvement in murders of Catholics; government says they may return if UFF maintains ceasefire
29 January	Blair announces setting up of Saville Inquiry into Bloody Sunday
20 February	SF expelled from talks over two recent PIRA murders; promised re-admission in two weeks if no further breaches of ceasefire
20 February	Car bomb injures eleven in Moira, County Down
23 February	300-pound car bomb in Portadown, County Armagh; extensive damage; UDA rejoin talks
24 February	250-pound bomb found in field in County Cavan
3 March	Car bomb found on farmland in County Louth; sectarian murder by LVF of two young men (one Catholic; one Protestant) in Poyntzpass, County Armagh; joint visit the following day to families by UUP leader David Trimble and SDLP deputy leader Seamus Mallon
10 March	Mortar attack on RUC base in Newry Road, Armagh
20 March	Bomb thrown into bank in Derry fails to explode
23 March	SF rejoins talks
10 April	Belfast Agreement reached and includes the provisions: NI's constitutional future should be determined by majority vote; all parties will use exclusively peaceful and democratic means; an NI Assembly with devolved powers be set up along with a power-sharing Executive; a British–Irish Council and a British–

Irish Inter-governmental Conference be established; release within two years of paramilitary prisoners of organisations on ceasefire; there be a two-year target for decommissioning of paramilitary weapons; RoI abolish its constitutional claim to NI; there be new legislation on policing, human rights and equality

12 April	RSF call for No vote in planned referendum
21 April	32CSM reject Agreement as 'fundamentally undemocratic, anti-Republican and unacceptable'
30 April	Army defuses 600-pound bomb in Lisburn, County Antrim; PIRA say they will not be decommissioning
1 May	RIRA member Ronan MacLochlainn shot by gardaí during robbery in County Wicklow
9 May	Two mortar tubes found in car park of hotel in Belleek, County Fermanagh; RIRA claims responsibility, thus formally announcing it exists
15 May	Car and trailer bomb abandoned in Kinawley, County Fermanagh; LVF announce ceasefire
16 May	Army defuses bomb near Armagh RUC base
22 May	Yes to agreement in referendums in NI (71 per cent) and RoI (94 per cent)
3 June	UK government sets up Independent Commission on Policing in Northern Ireland (Patten Commission)
24 June	200-pound car bomb causes two injuries and £3 million of damage in Newtownhamilton, County Armagh
25 June	Assembly election MLAs: UUP 28; SDLP 24; DUP 20; SF 18; Alliance 6; UKUP 5; PUP 2; Women's Coalition 2; Independent unionists 3
1 July	At Assembly meeting, Trimble elected FM (Designate); SDLP's Mallon Deputy FM (Designate); direct rule from London continues during negotiations about devolution
5 July	Orange parade blocked from going down Garvaghy Road; widespread loyalist rioting
12 July	Three Catholic boys (Jason (8), Mark (9) and Richard (10) Quinn) burned to death by a loyalist firebomb
18 July	Andrew Kearney bleeds to death in Belfast after unauthorised PIRA shooting
1 August	500-pound car bomb in Banbridge; two police, thirty-three civilians injured; £4 million estimated damage
15 August	Omagh bomb kills twenty-nine and unborn twins and devastates town
18 August	RIRA announces 'suspension' of operations

19 August	Bertie Ahern promises introduction of 'draconian' anti-terrorist measures
22 August	INLA announce ceasefire
26 August	Blair visits Omagh and promises draconian legislation to deal with paramilitaries not on ceasefire
1 September	Gerry Adams, SF President, says the war is over
2 September	Reports that PIRA have threatened RIRA and the 32CSM
3 September	President Clinton and Blair visit Omagh; Criminal Justice (Terrorism and Conspiracy) Bill passed in London; Offences Against The State (Amendment) Bill passed in Dublin
4 September	Gun attack on RUC Land Rover near Portadown, County Armagh
5 September	Frank O'Reilly injured by loyalist blast bomb and dies a month later; last paramilitary RUC victim (until 2009)
8 September	RIRA announces 'complete cessation of violence'
14 September	The NI Assembly meet for the first time since June; formation of Executive postponed because of stand-off over decommissioning
17 October	Announcement that John Hume and David Trimble have been awarded Nobel Peace Prize
2 November	Loyalist splinter group kill Catholic

1999

14 January	Gun attack on West Belfast RUC station
27 January	Informer Eamon Collins beaten to death in Newry, County Down, by PIRA members
16 February	Deadline of 10 March set to establish the Executive
15 March	Rosemary Nelson murdered by fringe loyalist group
1 April	'Hillsborough Declaration' agreed by Ahern and Blair sets out framework for progress towards establishing the Executive; UUP insists on IRA decommissioning before SF can sit on an Executive; SF says decommissioning possible only after Executive formed; Declaration suggests compromise
4 May	Gun attack on Lisnaskea RUC station, County Fermanagh
20 May	Blair sets absolute deadline of 30 June for deal on forming an Executive; failure will have Assembly suspended
30 June	Blair agrees to extension
2 July	British and Irish governments issue 'The Way Forward' suggesting method of establishing inclusive Executive and achieving arms decommissioning
12 July	Legislation put before British Parliament designed to act as a safeguard for the decommissioning of arms and the devolution of power in NI. Rejected subsequently by both UUP and SF

15 July	Attempt to form Executive fails because no unionists attend
30 July	Charles Bennett murdered by PIRA
14 August	Violence in Belfast and Derry following Apprentice Boys' parades
26 August	Mowlam says PIRA involved in the murder of Mr Bennett and implicated in Florida gun-running operation, but ceasefire nonetheless not breached
6 September	Beginning of review of Good Friday Agreement chaired by Senator George Mitchell, which takes ten weeks
9 September	Publication of Patten Report, which is denounced by unionists
12 October	Peter Mandelson succeeds Mowlam as Secretary of State
13 October	Murder of RIRA member Joe O'Connor in West Belfast by PIRA members
20 October	Weapons shipment seized and underground firing range uncovered in County Dublin
25 October	Rocket launcher and Semtex found in County Meath
26 October	Further arms recovered at same location
23 November	RUC awarded George Cross
27 November	UUP agrees to go into power-sharing Executive on understanding that PIRA will then decommission
29 November	Assembly meets; ten ministers nominated to Executive: Trimble FM; Mallon DFM; Martin McGuinness Minister for Education; DUP accept ministries but will not actually sit in Cabinet
2 December	Executive meets; PIRA say they have appointed a representative to the international decommissioning body
27 December	Kempton Park Racecourse, Sunbury-on-Thames, London, evacuated after hoax

2000

21 January	RIRA statement denounces NI Executive and those giving allegiance to 'corrupt, treacherous administration'; pledges to 'struggle' (though does not officially end cessation)
23 January	Gardaí find van in Cahir, County Tipperary, containing two primed Semtex bombs
24 January	Significant arms cache uncovered in Limerick; arrests
6 February	Bomb damages hotel in Irvinestown, County Fermanagh
11 February	Failure of PIRA to decommission causes Peter Mandelson to suspend the Assembly
25 February	Bomb outside Ballykelly Barracks, County Londonderry, fails to detonate fully
29 February	Rocket launcher and warhead recovered from near army base in Dungannon, County Tyrone

16 March	500 pounds of explosives captured at Hillsborough, County Down
27 March	First day of Bloody Sunday Inquiry
6 April	Bomb attack on Ebrington Barracks, Londonderry
12 April	Failed mortar attack on RUC station in Rosslea, County Fermanagh
6 May	PIRA promise to begin decommissioning if Assembly and Executive restored
9 May	Chief Constable Ronnie Flanagan announces five military installations to close
10 May	Statement calls on PIRA to disband and give its arms to those 'prepared to defend the Republic'
19 May	Bomb alerts cause widespread disruption in Belfast
24 May	Failed mortar attack on army observation post near Crossmaglen, County Armagh
30 May	Devolution restored
1 June	Bomb damages Hammersmith Bridge, west London
20 June	Partially exploded bomb found in ground of Hillsborough residence of Secretary of State
24 June	32CSM conference attacks PIRA's 'first stop in a decommissioning surrender process'
26 June	Having visited PIRA arms dumps, two international arms inspectors report arms could not be used without being detected
30 June	Bomb explodes on Belfast–Dublin railway line in south Armagh
9 July	Car bomb explodes outside RUC station, Stewartstown, County Tyrone
19 July	Controlled explosions of bomb near Ealing Broadway tube station, west London, and suspect package in Whitehall
28 July	Report from Croatia on 13 July of confiscations of substantial weaponry thought to be bound for NI
11 August	500 pounds of explosives apparently destined for Apprentice Boys' Derry march following day recovered by RUC
21 August	Two killed in loyalist feud; five more die in next four months
12 September	80-pound bomb partially explodes at army base at Magilligan, Londonderry; soldier treated for shock
13 September	Mortar attack on RUC station in Armagh city
20 September	Rocket-propelled grenade attack on MI6 HQ in London
25 September	Train services from Belfast disrupted when 50-pound bomb partially explodes
4 October	Liam Campbell arrested
9 October	BBC's *Panorama* accuses four men of involvement in Omagh bomb (Subsequent contempt of court proceedings settled on statement that presumption of innocence applies.)

13 October	PIRA murder RIRA's Joseph O'Connor
24 October	600-pound partially constructed bomb seized in West Belfast; subsequently alleged to be bound for London
1 November	Booby-trap bomb in Castlewellan, County Down, seriously injures RUC officer
11 November	Three men arrested after 200-pound mortar bomb found by RUC in van near Derrylin, County Fermanagh
12–13 December	President and Mrs Clinton in NI

2001

14 January	Police car damaged by bomb in Cookstown, County Tyrone
17 January	Police defuse 1,100-pound bomb near Armagh; booby-trap bomb damages RUC station in Claudy, County Londonderry
23 January	Mortar bomb fired at Ebrington Barracks, Londonderry, fails to explode
24 January	Mandelson replaced by John Reid as Secretary of State
17 February	Reported explosions force closure of Belfast–Dublin railway line
21 February	Stephen Menary, a fourteen-year-old cadet, maimed by bomb attack on west London Territorial Army base
26 February	Brian Keenan, reputed to be PIRA Chief of Staff, warns armed conflict could return if political process collapses
4 March	Substantial damage to BBC TV Centre in west London; one injury
29 March	Michael McKevitt arrested and charged by gardaí
3 April	RUC defuse 60-pound bomb in Derry
12 April	Fully primed 200-pound mortar bomb found in Gallbally, County Tyrone; defused
13 April	RIRA statement
14 April	Small bomb causes minor damage at postal sorting office in Hendon, north London
21 April	Grenade attack on a Derry RUC station
27 April	Vandalising of Omagh memorial garden
6 May	Small bomb in Hendon, west London, injures one
8 May	At launch of general election campaign, Trimble promises he will resign as FM if there has been no progress on PIRA decommissioning
14 May	Suspected attack on Bessbrook Mill Barracks in south Armagh
16 May	RIRA designated by US government as foreign terrorist organisation
26 May	Rocket attack on Strabane RUC station, County Tyrone

7 June	Blair re-elected at general election. NI MPs: UUP 6; DUP 5; SF 4; SDLP 3
1 July	Trimble resigns: nominates a UUP caretaker, which triggers a six-week period in which to resolve crisis
14 July	Political talks to rescue the peace process break down at Weston Park, Shropshire/Straffordshire border
17 July	President Bush calls for PIRA decommissioning
19 July	Bomb thrown at Castlewellan RUC station, County Down
1 August	Controlled explosion of 40-pound primed bomb at Belfast International Airport
2 August	100-pound bomb at Ealing Broadway, west London, injures seven
10 August	After inter-governmental proposals following on talks at Weston Park, the refusal of PIRA to decommission causes Reid to announce a technical suspension of devolution for twenty-four hours; Omagh families file their writ at the High Court
12 August	Devolution restored: six-week deadline for a deal
21 September	Second technical suspension
17 October	Primed 350-pound bomb found near Sixmilecross, County Tyrone
23 October	PIRA says it has begun process of putting arms beyond use; some arms decommissioned
23 October	Liam Campbell jailed
24 October	Trimble renominates UUP ministers, thus preventing the collapse of Executive
30 October	11-pound bomb detonated on bus outside West Belfast police station
3 November	Trimble re-elected FM; SDLP's Mark Durkan DFM; explosion in Birmingham causes minor injuries to police
4 November	Royal Irish Constabulary becomes Police Service of NI
7 November	Twenty million contraband cigarettes seized in Dundalk believed to have come from Estonia
8 November	Forty million cigarettes found in Warrenpoint, RoI, on cargo ship from Latvia
19 November	Weapons seized in Lurgan, County Armagh
20 November	Fully primed large car bomb found near Armagh
21 November	Incendiary device partially explodes in shop in Newry, County Down
5 December	Army defuses 80-pound bomb under railway line between Newry and Dundalk
16 December	Bomb attack damages Fermanagh Customs and Excise office

CHRONOLOGY: POLITICS AND TERROR

2002

3 January	Pipe bomb attack on policeman's home in County Down
24 January	Colm Murphy sentenced
8 February	Civilian security guard Peter Mason loses arms, hearing and sight when he picks up a booby-trapped flask near an army training centre, County Londonderry
3 March	Small bomb slightly injures two boys in County Armagh
29 March	Booby-trap bomb found under car in County Tyrone
8 April	PIRA says it has put more weapons 'beyond use'
12 April	Two bomb attacks on County Down police stations
16 April	Bomb attack on Belfast police training college
26 April	Large firebomb abandoned near Belfast city centre
28 April	150-pound bomb attack on Maghaberry prison, County Antrim
7 May	Three men from County Louth jailed for thirty years each for seeking arms for RIRA in Slovakia from MI5 operatives pretending to be Iraqi agents
5 June	Booby-trap bomb attack on Catholic police recruit in Antrim
2 July	Commons NI Affairs Committee report on financing of terrorism estimates that all terror groups combined make £18 million from criminality; RIRA annually has 'running costs' of £500,000, but makes £1.5 million
3 July	News that leading NI politicians have been warned that dissidents are planning assassinations
17 July	Bomb thrown at police car near Downpatrick, County Down
24 July	Bomb explodes on estate of unionist peer Lord Brookeborough, a member of the policing board
26 July	Serving of writs in Omagh bombing civil case
1 August	Builder David Caldwell killed by booby-trapped lunchbox at Territorial Army base in Londonderry
18 September	Two bombs seized from car near Newry, County Down
21 September	Trimble says UUP will leave Executive on 18 January if PIRA does not show they have permanently abandoned violence
4 October	Police investigation produces evidence of PIRA spy ring at Stormont: nobody charged as a result
5 October	Arrests in Cork
15 October	Devolution replaced by direct rule from London
20 October	It becomes public that the McKevitt faction accuses the RIRA leadership of corruption and demands it 'stand down with ignominy'; police defuse bomb at Castlederg station, County Tyrone
24 October	Reid replaced by Paul Murphy

25 October	Controlled explosion of van bomb in Belfast city centre
5 November	Taoiseach denies any deal with Real IRA after Omagh
6 November	Arrests and weapons seizure in Limerick

2003

8 January	Large firebomb defused at waterworks in Keady, County Armagh
13 January	Firebomb defused in Dungannon, County Tyrone
2 February	Bomb explodes at Territorial Army base in Belfast
7 February	Controlled explosion of bomb in stolen car in Belfast
10 February	Six police injured in bomb in Enniskillen, County Fermanagh
14 February	Bomb thrown over fence of police station in Belfast defused
18 February	One of two nail bombs thrown over fence of Belfast police station explodes
20 February	Weapons seized and arrest made in Donagh, County Fermanagh
12 March	Huge firebomb outside Belfast courts defused
9 April	Five men jailed for between sixteen and twenty-two years for orchestrating 2001 bombing campaign in England
16 April	Bomb outside offices of DUP politician defused
1 May	Blair postpones Assembly elections until the autumn, accusing the PIRA of refusing fully to abjure paramilitarism; governments propose blueprint for breaking impasse
5 May	Bomb found outside Belfast government building
7 May	Bomb thrown at police car in Armagh defused
13 June	Gardaí find 500 pounds of explosive in County Monaghan
15 June	PSNI intercept 1,200-pound bomb in Londonderry
17 June	Trimble wins narrow UUP acceptance of government proposals; three MPs resign the whip
23 June	Beginning of McKevitt trial
2 July	Police claim to have smashed a dissident republican 'spy ring' operating at the Royal Victoria Hospital in Belfast: nobody charged as a result
8 July	Marian Price speaks for Maghaberry dissident prisoners on 'dirty protest' to gain segregation from loyalists
16 July	Arrests in Dundalk and Netherlands; fifty-five million cigarettes found in County Monaghan
3 August	Training camp uncovered in County Tipperary; nine men later jailed
6 August	McKevitt found guilty; subsequently sentenced to twenty years in prison
11 August	Arrests and weapons seizures in England
17 August	Daniel McGurk murdered in Belfast

22 August	Car bomb explodes in Newry
29 August	Bomb found on County Down roadside
4 September	Four-man Independent Monitoring Commission set up to scrutinise paramilitary ceasefires; parties engaged in exploratory talks about restoration of devolution
6 September	Sean Hoey in court (later acquitted)
16 September	Threats to members of policing partnership cause a resignation
17-19 September	Intimidation of members of district policing partnerships results in resignations
14 October	Taoiseach admits Mansergh met McKevitt; BBC report dissidents smuggling weapons into Britain; bomb attack on Belfast police station
18 November	45-pound bomb found in Newcastle, County Down
24 November	Bomb injures two police officers at army base in Dungannon, County Tyrone
26 November	Despite protests from Trimble about the need first for more movement from PIRA, Assembly election takes place: DUP and SF replace UUP and SDLP as the largest parties
28 November	Police seize several million cigarettes in County Louth
8 December	McKenna sentenced to six years

2004

3 February	All-party talks reviewing working of Agreement begin at Stormont
4 February	Controlled explosion of bomb planted at Derry barracks
13 February	Explosives discovery and arrest in Limerick
24 February	Secretary of State asks IMC to investigate the abduction with apparent intent to murder by PIRA members of dissident Bobby Tohill
26 February	Seamus Daly pleads guilty; sentenced to three and a half years
2 March	Talks stall when UUP leave Executive because no action taken against SF over Tohill; Daly jailed for three and a half years
23 March	Blair and Ahern meet parties and call for breakthrough before June European elections
25 March	Charges dropped in Dublin against four accused of RIRA membership
24 April	Government accepts IMC recommendation to impose financial sanctions on SF and PUP because of PIRA and UVF violence

29 April	Bomb-making base found in Strabane, County Tyrone; four arrests
24 May	Liam Campbell found guilty; jailed for four years with eighteen months suspended
26 May	Review put on hold; ruling that the Real IRA was technically not proscribed, a Belfast judge acquits four of membership – ruling overturned June 2004
11 June	DUP and UUP hold European seats; SDLP lose to SF
14 June	70-pound bomb explodes at golf club, Lurgan, County Armagh
15 June	Review talks resume
1 July	Belfast rush hour halted by bomb hoaxes
13 July	CIRA designated by US government as foreign terrorist organisation
8 September	Three days of intensive all-party talks at Leeds Castle, Maidstone, Kent, end with the only agreement being to have more talks; DUP demands visible decommissioning of PIRA weapons; gun attack on Derry police station
28 October	IMC says the PIRA maintains full capability and all paramilitaries remain involved in violence
17 November	After two months of negotiations, governments put proposals to DUP and SF; parties agree to consult memberships; main stumbling blocks are visible decommissioning and Paisley's call for PIRA to 'wear sackcloth and ashes'; controlled explosion of firebomb in Belfast shop
21 December	A PIRA armed gang steals £26.6 million from Belfast's Northern Bank

2005

1 January	Taxi driver forced to drive firebomb to Belfast police station
7 January	PSNI Chief Constable says PIRA carried out the Northern Bank robbery; Ahern says trust and confidence in the peace process has been damaged
20 January	Pipe bomb under van in Dublin
30 January	PIRA members kill Robert McCartney in front of numerous witnesses in Belfast, which sets off a campaign by his five sisters and his partner to bring the murderers to justice.
8 February	Five in court in Ballymena, County Antrim, charged with possession of incendiary devices and Real IRA membership
24 February	Weapons seized and two arrested in North Belfast
17 March	Northern Ireland politicians excluded from White House St Patrick's Day party at which the McCartney campaigners are honoured guests

20 March	Report that MI5 warning dissident threat level 'substantial'
6 May	General election: DUP 9 MPs; SF 5; SDLP 3; UUP 1; Trimble loses seat; resigns as leader following day; Blair re-elected PM: Paul Murphy replaced by Peter Hain
13 June	Five jailed in Dublin as members of RIRA
9 July	Controlled explosion of pipe bomb at Coalisland police station, County Tyrone
12 July	Eighty police injured by blast and petrol bombs during Belfast riots
28 July	PIRA promises henceforth to pursue an exclusively democratic and peaceful path
1 August	British government promise extensive reductions in army presence in NI, the closure of barracks, the defortification of police stations and repeal of counter-terrorist legislation peculiar to NI
26 September	After a report from Father Alec Reid and the Reverend Harold Good, who have witnessed the process, the decommissioning body says PIRA has put all its weapons beyond use; Paisley sceptical
6 November	Down Royal Racecourse evacuated after suspect device found
8 December	Controlled explosion on car bomb near Dublin
16 December	Senior SF figure Denis Donaldson, one of three men against whom charges of spying at Stormont on behalf of PIRA had been dropped, admits to having been a British agent but denies any republican spy ring
26 December	Down Royal Racecourse again evacuated after telephone bomb warning; no device found

2006

6 April	Blair and Ahern arrive in NI two days after murder of Denis Donaldson and propose blueprint for restoring devolution: MLAs to be recalled on 15 May and given a deadline of 24 November to restore devolution or have salaries stopped
19 April	250-pound bomb seized in Lurgan, County Armagh; four arrested
2 July	Bomb in Bellaghy, County Derry
August onwards	Persistent attacks on Orange halls in Counties Armagh and Antrim
9 August	Firebomb attacks in Newry, County Down
16 August	Partially detonated bomb at site belonging to unionist peer
4 October	IMC says CIRA, ÓnH and other dissident groups are active and RIRA a 'real threat'

13 October	After intensive multi-party talks at St Andrews in Scotland, governments unveil roadmap with 10 November deadline for the parties to respond and target date of 26 March for restoration of devolution; main divisive issue now SF's attitude to policing
28 October	Gardaí announce major find of explosives in County Carlow
9 November	Shots fired at PSNI station in County Armagh
24 November	Transitional Assembly installed
4 December	Failed mortar attack on PSNI in Craigavon, County Armagh
7 December	Pipe bomb at PSNI station Lurgan, County Armagh, fails to explode

2007

28 January	SF special party conference votes to support the PSNI
30 January	IMC warn ÓnH has become 'more dangerously active'
7 March	Assembly election: DUP 36; SF 28; UUP 18; SDLP 16; Alliance 7
12 March	Two former CIRA members killed by ex-colleagues
24 March	DUP agree to share power with SF
26 March	Ian Paisley and Gerry Adams announce power-sharing will return to NI on 8 May
8 May	Direct rule over NI by Westminster ends after four years and seven months: Paisley FM; Martin McGuinness DFM
31 May	SF takes seats on the Policing Board.
14 June	Ahern wins third term as Taoiseach
27 June	Blair succeeded by Gordon Brown
15 July	Two bombs in Newry, County Down, fail to injure army unit
8 November	Police officer shot and injured in Londonderry
12 November	Police officer shot and badly injured in Dungannon, County Tyrone
7 December	Formation of anti-agreement party: Traditional Unionist Voice
15 December	Pipe bomb thrown at PSNI station in Strabane, County Tyrone, fails to explode
24 December	Adams says transfer of policing and justice powers from Westminster to Stormont must be priority

2008

7 February	RIRA announces it intends to 'go back to war' by launching new offensive against 'legitimate targets'. It also denies anything other than a peripheral role in Omagh bombing
12 February	Murder in Donegal; would later be attributed by the IMC to ÓnH

24 February	DUP says devolution of policing and justice powers will not happen until there is 'adequate public confidence', rejecting a government target date of May
4 March	Ian Paisley says he will resign in May as FM and leader of DUP
14 March	Four men from Londonderry arrested in County Donegal while being interviewed by the BBC later charged with membership of an illegal organisation; the trial collapses in December 2008
7 May	Brian Cowen replaces Bertie Ahern as Taoiseach
9 May	Incendiary device in store in Cookstown, County Tyrone
12 May	Police officer badly injured near Castlederg, County Tyrone, by bomb underneath his car
21 May	Two incendiary devices found in McDonald's in Cookstown, County Tyrone
26 May	Punishment shooting of drug dealer in Armagh city; incendiary device in Belfast store
5 June	Peter Robinson succeeds Paisley as First Minister
14 June	Two PSNI officers lured to site of 150-pound bomb near Roslea, County Fermanagh, escape when it malfunctions
19 June	NI Executive meets for the last time before impasse over the devolution of policing and justice powers deadlocks business
30 July	McKevitt loses appeal
31 July	Sinn Féin politicians assaulted in Ballymena, County Antrim
16 August	Attack on PSNI foot patrol in Lisnaskea, County Fermanagh; two officers slightly injured; rocket-propelled grenade fails to fire
26 August	Rioting in Craigavon, County Armagh, followed by gun attack on police patrol
11 September	Car bomb mistakenly targeted at a school teacher in Lisburn, County Antrim, fails to detonate
13 September	220-pound bomb found in hedge in Jonesborough, south Armagh
16 September	Gun attack on Belfast house
25 September	Alleged drug dealer shot in Donegal
28 September	Reports that a 'revived IRA' operating in Dungannon has expelled nine alleged drug dealers
29 September	Gerry Adams describes deadlock in NI Executive as 'very serious'
4 October	Bomb found near Newtownbutler, County Fermanagh
23 October	Serious rioting in Craigavon, County Armagh
18 November	After a deal to resolve the stalemate over the devolution of policing and justice, the Executive meets after a 152-day hiatus

2009

4 January	Seven guns and ammunition seized in Dublin
31 January	300-pound car bomb found in Castlewellan, County Down
6 March	Chief Constable says as threat posed by dissident republicans is at a 'critical' level, he has requested deployment of members of the Special Reconnaissance Regiment in Fermanagh; Gerry Adams says this a 'retrograde decision'
7 March	Sappers Mark Quinsey and Patrick Azimcar murdered at Massereene army barracks in County Antrim; two other soldiers and two pizza delivery men seriously injured
9 March	PSNI Constable Stephen Carroll murdered in a gun attack in Craigavon, County Armagh
10 March	Martin McGuinness, standing alongside Hugh Orde and Peter Robinson, condemns those responsible for the murders as 'traitors to the island of Ireland'
27 March	Colin Duffy, prominent former Provisional from Lurgan, charged with murder of soldiers, five counts of attempted murder and possession of gun and ammunition
9 April	BBC reports rise in the number of punishment attacks in republican areas
12 April	Real IRA statement on Easter Monday in Londonderry claims responsibility for 2006 murder of Denis Donaldson, threatens members of the PSNI and ex-IRA informers; pledges to carry out attacks in Britain
24 April	It is reported that Martin McGuinness has been warned by the PSNI of a threat to his life
11 May	Martin McGuinness calls on the 32CSM to condemn attacks on the home of local SF politician Mitchel McLaughlin
12 May	Spokesman for the 32CSM condemns the attack on McLaughlin's home
14 May	Report of discovery of 100-pound roadside bomb in County Fermanagh
22 May	Liam Campbell arrested by PSNI
4 June	Attack on home of SF MP Conor Murphy
8 June	SF top poll in EU NI election and lose seat in RoI; Omagh judgement

CHRONOLOGY:
LEGAL PROCEEDINGS

As my friend Matthew Jury of H2O has pointed out, no self-respecting lawyer could approve this laywoman's attempt to put into simple language what went on between writ-serving and trial. Since, however, the purpose of this chronology is merely so readers can marvel at the strange ways of the law, any minor inaccuracies must be overlooked.

D (Defendant); P (Plaintiff); NI (Northern Ireland); RoI (Republic of Ireland)

Northern Ireland: HCNI (High Court of Northern Ireland); CA (Court of Appeal); HoL (House of Lords); LSC (Legal Services Commission)

Republic of Ireland: SCC (Special Criminal Court); CCA (Court of Criminal Appeal); HCROI (High Court of the Republic of Ireland); CARoI (Court of Appeal, Republic of Ireland); SC (Supreme Court).

In the High Court of Justice in Northern Ireland, Queen's Bench Division

Between:
Mark Christopher Breslin (by himself and on behalf of the Estate of Geraldine Breslin)
Catherina Anne Gallagher
Michael James Gallagher (by himself and on behalf of the Estate of Adrian Gallagher)
Patricia Gallagher – discontinued 28 February 2002
Audrey Martha Mooney (née Gibson) – discontinued 20 July 2007
Caroline Faith Martin (née Gibson) – discontinued 20 July 2007
Edmund William Gibson
Elizabeth Catherine Gibson – discontinued 20 July 2007
Robert James Gibson – discontinued 20 July 2007
William James Gibson (by himself and on behalf of the Estate of Esther Norah Gibson) – discontinued 20 July 2007
Wilma Selina Kyle (née Gibson) – discontinued 20 July 2007

Stanley James McCombe (by himself and on behalf of the Estate of Ann McCombe)

Gerald George McFarland (by himself and on behalf of the Estate of Samantha McFarland) – discontinued 20 July 2007

Marion Elaine Radford (by herself and on behalf of the Estate of Alan Radford)

Paul William Radford

Laurence Rush (by himself and on behalf of the Estate of Elizabeth Rush) – discontinued 28 February 2002

Edith White (by herself and on behalf of the Estates of Thomas Frederick White and Bryan White) – discontinued 29 September 2006

Colin David James Wilson

Denise Francesca Wilson

Garry Godfrey Charles Wilson

Geraldine Ann Wilson (by herself and on behalf of the Estate of Lorraine Wilson)

Godfrey David Wilson (by himself and on behalf of the Estate of Lorraine Wilson)

PLAINTIFFS

-and-

Seamus McKenna (The First Defendant)

The Real Irish Republican Army (The Second Defendant)

John Michael McKevitt (sued on his own behalf and/or as representing the Real Irish Republican Army ('RIRA') and/or the Army Council and/or leaders and/or members of RIRA) (The Third Defendant)

Liam Campbell (sued on his own behalf and/or as representing RIRA and/or Army Council and/or leaders and/or members of RIRA) (The Fourth Defendant)

Michael Colm Murphy (The Fifth Defendant)

Seamus Daly (The Sixth Defendant)

DEFENDANTS

1998
15 August   Omagh bomb

1999
24 February   **Colm Murphy** charged with conspiring to cause an explosion

2000
6 September – 5 October Coroner's inquest

4 October   **Liam Campbell** arrested and charged in the RoI with membership of an illegal organisation

2001

29 March	**Michael McKevitt** arrested and charged in the RoI with membership and directing of an illegal organisation
31 July	**Liam Campbell** and three others charged with membership of an illegal organisation
10 August	Writ of Summons filed with the HCNI
3 October	**Campbell** convicted at the SCC of membership on 3 October 2000 of an unlawful organisation; sentenced to five years' imprisonment
12 October	**Murphy** trial begins at the SCC
November	**Murphy** trial adjourned as a result of a judge's ill health

2002

January	**Murphy** trial resumed; **Murphy** convicted of unlawfully and maliciously conspiring with another person to cause an explosion likely to endanger life or cause serious injury to property; sentenced to fourteen years' imprisonment
20 February	**Seamus Daly** arrested in the RoI and charged with membership of an unlawful organisation between 29 April 1998 and 20 November 2000
28 February	Ps Laurence Rush and Patricia Gallagher discontinue proceedings
25 July	*Ex-parte* motion filed with the HCNI to amend the writ and concurrent writ (for service outside of the jurisdiction) to include additional remedies of injunction
26 July	Writ served by hand by H2O on **Daly** at Kilmurray, Culloville and Drumcatton, Inniskeen, and on **Seamus McKenna** at Dublin Road, Dundalk (service against McKenna was deemed effective); **McKevitt** and **Campbell** accept service of writs at Portlaoise (**McKevitt** on his own behalf and on behalf of the RIRA)
30 July	Attempted service of writ on **Murphy** by H2O via letter to Portlaoise prison and by hand to the prison Governor
31 July	Note from Governor of Portlaoise prison stating **Murphy** had refused to accept service of writ by hand or by mail; letter from Deputy Governor stating that **Murphy** had refused to accept or sign for letter containing service of writ and had requested it be returned to sender
1 August	Upon application by the Ps, Master McCorry orders that service of notice of writ of summons is effective upon **McKenna** and that substituted service may be effected on the other Ds, who must pay the Ps' costs of – and incidental to – this application

3 August	Service advertisements placed in the *Irish Independent*, the *Irish Times* and the *Daily Mirror*
16 August	Memorandum of appearance filed with the HCNI by Kevin R. Winters & Co. Solicitors on behalf of **McKevitt** and by McShane & Co. Solicitors on behalf of **Campbell**
10 October	Upon application by the Ps, and upon objection by **McKevitt**, Master McCorry orders that the time for the Ps to serve their claim be extended until 16 January 2003
21 October	Ps served with notice that legal aid has been issued to **McKevitt**.
24 October	Ps served with notice that legal aid has been issued to **Campbell**; Ps file Statement of Claim with HCNI; Statement of Claim served on **Murphy** and **Daly** via letter

2003

3 February	Note received by Ps from Portlaoise Governor stating that **Murphy** had refused to accept service of Statement of Claim
5 February	**McKevitt** files his Defence with the HCNI
11 February	**Campbell** files his Defence with the HCJ
13 February	Ds served with Ps' Notice of Intention to proceed (within one month)
18 June	**McKevitt** trial begins at SCC
7 August	**McKevitt** convicted of offences of membership and directing of, between 29 August 1999 and 28 March 2001, an unlawful organisation against which a suppression order has been made; sentenced to concurrent sentences of six and twenty years to run from 29 March 2001
8 August	**McKevitt**'s legal aid certificate revoked on the bases that: his actions link to his criminal conviction; he is a man of straw; he has independent means
2 September	Sean Hoey arrested in NI and charged with possession of explosives and a timer for use in an explosive weapon
18 December	The decision of the LSC to suspend **McKevitt**'s legal aid is upheld and his legal aid revoked
19 December	**Campbell**'s conviction quashed on appeal at the CAA; retrial ordered

2004

8 January	Ps make application to the SCC for production of the transcripts and books of evidence relating to the criminal proceedings before the SCC of **McKevitt**, **Campbell**, **Murphy** and **Daly**

4 February	Direction issued granting legal aid to Ps
2 March	**Daly** pleads guilty at the SCC to membership on 20 November 2000 of an unlawful organisation; sentenced to imprisonment of three and a half years
25 March	Memorandum of appearance filed with the HCNI by Tara Walsh Solicitors on behalf of **McKenna**
23 April	First directions hearing at HCNI in front of Higgins J; **McKenna** and **Campbell** represented jointly; **McKevitt** on his own
18 May	**Campbell** pleads not guilty at his retrial at the SCC but tenders no evidence by way of defence; also pleads not guilty to a separate charge of membership on 29 July 2001, which is to be tried on 13 July 2004
24 May	**Campbell** found guilty of two counts of membership of, between 3 October 2000 and 29 July 2001, an unlawful organisation; sentenced to eight years to run from 1 May 2001 to take account of time already served, with final eighteen months suspended
27 May	Letter from Portlaoise Governor stating that **Murphy** and **Daly** had refused to accept letters of 4 March 2004
9 June	Summons issued by Ps for attendance of hearing on 11 June 2004 of an application by the Ps for an order that the evidence of David Rupert may heard by use of video conferencing
11 June	HCNI hearing on Ps' application re Rupert adjourned pending review of legal aid status of **McKenna**, **McKevitt** and **Campbell** (all separately represented); rescheduled for 24 June
23 June	Following a hearing on 18 June 2004, **McKenna**'s and **Campbell**'s legal aid certificates are revoked on the basis that they have adequate financial means; both state they will appeal
24 June	HCNI hearing on Ps' application re Rupert; hearing adjourned pending decision on legal aid status of **McKenna**, **McKevitt** and **Campbell** (separately represented)
9 July	Summons issued by **Campbell** for attendance of hearing on 22 July on an application for McShane & Co. to be granted leave to come off the record; hearing eventually rescheduled for 7 September
20 July	Summons issued by **McKevitt** for attendance of hearing on 7 September on the application for a ruling that he would be deprived of effective access to the court in the absence of legal assistance for the purpose of defending the action
27 July	Letter from Portlaoise General Office stating that **Murphy** and **Daly** are refusing to accept any correspondence and requesting that it be returned

28 July	Hearing of the Ps' application before the SCC for notes, transcripts, books of evidence and all documents relied on in the Ds' criminal proceedings at the SCC; **Murphy**'s and **Daly**'s solicitors apply for an adjournment so that they can apply for legal aid
7 September	Attended by lawyers for **McKevitt** and **Campbell**; hearing at HCNI on application by the Ps re Rupert; re-listed by Morgan J until after LSC ruling on whether **McKenna**'s and **McKevitt**'s legal aid should be reinstated; as no substantive arguments have been made on **McKevitt**'s application of 20 July, it is declined; **Campbell**'s application for his solicitors to come off the record as without legal aid he cannot afford to pay for representation is granted and he says he will not challenge the legal aid position
4 October	Hearing for mention of application adjourned from 30 July: Mr Justice Johnson appears to favour the contention that the application would be best made before the CCA
10 October	Ps' application to the SCC for documents pertaining to the Ds' criminal proceedings at the SCC listed for mention but postponed as **Murphy** and **Daly** are still waiting to be granted legal aid
8 November	Hearing at SCC to fix date for Ps' application for documents; date fixed for 11 January 2005
12 November	Upon application by **McKevitt** that he would be denied effective access to the court in the absence of legal assistance for the purpose of defending the action, Morgan J upholds the decision to revoke his legal aid
23 November	Summons issued by Ps for attendance of hearing on 29 November on the application for discovery documents arising from the Ds' criminal proceedings at the SCC
24 November	The Ps serve on the Ds a list of documents which they are free to come and inspect at the offices of H2O NI on a date to be mutually agreed
29 November	Hearing at HCNI on Ps' application re Rupert video link is adjourned by judge (Morgan J) pending resolution of legal aid positions of **McKenna**, **McKevitt**, **Murphy** and **Daly**; Morgan J directs that he is unable to consider this application until the PSNI have produced a security-risk assessment that demonstrates that Rupert cannot be expected to give evidence in person; Ps state they will be able to produce a Case Summary once the Ds have fulfilled their discovery obligations; judge directs that the Ps issue a summons for the hearing of an application for an order that the Ds discover documents relating to any matter in question in this action

7 December   **Murphy** appeals his conviction to the CCA

8 December   **McKenna** pleads guilty at the SCC of, on 13 June 2003, at Thronfield, Inniskeen, County Louth, unlawfully and maliciously possessing an explosive substance with intent by means thereof to endanger life or cause serious injury to property; sentenced to six years imprisonment to take effect from 15 June 2003

13 December   Summons issued by Ps for the hearing of an application for an order requiring **McKevitt**, **Campbell**, **Murphy** and **Daly** to verify, by affidavit, whether any of the documentation specified in the Ps' schedule (namely books of evidence and transcripts from the Ds' criminal proceedings in the RoI) is within their possession, custody or power

23 December   Summons issued by **McKenna** for the hearing of an application by his solicitors Tara Walsh to come off the record

2005

January   **Daly** denied legal aid; appeals

6–7 January   HCNI hearing on Ps' application of 13 December 2004; before giving such order Morgan J requests that expert opinion be obtained as to whether: (i) it is permissible for these documents to be used in proceedings other than the Ds' criminal proceedings; (ii) there is an impediment to the release of these documents as a result of ongoing criminal proceedings; (iii) under the law of the RoI, the Ds will be held in contempt of court if they release these documents in the absence of authorisation from the SCC; the court also states that the material must also be found to be relevant, i.e. contain material which may enable the party applying for discovery to advance their case; video link application re Rupert re-listed to 4 February pending outcome of Ds' various appeals re legal aid; leave given to **McKenna**'s solicitors (Tara Walsh) to come off record

11 January   Hearing at the SCC of Ps' application for an Order for production by Ds of documents arising from the Ds' criminal proceedings at the SCC

21 January   The CCA quashes **Murphy**'s conviction because two gardaí are alleged to have committed perjury; he is freed on bail pending retrial

28 January   Morgan J hands down preliminary ruling on Ps' application of 13 December 2004 that discovery should be granted and that there is no legal impediment to such discovery but notes Ds will have

	twenty-eight days to make any further representations on this matter
4 February	Scheduled HCNI directions hearing cancelled due to Ds' various legal aid applications
7 February	On the matter of Ps' application for an order for discovery of documents arising from Ds' criminal proceedings at the SCC, the SCC rules that it lacks the jurisdiction to make such an order and that it is, instead, for HCNI to do so
23 February	**Murphy** and **Daly** apply to HCNI for an extension of time in relation to their response to Morgan J's preliminary ruling of 28 January; extension granted until 4.30 p.m. on 11 March
7 March	Ps served with notice that **Murphy** and **Daly** have been granted legal aid to defend the proceedings; Ps served with a Memorandum of Appearance by Higgins, Hollywood & Deazley, solicitors for **Murphy** and **Daly**
11 March	HCNI review hearing. Morgan J states that he will affirm his preliminary ruling of 28 January 2005 and that if the Ds fail to comply, the Ps will have remedies; once matter of discovery is resolved then Ps will provide a 'Case Summary of Evidence' and the court will be open to make recommendations to the LSC on the issue of Ds' legal aid; Ps' application for an order granting a video link for Rupert is again re-listed pending resolution of the matter of **McKenna**'s and **McKevitt**'s legal aid
16 March	Upon considering submissions by **McKenna**, Morgan J orders that **McKenna, McKevitt, Campbell, Murphy** and **Daly** each serve on the Ps, within twenty-eight days, an affidavit stating whether he has the book of evidence served on him in his criminal proceedings before the SCC and, if not, what has become of it and in any event whether he has any objection to producing it together with the grounds for such an objection
5 April	**Murphy** and **Daly** make application to the CA for leave to appeal Morgan J's order of 16 March
19 April	Notes of Appointment of Tara Walsh as solicitors for **McKenna** is filed with court and served on Ps
29 April	HCNI review hearing in front of Morgan J. Ps request that **Murphy**'s and **Daly**'s appeal against the discovery order of 16 March be expedited; appeal listed for 19 May; Ps request that a hearing on their application for an order permitting Rupert to be heard via video link be re-listed for the soonest possible date – it is re-listed for 25 June; Ps request that Ds consent to telephone companies releasing their telephone records – this also to be dealt

with on 24 June; Ps request that **McKenna, Murphy** and **Daly** file defences in response to Statement of Claim – Morgan J directs them to do so **McKevitt**'s application for leave to apply for judicial review to challenge the LSC's decision to grant Ps exceptional funding is granted by Weatherup J

3 May   **McKevitt** files his defence with the HCNI

17 May   Summons by Ps for **McKevitt** and **Campbell** to attend a hearing on 3 June on an application by the Ps for the purpose of rectifying the Order made by Morgan J on 16 March against **McKenna, McKevitt** and **Campbell** so as to include reference to copies of any transcripts in their custody, possession or control thereby reflecting the intention of the court when the order was made

19 May   Hearing by the CA of **Murphy**'s and **Daly**'s appeal against Morgan J's order of 16 March; the CA varied Morgan's order and ordered that **Murphy** and **Daly** make and file affidavits stating whether any of the documents specifically described in the schedule are or have at any time been in their possession, custody, or power, and if not now in their possession, custody or power, stating when they parted with them and what has become of them

2 June   Following CA ruling of 19 May 2005, **Murphy** and **Daly** serve Ps with affidavits stating that, while the transcripts sought are in the possession and custody of their solicitors, it is not in their power to release then as they remain under the control of the SCC; Ds also object to the production of such documents on the grounds that: (i) their production is not necessary for the fair disposal of this action; (ii) they do not have the authority to release them as they remain within the control of the SCC and they have implied to have undertaken not to use them for any collateral purpose other than those purposes for which they were furnished without leave from the SCC, which has not been granted; (iii) the information contained in these documents is already known to and has been relied upon by the Ps and would be unlikely to assist them any further; (iv) that said documents have the tendency to be incriminatory and thus expose them to criminal prosecution in the UK; (v) that the documents are not admissible on the grounds that their prejudicial effect outweighs their probative value and re **Murphy** that his criminal proceedings are still ongoing; both deny having in their possession the books of evidence relating to their criminal trial

10 June   Summons for all parties to attend, on 17 June 2005, a hearing of the Ps' application for the following: an order that **McKenna,**

Murphy and **Daly** produce for inspection the documents set out in the schedule to the Order of Morgan J of 16 March 2005 and specifically referred to those affidavits of **Murphy** and **Daly** sworn on 23 May; an order that **McKenna**, **McKevitt**, **Campbell**, **Murphy** and **Daly** file affidavits stating whether any of the items in the Ps' attached schedule are, or have at any time, been in their possession, custody or power and if not now in their possession, custody or power, stating when they parted with them and what became of them

15 June   The Ds serve a repeat of their affidavits of 10 June though this time include a denial that they possess any material disclosed by the DPP during the course of their criminal proceedings

17 June   HCNI review hearing; Morgan J directs that Rupert video link application should be heard on 23 June together with **Murphy**'s and **Daly**'s application to strike out the writ on grounds that it contains a care-of NI address rather than H2O's London office address

23 June   HCNI refuses application by **Murphy** and **Daly** to strike out the writ; Ps' application for a video link for Rupert re-listed for 29 June

28 June   **Murphy**'s and **Daly**'s application for leave to amend the refusal to strike out the Ps' claim on grounds of the invalidity of the writ refused by Morgan J; the strike-out application is also refused; order that **Murphy** and **Daly** pay the Ps' costs of this application

29 June   Ps' application re Rupert video link is again re-listed when Morgan J requests that a summary of Rupert's evidence against **McKevitt** and **Campbell** be provided before an order can be made; Morgan J also states that the matter of issuing subpoenas to the PSNI will be dealt with on 9 September

30 June   Morgan J refuses **Murphy** and **Daly** leave to appeal the ruling of 28 June

26 August   On **McKevitt**'s application, the LSC's decision to grant the Ps legal aid is subject to judicial review: Weatherup J finds that the LSC's decision to grant legal aid to Ps was *ultra vires*

26 September   The CA hears **Murphy**'s and **Daly**'s appeal against Morgan J's order of 28 June that their strike-out application be refused

12 October   **McKenna** files list of discovery documents with the HCNI

25 November   CA rejects **Murphy**'s and **Daly**'s appeal against Morgan J's order that their strike-out application be refused

9 December   **McKevitt**'s appeal against conviction rejected by the CCA

13 December   **Murphy** petitions for leave to appeal to the HoL following the CA's ruling of 25 November

2006

13 February	The HoL rejects the Ds' application for leave to appeal against Morgan J's order of 28 June that their strike-out application be refused
14 February	Ps receive new funding under LSC authorisation
23 February	**Murphy** files notice for further and better particulars of each Ps claim
24 February	**Murphy** and **Daly** file notice with the HCNI for further and better particulars of each P's claim
March	**Campbell** released
7 March	Summons by **Murphy** and **Daly** for all parties to attend a hearing on 7 April of an application for: (i) an order for production of the documents in the Ps' list of documents; and (ii) an order requiring the Ps to disclose: (a) all documentation relating to any application for criminal injury compensation; (b) all documents relating to the engagement of a stenographer by the Ps for any of the criminal proceedings against **Murphy** and **Daly**; (c) all documentation relating to the Ps' investigation of **Murphy** and **Daly** in the Omagh bomb; (d) all documentation relating to the criminal investigation into the Omagh bomb by the RUC or PSNI; and (e) all documents relating to David Rupert
17 March	Ps file with the HCNI and serve on **Murphy** and **Daly** their replies to their requests of 23 and 24 February for further and better particulars; Ps also file a 'case summary' of evidence and allegations the Ps expect to rely upon to prove their case in response to an indication by Morgan J that it would assist in disposing of the various interlocutory issues; in response to **Murphy**'s and **Daly**'s application of 7 March 2006, Ps file a list of documents which they may come to inspect at a mutually convenient location and time
24 March	Summons by Ps for all parties to attend a hearing on 7 April 2006 on an application by Edith White to discontinue proceedings
7 April	HCNI review hearing: Edith White's application adjourned pending Ds' application for costs; Ps' application re Rupert and video link adjourned as Morgan J requests that Ps submit Rupert evidence against **Murphy**; inspection of material requested by **Murphy** and **Daly** on 7 March 2006 to be inspected on 26/27 April; Ds to notify Ps of any further documents required and Ps to respond with affidavit by 5 May
	The Ps respond to the disclosure request of 7 March via affidavit
13 April	**Murphy** and **Daly** serve the Ps with a notice to produce for inspection documents set out in an attached schedule

19 April   Summons by Ps for all parties to attend a hearing of an application for: (i) an order that **Murphy** and **Daly** produce for inspection certain documents on the list of documents served by **Murphy** and **Daly** on 23 May 2005; (ii) an order requiring **McKevitt, Murphy** and **Daly** to disclose whether certain specified documents served on them by the prosecution at their trials are or have at any time been in their possession, custody or power

20 April   Summons by **Murphy** and **Daly** for all parties to attend a hearing on 5 May of their application to compel the Ps to furnish proper replies to their Notice for Particulars dated 24 February 2006

26 April   SCC fixed a date of 11 January for **Murphy**'s retrial

26–28 April   Ps make available for inspection by the Ds all material that is neither legally privileged or irrelevant

3 May   Defence of **McKevitt** filed with the HCNI by Kevin R. Winters & Co.

5 May   Ps file and serve 'summary of evidence' of Rupert in relation to **Murphy**

16 May   Ps file with the HCNI and serve on **Murphy** and **Daly** their reply to their application of 24 February for further and better particulars

19 May   HCNI review hearing to deal with outstanding matters from previous review: Ds to serve amended application for Notice for Particulars; Ps to respond to **Murphy**'s and **Daly**'s application for response to Notice for Particulars; in relation to the Ps' application for inspection of 19 April 2006, Ps to submit skeleton arguments by 6 June and **McKevitt, Murphy** and **Daly** to submit skeletons by 13 June; adjournment of application by Edith White for Ds to get instructions re application for costs against her for discontinuance; Ds to submit objections to case summary and Rupert video link application

26 May   Summons by **Murphy** and **Daly** for all parties to attend a hearing on their application for orders (i) for the production of the documents in the Ps' list of documents dated 24 November 2004 and 17 March 2006; and (ii) requiring the Ps to produce (in addition to documents relating to Ds' criminal proceedings) all documentation relating to any application for criminal injury compensation, the engagement of a stenographer by the Ps for any of the criminal proceedings against **Murphy** and **Daly**, the Ps' investigation of **Murphy** and **Daly** in the Omagh bomb, the criminal investigation into the Omagh bomb by the RUC or PSNI: and Rupert

14 June   Summons by Ps for all parties to attend a hearing on 29 June of an application by the Ps for: an order for split trials so that the **RIRA, McKevitt** and **Campbell** are tried as soon as reasonably possible and **McKenna, Murphy** and **Daly** are tried on a date thereafter

21 June   Application made by **Murphy** and **Daly** challenging Ps' grant of legal aid by the LSC

29 June   Hearing of Ps' application for split trials; Morgan J adjourns application to next hearing to consider all issues

17 July   **McKevitt** granted leave to appeal to the SC against prior decision of the CCA of December 2005

31 July   RoI Director of Public Prosecutions fails in his bid to have **McKenna**'s prison sentence increased

6 September   Trial of Sean Hoey begins at Belfast Crown Court; adjourned until 18 September because of illness of defence counsel

20 September   Video link with Omagh approved for Hoey trial

25 September   Hoey trial begins

29 September   Application on Ps' application for split trials refused; trial date set for 16 April 2007; application for Edith White to discontinue is granted; video link for Rupert agreed; service of any documents required to be served on **McKevitt** and **Campbell** can be effected respectively by serving notice at Portlaoise or an advertisement in the *Dundalk Democrat*

18 October   Start of trial at the SCC of Detective Garda Liam Donnelly and Detective Garda John Fahy on charges of forging notes of **Murphy**'s interview and perjuring themselves at his trial

23 October   Review hearing on Ps' application for video link against Ds to be granted subject to amendments to draft order (requiring more specificity as to the scope of the evidence); arguments put forward by parties regarding Ps' application for discovery

         In the SCC, Donnelly and Fahy found not guilty of perjury or forgery in the **Murphy** case on direction of the trial judge

29 October   **Daly** released

23 November   Hearing at HCNI: application for Rupert video evidence in relation to **Murphy** order to be made; court indicates that Ps' application for production for inspection be ordered; hearing on **Murphy**'s and **Daly**'s Notice for Particulars adjourned until 20 December; upon application by the Ps and objections from **Murphy** and **Daly**, Morgan J ordered that **Murphy** and **Daly** produce for inspection within fourteen days the relevant parts of the transcript and book of evidence in relation to their criminal trials; the

evidence of Rupert could be heard by use of video link in relation to **Murphy** as regards the following specific matters: that **Daly** was a member of the CIRA at the time of the Omagh bombing; that the CIRA was partly responsible for the Omagh bombing; that **Murphy** was involved in the Omagh bombing; that the CIRA denied involvement in the Omagh bombing whereas the RIRA accepted responsibility; that **Murphy** bore an animosity toward the CIRA and Republican Sinn Féin and that he retained contact with **McKevitt** after the D was charged with the Omagh bombing

5 December   Summons by **Murphy** and **Daly** for all parties to attend a hearing on 20 December for an order for production of certain documents listed which are referred to in the Ps' Statement of Claim

11 December   Summons by Ps for all parties to attend a hearing on 20 December for an application by the Ps for an order that **McKenna** produce for inspection certain documents from the list of documents he served on 12 October 2005 and an order relating to the failure of **McKevitt** and **Campbell** to produce any documents for the purpose of inspection

13 December   **McKevitt** lodges application to appeal his conviction to SC

14 December   Ps file with the HCNI and serve on **Daly** their reply to his Notice for Particulars of 24 February 2006; summons by **Murphy** and **Daly** for all parties to attend a hearing on 20 December 2006 of an application for an order that the Ps' claim be struck out in whole or in part on the basis that it is an abuse of process

20 December   **Murphy** and **Daly** appeal Morgan's order of 23 November to the CA

21 December   HCNI review in front of Morgan J: application by **Murphy** and **Daly** to strike out claim citing abuse of process adjourned until next hearing; it is found that **Murphy**'s and **Daly**'s recent application for discovery ignored the Ps' response to their original application of May 2006 – to be dealt with on 12 January 2007; Morgan J minded to grant order of discovery to P against **McKenna** but wishes to delay the order until the outcome of **Murphy**'s and **Daly**'s appeal to the CA

21 December   Upon application by the Ps and upon objection from **Murphy**, Morgan J ordered that **McKenna** produce within fourteen days the relevant documentation from his trial at the SCC in October 2004

2007

12 January	HCNI review hearing: application on part of **Murphy** and **Daly** to strike out claim citing abuse of process adjourned until later date; issue of admissibility of foreign convictions – adjourned as judge reluctant to make ruling without dealing with evidential detail of each case
16 January	**Murphy**'s and **Daly**'s CA hearing against disclosure order of Morgan J of 23 November 2006; judgement reserved
9 February	HCNI review hearing scheduled for 10.30 a.m. Court makes last-minute reschedule to 9.00 a.m start on hearing to raise issues to do with trial date: could convene for only thirty minutes so H2O unable to attend; matter re-listed for 15 and 20 February
15 February	HCNI hearing: **Murphy**'s and **Daly**'s application for case to be struck out citing abuse of process adjourned until 1 March pending submission of skeleton arguments by both parties; hearing to discuss matters surrounding the trial date listed for 12 March 2007; judge did not give ruling on admissibility of foreign convictions
20 February	HCNI hearing before Morgan J of **McKevitt**'s submissions to be granted legal aid on three discrete issues: the evidence of Rupert; whether the RIRA can be sued in a representative capacity; and issues arising out of the Hoey trial. Matter re-listed for 28 February so counsel for McKevitt can produce further submissions
28 February	Hearing on **McKevitt**'s submissions for legal aid are made; listed for further review on 9 March
1 March	Hearing on **Murphy**'s and **Daly**'s discovery and abuse of process applications: the Ds directed to serve an amended affidavit to that accompanying their application of 26 May as the original affidavit failed to outline the Ds' belief that the Ps, in the first instance, actually have the sought-after material in their possession. Matter to be heard again on 12 March. Abuse of process application adjourned due to time constraints and hearing carried over for further arguments to be made on 12 March
12 March	Hearing before the HCNI in which the Ps request a review in respect of all matters in relation to the trial date and further conduct of the action; judge directs that all outstanding applications be heard in the week commencing 16 April and that the trial be re-listed for 24 September. Also heard are **Murphy**'s and **Daly**'s discovery and abuse of process (pleadings and bias) applications. **McKevitt** finishes his submission relating to legal aid

15 March   **Murphy**'s and **Daly**'s appeal to the CA of Morgan J's order of 23 November 2007 re production of relevant documentation dismissed

28 March   Summons by Ps for the hearing of applications for: (1) an order for the examination on oath by the trial judge of the Ds at a place to be agreed in the Republic of Ireland; (2) the court to give leave to admit in evidence Rupert's written statements and those e-mails prepared by him and served on the Ds on or about 8 June 2004

29 March   Hearing to timetable the hearing of 23 April listed to deal with all outstanding interlocutory applications

4 April   **Murphy** and **Daly** apply to the CA for leave to appeal to the HoL re disclosure

5 April   Summons by the Ps for the hearing of an application for an order for the leave of the court to hear the matter of the admissibility of the Ds' foreign convictions prior to the hearing of the main action and for **McKevitt** and **Campbell** to produce for inspection certain listed documents

13 April   Summons by **Murphy** and **Daly** for the hearing of an application for an order that the publication of any report of the proceedings be postponed until the conclusion of **Murphy**'s criminal proceedings and for an order (in NI) for any person to be restrained from publishing or causing to be published any information concerning the case until after the conclusion of all criminal proceedings against **Murphy**; summons by **Murphy** and **Daly** for the hearing of an application for an order for the hearing of this action be transmitted by way of a video link to a suitable location in the RoI

16 April   Summons by **McKevitt** for the hearing of an application that the representative aspect of proceedings against him be discontinued

19 April   **Murphy**'s and **Daly**'s application to the CA for leave to appeal its ruling of 15 March re production of documentation brought before the CA and subsequently refused; summons by the Ps for the hearing of an application for an order amending the previous order of the court dated 29 September 2006 in respect of **Campbell**

23 April   Ds file letter with the Judicial Office of the HoL advising that they intend to lodge a petition for leave to appeal to the HoL re issue of production of documentation and asking for an extension of time until the final determination of the public funding application

23–24 April   The following application brought before Morgan J: by the Ps (i) for the matter of admissibility of foreign convictions to be dealt with as a preliminary point; (ii) for an amended order of production to make reference to **McKevitt** and **Campbell**; (iii) for an amended order of substituted service against **Campbell**; (iv) for an order for the court to sit on commission in the RoI and (v) for an order for the court to admit Rupert's written statement and e-mails; (vi) **McKevitt** makes an application for the representative aspect of proceedings against him to be dropped; (vii) **Murphy** and **Daly** apply for a bar on reporting, (viii) a video link and (ix) a finding of abuse of process (bias)

Judgements are: (i) would be dealt with at trial; (ii) orders would be issued; (iii) only be made if the Ps suggest an alternative means of service to advertising in the *Dundalk Democrat*; (iv) judge minded to grant; (v) the admissibility and weight given to Rupert evidence to be dealt with at the trials; (vi) ditto; (vii) **Murphy** and **Daly** directed to seek either an order or advice from the SCC or the RoI Attorney General on whether the civil proceedings might prejudice **Murphy**'s ongoing criminal proceedings; (viii) **Murphy** and **Daly** instructed to obtain a security risk assessment from the PSNI; (ix) effectively postponed until after the ruling on the judicial review of the Ps' funding following a letter from the Lord Chancellor's office confirming that **Murphy** and **Daly** exhibited material in these proceedings that should have been confined to the judicial review

Ds receive letter from the Judicial Office of the HoL advising them that their request for an extension of time until the question of public funding has been resolved was made out of time

May	Ds file petition for leave to appeal to the HOL re CA's ruling on the issue of production of documents
22 May	The Ps issue a special summons requiring the Ds to appear before the Master of the HCROI for the purposes of: (i) obtaining a declaration as to whether any impediment exists under Irish law that prevents the Ds from producing for inspection the documentation relating to their criminal proceedings before the SCC; and (ii) if necessary, an order granting the Ds leave to produce said materials; return date of 19 July 2007 given
22–23 May	At the judicial review at the HCROI **Murphy** argues that his retrial should not go ahead because (i) delays had prejudiced his right to a fair trial; and (ii) his capacity to defend himself was prejudiced by the short-term memory loss he sustained following an accident in 1988; judgement reserved
7 June	**Murphy** and **Daly** granted legal aid

13 June	**Murphy**'s and **Daly**'s request for judicial review of the Ps' legal funding dismissed
19 June	HoL Appeal Committee refuses **Murphy** and **Daly** leave to appeal the CA's judgement of 15 March re production of documentation
20 June	Summons by the Ps for the hearing of an application by Ps Audrey Mooney, Caroline Martin, Elizabeth Gibson, Robert Gibson, William Gibson, Wilma Kyle and Gerald McFarland for an order to discontinue proceedings
22 June	Hearing before the HCROI; Ps granted application for discontinuance, with costs reserved to trial
	Ps made renewed application for a split trial; ruling to be delivered by the end of July
2 July	At HCROI, because of the Ds' NI solicitors' refusal to accept service on their clients' behalf and an inability to locate a summons server willing to undertake the task of serving the Ds personally, the Ps made an application for an order of substituted service for the purpose of making an application for an Order of substituted service by way of ordinary post; judge ordered substituted service by registered post
6 July	Summons of proceedings at the HCROI served on the Ds by registered post
16 July	In the HCROI the Ps granted their second application for an order of substituted service by way of ordinary post since **McKevitt**, **Campbell** and **Daly** had refused to accept service by way of registered post
18 July	**Murphy** and **Daly** lodge appeal against judgement of 13 June in relation to the Ps' funding
19 July	The Ps returned before the Master of the HCROI where a request for an adjournment is made by a representative from the Portlaoise Law Centre (PLC) appearing on behalf of **McKenna**, **McKevitt** and **Campbell** to allow for clarification of these Ds' legal aid position; proceedings adjourned until 18 October
10 October	Memorandum of appearance in RoI proceedings entered by **McKevitt** and **Campbell**
15 October	Memorandum of appearance in RoI proceedings entered by **McKenna**
18 October	**McKenna**, **McKevitt** and **Campbell** granted request for a second adjournment to allow time for the filing of a responding affidavit to the Ps' special summons; proceedings adjourned until 15 November

> **Murphy** and **Daly** have not entered a memorandum of appearance as having yet to be granted legal aid in relation to this matter they are not ready to proceed

23 October   HCROI gives judgement on **Murphy**'s judicial review and orders retrial to go ahead

26 October   **Murphy** appeals the decision to the SC

15 November   **McKenna**, **McKevitt** and **Campbell** request further time in which to file responding affidavits; request granted and proceedings adjourned until 29 November

> Counsel on behalf of **Murphy** and **Daly** state that they were still unable to participate in these proceedings as – while the necessary applications have been made – their legal aid position has not been confirmed

29 November   It is directed that proceedings be allowed to progress through to the HCROI non-jury list on 11 December

> Counsel appearing on behalf of **Murphy** and **Daly** confirmed their legal aid position had yet to be clarified; they were given leave to file responding affidavits

11 December   At HCROI a request was made that proceedings be given a priority position on the non-jury list; **Murphy** and **Daly** given continued leave to file replying affidavits; matter listed for 7 March on the strict understanding that it would take no more than one day

20 December   Sean Hoey found not guilty on all charges

2008

7 January   Summons by the Ps for an application for an order striking out **McKenna**'s, **McKevitt**'s, **Campbell**'s, **Murphy**'s and **Daly**'s defence and entering judgement for the Ps by reason of the failure of the said Ds to obey Morgan J's order of 26 November 2006 compelling discovery of specific documents

10 January   Ps make an application for an order to strike out the Ds' defences on the basis that they have failed to comply with the court's orders to produce for inspection the documentation relating to their criminal proceedings before the SCC; court directs that this matter be adjudicated at the next proposed hearing of 25 January

> Court also directs that it would adjudicate on that date whether the proposed PSNI subpoenas could be issued as well as deciding whether it would invoke the letter of request procedure to the SC

18 January	Judge refuses **Murphy**'s and **Daly**'s application to strike out Ps' claim on the grounds that there were no reasonable grounds for bringing it; will deal at the trial with the issue of representative capacity, burden of proof, foreign convictions and with **Murphy**'s and **Daly**'s challenge of the basis upon which Ps claimed exemplary damages – asks Ps to set out at hearing on 25 January the basis upon which they seek to approach the assessment of damages; refuses **Murphy**'s and **Daly**'s application for a bar on publicity, because no risk of prejudice had been shown; a ruling on **Murphy**'s and **Daly**'s general abuse of process application to be delivered on 25 January, when he also requires that **Murphy**'s and **Daly**'s request for a video link be set out on a factual basis
25 January	Hearing of the Ps' application of 21 January 2008 for an Order for leave to issue a writ of subpoena *duces tecum* on Detective Chief Superintendent Norman Baxter; review of Ps' application of 28 March 2007 for an Order for the examination on oath by the trial judge of persons named in the attached schedule at a place to be agreed in the RoI; review of the Ps' application of 7 January 2007 for an order to strike out the first, third, fourth, fifth and sixth Ds' defences and enter judgement for the Ps for reason that the Ds failed to obey the Order of Morgan J of 26 November 2006 compelling discovery of specific documents
12–18 February	**McKevitt**'s appeal to the SC; judgement reserved
15 February	Morgan J orders that the judicial authorities in the RoI be formally requested to help with securing help from gardaí
12 March	In the HCROI, Gilligan J reserves judgement on the Ps' application for discovery from **McKenna**, **McKevitt**, **Campbell**, **Murphy** and **Daly**; DPP says he has 'no difficulty' in disclosing the required documentation
7 April	Civil case begins in Belfast High Court
October	Supreme Court reserves judgement on Colm Murphy's appeal against a retrial

2009

25 March	End of civil case
26 March	**McKevitt**'s appeal for a fresh appeal rejected by the Supreme Court
8 June	Judgement

INDEX